Baker
Barreca
Cone
Dellaperute
Marsh
McGinniss
Miles
Oglesby
Parle
Stallard
Twombly
Walker

BIBLICAL DISTINCTIONS APPLIED
Essays on Personal, Social, and Civic Responsibility

Edited by Christopher Cone and Mike Stallard

Biblical Distinctions Applied: Essays on Personal, Social, and Civic Responsibility

©2025 Agathon University Press
Fort Walton Beach, Florida

ISBN – 978-1-60265-106-7

All rights reserved. No part of this publication may be reproduced, stored in a retrieval system or transmitted in any form or by any means – electronic, mechanical, photocopy, recording, or any other – except for brief quotation in printed reviews, without the prior permission of the publisher.

All Scripture quotations, except those noted otherwise are from the New American Standard Bible, ©1960,1962,1963,1968,1971,1972,1973,1975, 1977, and 1995 by the Lockman Foundation.

Contents

	Editor's Preface – *Cone and Stallard*	i
1	**On Meaning and Purpose** – *Stallard*	1
2	**On Biblical Interpretation** – *Ogelsby*	25
3	**On Worldview and Method** – *Cone*	45
4	**On Morality** – *Walker*	67
5	**On Sexual Expression** – *McGinness*	83
6	**On Anxiety** – *Twombly*	111
7	**On Suffering** – *Marsh*	149
8	**On Race and Ethnic Diversity** – *Parle*	171
9	**On Antisemitism** – *Stallard*	227
10	**On Sexuality and Gender Identity** – *Dellaperute*	255
11	**On the Environment** – *Miles*	287
12	**On Diversity and Inclusion** – *Cone*	333
13	**On Social Justice** – *Parle*	365
14	**On Outreach and Mission** – *Barreca*	391
15	**On American Government** – *Stallard*	425
16	**On Civil Liberties** – *Cone*	445
17	**On Political Science** – *Baker*	467

Editors' Preface

In 2008 Mike Stallard led the launch of the Council on Dispensational Hermeneutics (CDH).[1] Stallard recognized that a forum was needed for scholars and practitioners working from the literal grammatical historical hermeneutic method[2] to work together to consider the important areas of hermeneutics, exegesis, and theological method, along with their applications and implications.

Consistent application of the LGH hermeneutic to the Biblical text has historically resulted in traditionally dispensational conclusions such as the centrality of God's doxological purpose and the clear distinction between Israel and the church. Because of this relationship between method and outcomes, the LGH hermeneutic has become synonymous with "dispensational hermeneutics." The LGH hermeneutic *is* the dispensational hermeneutic in the sense that its outcomes are dispensational, but it is not a dispensational hermeneutic in the sense of reading a theological pre-commitment into the Biblical text. In fact, to be pre-committed to a theological system and to infuse that system in any way into the exegetical

---

[1] The official website of the Council on Dispensational Hermeneutics is www.dispensationalcouncil.org.
[2] Literal grammatical historical, often referred to simply as the *grammatical-historical* method, hereafter: LGH.

process is the antithesis of LGH hermeneutic and would ultimately and completely undermine dispensational thought.

In recent decades, changes in hermeneutic theory and application have underscored the need for diligence, skill, and consistency in understanding and applying LGH principles that produce, through exegesis, understanding of the author's intended meaning. The CDH was designed to be a forum for dispensational thinkers[3] to refine their consistency and to revisit long-held conclusions, but also to consider contexts and implications that may not have been fully developed – or even considered, in some cases – by earlier thinkers.

While the papers presented and discussed at CDH conferences have covered broad and diverse topics – demonstrating dispensational thought as more well-rounded than some critics have been willing to admit – there is a requisite and thematic attention given to the details of *Biblical distinctions*. Seeking to understand Biblical distinctions and their implications is characteristic of dispensational thought. Especially in recent years, the CDH has focused on themes considering and evaluating applications of those distinctions for contemporary situations and current cultural contexts. While the word of God and its meaning remain unchanged, its significance and applications are timelessly relevant and provide God's trustworthy guidance for anyone facing any situation. *Biblical Distinctions Applied: Essays on Personal, Social, and Civic Responsibility* is a collection of essays, originally presented to, discussed, and refined by the CDH on topics that are deeply relevant to anyone. It is our hope that by reading this book, you will be encouraged in at least these ways:

---

[3] A dispensational thinker is a Bible student/scholar who seeks to consistently apply the LGH, who exegetes diligently, and who arrives at traditional dispensational conclusions because of the two methodological principles (consistency in applying LGH and faithfulness in exegesis instead of eisegesis).

1. That God has provided timeless guidance in His word, communicated in such a way that His audience can – and is expected to – understand.

2. That literal grammatical historical hermeneutics (or grammatical-historical) is the means whereby communication is designed to reliably convey meaning. Without that hermeneutic grounding, communication cannot be consistently understood.

3. That Biblical distinctions are evident through consistent application of the LGH hermeneutic in the exegetical process, and that they have significant implications for our everyday faith and practice.

We hope that you are encouraged by the essays that follow in this collection.

We hope that you are challenged to faithfully seek His guidance in Scripture as you steward the life He has given you.

We hope that through what has been written here your confidence in Him will grow as you are encouraged that His word is trustworthy – *that He is trustworthy* – and that His word is understandable at its core.

"…that the eyes of your heart may be enlightened, so that you will know what is the hope of His calling, what are the riches of the glory of His inheritance in the saints, and what is the surpassing greatness of His power toward us who believe." – Ephesians 1:18-19a

In His Grace,
Christopher Cone and Mike Stallard

Chapter 1 - On Meaning and Purpose

Prophetic Hope in the Writings of Arno C. Gaebelein: A Possible Demonstration of the Doxological Purpose of Biblical History[1]

Mike Stallard

Arno C. Gaebelein was a leading fundamental, dispensational Bible teacher in the early half of the twentieth century. He served as one of the associate editors of the Scofield Reference Bible and left us thousands of pages of material in his writings. The theological content of these many writings emphasized three things: inspiration of the Bible, the centrality of Christ at a personal level, and eschatological issues. It is fairly easy to determine a precise statement of the central interpretive motif or integrating idea in Gaebelein's thought. Bible inspiration can be ruled out simply because it does not integrate the content of Gaebelein's theology although it does provide a hermeneutical basis. The centrality of Christ is clearly stated. However, the sheer weight of discussion of eschatology, with its various emphases, speaks as forcefully as many direct statements. Nonetheless, it is possible to merge the theological statements about the centrality of Christ with eschatology to produce one statement clarifying the integrating theme of Gaebelein's theology. This can be done through the concept of prophetic hope which finds its fulfillment in the Second Coming of Christ. Thus, the central interpretive motif of Gaebelein's theological formulations can be stated as prophetic hope centered in the personal Second Coming of Jesus

---

[1] This chapter was originally delivered in December 1997 at the Pre-Trib Study Group in Dallas, Texas. This was a slightly modified version of a section of the writer's Ph.D. dissertation. Only minor modifications have been made but nothing substantive has been altered from the original presentation.

Christ. That this theme truly integrates Gaebelein's theological system will be seen by an examination of the individual and multiple expressions of prophetic hope which he outlined. However, it may be possible to see in these expressions, taken as a whole, the idea of a multi-faceted program of creation and redemption centered in Christ and leading to the glory of God. That is, unity from diversity can be seen in the light of this doxological purpose to biblical history as the greatness of our sovereign God is displayed.

THE OUTLINE OF BIBLICAL REVELATION

It is clear that Gaebelein emphasized the theme of redemption with respect to the multi-faceted program of God which he saw outlined in the Bible. The scheme begins in the Old Testament with the presentation of the four great subjects of revelation. It culminates in the New Testament with the outworking of redemption with respect to each of these subjects. Gaebelein saw this biblical outline of revelation in the plan of redemption as yielding proof for the doctrine of premillennialism.

> There is one more line of Scripture proof we would suggest. The Bible presents four great lines of revelation in the outworking of the divine purpose of redemption, viz.: Creation; the Gentiles or nations; Israel; the Church. This is the Old Testament order in its historical unfolding. The New Testament reverses the order and presents first the calling and destiny of the Church; then follows the restoration of the kingdom to Israel under the sway of Messiah's sceptre on David's throne; next the calling of the Gentiles or nations, and last the deliverance of creation from the bondage of corruption. Acts xv:13-18, gives the divine order of events. Each of these lines runs its predicted course of mingled imperfection and pain and suffering until the time of consummation –

"the dispensation of the fulness of times" — at the second coming of Him in whom "all things" shall head up (Ephes. i:10). There is no peace, no rest from suffering, no glory for any of these four great subjects of revelation till Christ comes again in power and great glory.[2]

Yet, in spite of this multi-track outline of what Gaebelein believed God was doing, he did not see this as devoid of unity. While discussing the inherent problems with postmillennialism, he remarked that

> Its [postmillennialism's] serious mistake is, that it confounds the accommodation and application of Scripture with the true interpretation, which in Bible study must have always the first place. Delitzsch well said, "Application is not interpretation. Application is manifold; interpretation is the very opposite, it is unitous. By the method of application the promises made to Israel are evaporated; in true interpretation Israel is given its rightful place in the purposes of God.[3]

In other words, Gaebelein believed that unity existed as each of the four great subjects of revelation were allowed to have their rightful, yet distinctive, place within the panorama of God's multi-faceted purposes. This is not far from saying that Gaebelein believed that the sovereign plan of God could not be understood or God given His due, until this valid interpretation was acknowledged.

THE EXPRESSIONS OF PROPHETIC HOPE

---

[2] 2 Arno C. Gaebelein, *Meat in Due Season: Sermons, Discourses and Expositions of the Word of Prophecy* (New York: Arno C. Gaebelein, Inc., n.d.), 19-20.

[3] Gaebelein, *Meat in Due Season*, 36. It is not clear in Gaebelein's quote of Delitzsch where the comments of Delitzsch end and Gaebelein's pick up again.

There are five major ways in which Gaebelein discussed the idea of *prophetic hope*. The method of presentation will adhere to the chronological order in which each element of hope is realized in his dispensational scheme flowing primarily from New Testament realization. One must always keep in mind that, in each case, this hope can only be fully realized when Jesus comes again.

The Hopelessness of the Present Age
The first area, while not technically a matter of positive hope, serves as an introduction to the four manifestations of hope which Gaebelein believed would take place in the future. The fact that hope exists implies that in the present there must be conditions which need to be changed. For Gaebelein, the present church age was characterized by such an unwanted environment.

In a series of five books beginning in the turbulent times of the 1930s, Gaebelein outlined for his readers a dark picture for the world. In *Conflict of the Ages* (1933), he portrayed the historic development of the mystery of lawlessness which was, in his mind, close to pushing the world to the precipice. His work, *World Prospects* (1934), held out final hope for Israel, the Gentiles, and the church, but not until a time of great darkness and difficulty.

Over half of the pages in the next book of the sequence, *Hopeless, Yet There is Hope* (1935), were devoted to a description of the bleak condition of the Twentieth Century due to war, financial chaos, and the rise of communism. *As It Was—So Shall it Be* (1937) compared the time before Noah's Flood to the present hour. Finally, the optimistic book, *The Hope of the Ages* (1938), described the present absence of kingdom-hope and noted that only by the Second Coming of Christ can this void be filled with lasting hope. A small booklet, *What Will Become of Europe* (1940), during the beginning days of World War II, observed that "there is no nation which does not tremble."[4] All that appeared from a human perspective on the horizon was darkness, distress, and destruction.[5]

For Gaebelein, the problem with the human race could always be identified with the existence of sin.[6] Specifically, two major areas of concern are emphasized. First, the present age is characterized by an increasing persecution of the Jews. After the destruction of Jerusalem in AD 70 and the subsequent scattering of the Jews throughout the nations, Gaebelein observed that "the fires of persecution burned fiercely in almost every century."[7] This persecution would culminate one day in the Great Tribulation or time of Jacob's trouble when the nation would go through its darkest hour.[8]

The second major characteristic of the present age was the increasing moral and religious declension.

> Morally the world sinks lower and lower. Christendom is turning more and more away from the supernatural, the foundation of true Christianity, turning from the spiritual to the material, giving up the message of power for social improvements . . . The faith as revealed in

---

[4] Arno C. Gaebelein, *What Will Become of Europe? World Darkness and Divine Light* (New York: Our Hope Publications, 1940), 9.

[5] Gaebelein, *What Will Become of Europe?*, 10.

[6] Arno C. Gaebelein, *The Conflict of the Ages, the Mystery of Lawlessness: Its Origin, Historic Development and Coming Defeat* (New York: Publication Office "Our Hope," 1933), 23.

[7] Arno C. Gaebelein, *World Prospects, How is it All Going to End? A Study in Sacred Prophecy and Present Day World Conditions* (New York: Publication Office, "Our Hope," 1934), 46.

[8] Gaebelein, *World Prospects*, 49-59. Gaebelein seems to use the expression "Great Tribulation" to refer to the entire seven-year period of Daniel's Seventy Weeks. Many pretribulationalists would be uncomfortable with this, preferring to see the Great Tribulation as referring to the last three- and one-half years of that period based upon Jesus's statement in Matthew 24:21. It may be that Gaebelein is simply being non-technical with his usage.

6   On Meaning and Purpose

> God's infallible Book is abandoned; apostasy is seen everywhere. World conversion, the world accepting Christianity? What mockery! The nations of the world were never as far away from accepting Christ as Saviour and recognize Him as Lord as in 1938.[9]

Both apostasy within Christendom, associated with moral decline, and the persecution of the Jews were understood by Gaebelein as a fulfillment of prophecy. Both called for a cry of hope, the former from the genuine Christian and the latter from the Jewish people. The divine line of revelation, for Gaebelein, began with creation, continued with God's work with the nations, took a turn with God's choosing of Israel, and culminated in the highest revelation of the church.[10] The fulfillment of hope for each takes place progressively in reverse order so that the first manifestation of hope is found in the church.

The Blessed Hope and the Rapture of the Church

Gaebelein believed strongly that the first manifestation in history of the fulfillment of prophetic hope would be the rapture of the church. This was the "blessed hope" of Titus 2:13 which was to be looked for expectantly by true Christians. It was a common topic in the pages of Gaebelein's magazine, Our Hope, especially the aspect of pretribulational timing, with more outside writers invited to address it than perhaps any other single issue.[11] This hope

---

[9] Arno C. Gaebelein, *The Hope of the Ages* (New York: Publication Office "Our Hope," 1938), 170-71. One wonders what Gaebelein's analysis would have been had he seen the fifty or so years since he made that statement.

[10] Gaebelein, *Meat in Due Season*, 19-23.

[11] Some examples would be Arno C. Gaebelein, "Opening Address," *Our Hope* 8 (September 1901): 93-96; "Notes on Prophecy and the Jews," *Our Hope* 8 (November 1901): 294-95; "The Patient Waiting for Christ," *Our Hope* 8 (January 1902): 345-46; "Editorial Notes," *Our Hope* 8 (February 1902): 394-95; "Who Will Be Caught Up When the Lord Comes," *Our Hope* 8 (February 1902): 408-17; "Editorial Notes," *Our*

was the catching up of New Testament believers to be with Christ. It included both those who had died in Christ and believers alive at the moment of the rapture. One aspect of the rapture which often received attention was its imminency. Gaebelein defined imminency with these words:

> Now the word 'imminency' or 'imminent' means that an event is impending, the matter in question is liable to occur at any moment. When we speak of the imminency of the coming of the Lord we understand by it that the Lord may come at any moment. This is the meaning of imminent.[12]

In light of the fact that Jesus could come for the church at any moment, no signs were expected to herald His coming in advance.[13] The significance of this doctrine for Gaebelein is clear when he warned that to do away with it was to rob the rapture of its "glory and power."[14]

The second aspect of the rapture of the church is its pretribulational timing. Another way of describing this doctrine is to note that the church

---

Hope 9 (August 1902): 116-21; "Editorial Notes," *Our Hope* 9 (October 1902): 225-27; "Will There be a Partial Rapture?" *Our Hope* 44 (August 1937): 100-4; John Nelson Darby, "What Saints Will Be in the Tribulation?" *Our Hope* 8 (May 1902): 597-605; Charles Campbell, "The Interval Between the Lord's Coming For Us, and His Coming With Us," *Our Hope* 9 (August 1902): 81-92; G. L. Alrich, "The Imminency of the Coming of Our Lord Jesus," *Our Hope* 9 (August 1902): 167-74; and I. M. Haldeman, "The Two Distinct Stages of the Coming of the Lord," *Our Hope* 9 (January 1903): 418-19. Many others can be cited. Most of the articles here appeared during the height of the controversy with Robert Cameron which helped to end the Niagara Bible Conference movement.

[12] Arno C. Gaebelein, "Editorial Notes," *Our Hope* 9 (October 1902): 225. See also Arno C. Gaebelein, "Editorial Notes," *Our Hope* 39 (August 1932): 76-77.

[13] Arno C. Gaebelein, "Notes on Prophecy and the Jews," *Our Hope* 8 (November 1901): 295.

[14] Gaebelein, "The Patient Waiting for Christ," 345. See also Gaebelein, "Opening Address," 96.

would not go through the Great Tribulation. The coming of Christ in the air to receive the church is a separate event from His coming to the earth to set up His kingdom seven years later. Gaebelein gave several reasons for his view with the discussions at times being extremely tedious. However, the following arguments appear to be the major support for a pretribulational rapture as taught by Gaebelein. First, he argued that the rapture had to come before the start of the Great Tribulation because the coming of the Lord for the church was imminent.[15] Second, there were exegetical reasons for pretribulationalism. In 1 Thessalonians 5:9 ("For God hath not appointed us to wrath but to obtain salvation by our Lord Jesus Christ"), there is a promise from God that church believers will not suffer the wrath of God during the Great Tribulation. The context of the book indicated to Gaebelein that the start of the day of the Lord or tribulation period is in mind.[16] Another passage (Rev 3:10) promised that the church would be kept from the "hour of temptation" which was interpreted to be the Great Tribulation of the latter days.[17]

---

[15] Arno C. Gaebelein, "The Attempted Revival of an Unscriptural Theory," *Our Hope* 41 (July 1934): 24-25. This argument stems from an understanding that watching for the coming of Christ, as Scripture exhorts, would be meaning-less without imminency. Gaebelein commented: "Looking for that blessed Hope [Titus 2:13] can mean only one thing, that daily we should look for Him and for His promised coming, not for death, but for Himself. But how is this daily looking possible if He cannot come at any moment?" (24).

[16] Arno C. Gaebelein, *The First and Second Epistles to the Thessalonians* (New York: Our Hope Publications, n.d.), 116-19. For a more recent approach with similar argumentation, see Zane C. Hodges, "The Rapture in 1 Thessalonians 5:1-11," in *Walvoord: A Tribute*, ed. Donald K. Campbell (Chicago: Moody Press, 1982), 67-79.

[17] Arno C. Gaebelein, *The Return of the Lord* (New York: Publication Office "Our Hope," 1925), 101. For perhaps the best description of how this passage plays a role in the rapture debate, see W. Robert Cook, *The Theology of John* (Chicago: Moody Press, 1979), 168-72. The exegetical arguments of Gaebelein with respect to 1 Thessalonians 5 and Revelation 3:10 appear to be the strongest and are based, in large measure, on grammatical-historical interpretation.

Third, the most frequent argument used by Gaebelein in the rapture debate was the fact that the Great Tribulation or time of Jacob's trouble, was exactly that, a period designated for Jacob's offspring, the Jews. Here the absolute distinction between Israel and the church prohibits the involvement of the church in a Jewish event. Gaebelein, in a representative remark, noted:

> All passages which have to do with the great tribulation prove that it is Israel's time of sorrow (Jer. xxx; Mark xiii:14-22; Rev. vii:1-14; Dan. xii:1; Matt. xxiv). "Jacob's trouble," not the Church's trouble. Christ saved us from wrath to come and will deliver us from that hour of trial that shall try them that dwell on the earth. When this takes place the Church will be far above the storm (John iii:36; 1 Thess. v:9; Rev. iii:10).[18]

The third aspect of the rapture of the church was found in the blessings which constituted the realization of the hope. First, the blessed hope pointed toward the resurrection of all saints who have died and the glorification of the bodies of those saints alive at the time of the rapture.[19] Second, the

---

[18] Arno C. Gaebelein, "The True Church: Its Translation Before the End," *Our Hope* 38 (September 1931): 184. See also "Editorial Notes," *Our Hope* 39 (August 1932): 78. This method of arguing is a use of a dispensational theological hermeneutic. The distinction between Israel and the church becomes the switch which helps to determine an interpretation. There are two problems (although they can be overcome) with using this argument which Gaebelein was not careful to address. First, as seen earlier, he included the Old Testament saints in the rapture of the church. An alert nondispensationalist might ask if the heavenly people can be mixed, what keeps the earthly people from being mixed in the tribulation? That is one reason that contemporary dispensationalists have come to view the resurrection of Old Testament saints at the end of the tribulation. Second, Gaebelein included the Gentiles in the tribulation (Revelation, 59). Since distinctions between Israel and the nations are made, why not between Israel and the church? This shows that the particular distinction between Israel and the church had priority for Gaebelein over all other distinctions.

[19] Gaebelein, "True Church," 184-85.

church will receive rewards at the judgment seat of Christ in heaven during the earthly Great Tribulation.[20] Third, the church saints will become rulers with Christ during the millennial kingdom. While living in heaven, they will be priests and kings who will reign and judge the world and angels.[21] Thus, the blessed hope of the rapture of the church is summed up in the encompassing truth that "the Church's glorious prospect is the eternal fellowship with the Son of God."[22]

The Hope of the National Restoration of Israel

It can readily be observed that Gaebelein's use of literal interpretation concentrated often on that portion of the Scriptures which prophesied the national restoration of Israel in the millennium. This literal promise provided hope for the nation, a hope that was a living hope.[23] One of the greatest evidences of that hope was the desire, stated during Passover ceremonies, to be in Jerusalem the next year. "And this has been going on generation after generation, century after century, during the darkest ages, during the times when satanic powers attempted their complete extermination. 'This year here—next year in Jerusalem.' The Jewish Hope is a never dying Hope. Israel is the nation of Hope."[24] In addition, this hope was not known by other nations.[25]

According to Gaebelein, the basis for this national hope was clearly outlined in prophetic Scripture: "The foundations of the Hope of Israel, that never dying Hope, are the two promises; the promise of the Messiah and the

---

[20] Gaebelein, "Unscriptural Theory," 24. This aspect of the blessed hope was considered by Gaebelein the greatest incentive for holy living (*Return*, 118).
[21] Gaebelein, *Return*, 118.
[22] Gaebelein, *World Prospects*, 166.
[23] Gaebelein, *Hopeless*, 156.
[24] Gaebelein, *Hopeless*, 157.
[25] Gaebelein, *Hopeless*, 160.

promise of the land in the dimensions as given in the [Abrahamic] covenant."[26] In this way, the future restoration of Israel is tied to the coming of Messiah, which from a Christian perspective, meant the Second Coming of Jesus Christ.

Although the focus of this hope is on the unique relationship between God and the Jewish people, it is also the basis of hope for other nations. Gaebelein observed:

> And the people Israel have been thus preserved because the other great promise of Hope and Glory, the promise of the land, their national restoration, spiritual regeneration, and the promise of future blessing to "all the families of the earth" will have to be fulfilled. Such is Israel's Hope, and, when it is reached, it will mean the Hope and blessing for all the world.[27]

The realization of the national restoration of Israel with its overflowing blessings upon other nations awaits fulfillment when Jesus, Israel's Messiah comes again.

The Hope of the Nations

Hope for the nations of the world was seen above as a side effect of the restoration of Israel. Gaebelein outlined the history of God's dealings with the Gentile nations beginning with Israel's own apostasy and resultant judgment via the Babylonian captivity.[28] The setting aside of "Israel as a nation in government and dominion" started with Nebuchadnezzar.[29] The

---

[26] Gaebelein, *Hopeless*, 162.
[27] Gaebelein, *Hopeless*, 165.
[28] Gaebelein, *World Prospects*, 101-8.
[29] Gaebelein, *World Prospects*, 108.

book of Daniel yields the prophetic account of the history of the dominion of the Gentiles during a period known as the times of the Gentiles.[30]

However, this period of Gentile supremacy was only temporary. Again, following closely the prophecies in Daniel (especially chapters two and seven), Gaebelein noted the future defeat of Gentile domination culminating in the setting up of the kingdom of God on earth.[31] This was preceded by the seven-year time of Jacob's trouble which also included the wrath of God poured out on Gentiles. However, during this time many Gentiles will come to know the Lord, mainly due to the witness of the Jewish remnant which also follows Him.[32] However, this is not the great hope of the Gentiles. At the coming of Christ at the end of the tribulation, the conversion of the world will take place.

> But there are other nations; though missionaries went and brought them the message of salvation, as nations they were hardly touched by the Gospel. Millions upon millions never heard it. Humanly speaking, as conditions are today they would never hear that Gospel of Grace. There is not the remotest chance of the conversion of these great nations of Asia, Africa and other parts of the world.
> Now these nations, such as China, Japan and the millions of India and the millions living in Africa, will heed this Gospel of the Kingdom, they believe, and then turning away from their idols and their false system will learn righteousness. The great revival comes to the unevangelized masses of the heathen world. Out of them comes the great multitude; though they suffer in the great tribulation, they come out of it

---

[30] Gaebelein, *World Prospects*, 109-23.
[31] Gaebelein, *World Prospects*, 124-42.
[32] Gaebelein, *World Prospects*, 151.

victoriously and enter as saved nations the earthly Kingdom of our Lord.[33]

Gaebelein associated this conversion with the judgment of the nations found in his interpretation of Matthew 25:31.[34] As with the national hope of Israel, the ultimate realization of this hope of the nations occurs when Jesus returns to earth.

The Hope for Renewal of Creation

Gaebelein marveled at the wonder of God's creation. However, the existence of sin in the universe led to another less beautiful facet of nature. What about the other side? Cyclones and tornadoes sweep over God's fair creation, working a terrible destruction. Earthquakes devastate many regions of different continents; volcanoes emit their streams of hot lava inflicting sufferings on man, beast, and vegetation. There are droughts and dust storms which turn the most fruitful lands into a hopeless wilderness. Ferocious animals attack man, poisonous snakes and insects claim many thousands of human victims . . . There is a terrible blight upon all creation. Did a kind and loving Creator create such things for His own pleasure and glory?[35] As in the case of the church, Israel, and the nations, only the intervention of God could correct the situation and give cause for hope. Gaebelein expected a reversal of the fortunes of creation in a literal fashion. Two key passages were Isaiah 11:6-9 and Romans 8:19-22. The first passage predicted a time when wolves would dwell in peace with sheep and, among other changes, children would be able to play with and around what used to be dangerous animals. Gaebelein's literal interpretation is indicated by his rhetorical question: "Who

---

[33] Gaebelein, *World Prospects*, 153-54.
[34] Gaebelein, *World Prospects*, 154.
[35] Gaebelein, *Hope of the Ages*, 68.

authorizes the expositor to say that these words have not a literal meaning but they must be understood allegorically and given a spiritual interpretation."[36]

Gaebelein believed that "the hope of Creation" was evinced in the second passage (Ro 8:19-22). There, the Pauline picture is one of the entire creation groaning and longing for the day when the sons of God (believers) will be manifested.[37] The theme of hope dominates the context of this passage and takes in not only creation, but the church (Romans 8) and the hope of Israel and the Gentiles (Romans 9-11).

When will the hope of a renewed creation be realized? In the context of a commentary on the crown of thorns, Gaebelein highlighted the answer.

> That crown of thorns is emblematic of creation's curse. Not science with its inventions and discoveries can arrest or even ameliorate the curse of sin. Only One can remove it. He is Creation's Lord who paid the price of redemption and whose redemption power can alone deliver groaning creation. But it will never come till He comes again, no longer wearing the crown of mockery, but crowned with many diadems.[38]

Renewal of creation will then be the last hope to come to fruition when Jesus comes again.

---

[36] Gaebelein, *Hope of the Ages*, 69. This literalism with respect to the restoration of creation is also evident in passages such as Zechariah 14:1-4. There the topographical changes in the Mount of Olives are taken literally. See Gaebelein's exposition, *Studies in Zechariah*, 8th ed. (New York: Publication Office "Our Hope," 1911), 140-46. However, he is not consistent throughout the passage. Later in verse eight, living waters flow out of Jerusalem into the Mediterranean and Dead Seas (149-50). The association is made with the pouring out of the Holy Spirit as mentioned in the description of John 7:38-39.

[37] Gaebelein, *Hope of the Ages*, 69-71.

[38] Gaebelein, *Hope of the Ages*, 75.

SIGNIFICANCE FOR THE DOXOLOGICAL PURPOSE OF BIBLICAL HISTORY

In *Dispensationalism Today* (1965), one of the most important books on dispensationalism written in the twentieth century, Charles Ryrie taught us that there were three essential principles which distinguish a dispensationalist from a nondispensationalist.[39] The first in his presentation was a distinction between Israel and the church. The second—which formed the basis for the firs— was consistent literal interpretation. Prophetic portions of the Bible should be interpreted using grammatical-historical interpretation just like historical and other sections of the Bible should also be. The third essential principle is what we are referring to as the doxological purpose of biblical history. Ryrie said it this way:

> A third aspect of the sine qua non of dispensationalism . . . concerns the underlying purpose of God in the world. The covenant theologian in practice makes this purpose salvation, and the dispensationalist says the purpose is broader than that, namely, the glory of God. To the dispensationalist the soteriological or saving program of God is not the only program but one means God is using in the total program of glorifying Himself. Scripture is not man-centered as though salvation were the main theme, but it is God-centered because His glory is the center.[40]

Ryrie expanded this thought in a later chapter in which he answers the charge from covenant theologians that dispensationalists had no unifying principle

---

[39] Charles Ryrie, *Dispensationalism Today* (Chicago: Moody Press, 1965), 43-47.
[40] Ryrie, *Dispensationalism Today*, 46.

to their theological system. In fact, in the thinking of covenant theologians, dispensationalism could be compared to higher criticism's parceling out of the Bible into different unrelated sections.[41] These covenantalists saw individual redemption as the unifying principle of the Bible. Ryrie noted that many of these nondispensationalists acknowledged the glory of God as the ultimate theme, but in practice that theme was addressed only from a soteriological, rather than a fully doxological vantage point.[42]

This third essential principle of dispensationalism has largely been ignored for several years by both covenant and dispensational theologians. One such recent and thoughtful dismissal of Ryrie's third point was worded this way by Craig Blaising:

> It would be difficult to identify this perspective as a particularly distinctive feature of earlier dispensationalism. Most evangelicals, especially among the Reformed, would have agreed on the comprehensive doxological purpose of God. Ryrie's insistence on this point can be seen as a calculated response to covenantalist criticisms that dispensationalism (Scofieldism) divides up the salvific unity of the Bible. Ryrie distinguishes dispensationalism from covenantalism as the difference between a doxological versus a soteriological perspective. The fundamental issue was whether or not the divine purpose is broader than the salvation of individual souls and the spiritual communion of the church. The proposed doxological unity was supposed to embrace these broader purposes, which include Israel's national and political future. But in spite of its categorical breadth, divine self-glorification does not seem particularly useful for explaining changes within history. At Niagara, the unity of the dispensations was found in the person and

---

[41] Ryrie, *Dispensationalism Today*, 98-105.
[42] Ryrie, *Dispensationalism Today*, 103-04.

history of Jesus Christ. Scofield saw history in terms of human failure, a notion that Ryrie dismisses as secondary and inappropriately anthropocentric. Other dispensationalists used salvation and redemption as integrating themes but defined them to include national and political salvation and even the redemption of the entire creation.[43]

The last couple of years this writer has revisited this issue and has come away with the conviction that there is a core of truth to Ryrie's observation, although much remains to be said in this area. In fact, there are several questions that could be raised with respect to Blaising's response to Ryrie in the above quote.

First, Blaising has acknowledged that the covenantalists have in their approach often emphasized the glory of God. However, we showed that Ryrie had done the same pointing to Hodge's and Shedd's theologies.[44] What Ryrie has noted is that the practice of covenant theologians yields the conclusion, not their statements: "But covenant theology makes the means of manifesting the glory of God the plan of redemption. Thus, for all practical purposes, covenant theology uses redemption as its unifying principle."[45] Appeals to certain statements affirming that one's theology is unified by the theme of God's glory may simply not be sufficient on either side. For example, it is clear that Gaebelein's statements focus on the word *redemption,* but his overall outline leaves open the possibility of a broader interpretation.

Second, it seems that Ryrie may not merely be responding to charges that dispensationalism has divided up the salvific plan of God and destroyed

---

[43] Craig Blaising, "Dispensationalism: The Search for Definition," in *Dispensationalism, Israel, and the Church* (Grand Rapids, MI: Zondervan, 1992), 27. See also Craig Blaising, "Development of Dispensationalism by Contemporary Dispensationalists," *Bibliotheca Sacra* 145 (1988): 267-69.

[44] Ryrie, *Dispensationalism Today*, 104.

[45] Ryrie, *Dispensationalism Today*.

biblical unity. Such attacks upon dispensationalists have taken many forms and a response to them is certainly part of what has happened historically.[46] However, what may lie behind the statements of Ryrie and other dispensationalists who are in agreement with him is, in fact, a reaction to the false theology flowing from the theological covenants which govern covenant theology.[47] The covenant of works and the covenant of grace are theological constructs which govern all of biblical history for the covenant theologian. Especially, the covenant of grace, which has been operative since the Fall in Genesis 3, provides a kind of unifying program based upon individual election. It is this focus on individual election that does not really fit the emphasis of Old Testament biblical history with its focus on national and community promises. Consequently, the covenant theologian is uncomfortable in that domain, and his reading of the Old Testament text is colored by his reading of the New Testament where he does feel comfortable with his focus on individual election.[48] The dispensationalist is not necessarily denying individual election. He is rejecting the idea of making it the central interpretive motif for the entire Bible. It is this rejection that may be at the heart of Ryrie's third point in the essentials of dispensationalism.[49]

---

[46] John Gerstner, *Wrongly Dividing the Word of Truth* (Brentwood, TN: Wolgemuth & Hyatt, Publishers, Inc., 1991), 149-69.

[47] Ryrie, *Dispensationalism Today*, 177-91.

[48] This present writer deals with the basic mistakes of theological method found in covenant theology in "Literal Interpretation, Theological Method, and the Essence of Dispensationalism," *The Journal of Ministry and Theology* 1 (Spring 1997): 5-36.

[49] It must be admitted that this third point distinguished dispensationalism from covenant theology but may not distinguish it from other forms of nondispensationalism. It may also be true that some covenant theologians have tried to develop their theological system with the glory of God in mind as part of an integrating grid. However, the common approach to covenant theology with its focus on individual redemption via election can certainly be responded to with Ryrie's third point.

Further, it is possible to see the doxological purpose to biblical history as a corollary to the distinction between Israel and the Church. Although the multi-track approach to biblical history as cited in Gaebelein's five-fold presentation above is clear, the primary distinction in the list is that between Israel and the Church. Simply put, the dispensationalist is open to the diversity which the biblical text yields because of his belief in a great sovereign God who can coordinate multiple tracks in His will and way. By implication the covenant theologian may not be so open to such diversity since he has a tendency to unify every aspect at the point of individual election.

Third, Blaising's comments point to a discussion of the usefulness of the doxological purpose as an integrating principle. In this he is only right to a point. He shows that some dispensationalists have integrated their theology around redemption as a category. Their category is just broader than most covenantalists and perhaps not broader than other theologians. In the end he feels, there really is not a lot to argue about. Gaebelein's example seems to cut both ways on this issue. It is true that Blaising's reminder about the Niagara Bible Conference focus on a Christological center is instructive especially as we look at Gaebelein who was certainly a child of the Niagara movement. Gaebelein surely talked about biblical history as God's plan of redemption through Christ.

Yet the stress on redemption tied to Christology should not rule out other emphases. Gaebelein believed that God had a plan for lost men and for angels[50] as well. In his discussion on angels, which highlights the issue of God's glory, Gaebelein betrayed a possible way of thinking about the many things that God does: "If man is God's only creature, gifted by Him with powers to search out His creation, to admire His works and to praise Him

---

[50] Arno C. Gaebelein, *The Angels of God* (New York: "Our Hope" Publication Office, 1924).

for them, how little is the praise and glory He gets from His creatures!"[51] In other words, if the plan of God involved only mankind, then one's view of the glory of God should be diminished. Couple this with his earlier statement about the need to understand the distinctive place of each of the four great subjects of the Bible (creation, the nations, Israel, and the church) in order to fathom the purposes of God. It is easy to imagine Gaebelein believing that the loss of these distinctions would somehow diminish the glory of God.

Although, in the end, there may be only a difference in degree between covenant theology and dispensationalism on the matter of the glory of God, the difference does seem to exist. The dispensationalist sees biblical history as following a multiple track scheme which highlights the glory of God as he fulfills his purposes of prophetic hope. Such a multiple track approach simply cannot be handled by covenant theology. However, dispensationalists who want to affirm the third essential principle of Ryrie's sine qua non can demonstrate that the doxological purpose is undergirded with both redemptive and Christological threads. This is, in essence, what Gaebelein outlined for us. One of its side benefits is a theological warmth which prevents dispensational theology from being merely an academic enterprise.

THE CHRISTOLOGICAL FOCUS OF HOPE

The theme of prophetic hope expressed, in spite of the hopelessness of the present age, to the church, Israel, the Gentile nations, and creation is the thread that unites the theological system of Gaebelein.[52] It is not surprising

---

[51] Gaebelein, *The Angels of God*, 10.
[52] The consistency of Gaebelein's theology over the years can be seen by comparing the books mentioned above from the 1930s to an earlier article in *Our Hope*. See Arno C. Gaebelein, "The Coming of the Lord, the Hope of Israel, and the Hope of the Nations and Creation," *Our Hope* 8 (September 1901): 194-99. This article was actually the publication of an address given at the first Sea Cliff Bible conference.

then to find the name of his Jewish outreach ministry to be *The Hope of Israel Movement* or to note that the highly significant expository magazine which he edited for over half a century was named *Our Hope*.

However, this thread has a Christological focus. While the evangelical character of Gaebelein's theology shows that the benefits of God for the human race are grounded in the work of Christ on the cross, the Christological spotlight falls on the doctrine of the Second Coming.[53] In a chapter entitled "Hundreds of Questions But Only One Answer,"[54] the message is unblurred,

> There is but one answer to all these questions concerning the promised hope for Israel, for the nations of the earth and for all creation. That answer is:
>
> *The Lord Jesus Christ.*
>
> He alone is the only answer, the completest answer, the never-failing answer to all our questions. But what do we mean when we give His ever blessed and adorable Name, the Name above every other name, as the only answer? We do not mean that the answer is a practical application of the principles of righteousness declared by the infallible teacher in the sermon on the mount. We do not mean the practice of what has been termed the golden rule. We do not mean a leadership of

---

[53] Gaebelein viewed the atonement on the cross by Christ as the greatest event in human history while the Second Coming of Christ was the second greatest event (*Hope of the Ages*, 76). Yet the Second Coming is "the great hope, the only hope, for all the earth . . . All waits for that coming event" (76). It is the work of Christ in the Second Coming, rather than the first advent, which serves as the focus of the unifying theme of hope.

[54] Gaebelein, *Hope of the Ages*, 54-76.

Jesus. We do not mean that these questions will be answered by future spiritual revivals, nor do we mean that a blasted Western civilization, misnamed Christian, will influence heathen nations to accept Christianity and turn to God from their idols. The sorrowful fact is that what military Christendom has done and is doing, and the shameful failures of Western civilization, has been a curse to heathen nations. What we mean, the only answer, the completest and neverfailing answer to all our questions, is

> *The Glorious Reappearing of the Lord Jesus Christ*

This future event will answer every question, solve every problem which humanity faces today, and all the existing chaotic conditions, and bring about that golden age of which heathen poets dreamed, which the Bible promises is in store for the earth.[55]

In light of such an emphasis, it is no wonder that for many years the cover of *Our Hope* magazine had on it the words "The Lord Jesus Christ, Who is Our Hope." The central interpretive motif, prophetic hope through the Second Coming, was best captured in a prayer which closed Gaebelein's volume, Hopeless, Yet There is Hope,

> Even so Come, Thou Hope of the hopeless, Thou Hope of Israel, Thou Hope of the World, all Nations and Creation. Even so, Come Lord Jesus.

---

[55] Gaebelein, *Hope of the Ages*, 71-72.

CONCLUSION

Arno C. Gaebelein believed in a sovereign God who controlled history. Predictions God had made came true because of His great power and plan. The "plan" is a multi-faceted one which highlighted prophetic hope in the personal Second Coming of Jesus Christ as God's redemptive plan is accomplished on several fronts. It may be possible to see in Gaebelein the makings of our understanding of the doxological purpose of biblical history. If so, then Ryrie's third point in the essentials of dispensationalism may have some merit.

24 On Meaning and Purpose

Chapter 2 – On Biblical Interpretation
The Biblical Roots of the Hermeneutic in Revelation[1]
John Oglesby

The author of Revelation begins with arguably the most pressing introduction within all of divine literature,

> The Revelation of Jesus Christ, which God gave Him to show to His bond-servants, the things which must soon take place; and He sent and communicated it by His angel to His bond-servant John, who testified to the word of God and to the testimony of Jesus Christ, even to all that he saw. Blessed is he who reads and those who hear the words of the prophecy and heed the things which are written in it; for the time is near.[2]

John the Apostle begins by identifying the source of the revelation, the stance by which to receive it, the result of those who read and keep its contents and repeats the urgency which defines the information of the revelation.

The book of Revelation is a critical part of the Biblical canon,[3] yet often misunderstood due to either a shift in hermeneutics when approaching the

---

[1] Originally presented to the Council on Dispensational Hermeneutics as "The Internal Precedent for the Utilization of the Literal Grammatical-Historical Hermeneutics as Found in the Book of Revelation," September 15-16, 2021.

[2] Revelation 1:1–3 (NASB). All Scripture references are from the New American Standard Bible unless otherwise noted.

[3] Revelation 1:1–3, 22:10; 1 Thessalonians 4:13–17; Christopher Cone presents a convincing paper on the necessity of Biblically derived premillennialism within the study of socio-political thought. While his topic is not specific to Revelation,

book or simply a poor hermeneutic consistently used throughout the Bible as a whole.[4] Reformed theologian, Louis Berkhof, points this out in his critique of premillennialism, "The theory [premillennialism] is *based on a literal interpretation of the prophetic delineations* of the future of Israel and of the Kingdom of God, which is entirely untenable [*emphasis mine*]."[5] While Berkhof disagrees with the conclusion of premillennialism, or a literal interpretation of prophecy, he recognizes the battlefield of a proper view of prophecy is that of interpretation or hermeneutics.

Hermeneutics finds its proper place in epistemology, the foundational category of one's worldview.[6] Within epistemology (the study of knowledge/certainty), the source of authority and how to interpret or

---

Revelation is a major source of understanding for Biblically derived premillennialism. Christopher Cone, "Biblically Derived Premillennialism as a Necessary Condition for a Biblical Socio-Political Model" at drcone.com, https://www.drcone.com/2014/09/18/biblically-derived-premillennialism-as-a-necessary-condition-for-a-biblical-socio-political-model/.

[4] Andy Woods writes an article regarding Revelation 17–18 and addresses Apocalyptic literature exploring the genre of Revelation. Within this context, Woods establishes the different hermeneutic approaches to Revelation and connects it with one's understanding of the acceptance of the apocalyptic genre. Andy Woods, "What is the Identity of Babylon in Revelation 17–18?" Pre-trib Research Center, https://www.pre-trib.org/articles/dr-thomas-ice/message/what-is-the-identity-of-babylon-in-revelation-17-18/read#_ftnref214; For an example of this in practice, see Kevin DeYoung, "Theological Primer: The 144,000" The Gospel Coalition, https://www.thegospelcoalition.org/blogs/kevin-deyoung/theological-primer-the-144000/; Steve Gregg, ed., *Revelation: Four Views, a Parallel Commentary* (Nashville: Thomas Nelson, 1997); Louis Berkhof, *Systematic Theology* (Grand Rapids: Eerdmans Publishing Co., 1938).

[5] L. Berkhof, *Systematic Theology* (Grand Rapids, MI: Wm. B. Eerdmans Publishing Co., 1938), 712.

[6] One could argue for metaphysics being foundational, but before one could understand reality, one must understand *how* to understand reality. Without a proper understanding of how to view, it would be impossible to study metaphysics with any certainty. Christopher Cone addresses this issue extensively in *Priority in Biblical Hermeneutics and Theological Method*, 1–4.

understand that authority is established. How should one understand the book of Revelation? Berkhof was correct – the varying answers to this question lead to varying disagreements within the metaphysics topic of eschatology. However, the more foundational question is "How should one understand the book of Revelation *based on the proper authority?*"

Hermeneutics is an important study but must be established on the proper authority. If the hermeneutic theory is not grounded upon God's word, it is fallacious and insufficient for a proper understanding of the Bible – if indeed the Bible is the word of God.[7]

Berkhof posits the idea that understanding prophecy using a literal methodology is entirely untenable. Berkhof presents a methodology for interpreting prophecy which goes against a normative understanding.[8] For example, Berkhof posits, "Moreover, he should not proceed on the assumption that prophecies are always fulfilled in the exact form in which they were uttered. The presumption is that, if they are fulfilled in a later dispensation, the dispensational form will be disregard in the fulfillment."[9] Interestingly, though Berkhof argues for the illegitimacy of understanding prophecies in a normative fashion, he defines a prophecy as a proclamation of that which God has revealed.[10] The claim, then, can be understood that within this specific genre, that which God has revealed should not always be taken normatively based on the context of when it was said and the

---

[7] Understandably some may object due to circular reasoning. However, the purpose of language presupposes a basic nature of understanding. As God created language with the purpose of understanding, a basic level of understanding is presupposed.

[8] Cf. "In such cases the prophetic horizon was enlarged, they sensed something of the passing character of the old forms, and gave ideal descriptions of the blessings of the New Testament Church." *Principles of Biblical Interpretation*, 152.

[9] Ibid, 153.

[10] Ibid, 148.

surrounding literature. This, however, goes against the exegetical evidence found within various places of the Bible.

Christopher Cone illustrates this point well in a similar study throughout the books of Genesis and Job.[11] Cone observes an exegetically derived basis for a normative approach to the Biblical canon through examining each speech act of God and the response to that speech act. Cone concludes "because of the two-thousand-year precedent evident in Genesis and Job, any departure from the simplicity of this method bears a strong exegetical burden of proof, requiring that there be *explicit exegetical support for any change one might perceive as necessary in handling later Scriptures.*"[12]

Cone demonstrates the necessity of a normative understanding in two books which are commonly recognized as narrative.[13] Many have made the claim that all messianic prophecies pointing to Jesus's first advent were fulfilled in a literal or normative fashion. Charles Ryrie says it this way, "The prophecies of the first advent of Christ were all fulfilled literally. This obvious but extremely significant fact argues for the validity and use of the literal hermeneutics in all of biblical interpretation."[14]

---

[11] Christopher Cone, *Priority in Biblical Hermeneutics and Theological Method*, (Raymore, MO: Exegetica Publishing, 2018), 17-36.

[12] Ibid, 35.

[13] This is not necessarily true for all of Genesis and Job. An example of a specific area contrary to the given statement is the understanding of Genesis 1–3. Many debates are had regarding the genre of writing for the Creation account. For an exegetical and quantitative study on the genre of Genesis 1–3, see Larry Vardiman, Andrew A. Snelling, and Eugene F. Chaffin, *Radioisotopes and the Age of the Earth: A Young-Earth Creationist Research Initiative*, (Dallas: Institution for Creation Research, 2000).

[14] Charles Caldwell Ryrie, *Basic Theology: A Popular Systematic Guide to Understanding Biblical Truth* (Chicago, IL: Moody Press, 1999), 129; It is worth noting the lack of citations showing one's work within the topic of Christ's fulfillment of messianic prophecy. Some have disputed this claim, but upon further investigation, it seems they have misunderstood what is meant by the term "literal." For further understanding, see Thomas D. Ice, "The Literal Fulfillment of Bible Prophecy" Scholars Crossing,

RECENT DEPARTURE FROM NORMATIVE UNDERSTANDING

As Cone and Ryrie have demonstrated, there is much exegetical support within Genesis, Job, and various prophecies for a normative understanding of the Scriptures. However, within fairly recent development, the genre of apocalyptic literature has taken root and spread throughout the theological community.[15] Due to various reasons such as the ambiguity of the definition of "apocalyptic," many theologians have assumed an apocalyptic genre designation and consequently an allegorical understanding of the book of Revelation. But if the genre diagnosis is incorrect, then what about the resulting hermeneutic method?

Robert Thomas points out, "no consensus exists as to a precise definition of *genre*."[16] Thomas recognizes an important consequence: "…so attempts to classify portions of the New Testament, including Revelation, are at best vague." While in some kinds of literature genre designations may be ambiguous, the Biblical author seems to leave no room for ambiguity within the book of Revelation.[17] Andy Woods presents an argument for the

---

https://digitalcommons.liberty.edu/cgi/viewcontent.cgi?article=1100&context=pretrib_arch.

[15] William W. Klein, et. al, *Introduction to Biblical Interpretation* (Nashville: Thomas Nelson Inc. 2004), 444–448; Roy Zuck, *Basic Bible Interpretation* (Colorado Springs: David C Cook, 1991), 243; Grant R. Osborne, *The Hermeneutic Spiral: A Comprehensive Introduction to Biblical Interpretation* (Downers Grove: InterVarsity Press, 2006), p. 275–290; Leland Ryken, *How to Read the Bible as Literature…and Get More Out of it* (Grand Rapids: Zondervan, 1984); Gordon D. Fee, Douglas Stuart, *How to Read the Bible for All Its Worth* (Grand Rapids: Zondervan, 2014); J. Scott Duvall, J. Daniel Hays, *Grasping God's Word: A Hands-On Approach to Reading, Interpreting, and Applying the Bible* (Grand Rapids: Zondervan, 2012).

[16] Robert Thomas, *Evangelical Hermeneutics: The New Versus the Old* (Grand Rapids: Kregel, 2002), 324.

[17] Rev. 1:3; This author recognizes the external factors in establishing genres. The nature of genres would involve finding commonality among writings, grouping them under a heading pointing to those similarities, and calling that a genre. As an exegete, it

prophetic delineation of Revelation where he establishes the necessity to consistently use the literal grammatical historical hermeneutic.[18] Robert Thomas, likewise in his commentary on Revelation states:

> Most distinctive of all, however, is that this book calls itself a prophecy (1:3; 22:7, 10, 18, 19). Its contents fully justify this self-claim. Of the thirty-one characteristics that have been cited in attempts to define apocalyptic, all when properly understood could apply to prophecy as well, with the possible exception of pseudonymity (which does not apply to Revelation). Alleged differences between the Apocalypse and generally accepted works of prophecy often rest upon inadequate interpretations of the Apocalypse.[19]

While the correct genre designation of the book of Revelation is not the primary purpose of this writing, it seems necessary to give some background information regarding departures and disagreements about the proper interpretation of the book. Still, the primary question is whether or not God provides an interpretive method *within* the book of Revelation. If so, it would seem the genre classification of the book of Revelation has little to no effect on the necessary interpretive approach, especially as the apocalyptic genre is

---

is this author's intention to let God's word reign authoritative whenever it speaks. Some theologians have made the case that John does designate the genre as apocalyptic due to the first word of the book. However, after further study, there isn't any reason to believe John was dealing with genre as the Greek word simply means to reveal as J. Ramsey Michaels clear points out in his work. Cf. Michaels, J. Ramsey, *Revelation*, vol. 20, The IVP New Testament Commentary Series (Downers Grove, IL: InterVarsity Press, 1997); N. T. Wright, *The New Testament in its World* (Grand Rapids: Zondervan, 2019), 821.

[18] Andy Woods, "What is the Identity of Babylon in Revelation 17-18?"

[19] Robert L. Thomas, *Revelation 1-7: An Exegetical Commentary* (Chicago: Moody Publishers, 1992), 25.

an extra-biblical designation. In fact, an external designation which requires interpretive variation from the normative understanding of Scripture places that external data as authoritative, usurping the rightful authority of God.

A brief note on the sufficiency of Scripture is necessary at this point to justify the priority of internal evidence for an appropriate interpretive method. Solomon establishes *the* prerequisite for knowledge and wisdom: the fear of the Lord.[20] Solomon continues to provide the source of that wisdom and knowledge: the mouth of God.[21] This leads to superiority of God's special revelation for gaining true knowledge and wisdom. In this current era, with a closed canon, that special revelation is found in written form – namely the Bible.[22] The Bible is sufficient to equip the believer (and contains the necessary information to convert the unbeliever) for the good works which God has prepared beforehand.[23] Similarly, God has given the believer everything pertaining to life and godliness which is through the knowledge of Him,[24] which we understand to proceed from the mouth of God. Because of this, the Bible should be considered sufficient to provide its own interpretive method. After all, if external data was needed to ascertain the knowledge and understanding of the Scriptures, then how could the Scriptures themselves be sufficient to transform the believer through the renewing of the mind?[25] Would the Bible alone be able to provide true knowledge and certainty? The answer seems clear enough. It would lack capacity for certainty and could only provide understanding to the level that fallen humanity's reasoning is able to deliver.

---

[20] Proverbs 1:7, 9:6.
[21] Proverbs 2:6.
[22] 2 Timothy 3:16–17; 2 Peter 1:16–21.
[23] Ephesians 2:10.
[24] 2 Peter 1:3–4.
[25] Romans 12:1–2.

AN INTERNAL MODEL FOR UNDERSTANDING THE BIBLE

In order to derive an internal precedent for a normative interpretive approach to the book of Revelation each speech act is recorded, and the responses are noted.[26] By identifying a normative understanding of the speech act one can consider the response and observe whether the intended audience understood the speech act normatively. Each response is categorized in one of two groups: Category 1 (C1) which is regarded as a normative response or Category 2 (C2) which is regarded as a response not based on a normative understanding.[27]

Various conjugates of *lego* (λέγω) appear 94 times in 90 verses of Revelation. Among these instances, 22 of them receive a response in the immediate context. Of the verses containing the responses, another 9 instances are accounted. Twenty of the 94 instances appear in Revelation 2–3. In these contexts, there are no responses because the recipients hadn't yet received the communication. The remaining 43 speech act contexts do not provide responses.

Speech Acts and Responses
Speech Act – Revelation 1:11
Jesus commands John to write about everything he sees and send it to the seven churches.

---

[26] This writer is not invoking speech act theory. The terminology, "Speech act," is simply pointing to an occurrence of one speaking to another.

[27] It is worth noting, this study does not identify specific types of responses outside of one based on a normative understanding. It will either be normative or not. If it is not, it will be the burden of the next student to identify specifically what type of understanding was utilized based on the response.

Biblical Distinctions Applied 33

Response — Revelation 1:4; 2:1, 8, 12, 18; 3:1, 7, 14
John provides a C1 response as he writes the book of Revelation and specific sections addressed to the seven churches. The absence of a C1 response recorded for the sending of the letter does not show a C2 response, but the act of sending the book of Revelation would not be expected to have been recorded elsewhere in the Bible as Revelation is the conclusion of the canon.

Speech Act — Revelation 1:19
Jesus implores John to write the things he has seen, the things which are present, and the things to come which will be shown him.

Response
There are two ways to address the response. First, the existence of the book of Revelation shows a C1 response as John wrote the things he was told to write. Second, John wrote the book of Revelation in the three mandated categories. He wrote the things which he had seen (Rev 1), the things which are (Rev 2–3) and the things to come (Rev 4–22).

Speech Act — Revelation 4:1b
"The first voice" commanded that John ascend or come up to see what must take place in future events.

Response — Revelation 4:2
John provides a C1 response by ascending immediately to the throne room of God where he begins his journey of future events.

Speech Act — Revelation 5:2
"A strong angel" asks a question regarding the opening of the scroll which is in the hand of the one who sits on the throne.

Response – Revelation 5:3
John shows a C1 response by weeping as he found no one worthy of opening the scroll. Furthermore, the angel comforts John by showing him One who is able to open the scroll and break the seals.

Speech Act – Revelation 5:5
As John weeps from not being able to identify anyone worthy of opening the seals within the scroll God holds, the angel comforts John by identifying One who is worthy. He further implies that the Lion of the tribe of Judah, the Root of David, the Lamb of God, will open the scroll because He has overcome.

Response – Revelation 5:6–7
We see Jesus provide a C1 response as He does, in fact, get up, take the scroll, and begin breaking the seals within.

Speech Act – Revelation 7:13
One of the elders approaches John and asks him "what is the identity of the multitudes dressed in white robes?"

Response – Revelation 7:14
After John responds that the elder already knows, the elder provides a C1 response to his own question by answering the question in a normative way. The elder identifies the multitudes and why they have white robes.

Speech Act – Revelation 8:13
The eagle flies over the earth and proclaims a woe to all the earth for the three trumpets that remain.

Biblical Distinctions Applied 35

Response – Revelation 9:1, 13; 11:15
The angels provide a C1 response to the eagle's warning as they blow the remaining three trumpets. The result of the trumpets is mass destruction and woeful events for those on the earth.

Speech Act – Revelation 10:4
After "seven peals of thunder" spoke, John was about to write what was spoken but a voice from heaven told him not to.

Response – Revelation 10:4–5
The absence of what was said by the peals of thunder provide a C1 response. While this instance is an argument from absence or silence, silence was the imperative and provides adequate evidence for a C1 categorization.

Speech Act – Revelation 10:8
The voice from heaven tells John to approach the angel who was previously described in verses 1–7 and take the scroll from his hand.

Response – Revelation 10:9a
John provides a C1 response as he immediately approaches the angel and takes the scroll from his hand.

Speech Act – Revelation 10:9b
After John takes the scroll from the angel's hand, the angel tells John to eat the scroll. He also communicates that the scroll will be bitter in his stomach and sweet in the mouth.

Response – Revelation 10:10
John provides another C1 response by eating the scroll and describes the experience as bitter in the stomach and sweet in the mouth.

Speech Act – Revelation 11:12
After the two prophets of Revelation 11 are resurrected, they hear a voice from heaven giving the imperative to "come up here."

Response – Revelation 11:12
The two prophets provide a C1 response as they "went up into heaven in the cloud."

Speech Act – Revelation 11:15
Loud voices in heaven proclaim the beginning of the kingdom and the truth of Christ's reign forever.

Response – Revelation 11:17
The twenty-four elders respond by praising God for His reign. While the elders are not acting, their response to the truth proclaimed by the multitude of voices provide precedent for categorizing their response as a C1.

Speech Act – Revelation 14:15
"One like a son of man" was sitting on a cloud, crowned with a sickle in His hand. An angel, leaving the temple, tells him to swing the sickle across the earth for it was ripe.

Response – Revelation 14:16
"The one like a son of man" provides a C1 response as He swings His sickle across the earth as directed.

Biblical Distinctions Applied   37

Speech Act – Revelation 14:18
Similar to the previous speech act, another angel tells the "one like a son of man" to swing the sickle and gather the grapes from the earth.

Response – Revelation 14:19–20
He swings His sickle and gathers the grapes, providing another C1 response.

Speech Act – Revelation 16:1
A loud voice comes from the temple commanding seven angels to pour out seven bowls of judgement on the world.

Response – Revelation 16:2, 3, 4, 8, 10, 12, 17
A C1 response is provided as the seven angels are recorded pouring out the bowls on the earth.

Speech Act – Revelation 17:1–2
One of the seven angels tells John that he is going to carry him away to see "the judgement of the great harlot…"

Response – Revelation 17:3
A C1 response is provided in 17:3 as John is immediately carried away into a wilderness and shown the details of the great harlot.

Speech Act – Revelation 17:7
As John is being shown the details of the great harlot, he "wondered with great wonder." As the angel responsible for revealing these things to him sees his wonder, he responds by telling John that the angel will explain everything regarding what John has seen in the previous six verses.

Response – Revelation 17:8–18
The angel intends a C1 understanding, as the angel then proceeds to explain in detail what John has just seen. The highly figurative language has a normative meaning, and the angel explains the metaphor.

Speech Act – Revelation 19:5
After the fall of Babylon, a voice from the throne gives the imperative to praise God.

Response – Revelation 19:6
The multitude of God's bond-servants provide a C1 response as they praise God by saying, "Hallelujah! For the Lord our God, the Almighty, reigns."

Speech Act – Revelation 19:9
John is commanded to write "Blessed are those who are invited to the marriage supper of the lamb."

Response – Revelation 19:9
The fact that the words are recorded in the book of Revelation shows John's C1 understanding.

Speech Act – Revelation 19:17–18
As Christ returns to earth for the great war, an announcement is made for all the birds of heaven to come so they can feast on the fallen kings and beasts.

Response – Revelation 19:21
The birds responded in a C1 fashion as they were "filled with their flesh."

Speech Act – Revelation 21:5
John is commanded to write the words which God had previously spoken in verses 3–4.

Response – Revelation 21:3–4
The presence of the words in verses 3–4 provide adequate evidence to categorize John's understanding as a C1 interpretation.

Speech Act – Revelation 21:9
One of the seven angels tells John to come so that the angel could show him the "Bride of the Lamb."

Response – Revelation 21:10–11
A C1 response is recorded in verses 10–11 as the angel carried John away and showed him the details of the "Bride of the Lamb."

Results

After reviewing each speech act within the book of Revelation and the response to each, where one is provided, 22 of the 22 responses should be considered C1 responses. It is evident that one hundred percent of the responses within the book of Revelation show a normative understanding of communication providing overwhelming evidence for an internal model of interpretation. Communication should be understood in a normative, common-sense fashion. The method of interpretation which models this straightforward approach has become known as the literal grammatical historical method, utilizing grammar and context to understand the normative usage of language in the communication.

Among the various speech acts and responses, many of them are found in contexts with figurative language. To understand Scripture in a normative way is not to disregard figurative language, but to utilize the context provided by the Scriptures themselves in order to understand when a figure of speech is used. A great example of this is found in Revelation 17:7–18. As John is being shown this vast metaphor, he stands in wonder as to how he should understand what is taking place. The context reveals the obvious use of metaphor as the angel follows up by explaining what the metaphor is intended to communicate. There is a literal meaning behind the figurative language, and the presence of figures of speech should not change the hermeneutic employed by the reader.

A BRIEF LOOK AT OTHER VIEWS

After examining the text for an internal model of interpretation, it is worth interacting with other scholars regarding various passages, for illustrating the importance, examining reasons to disagree with the proposed model, and evaluating the worldview implications (specifically within epistemology).

Charles Hodge, a reformed theologian, makes the claim that "prophecy makes a general impression with regard to future events, which is reliable and salutary, while the details remain in obscurity."[28] As an example of this, Hodge utilizes the failure of the first-century Jews to recognize the details of Jesus's first advent. While, admittedly, in many ways the religious leaders of Jesus's day got it wrong, to base the argument on the response of leaders whom Jesus consistently rebuked for their lack of understanding and misplacement of God's word proves to be an unreliable foundation for

---

[28] Charles Hodge, *Systematic Theology*, vol. 3 (Oak Harbor: Logos Research Systems Inc., 1997) 791.

argumentation.²⁹ As one examines the fulfillment of prophecies regarding Jesus's first advent, the details are evident enough, although admittedly what one might consider detail versus vagueness does come into play.³⁰ The examples Hodge uses to justify his argument come from a misunderstanding of the prophecies themselves. For example, Hodge argues that first-century Jews misunderstood the prophecies regarding Jesus subduing the nations, as Hodge states, "He is to subdue all nations, not by the sword, as they supposed, but by truth and love."³¹ This conclusion assumes that the prophecies referenced are in fact regarding Christ's first advent alone. If one takes later revelation into consideration, the book of Revelation clearly shows that Jesus will, in the future come back and subdue the nations.³² This type of interpretive method leads Hodge to spiritualize much of the prophecy found within the book of Revelation, including the nature of the millennial kingdom.³³ One's metaphysical understanding of the Kingdom has critical impact on one's ethical and socio-political understandings of worldview.

N. T. Wright models the importance of an internal precedent for interpretive method and genre classification. Wright posits the idea that the book of Revelation is apocalyptic literature and should be interpreted accordingly, just as one might interpret other apocalyptic literature from the same era.³⁴ Because of this, Wright concludes, "At the same time, as with biblical prophecy more generally, the rich symbolic language invites *multiple*

---

²⁹ It is important here to note the difference between descriptive and prescriptive text. While models of interpretation may be derived from descriptive passages, context and details of speakers/recipients is a critical part of deriving a proper model.
³⁰ Isaiah 53 is a great example of these prophecies. See Isaiah 53:3 and John 1:11; Isaiah 53:4-5 and Matthew 27:35; Isaiah 53:6 and Romans 4:25; etc.
³¹ Ibid.
³² Revelation 19:11-16.
³³ Hodge, *Systematic Theology*, 841-842.
³⁴ Examples of these would be other pseudepigraphal books such as Ascension of Isaiah and Apocalypse of Peter.

'applications' and 'interpretations' as the various systems of pagan power behave in characteristic ways and the church is faced with the challenge both of understanding what is happening and acting appropriately *[emphasis mine]*."[35] Many scholars rightly disagree with the idea of multiple interpretations for various reasons – one being the loss of all effective communication and meaning. However, because Wright considers the book of Revelation as apocalyptic literature, the text has a meaning for the time it was written and for future events. Note that Wright is not simply advocating for multiple applications but is also advocating for multiple correct interpretations.

This idea plays a role in Revelation 17-18 as Wright identifies Babylon the Great as symbolic for the nation of Rome contemporary to the time of the writing of Revelation. He then contends that "We appropriate this vision for our twenty-first-century context by remembering that there are many Babylons and beasts, and we need to resist them all."[36] Interestingly, Wright makes the claim of ancient Rome being the true Babylon the Great but only defends his position by drawing parallels using further symbolism.[37] What is problematic is the lack of any internal evidence for interpreting the symbols this way. No doubt, Wright's precommitment to the use of symbolism comes from his understanding of apocalyptic literature and his precommitment to the book of Revelation as apocalyptic.

Lastly, the 144,000 of Revelation 7 provides another useful case study. As Revelation presents the 144,000 as the "bond-servants of God"[38] coming from the "Tribes of Israel"[39] and continues by listing how many bond-servants from each tribe, a normative understanding of the passage would lead one to believe that the 144,000 are actually 144,000 Jews. However,

---

[35] N. T. Wright, *The New Testament in its World*, 828.
[36] Ibid, 844.
[37] Ibid, 838-839.
[38] Revelation 7:3.
[39] Revelation 7:4.

Ryken posits "The number of the redeemed – 144,000 – symbolizes completeness (foursquare symbolism of 12 times 12, and all 12 tribes represented) and magnitude (inasmuch as 1,000 symbolized a multitude in ancient times)."[40] Ryken provides the 144,000 as an example of how numbers should be taken figuratively within the book of Revelation. Ryken's reasoning for the symbolic nature of numbers is based upon other *extra-biblical* apocalyptic sources.

Wright likewise states, "The number of 144,000 from the twelve tribes is symbolic for the church as the continuing expression of Israel," yet provides no basis for his understanding. If one is understanding the Bible using a normative methodology, a symbolic understanding must be warranted within the context of the passage.[41] To establish a passage as symbolic simply because of an external genre designation places the genre – not the Bible – as authoritative, leading to a Genre Hermeneutic.

CONCLUSION

Regardless of genre the book of Revelation presents an internal precedent for a normative (literal grammatical historical) interpretive method. Genre is an important consideration for studying books of the Bible, but because of the internal interpretive precedent established, genre simply does not play a role in interpretive methodology. Beyond this, to deviate from a normative interpretive method whenever approaching the Scriptures as a whole would demand strong exegetical evidence. To deviate from the literal

---

[40] Leland Ryken, *Symbols and Reality: A Guided Study of Prophecy, Apocalypse, and Visionary Literature: Reading the Bible as Literature* (Bellingham: Lexham Press, 2016), 99.

[41] For further study on how to identify symbolism, see Roy Zuck, *Basic Bible Interpretation* (Colorado Springs: David C. Cook, 1991) or Milton Terry, *Biblical Hermeneutics: A Treatise on the Interpretation of the Old and New Testaments* (Grand Rapids: Zondervan, 1976).

grammatical historical hermeneutic without exegetical roots is to enthrone oneself as a source of authority in the worldview. The consequence is an altogether different epistemology and ultimately a catastrophic deviation from the Biblical worldview.

Chapter 3 – On Worldview and Method
The Double-Edged Sword of Dispensationalism:
Destructive as Methodology, Constructive as Outcome
Christopher Cone

INTRODUCTION

As Charles Ryrie catalogued the three aspects of dispensationalism's *sine qua non*, he prefaced the three distinctives by emphasizing a critical methodological difference between dispensational thinkers and covenant (theology) thinkers: "the covenant theologian finds biblical distinctions a necessary part of his theology even though the covenant of grace is the ruling category…the dispensations supply the need for distinctions in the orderly progress of revelation throughout Scripture."[1] Ryrie cites the need for distinctions as the occasion for developing theological systems, and the basis of those distinctions as the covenant of grace for covenant theology and the progress of Scripture for dispensational theology.

The implication is evident: Ryrie asserts that covenant theology is primarily a *theological predetermination* because the theological covenant undergirding covenant theology is the ruling category, while dispensational theology is an exegetically based *theological outcome*, because it is derived by observing the progress of Scripture. Ryrie further observes that "Only dispensationalism does justice to the proper concept of the progress of revelation."[2] Ryrie further recognizes dispensationalism as an outcome when

---

[1] Charles Ryrie, *Dispensationalism* (Moody Press, 1995), 16-17.
[2] Ibid., 19.

he affirms that, "If plain or normal interpretation is the only valid hermeneutical principle, and if it is consistently applied, it will cause one to be a dispensationalist."[3] The primary emphasis of Ryrie's opening chapter (entitled "*Dispensationalism: Help or Heresy?*") is that dispensationalism is a help because it is a *product* of the Bible interpreted in a normative way.

If Ryrie is correct in his assertion that dispensationalism is helpful because of its scriptural derivation and as an outcome of exegetical work, then his firm yet gracious critique of covenant theology as a theological rather than exegetical precommitment is likewise warranted. Ryrie's evaluation occasions examining the impact and value of the dispensational theological system when reckoned as an outcome of hermeneutics applied (as Ryrie advocates) or by contrast, as a theological precommitment.

As Ryrie critiques theological precommitments by critiquing a popular example (covenant theology), it is fair to scrutinize dispensational thought, seeking to understand whether it is precommitment or product. If a precommitment, then dispensationalism deserves every bit of the criticism Ryrie (and others) direct toward covenant theology. It is curious then to discover the diversity of opinions on which of the two characterizations is true – among both critics and adherents of dispensational thought.

PRECOMMITMENT OR PRODUCT: SOME OUTSIDE PERSPECTIVES ON DISPENSATIONAL THOUGHT

Perhaps the most commonly accessed definition of dispensationalism asserts that the system is in fact a unique hermeneutic that is distinct from yet based on a literal translation of the Bible. Wikipedia's entry on the system reads, "Dispensational-ism is a particular hermeneutic or analytical system for interpreting the Bible based on a literal translation, and which stands in

---

[3] Ryrie, *Dispensationalism*, 20.

Biblical Distinctions Applied 47

contrast to the earlier Calvinist system of covenant theology used in fundamentalist biblical interpretation."[4]

Varner Johns exemplifies the staunchest critics of dispensationalism in his assertion that CI Scofield "imposed upon the Bible a system of error as subtle and Satanic as any that has ever been invented by the master deceiver."[5] Robert Harbach goes a bit further in describing exactly how the dispensational system is in error, noting that

> the line Dispensationalism makes through Scripture is disjointed, slip-knotted, sheep-shanked, strained and broken with many gaps intervening along its shabby, ludicrous length…they become **guilty of approaching the Bible according to modernistic methods. For both Dispensationalism and Modernism have a subjective theory of Bible structure**…reads the Gospel According to Matthew **applying its subjective hypothesis,** and decides that the Sermon on the Mount is not intended for the Church today, but for a future age, after the Church has gone…Dispensationalism is a questionable hermeneutical method…[emphasis mine].[6]

Harbach considers dispensationalism to be a hermeneutic method, and a highly problematic one for sure. If Harbach is right, then dispensationalism represents a precommitment that demands a particular interpretive method

---

[4] Wikipedia, "Dispensationalism" https://en.wikipedia.org/wiki/Dispensationalism.

[5] Varner Johns, "Sevenfold Errors of Dispensationalism," *Ministry Magazine*, November, 1942, https://www.ministrymagazine.org/archive/1942/11/sevenfold-errors-of-dispensationalism.

[6] Robert Harbach, "Dispensationalism: An Ancient Error" PRCA website, originally January 1, 1967, in *The Standard Bearer*, http://www.prca.org/resources/publications/articles/item/3741-dispensationalism-an-ancient-error.

in order to justify its conclusions. In fact, this is reminiscent of Ryrie's critique of covenant theology (though Ryrie is certainly much more gracious than Harbach attempts to be).

Adam Graham furthers the discussion elucidating what he believes to be wrong with dispensationalism:

> It is clear that literal interpretation of scripture, as a rule, is a valuable principle, but only when it is tempered with a consistent understanding of context and the progressive nature of revelation. **It is also clear that dispensationalism does not and cannot fully adhere to this principle consistently.** We should therefore not be afraid to both espouse the merits of literal interpretation of scripture and deny the exclusivist claims that many in the dispensational camp often make.[7]

Graham recognizes the merit of "literal interpretation," but suggests that dispensationalism simply doesn't follow that method. The "exclusivist claims" of many dispensationalists, according to Graham, are rooted in theological loyalties rather than sound exegetical process.

John Gerstner helps put the hermeneutic issue in focus, as he specifies that,

> We all agree that most literature, including the Bible, is usually meant to be understood according to the literal construction of the words which are used...At the point where we differ, there is a tendency for the dispensationalists to be literalistic where the

---

[7] Adam Graham "What is Wrong With Dispensationalism" No King But Christ, June 21, 2018, https://www.nokingbutchrist.org/what-is-wrong-with-dispensationalism/.

non-dispensationalist tends to interpret the Bible figuratively. But to say on the basis of that limited divergence of interpretation that the two schools represent fundamentally different approaches is not warranted. Many on both sides think that this minor "hermeneutical" difference is a more foundational difference than the theological. We profoundly disagree for we believe that **the dispensational literal hermeneutic is driven by an *a priori* commitment to dispensational theological distinctives** [emphasis mine].[8]

Gerstner conceives dispensationalism to be a theological precommitment that drives a version of a literal hermeneutic – what Gerstner calls "the *dispensational* literal hermeneutic."

PRECOMMITMENT OR PRODUCT: SOME INSIDE PERSPECTIVES ON DISPENSATIONAL THOUGHT

Outside perspectives are not the only ones that seem to indicate that dispensationalism might be a precommitment based on hermeneutic applications, though it is noteworthy that none (of which are cited here) would *directly suggest* that the system of thought is a theological precommitment. Self-affirmed dispensationalist David Guzik illustrates the difficulty as he describes dispensationalism as "a way of looking at the Bible that understands God's unfolding plan—that He has worked in somewhat different ways with and through different peoples...I'm a

---

[8] John Gerstner, *Wrongly Dividing the Word of Truth* (Morgan, PA: Soli Deo Gloria, 2000), 92-93.

dispensationalist…"[9]. It is unclear whether "a way of looking at the Bible" refers to the outcome of exegesis or the methodology.

Tommy Ice addresses the challenge a bit in his article *Dispensational Hermeneutics*, in part by distinguishing between macroliteralism and microliteralism. Ice explains that "The system of literal interpretation is the grammatical-historical, or textual, approach to hermeneutics. Use of literalism in this sense could be called macroliteralism."[10] He adds that,

> Within macroliteralism, the consistent use of the grammatical-historical system yields the interpretative conclusion, for example, that Israel always and only refers to national Israel. The church will not be substituted for Israel if the grammatical-historical system of interpretation is consistently used because there are no indicators in the text that such is the case. Therefore, one must bring an idea from outside the text by saying that the passage really means something that it does not actually say. This kind of replacement approach is a mild form of spiritualized, or allegorical, interpretation.[11]

Ice concludes that those who replace Israel with the church so do in violation of macroliteralism.[12] At the same time, within macroliteralism, the attention to individual passages and whether or not they might include figures of speech and how those should be handled in each instance, Ice refers to as microliteralism.[13] Ice makes it clear that dispensational thought is an outcome

---

[9] David Guzik, "Pitfalls of Dispensationalism" Calvary Chapel, May 14, 2015, https://calvarychapel.com/posts/pitfalls-of-dispensationalism/.

[10] Thomas Ice, "Dispensational Hermeneutics," *Scholars Crossing*, Liberty University, May 2009, 3.

[11] Ice, "Dispensational Hermeneutics."

[12] Ibid.

[13] Ibid.

that is rooted in macroliteralism (a broad and consistent commitment to LGH[14]), even though there may be some differences and disagreements at the microliteral level. Ice thus absolves of theological precommitment exegetes who arrive at dispensational conclusions broadly and yet have some differences in various details not contrary to macroliteralism, as he perceives such exegetes to be working within the framework of LGH. On the other hand, while Ice resolutely recognizes that LGH is an essential of dispensationalism,[15] he curiously and in passing refers to the literal hermeneutic as "a development of dispensationalism"[16] – a reference that seems to imply that the system of dispensationalism, at least in some sense, precedes the hermeneutic. Perhaps he was meaning that hermeneutic ideas at the *microliteral* level have been advanced by dispensational thought, but either way, Ice's comments underscore the difficulty of the relationship of dispensational thought to hermeneutic methodology. Ryrie's sine qua non positions dispensationalism as utterly dependent on the consistent application of LGH, yet other dispensational thinkers seem to imply at least an occasional interdependence between dispensational thought and LGH.

In a recent statement affirming its commitment to dispensational thought, the IFCA asserts that "Dispensational theology emerges from_a consistent literal- grammatical-historical hermeneutic."[17] This statement reflects that dispensationalism is the theological egg that comes from the hermeneutic chicken. At the same time, the statement adds that, "IFCA International has been committed since its inception to a Dispensational

---

[14] Literal Grammatical Historical.
[15] Ibid., 13.
[16] Ibid., 14.
[17] IFCA, "Resolution on Dispensational Theology and Hermeneutics," adopted July 1, 2020, https://www.ifca.org/blog/Advancing%20the%20Cause/2020-resolution-on-dispensational-hermeneutics.

understanding of Scripture."[18] One might wonder the value of referring to a dispensational understanding of Scripture while affirming that dispensationalism emerges from viewing the Scriptures through a particular hermeneutic lens. While it is clear that the IFCA is comprehensively committed to LGH in its most normative form,[19] the description of the view of Scripture as dispensational blurs the relationship of cause to effect.

Michael Vlach describes (in a Reformed-theology venue) dispensationalism as "a distinctive hermeneutic."[20] Vlach expands on that assertion, noting that dispensationalism is "primarily about a hermeneutic for Bible interpretation, especially involving Old Testament prophecies concerning ethnic/national Israel."[21] Again one might ask whether dispensationalism is the outcome of a hermeneutic or whether it is about a hermeneutic. At the very least equating the system (dispensationalism) with the hermeneutic (LGH) by describing dispensationalism *as* a distinctive hermeneutic is problematic.

Andy Woods rightly explains that "dispensationalism has more to do with commitment to a particular hermeneutic then it does to adherence to a theological model."[22] Woods is clear that "the Dispensational theological system arises out of a hermeneutic rather than from a theology imposed upon Scripture."[23] His thesis in the article is "to explain the hermeneutics of

---

[18] Ibid.

[19] The IFCA affirms in the Resolution that "we commit ourselves to the search for the authorial intent, both divine and human, behind every biblical text, through the careful use of the interpretation principles found in the literal- grammatical-historical approach to hermeneutics."

[20] Michael Vlach, "Dispensational Theology" The Gospel Coalition, https://www.thegospelcoalition.org/essay/dispensational-theology/.

[21] Ibid.

[22] Andy Woods, "Dispensational Hermeneutics" SpiritAndTruth.org, 2005, https://www.spiritandtruth.org/teaching/documents/articles/25/25.pdf?x=x.

[23] Ibid.

dispensationalism,"[24] yet the title itself ("Dispensational Hermeneutics") can be understood in two ways – and both are ways that dispensational thinkers have utilized. Woods certainly meant it – as did Ice in his identically titled article – to describe, as his thesis states, the hermeneutics of dispensationalism. Woods is otherwise careful not to blur the lines between cause and effect.

GREAT IMPLICATIONS OF A SUBTLE DISTINCTION

At this point it is important note the vital distinction between (1) a hermeneutic which results in a theological system and (2) a theological system which prescribes a hermeneutic. The latter is found in most worldviews, and is easily identifiable in other Christian denominations and theological systems (e.g., the allegorical/ theological hermeneutic of covenantalism, the canonical/dogmatic hermeneutic of Catholicism, etc.). Yet dispensational thought is grounded and rooted in the former: a hermeneutic which results in the theological system. The moment the theological system prescribes a hermeneutic, the theological system can no longer be considered a product of exegesis. Dispensationalism as a theological methodology is self-defeating at best and destructive at worst. Yet if it is an outcome, then it is constructive and useful, as Ryrie characterized it.

If dispensationalism *is* the hermeneutic, then dispensationalism is the lens through which dispensationalists seek to read Scripture, and if so, that is precisely the error Ryrie rebukes in his criticism of covenantalist thought. Especially in light of the conflating of the two (the theological system and the hermeneutic methodology) by those outside of dispensational thought, it would seem advisable to avoid any appearance of conflation and to

---

[24] Ibid.

consistently acknowledge and maintain the cause and effect boundaries and the distinctness of the hermeneutical cause and the theological effect. If one recognizes the Biblical model and consistent prescription of the LGH as integral to **Biblical epistemology,** and interprets all of Scripture through that lens, the outcome will be (at least the basic) traditional dispensational concepts. Critics of dispensationalism unashamedly affirm this (e.g., Berkhof, Gerstner) but believe the theological conclusions to be untenable and thus advocate a different hermeneutic approach.

A vital component of the epistemology modeled and prescribed in the Bible is the model for interpreting communication – the hermeneutic. LGH is modeled in every book of the Bible, and no alternative is announced nor extoled. If one consistently applies that hermeneutic, then they are putting into practice *Biblical* epistemology – they are thinking the way God revealed that He intended for humanity. If one applies those principles consistently, their theological outcome will look (at least) quite a bit like traditional dispensational thought. Thus, it is fair to say that there is a distinctive hermeneutic (LGH) that results in the dispensational system. Some refer to this as a "dispensational hermeneutic," but that is at best confusing. There is a distinctive hermeneutic (LGH) that results in the dispensational system. It is the basis of the dispensational system, but *it is not part of the system*, it is simply part of the *sine qua non* of the system. Ryrie's *sine qua non* recognizes LGH consistently applied as a necessary prerequisite of dispensational thought but never describes it as *part of the thought-outcome or theological system*. As LGH is directly contra the theological hermeneutic, if the hermeneutic of dispensationalism is a product of the theological system, then it cannot be LGH. Dispensationalism would be a self-defeating and hypocritical system (particularly in its critiquing other systems for embracing that very theological hermeneutic). The hermeneutic of dispensationalism is not *dispensational,* rather it is simply integral to communication as God created it and revealed it in the Bible, thus undergirding the Biblical worldview.

On the other hand, Kevin DeYoung argues that the "insistence on making the path between exegesis and theology a one way street is untenable and unwise."[25] He suggests that "Theology does not have to distort exegesis. Done well, it can help provide **guardrails for the interpretive process** [emphasis mine], honor the unity of Scripture, and throw a spotlight on the most important and most difficult issues arising from the Word of God."[26] These guardrails provided by theological conclusions would keep us from what errors, I wonder. And who will guard the guardrails? De Young provides an answer to that conundrum, as he muses, "As a Christian I hope that my theology is open to correction, but as a minister I have to start somewhere. We all do. For me that means starting with Reformed theology and my confessional tradition and sticking with that unless I have really good reason not to."[27] DeYoung joins many scholars in beginning with a system of theology in order to "better" understand the Scriptures. But at what cost. Even if the starting theological system is completely reliable, that preunderstanding shortens or short circuits the exegetical process. Theology comes last, not first, and if it attempts to do both (as DeYoung prescribes) then it comes first.

Finally, Tim Challies illustrates how a theological system as a method (rather than outcome) can be destructive. Challies's reflection on why he is not dispensational in his theology is noteworthy:

---

[25] Kevin DeYoung, "Your Theological System Should Tell You How to Exegete," The Gospel Coalition, February 2012, https://www.thegospelcoalition.org/blogs/kevin-deyoung/your-theological-system-should-tell-you-how-to-exegete.
[26] Ibid.
[27] Ibid.

So why am I not dispensational? I'd like to say that I have studied the issue very closely, that I have read stacks of books on eschatology, and that I can thoroughly defend my position against every alternative. But that's not the case. It's more that **my reading of the Bible**, my years of listening to sermons, and my study of Christian theology **has not been able to shake or displace the amillennialism of my youth** [emphases mine]. To the contrary, it has only strengthened it. Paul Martin's recent sermon series through Revelation strengthened it all the more. The very framework of dispensationalism appears to me to fall into a similar category as paedobaptism in that they both, in the words of Tom Hicks, "wrongly allow the Old Testament to have priority over the New Testament."[28]

Challies began with an infusion of (amillennial) theology, and presupposing the principle of New Testament primacy, has found no good reason to abandon his original theology. Further, he is strengthened in his theological conclusions. It is worth noting that New Testament primacy could be characterized as *sine qua non* for amillennial thought. If that is so, then Challies justifies his rejection of dispensationalism based on a fundamental necessity of amillennial thought. In other words, the theological precommitment precludes hermeneutic objectivity and is self-authenticating. This is destructive, because it does not allow the interlocutor to be objective in study and can obfuscate realities which might otherwise be readily recognizable in the text. If dispensational thought is guilty of theological precommitment, then it is no better off and no less destructive.

---

[28] Tim Challies, "Why I Am Not Dispensational," June 23, 2016, https://www.challies.com/articles/why-i-am-not-dispensational.

On the other hand, dispensational thought matters as a way of synthesizing history *because* it is the outcome of the Bible interpreted in a manner consistent with the hermeneutic principles described and prescribed in the Bible itself. Only insofar as dispensationalism is the outcome of that methodology can it provide a useful perspective of history, because as dispensational thought corresponds with Biblical methodology, it corresponds with truth. At any point at which the system trumps Biblical methodology that system is prone to error. The power of dispensationalism is not the system itself, but its distinctiveness as a comprehensive product of the Bible handled consistently according to the basic principles of normative communication (the LGH).

CASE STUDY: METHODOLOGY AND OUTCOME PERTAINING TO THE CHARACTER OF GOD, LAW, AND IMPLICATIONS

The Premise

Basic dispensational thought asserts its derivation as Scriptural and as arrived at through the exegetical process, and consistently applied LGH principles. Because of this fundamental principle of origination, dispensationalism cannot simply be an eschatological addendum to an already established system – it must be the direct product of Biblical study. Thus dispensational thought should be philosophically and theologically comprehensive and have great interdisciplinary importance. It ought to be synonymous with Biblical worldview

This idea is nowhere more evident than in relation to the basic understanding of the character of God and how He works. If dispensationalism is the product of Biblical exegesis according to the LGH, then *any and every theological affirmation* ought to be not just subject to scrutiny by Biblical content, but the Biblical origin of the idea should be demonstrable and readily connected to the most normative understanding of passages being studied.

Testing the Premise

There are three historical views, and perhaps three logical possibilities pertaining to God and His relationship to His legislation: (1) God is under good (authority is under law), (2) God is good (authority is law), and (3) God is over good (authority is over law). Plato took up this discussion (in the *Euthyphro*), arguing that if the gods were under good, then they were merely intermediaries and the idea of good was supreme. Plato also critiqued the second option, suggesting that the gods being good would illustrate good but would offer no actual definition of good. He also challenged the third view, noting that if the gods were over good, then when they disagreed with one another how could anyone ever know what was the good in that case. Plato didn't answer the question for the reader, he simply showed the problems with the three logical options. But there was one aspect Plato did not consider (a singular, authoritative Deity sovereignly declaring what is good). Unfortunately, some theological systems have not considered the issue with even as critical an eye as did Plato, and have come to some destructive conclusions.

The three perceptions of the relationship of God to good naturally lead to three views on the present applicability of the Mosaic Law, for example. The view that God is under (or bound by) good leads to a **Continuity** view – that all three categories[29] of Law are still in effect. God legislates from His character. His character does not change, therefore His legislation cannot change, thus we are still under the entirety of the Law. Theonomy and

---

[29] Some suggest the Law should be divided into moral, civil, and ceremonial categories. Yet in doing so face the dilemma of James 2:10.

reconstructionism have taken this approach. The **Semi-Continuity** view is rooted in the idea that God is good (as a definition, being good is being like God) and affirms that the moral aspects of the Law are still in effect. God's legislation is an expression of His character, and His character remains unchanged, thus the Law must also remain applicable even if some aspects are no longer in force. Reformed/Covenant theology affirms this view and its premises. Both the Continuity and Semi-Continuity views rely on a theological precommitment to a particular view of the relationship of God to good and legislation, and both employ their respective precommitment as a hermeneutic by which to understand not only God's relationship to the Mosaic Law, but also the relationship of the Mosaic Law to the church. On the other hand, the **Discontinuity** view recognizes that God as sovereign has authority to determine what is and is not good. He has the freedom to change His legislation without changing His character. Consequently, the Mosaic Law need not be applicable based on a universal constant. That God is sovereign and has such authority to determine and communicate good is exegetically derived,[30] as is the fact that the Law was within a covenant given to Israel as a nation.[31] God reveals His ultimate purpose for the Law,[32] communicates that the Law has been fulfilled by Christ on the cross,[33] and emphasizes that the church is not under that Law.[34]

Greg Bahnsen, affirming the Continuity view, appeals to Matthew 5:17 to argue against three categories of Law with different applicability. He refers to the abiding validity of the Law,[35] though he does recognize there needs to

---

[30] E.g., Genesis 1, Micah 6:8.
[31] Exodus 19:3-6.
[32] Galatians 3:19-24.
[33] Ephesians 2:15.
[34] Romans 6:14-15, Galatians 3:24.
[35] Greg Bahnsen, *Theonomy in Ethics,* 3rd edition (Covenant Media Press, 2021), chapter 2.

be changes in how that Law is expressed, because "The accomplishment of redemption changes the way in which we observe the ceremonial law, and the change of culture and times alters the specific ways in which we observe the case laws. The cases are different, but the same moral principles remain."[36] Though he tries to avoid it, Bahnsen's view is subject to the James 2:10 problem – the Law is all or nothing, and one does not have liberty to change how the Law is administered (unless there is clear exegetical warrant to do so).

David Jones calls the Semi-Continuity view "the prevailing view of the church."[37] This view appeals to Acts 15 to suggest that ceremonial law is not applicable to believers, and he appeals to several other passages[38] to assert that civil law is not applicable. Yet, the moral law is applicable today for sanctification.[39] Jones and others recognize that the undergirding principle is that *authority is law*. Some aspect of God's legislation must stay in effect if His character is to remain intact. Jones adds that, "Since the Decalogue is a reflection of God's moral character, the norms codified in the Ten Commandments are universally applicable and demonstrable both before and after their issuance on Mount Sinai."[40] Yet again, the James 2:10 problem is in view – the Law didn't codify norms, it codified legal mandates, and those mandates were (mostly) *not* evident before the Law was put in place. Samuel Bolton recognizes that placing believers under the Law seems to conflict with freedom in Christ, but he addresses that conflict almost poetically: "The law

---

[36] Greg Bahnsen, "The Faculty Discussion of Theonomy," Question 9, 1978, at RTS, http://www.cmfnow.com/articles/pe192.htm.
[37] David Jones, *Introduction to Biblical Ethics* (B&H Academic, 2013), 76.
[38] E.g., Romans 13:1-5, 1 Peter 2:13-17.
[39] Jones, 139.
[40] Jones, 139.

Biblical Distinctions Applied 61

sends us to the gospel that we may be justified, and the gospel sends us to the law again to enquire what is our duty in being justified."[41]

Because the Semi-Continuity view is not exegetically derived, it runs into significant exegetical problems, not the least of which relates to the Sabbath. Jones attempts a resolution, but has to do some contortions with the text to get there:

> For Christians, then, the Sabbath is a sign of redemption and, as such, it depicts the eternal rest they have received from Jesus in salvation...Keeping the Sabbath ought not to be a legalistic burden, characterized by lists of permitted and forbidden activities. Rather the Sabbath ought to be a joyous celebration and a blessing...In a specific sense the fourth commandment calls believers to observe a regular day of worship...not to observe the Sabbath, in either a broad or a specific sense, is to behave in a distinctly un-Christlike manner...in the NT...the early church moved the day of Sabbath observance to the first day of the week."[42]

Jones's assertion that the Sabbath is celebration rather than legal burden doesn't square with the text. The Sabbath was by its very nature as part of the Law a legal burden. The claim that the Sabbath calls believers to a day of worship seems to miss entirely that the Sabbath mandated rest, not worship specifically. The idea that the church moved the Sabbath, borders on absurd, and begs the question of where such a move was prescribed and upon what authority. Theological precommitments lead to continual (and destructive) theological supremacy over exegesis.

---

[41] Samuel Bolton, *True Bonds of Christian Freedom* (London:UK, Banner of Truth, 1964), 80.
[42] Jones, 166.

Illustrating how a self-proclaimed (leaky) dispensationalist can apply the same methodology (theological precommitments predetermine outcomes), John MacArthur states the precommitment this way: "God's law is a manifestation of His nature. What God has commanded, moral attitudes and behaviors, is a reflection of His nature."[43] MacArthur recognizes this (pre)commitment has implications and explains them as follows:

> So, to come along and say that the law is unimportant is to say that the very nature of God and the will of God as reflected in His law is insignificant and unimportant, which I see as a blow or a strike against the very character of God. That is why, at the end of Romans 3, Paul says, after talking about justification by grace through faith alone, he says, "Do we nullify the law?" And then he says, *me genoito*, "No, no, no, God forbid: but we establish the law."[44]

The (semi) continuation of the Law is now a necessary consequence of the precommitment, and it impacts how MacArther views the new nature (and is one of the reasons he rejects the dual nature idea): "…And that new nature is a new, divinely created disposition infused with power from the Holy Spirit so that you can now, for the first time, actually obey the law. And not just obey the law, but love to obey the law."[45] In asserting the new nature's ability (and design) to obey the law, MacArthur seems to recognize that his words are conflicting with Paul's, so he clarifies to resolve that apparent contradiction. Notice he doesn't clarify his own words, but Paul's:

---

[43] John MacArthur, "Sanctification, Sin, and Obedience", https://www.gty.org/library/sermons-library/GTY164/sanctification-sin-and-obedience.

[44] MacArthur, "Sanctification, Sin, and Obedience."

[45] Ibid.

Biblical Distinctions Applied 63

> …when Paul says you're not under the law, he first means you're not under the law as a means of salvation. You've come out from under the law, and you are no longer defining your relationship to God by your ability to keep the law satisfactorily, which was impossible.[46]

Based on MacArthur's theological precommitment to God's law as a manifestation of God's nature (an assumed premise of both Continuity and Semi-Continuity), MacArthur asserts that believers are now enabled, equipped, and designed to keep the law, though not for justification. But it is noteworthy how on the one hand he distinguishes between justification and sanctification (not wanting to affirm justification by works of law), yet in the immediate context joins the two together again:

> …salvation is both a forensic reality – that is, God declares you righteous by imputing His righteousness to you – and it is also a real change so that you now are given the ability to live righteously, which is to live in conformity to the law of God and do so willingly from the heart.[47]

On the one hand it is a forensic reality, on the other it is a "real" change. The unbeliever has "broken the law of God and He's angry about it. Unless something happens to change your condition, you're on your way to eternal hell."[48] That something is faith *and* repentance, which MacArthur (problematically) defines as "turning from sin."[49] Yet he adds that true

---

[46] Ibid.
[47] MacArthur, "Sanctification, Sin, and Obedience."
[48] John MacArthur, "Saved. From What?" https://www.gty.org/library/articles/A242/saved-from-what.
[49] John MacArthur, *Faith Works: The Gospel According to the Apostles* (Word Publishing, 1993), 74.

repentance inevitably results in a change of behavior."[50] MacArthur begins with a theological precommitment that results in several theological-over-exegetical affirmations. When following this methodology, it becomes apparent that objective exegesis can no longer be possible, because the theological precommitments are too influential. Often God's character and His gospel are defined outside of the normative principles of communication because of those precommitments.

The Discontinuity view, on the other hand, is consistent (and even synonymous) with a dispensational understanding of God's character and His relationship to good and legislation. These two ideas are consistent because they both rely on LGH and objective exegesis to derive their affirmations. Nowhere in Scripture does God reveal any ontological limitations for His declarations of good nor of His legislations, thus any assertions of such limitations would be speculative theological constructs. Discontinuity and dispensational thought attempt to avoid these because they have no exegetical basis. Further, there is no exegetical case to be made for the three-fold division of the Law, and there is no exegetical case to be made for the church to be under the Law of Moses. Instead, we discover when applying normative communication principles that God is holy,[51] that God determines and reveals what is good,[52] and that He works all things for His glory.[53] If He desires to change, fulfill, end, or apply legislation He has sovereign rights as the Creator and as the Legislator to do so.

This particular case study is intended to illustrate how one seemingly innocuous theological precommitment can greatly impact one's theological outcomes. If one predetermines theology and uses those predeterminations

---

[50] Ibid., 75.
[51] Isaiah 6:3.
[52] Genesis 1, Micah 6:8.
[53] E.g., Romans 11:36.

to direct their exegesis, then they must do so at the abandonment of normative communication principles (LGH) and with a departure from the exegetical process. Any theological precommitment great or small that preempts hermeneutics and exegesis is destructive *if* we are designed to understand truth by hermeneutic principles and through the exegetical process.

Dispensationalism is no exception. As an outcome, (traditional) dispensationalism is an excellent and helpful way to organize and understand Biblical and historical data. Yet if used as a method, dispensationalism becomes credal (just like every other theologically driven system), locking in any theological error for future interlocutors, darkening the path of exegesis. This state of affairs would necessitate constant reformation to once again return our focus to the very words that God provided for our accurate understanding of Himself and His plan insofar as He has revealed these to us. It is significant that He revealed these things employing the principles of normative communication. Consequently, dispensational thought matters and is thus constructive when those same principles are acknowledged and consistently applied.

Chapter 4 – On Morality
The Root of Moral Epistemology: Dispensationalism's Relevance in Establishing Moral Truth in a Relativistic World
Taylor Walker

INTRODUCTION

Western societies were once strongly rooted in the Judeo-Christian values that emanated from the religious foundation of their culture. Beginning with the Enlightenment in the late eighteenth century, these cultures began to shift away from the proclamations of the Bible, preferring to root themselves in the ever-evolving promises of science. This affirmation of science as the sole basis of fact became the cornerstone of modernist philosophy and had significant epistemological implications for questions of ethics and morality. Whereas the Scriptures were once seen by the masses as the authority on moral conduct, the scientific revolution seemingly dismantled this claim. The concept of moral relativity has pervaded modern academic institutions and has become a predominant viewpoint of secular Americans. This trend has increased as the secularists replaced the hard sciences with the social sciences as the means of developing their epistemology. This fact is demonstrated by a study conducted by philosopher Thomas Pölzer and psychologist Jennifer Wright, which concluded that sixty-four percent of participants surveyed identified moral questions as entirely subjective with divergent ethical positions being identified neither as right nor wrong regardless of the respondent's personal stance on the subject.¹

Now much of the church exists within the confines of moral relativism as many traditional protestant denominations have affirmed the social tenants of modernism and postmodernism through their acceptance of biblically untenable positions that align with the social whims of secularists. The justifications for these amoral positions are typically based upon a faulty hermeneutical process. Moreover, the hermeneutical framework employed to support these unscriptural conclusions reveals a deeper philosophical flaw influenced deeply by the moral relativism of secular belief systems. Specifically, these philosophies reject the Bible's authority on epistemological matters, instead looking towards the advances of the hard sciences and social sciences to form the nucleus around which Scripture is understood. Dispensational theology stands the best chance of combating these shifting cultural paradigms within the church. This chapter will examine dispensationalism's relevance in combating moral relativism in the twenty-first century church by reviewing errant positions of the mainstream denominations and defining a dispensational moral epistemology based upon the literal- historical-grammatical hermeneutic.

MORAL RELATIVISM IN THE CHURCH

That moral relativism is a popular position within secular society should not be a surprise. Scripture has warned Christians that those who live while rejecting the Lord will be unable to discern the truth despite it being made evident to them (Ro 1:18-20). Paul reiterates this fact in his instructions to

---

¹ Thomas Pölzer, "Is Moral Relativism Really a Problem? Psychological Research Suggests it is Not," *Scientific American*, https://blogs.scientificamerican.com/observations/is-moral- relativism-really-a-problem/.

Timothy, as he predicts the coming time when people would seek out teachers that simply affirm their internal desires with a complete disregard for the truth (2Ti 4:3-4). The roots of moral relativism within the body of Christ are found through both an understanding of the principles of moral relativism and the hermeneutical processes which underly this philosophy. The pervasiveness of moral relativism within the church has given way to the affirmation of sinful positions within mainline protestant denominations with justification found in the faulty application of Scripture.

Philosopher J. David Velleman essentially defines moral relativism as the inability to determine a universal understanding of morality on the basis that people devise rules around common themes that vary between communities due to cultural differences and share so little in common, they cannot be rightly invalidated.[2] Thus, based upon Velleman's definition, ethical relativity exists regardless of the claims of exclusivity by certain peoples regarding a moral theme. Further, it would appear, based upon Velleman's argument, that the incongruency of the subjects deemed moral by these different groups is the reason ethical absolutes cannot be objectively determined. Therefore, moral relativism finds its foundation within the supposed inability to discredit the norms of a people based on apparent cultural differences in practical ethics. To this point, the moral relativists, such as Velleman, regard culture as the lynch pin of morality. Further, they claim culture is a concept defined by the external environment be it political, social, or even historical which underlie the validation of local beliefs.[3] It is through the moral relativists' concept of culture, that many of denominations affirm the words of Scripture within their cultural-historical position, while

---

[2] J. David Velleman, *Foundations for Moral Relativism: Second Expanded Edition* (Cambridge, UK: Open Book Publishers, 2015), 1-3.

[3] Velleman, *Foundations for Moral Relativism*, 75-76.

maintaining that they are no longer applicable to the modern church.[4] That is to say, the moral positions taken by the characters within the Biblical narratives were correct in their historical context, but their stances on ethical topics are not acceptable nor Biblical in a modern western context.

Moral relativism within the church found justification through the hermeneutical practices of theologians and religious philosophers who reject a normal hermeneutical process based upon the literal-historical-grammatical understanding of the Bible. Merold Westphal, a graduate of Wheaton College, adjunct professor at Fuller Theological Seminary, and guest lecturer at the Harvard Divinity School supports the idea that there are several valid moral interpretations of Scripture's ethical teachings. The basis of his position is the dismissal of a plain interpretation of the biblical text due the supposed inability of this hermeneutic to capture the spiritual meanings of God's word.[5] In his book, *Whose Community? Whose Interpretation? Philosophical Hermeneutics for the Church*, part of a series entitled *The Church and Postmodernism*, Westphal sought to undermine the concept of objectivity in Biblical interpretation by turning the reader towards a hermeneutic that understands the meaning of Scripture as being derived from the cooperative effort of the author and the reader in a contemporary context.[6] Westphal notes that this position is strongly influenced by the hermeneutical practices of Hans-Georg Gadamer, both of who sought a philosophical interpretation of Scripture.[7] Therefore, Westphal seeks to promote a hermeneutic which is not centered

---

[4] Anna-Marie Lockard, "Homosexuality: Legally Permissible or Spiritually Misguided?" *Conspectus* 05:1 (Mar 2008), 156.

[5] Merold Westphal, *Whose Community? Which Interpretation? Philosophical Hermeneutics for the Church* (Grand Rapids, MI: Baker Academic, 2009), 17-18.

[6] Nathan D. Shannon, "His Community, His Interpretation: A Review of Merold Westphal's 'Whose Community? Which Interpretation?'", *Westminster Theological Journal* 72:2 (Fall 2010), 423-424.

[7] Shannon, "His Community, His Interpretation."

at exegeting the Bible within its proper context, but instead to base the understanding of Scripture through a completely modern interpretation subject to the cultural conditions of the reader. This makes Scripture out to be a collection of ethical teachings which are malleable based upon the reader's situation and therefore allows for identifying multiple, often conflicting, meanings of Biblical passages as equally valid.

There are severe epistemological consequences associated with relativism. Relativist positions requires disavowing the possibility of objective truth, specifically in the areas of morality and ethics.[8] Postmodernists even deny the ability to affirm objective truth derived from history and the hard sciences, instead believing that the historical and scientific narratives are in fact constructs from individual perceptions and therefore malleable.[9] On the surface this type of philosophy is wholly incompatible with the Christian worldview, as Christianity requires the assent of specific facts that are objectively chronicled in the historical record such as the life, death, and resurrection of Christ Jesus. The Apostle Paul summarized the importance of affirming these historical facts in 1 Corinthians 15:14 by stating, "And if Christ has not been raised, our preaching is useless and so is your faith" (NIV).

Despite the apparent conflict with these philosophies and the Christian worldview, they have been synthesized in the progressive moral positions of many mainline protestant denominations. The language of moral relativism is made apparent in the proclamations of these denominational groups regarding such topics as same-sex marriage. For example, the Presbyterian Church (U.S.A.) declared in their doctrinal summary on sexuality, "By its

---

[8] Ted Cabal, "An Introduction to Postmodernity: Where are we, how did we get Here, and Can we get Home?" *Southern Baptist Journal of Theology* 05:2 (Summer 2001), 9.

[9] Rick C. Shrader, "Postmodernism," *Journal of Ministry and Theology* 03:1 (Spring 1999), 26-27.

actions the Presbyterian Church (U.S.A.) has decided that strongly differing convictions about sexuality and faithful sexual relationships are granted equal standing within this denomination…"[10] Thus, the Presbyterian churches in the United States have taken an official stance on sexuality that affirms any position to be equally valid. This stands in stark contrast to a plain interpretation of Scriptural teachings on the subject such as Paul's admonition against homosexual practices in 1 Corinthians 6:9, Romans 1:26-27, and 1 Timothy 1:9-10. Likewise, the Evangelical Lutheran Church in America (ELCA) in their 2009 statement entitled "Human Sexuality: Gift and Trust", which it claims to be their denominational guidelines on this social issue, affirmed four opposing positions on homosexuality under the guise of being unable to faithfully discern the moral imperatives from Scripture alone.[11] This is particularly alarming because a plain interpretation of the Scriptures would make God's position on the matter evident.

Besides showing a common philosophical framework for the decision to affirm diametrically opposed positions within the same denomination, neither the Presbyterian Church (U.S.A.) nor ELCA cite any Scripture in support of their position. While not directly stated, the Scriptural justification for ELCA's position appear in a 2004 article in the Journal of Lutheran Ethics entitled "The Church and Homosexuality." Within this article, the author cites a hermeneutical process through which Scripture should be interpreted by weighing Jesus's personal statements over all other claims within the Bible and then evaluated within the context of twenty-first century western

---

[10] Presbyterian Church (U.S.A.), "Sexuality and Same-Gender Relationships," https://www.presbyterianmission.org/what-we-believe/sexuality-and-same-gender-relationships/.

[11] Evangelical Lutheran Church in America, "Human Sexuality: Gift and Trust" (Minneapolis, MN: ELCA, 2009), 18-21.

culture.[12] Likewise, the article's author claims that because Christ rejected certain aspects of the Levitical Law, an application of Jesus's ethic "can never produce universal rules."[13] This position not only removes the historical context of the Bible, but it also undermines the role God played in the inspiration of the entire text. Moreover, the absence of Jesus's words on a subject in the Bible do not eliminate the possibility that He spoke on the subject as is reflected in John 21:25 where John states not everything Jesus did was recorded which also insinuates not everything He said was written down for posterity. It follows that if God inspired the words of the Bible and worked through the human authors to construct the Holy Scriptures, then God's position on what constitutes sin can be clearly discerned through the Bible regardless of such positions not being written in red letters (2Ti 3:16-17). The acceptance and even glorification of homosexuality, an act condemned as sinful throughout the Old and New Testament, by these mainline denominations is but one example of flawed hermeneutics hinging upon contemporary sensibilities leading to the affirmation of moral relativity within the body of Christ.

Ultimately, moral relativism undermines the authentic witness of God's word to His church. This has severe philosophical ramifications for traditional Biblical doctrines such as the concept of Scripture's inspiration and inerrancy. Judging the biblical text within the confines of modern philosophical and scientific frameworks which appear to refute the scriptural narrative would negate God's inspiration of the text, thus making the Scriptures merely the work of fallen man susceptible to moral, historical, and scientific errors. This further undermines the doctrine of inerrancy. The

---

[12] John Wickham, "The Church and Homosexuality," *Journal of Lutheran Ethics* 4:8 (August 2004).
[13] Ibid.

negation of the doctrine of inerrancy opens the Bible to legitimate criticism regarding its reliability and authority.[14] The evidence of the mainline protestant denominations refusing to remain steadfast to Scripturally supported moral standards demonstrates the necessity of the church to reject any philosophical or hermeneutical doctrine that apparently rejects God's authority on ethical matters. Therefore, a hermeneutical system from which a consistent Christian philosophy can be derived which affirms Scripture as the root of moral epistemology is required.

EPISTEMOLOGICAL IMPLICATIONS OF DISPENSATIONALISM

Dispensationalism is rooted in its hermeneutical process which treats the biblical text as communication between God and His creation. Thus, dispensationalism maintains Scripture has a concrete meaning that is derived from the literal interpretation of the word within its historical context while accounting for the grammatical nuances of the original languages.[15] Due to its focus on developing the interpretation of Scripture entirely from exegesis, a sound Christian philosophy emerges from the application of the dispensational hermeneutical framework. Moreover, dispensationalism's philosophical principles stand in stark contrast to those employed by Christian moral relativists because they are being extracted from biblical doctrine and not being read into biblical doctrine. The two of the most important philosophical conclusions from a dispensational interpretation of Scripture are that truth emanates from God's essence and that truth is objective. Thus, this position eliminates the moral relativists' reliance of self-

---

[14] Augustine, *Letters: The Works of Saint Augustine*, trans. Roland Teske (New York, NY: New City Press, 2001), 92-93.

[15] Charles C. Ryrie, *Basic Theology: A Popular Systematic Guide to Understanding Biblical Truth* (Chicago, IL: Moody Publishers, 1999), 155-156.

perception for discerning and validating multiple versions of "truths." Moreover, it squashes the possibility of truth's malleability which would be a rational conclusion of Christian theologies that rely on a spiritual or allegorical interpretation of certain portions of the Bible.

Epistemology is the "theory of knowledge," and within the philosophical realm it refers to the concepts that determine that which can be known and through which modes it can discovered.[16] The foundation of epistemology is the concept of "knowing" and experiencing knowledge in its concrete sense. Moral relativists, particularly of the postmodern variety, willingly assert a logical fallacy by claiming that truth cannot be known. However, this is a specific claim to objective truth. This points, on a philosophical level, to the necessity of objective knowledge. The implication of this for the Christian is the necessity of being able to receive and discern knowledge from an authoritative source. Scripture teaches clearly that this knowledge is revealed to man through God's written revelation and has also been made apparent through nature itself which was created by God thereby infused with His essence (2Ti 3:16-17, Ro 1:18-21).

The categorization of something as objective rather than subjective is that its existence is not contingent upon or influenced by internal sources.[17] Christian Philosopher, J. P. Moreland would further classify objectivity in truth as the understanding of knowledge that remains factual regardless of its perception.[18] This means a person's feelings towards a fact or inability to understand that fact do not undermine its objective truth. A simple example

---

[16] "Epistemology," *Standford Encyclopedia of Philosophy*, https://plato.stanford.edu/entries/epistemology/.

[17] Scott Newman, "The Appeal of God's Truth to the Mind: Theological and Exegetical Answers to Post- Modern Trends within Evangelical Thought," *Conservative Theological Journal* 01:2 (Aug 1997), 145.

[18] J. P. Moreland, "Truth, Contemporary Philosophy, and the Postmodern Turn," *Journal of the Evangelical Theological Society* 48:1 (Mar 2005), 78.

of this objectivity in truth is found in mathematics which would maintain the sum of two and two is four. Therefore, a person's inability to conduct or understand the arithmetic function of addition does not affect the mathematical fact. Given that objective facts cannot be influenced by internal processes, it would bear to reason that the source of these truths must exist outside of those internal forces. Furthermore, objective truth cannot be formed based upon the external influences of the environment, which affect one's internal perception of physical phenomena and understanding of metaphysical experiences. Only one entity exists outside of the influence of these internal and external forces: the three persons of the Holy Trinity.[19] Thus, because any objective truth must be determined from a source that is uninfluenced by these internal and external processes which affect perceptions, and there is but one entity that exists entirely free of these factors, that entity must therefore be the source from which truth is derived. This right identifies God as that source.

In general, objective epistemology rests on the existence of God and is revealed through His attributes. One of God's attributes is aseity. God's aseity means that His existence is derived only from Himself and His fullness is due to nothing outside of Himself.[20] This necessitates that God exists outside of any cause, but it also requires that God be unmoved by external forces. The most apparent evidence for God's claim to aseity is in John 5:25-27. As Jesus replies to the Jewish leaders, He affirms that God has "life in himself" which reflects His independence of existence outside of other factors (Jn 5:26). Moreover, because the Father has life in Himself and has given the life within Himself to the Son, they alone have the power to give

---

[19] John S. Feinberg, *No One Like Him: The Doctrine of God* (Wheaton, IL: Good News Publishers, 2001), 241-242.

[20] John Piper, "I Believe in God's Self-Sufficiency: A Response to Thomas McCall," *Trinity Journal* 29:2 (Fall 2008), 227.

life to the dead, which shows they are givers of life to whom they please (Jn 5:21, 26-27).[21] The Father's and Son's giving of life to whom they please reflects on the will of God being solely from within Himself. This is further made apparent by God's creation of the world and everything in it making Him the origin of all things including objective truth (Jn 1:3, Ac 17:24-27).

While nearly all Christians agree on God's aseity, the appearance of moral relativism within the church makes it evident that segments of the body of Christ do not understand the connection between this divine attribute and epistemology. Specifically, God's aseity ensures His reliability because of the immutability of His character. Because God is the author of truth and it is objective, man's discernment of that truth is reliant upon the evidence of the consistency of His attributes. The disconnect between moral objectivity and God's reliability appears to be hermeneutically based. Moreover, it is not merely liberalized denominations that are prone to hermeneutical errors which are prone to undermine God's reliability and therefore His position as the objective source of truth. Covenantal theology, a position held by many conservative Christians, undermines the reliability of God. For example, in the case of the Abrahamic Covenant, covenant theology, in both its amillennial and premillennial varieties, disregards the fulfillment of this covenant in the literal sense as recorded in the Old Testament.[22] This subverts a tenant of biblically derived epistemology because it gives God the ability to amend or ignore the terms of unconditional covenants, thus making Him unreliable. Being that epistemology emanates from God's essence, and its objectivity is rooted in God's immutability, any evidence against the reliability of God would also point to the idea that truth would be malleable. However, God's reliability, and thereby His faithfulness to His covenants, is

---

[21] Piper, "I Believe in God's Self-Sufficiency," 242.
[22] Gary R. Gromacki, "The Fulfillment of the Abrahamic Covenant," *Journal of Ministry and Theology* 18:2 (Fall 2014), 99 and 107.

well accounted for in both the Old and New Testaments (Dt 7:9, Ro 3:1-4, Heb 13:8).

Just as truth is found in God's essence, so is objective morality. In his dialogue, *Euthyphro*, Socrates, as recorded by Plato, introduces a moral dilemma, "... whether the pious or holy is beloved by the gods because it is inherently holy or is it holy because it is beloved by the gods."[23] This discourse in *Euthyphro* is centered around the morality of specific actions and assumes within the contextual confines of the Greek pantheon that these are the only two viable perspectives from which to understand the questions of ethics. However, Scripture reveals a different nature of morality than that which could be conceived through Euthyphro's dilemma. Morality is neither an arbitrary value placed on a particular action nor is it simply a preference of God as suggested within Euthyphro but is instead the reflection of the righteous God.[24] Thus, Christian morality is objectively derived solely from the character of God, which is the basis upon which believers are called to live holy lives (Lv 11:44, 19:2; Heb 12:14; 1Pe 1:16; 1Th 4:7).

Because morality is based in the essence of God, it is revealed through both nature and in God's self-revelation to mankind through His word. In this latter respect, dispensationalism emerges as the most reliable means through which assertions of a universal and objective morality can be made. The literal-historical-grammatical hermeneutic correctly places the emphasis on the unity of God's word through His character while recognizing distinctions between God's peoples. The most prominent example of this is

---

[23] Through this dialogue, Socrates demonstrates that the basis for the dilemma is the inability to understand a universal morality due to the disagreements and wars that occur among the gods of the Greek pantheon. Thus, from this cultural perspective, this is a legitimate proposition, but it falls short from the perspective of monotheism. Plato, *Euthyphro*, trans. by Benjamin Jowett (South Bend, IN: Infomotions Inc, 2000), 8.

[24] Larry D. Pettegrew, "Theological Basis of Ethics," *Master's Seminary Journal* 11:2 (Fall 2000), 149.

the relationship between the decalogue and the church. Dispensationalism recognizes the Mosaic Law as being bestowed specifically upon Israel during that age, while also understanding that the Law was merely a tool for Israel to understand morality rooted in God's character.[25] This is reflected in Romans 7:7-25, in which Paul cites the value of the law for helping him to understand the moral will of God, but the universal fact of righteousness being credited to a person by faith.[26] Thus, in the tradition of Paul, the dispensationalist recognizes the Law as a series of ordnances that were given specifically to Israel which reveal God's moral will, while also maintaining that the law was fulfilled in Christ, thus not applicable in its legal sense to the church but still applicable in defining sin. Further, dispensational theology recognizes that adherence to the law prior to the incarnation of Christ and adherence to the moral imperatives stated by Christ, which summarize the law, were only possible through a faithful relationship to the Lord (Mt 22:35-50, Mk 12:28-31, Lk 10:25-28).

The consistency of what constitutes sin through these different dispensations highlights that ethics are universal and objective based upon the word of God. Therefore, dispensationalism is the only viable theological framework which fully espouses an epistemology that affirms objective truth. From the literal-historical-grammatical hermeneutic of dispensationalism, God's essence is understood to the extent of man's ability to comprehend an infinite being leading to a sound biblical epistemology.[27] Specifically, dispensationalism recognizes that all truth is derived from God and is authoritative as revealed in Scripture. This further provides the foundation

---

[25] Roy L. Aldrich, "A New Look at Dispensationalism," *Bibliotheca Sacra* 120:477 (Jan 1963), 47.

[26] Charles C. Ryrie, *Ryrie Study Bible* (Chicago, IL: Moody Publishers, 2020), Olive Tree Bible Study Software.

[27] Christopher Cone, "Presuppositional Dispensationalism," *Conservative Theological Journal* 10:29 (May 2006), 93-94.

for understanding morality as a reflection of God's character that is likewise objective, immutable, and discernable through various means of revelation.

CONCLUSION: DISPENSATIONALISM'S TWENTY-FIRST CENTURY RELEVANCE

In the midst of the growing popularity of moral relativism within secular society and mainstream protestant churches, dispensationalism has found its greatest practical relevance. Specifically, moral relativism within the church is dismantling long understood moral truths to be deemed as socially acceptable to contemporary secular culture. This is the single greatest threat to conservative Christianity and requires proper redress. Dispensationalism provides that redress because it applies a hermeneutical process that recognizes God as the eternal and absolute source of authority on ethical matters.[28] Thus, it characterizes truth as being immutable and discernable by mankind through various modes of revelation. Dispensationalism does this by consistently applying the literal-historical-grammatical hermeneutic which affirms doctrine that has been outlined in God's word.

Relativistic positions on morality within the church are wantonly justified through the misapplication or omission of Scripture.[29] Therefore, dispensationalism provides the soundest foundation upon which strong moral doctrine can be determined from God's self-revelation. With dispensationalism's emphasis on a faithful and consistent interpretation of Scripture through the literal- historical-grammatical framework, man may grow a deeper understanding of the character of God and thereby discern

---

[28] Philip Heideman, "Dispensational Theology," *Chafer Theological Seminary Journal* 04:3 (Jul 1998), 39-40.

[29] Nickolaus Kurtaneck, "Excellencies of Dispensationalism," *Grace Journal* 03:2 (Spring 1962), 9.

God's moral will for humanity. This requires faithful servants of the Lord to live in humility to recognize their limitations in understanding the eternal, righteous God while remaining steadfast to the truths that can be rightfully discerned from Scripture. This becomes increasingly important as the Christian educational system becomes increasingly liberal in its theology, molding preachers and theologians in a relativist framework which then mold the nature of Christian philosophy for generations. This risks further normalization and acceptance of sinful practices that have been adopted and even glorified by certain segments of the church.

Moreover, the theological framework of dispensationalism recognizes God's primary purpose is His own glorification, rightly placing man subordinate to Him as opposed to the soteriological focus of other theological motifs which place man as a necessary element of God's purpose.[30] As local churches become entrenched in affirming sinful lifestyles as a means of appeasing a small portion of society (that likely would not affirm the church's teaching regardless of its stance on contemporary social issues), they place humanity on a theological pedestal. By justifying homosexuality, transgenderism, abortion-on-demand, or any other immoral social issue through Scripture, these churches have allowed man to dictate morality for the purposes of defining a God whose primary purpose is the salvation of a fallen humanity. This is antithetical to the teaching of Scripture and seeks to glorify man, akin the humanism, instead of properly recognizing the primary motivation of God as His own glorification. Thus, dispensationalists have a responsibility to preach and teach that man's purpose is to glorify the Lord. One of the ways this is done is through the reliance on the indwelling Holy Spirt to live a life in accordance with the moral will of God, best discernable through a dispensational interpretation

---

[30] Douglas Brown, "The Glory of God and Dispensationalism: Revisiting the '*Sine Qua Non*' of Dispensationalism," *Journal of Ministry and Theology* 22:1 (Spring 2018), 35.

of the Bible.

Society bears the marks of moral relativism as the inhabitants of a broken and fallen world continually embrace positions that promote unethical behavior through the rejection of objective moral truths. That these positions have also become prominent in the church compounds the cultural decay, as God's elect have seemed to selectively reject aspects of God's self-revelation to appease contemporary western sensitivities. The church needs to be called back to a normal interpretation of Scripture which affirms the objective truth of God's morality. Moreover, the church needs to understand that it has been called to glorify God by presenting itself as the faithful, holy bride of Christ (Eph 5:25-27, Rev 19:7-9). This can only be achieved by recognizing the authority and purpose of God within history and shedding light on the fallacies of secular philosophy's undue influence upon the church.

Chapter 5 – On Sexual Expression

Hearing & Proclaiming Her Voice: The Not-So-Secret Longing of Female Sexual Desire in the Song[1]

Mark McGinniss

WRONG VOICES AND DEAFENING SILENCE

Evangelicalism as a whole (of which Dispensationalism is a part) cannot boast a stellar history as it relates to its treatment of women or their issues.[2] One area that has been woefully mishandled in the church at large is the area of female sexuality. The church's voice has generally been either silent or monotone to her female members along the lines of "no, no, no," "sex is

---

[1] Special thanks to A. W. Morris, John Vo (PhD students at BBS), Kasey J. Waite (PhD student in English at SUNY Albany and my daughter), Terry Perrine, (MDiv student at BBS), Kara McGinniss (my daughter-in-law) and my wife, Joy for their insightful comments on the first draft of this chapter.

[2] The denial or suppression of female sexuality is not a church only issue. Western culture may have a more checkered history than the church in this regard. Baumeister and Twenge observe, "The suppression of female sexuality can be regarded as one of the most remarkable psychological interventions in Western cultural history. According to Sherfey's (1966) respected statement of this view, the sex drive of the human female is naturally and innately stronger than that of the male, and it once posed a powerfully destabilizing threat to the possibility of social order. For civilized society to develop, it was allegedly necessary or at least helpful for female sexuality to be stifled. Countless women have grown up and lived their lives with far less sexual pleasure than they would have enjoyed in the absence of this large-scale suppression. Socializing influences such as parents, schools, peer groups, and legal forces have cooperated to alienate women from their own sexual desires and transform their (supposedly and relatively) sexually voracious appetites into a subdued remnant." "Cultural Suppression of Female Sexuality," *Review of General Psychology*, Vol 6, No. 2 (2002,):166.
https://pdfs.semanticscholar.org/26cf/592c500860d43ceab39d21816654e53e9c6c.pdf.

dirty, dirty, dirty" or "sex is simply for your husband."[3] While some have attempted to correct these incomplete or unbiblical "voices," they are competing with countless opinions that at times (unfortunately) are noisier and more compelling.

Linda Dillow and Lorraine Pintus record these well-intentioned (but woefully wrong) voices of moms to their daughters:

"Only 'those kinds' of girls enjoy sex."

"Sex is a man's thing. You just have to endure it."

"Wait until you've have been married twenty years, it gets old."

"After two years of marriage, the excitement vanishes. You'll see."

"Give him his sex so you can have his children."[4]

A female believer wrote to Kevin Leman: "I grew up in a really conservative, religious home. I was never told in so many words, but the message came across loud and clear: *Sex is dirty. And you're dirty if you ever think about it.*"[5] Gary and Barbara Rosberg share Jasmine's struggle: "My mom and grandmother pounded into my head that sex was dirty. How do I take all that

---

[3] This essay is dealing with female sexuality from a Western perspective. It is not interacting with the international church in areas where female sexuality is actually physically attacked as in the practice of female circumcision.

Interestingly, while the male gender may have heard the same voices, they do not generally suffer in the same way expressing their sexuality within marriage.

[4] Linda Dillow and Lorraine Pintus, *Intimate Issues: Conversations Woman to Woman* (Colorado Springs, CO: WaterBrook Press, 1999), 5.

[5] Kevin Leman, *Turn Up the Heat: A Couples Guide to Sexual Intimacy* (Grand Rapids, MI: Revell), 22.

training from the women in my life and still become the sexy woman I know my husband wants? As soon as I get in the mood, those messages bounce around in my head and I get turned off before I get started."⁶

Dannah Gresh and Juli Slattery write of one Christian who shared: "Growing up, I was one of those 'good Christian girls' who took the message of purity seriously. I had trained my mind and my heart to say no to sexual things through my teens and early twenties. When I got married, the wedding ring on my finger didn't suddenly erase all the 'no' messages."⁷ Another female believer wonders, "How can I get rid of old tapes in my head from my childhood about how defiled sex is? They make me feel inhibited every time I have sex. I feel like a prostitute."⁸

Judy, too, grew up in a religiously conservative home. Before she was to be married at twenty-one her mom pulled her aside for the sex talk (for the first time). Kim Eckert continues Judy's story, "Her mom described sex as something a wife did for her husband to keep him satisfied. Never did the mom mention the possibility that there could be sexual pleasure for the wife."⁹ Unfortunately Judy is not a lone case as Eckert reports, "I have counseled many women who have experienced a deep sense of disappointment and guilt about their inability to enjoy sex as a gift in marriage. Even though they know that sex within marriage is not a sin; it still feels like a sin."¹⁰ One Christian wife responded to a study of the sexual attitudes of Christian women and shared, "More than anything else I want to

---

⁶ Gary and Barbara Rosberg, *The 5 Sex Needs of Men and Women* (Carol Stream, IL: Tyndale House, 2006), 99-100.

⁷ Dannah Gresh and Juli Slattery, *Pulling Back the Shades: Erotica, Intimacy, and the Longings of a Woman's Heart* (Chicago: Moody Press, 2014), 103-4.

⁸ Archibald D. Hart, Catherine Hart Weber, and Debra L. Taylor, *Secrets of Eve* (Nashville, TN: Word Publishing, 1998), 11.

⁹ Kim Gaines Eckert, *Things Your Mother Never Told You: A Women's Guide to Sexuality* (Downers Grove, IL: IVP, 2014), 85.

¹⁰ Ibid., 13.

abandon myself to my husband when we make love. He is kind and gentle, and very patient with me. But something inside me tells me I am doing bad things… after two years of marriage I still feel like I am sinning."[11]

Juli Slattery tells the story of Holly. In a group of moms discussing how to "infuse excitement into the marriage after childbirth…. One of the women suggested going to the underwear store and mixing in some 'sexy undies' with the standard 'granny panties.' Holly was embarrassed and disgusted that her Christian friends would suggest wearing lacy underwear and thongs. Although she couldn't voice a logical or biblical reason why she was offended, she simply couldn't accept that God would be okay with this."[12]

Dillow and Pintus share the story of one woman who confided, "It's as if I live in a two-story house. The top floor is my spirituality and the bottom floor my sexuality. In between the two floors is a brick barrier separating my spiritual self from my sexual self. Because I want to be godly, I can't allow myself to be too earthly—and sex is definitely earthly. I allow myself to experience pleasure—but only so much. If I get really carried away, it would be 'too fleshly.'"[13]

My wife, Joy, and I counseled one young wife and her sexually frustrated husband, (with two kids) who truly believed that God never meant women to enjoy sex. As "Jean" sat on the couch across from us she vehemently challenged us to show her that he did!

Just a few years ago we were asked to conduct a single pre-marital session on "sex" for a young Christian pastor and his soon to be bride. The reason for only one session was because her pastor was too uncomfortable

---

[11] *Secrets of Eve*, 12.
[12] Juli Slattery, *No More Headaches: Enjoying Sex & Intimacy in Marriage* (Carol Stream, IL: Tyndale House, 2009), 50.
[13] *Intimate Issues*, 15.

and embarrassed to share with them openly, honestly, and biblically about physical intimacy within marriage.

While the reasons, motivations and historical influences can be debated concerning such individual stories, the reality is that many of our sisters in the Lord have not heard God's *full* voice concerning female sexuality. What is surprising is that with the sexual revolution of the 1960s and the plethora of sexual information (both good and awful) a few mouse clicks away a mere few decades later, one wonders why Christian women are struggling so in this area. One reason is that these women (generally) have been taught that the Bible should be followed in all areas of life. And many endeavor to obey the biblical text. However, in the area of sexuality, outside the "Thou shalt not" passages and 1 Corinthians 7:3-5, the church has been monotone in her prohibitions. One sister observes, "The church is behind the times in many respects. Certainly, it has not helped to educate its adherents to a healthy and biblically acceptable form of sexuality. The church needs to counter hundreds of years of 'shame-based' theology connected with sexuality. I want my daughters to have a healthier view of sexuality than I grew up with."[14]

While not true of every church or family, this sister recognizes that while the church has nailed the negatives, it has in many cases avoided the teaching of the positives. Ellison and Brown submit, "If the Christian response to sex has long been fear and suspicion, and if the prevailing watchwords are control and restraint, then contemporary Christians must look long and hard to find theological affirmation of erotic pleasure and even longer and harder to find theological interest in *women's* sexual pleasure."[15]

---

[14] *Secrets of Eve*, 9.
[15] Marvin M. Ellison and Kelly Brown Douglas eds. "Introduction to Part 4," *Sexuality and the Sacred: Sources for Theological Reflection*, 2nd edition (Louisville, KY: Westminster John Knox Press, 2010), 241.

For women, the church's silence is deafening; and other voices are all too eager to fill this void. As Carolyn Mahaney observes, "If you watch TV, go to the movies, or read magazines today, you can get the impression that the only people having sex (or good 'sex') are the ones who aren't married. If married sex is even portrayed in popular media, it seems bland or routine. Our culture demeans marital sex and instead celebrates immoral sex."[16] Following the siren song of culture creates its own set of poor consequences for the women of the church.

However, above this cacophony from culture rises a clarion voice from Scripture—an entire book about sexuality from the female perspective. It is my contention that the church needs to hear this voice and "sing" without embarrassment, shame, or blush the Song of Songs.[17] I also assert that this mostly ignored but divinely inspired poem from God's own lips needs to be the foremost voice women hear on the beauty and wonder of their sexuality.

Speaking for women, Mahaney rightly observes:

> It is important that we acquire a biblical perspective of sex. God intends for us to experience tremendous joy and satisfaction in our sexual relationship with our husbands. And what greater proof do we need than the fact that God included the Song of Solomon in Holy Scripture—an entire book of the Bible devoted to love, romance, and sexuality in marriage…. This little book portrays a physical relationship between husband and wife that is filled with uninhibited passion and exhilarating delight. This is God's heart and aim for our sexual experience.[18]

---

[16] Carolyn Mahaney, "Sex, Romance, and the Glory of God: What Every Christian Wife Needs to Know" in *Sex and Supremacy of Christ*, ed. John Piper and Justin Taylor (Wheaton, IL: Crossway Books, 2005), 202.

[17] Or allegory or spiritualizing.

[18] Ibid.

HEARING THE SONG IN ITS PROPER KEY

To hear the divinely inspired Song rightly, women (and others who want to teach it) must recognize how it teaches. Unlike the NT epistles or OT Law there are no commands or imperatives for the reader to follow. Instead as wisdom literature it instructs by holding up at the same time both a model and a mirror. As a model the Song implicitly instructs the reader that this is the type of wise, intimate relationship God desires you to enjoy. The model does not share the "normal" quantity of sexual experiences, various sexual positions, or best sexual techniques for a happy Christian marriage.[19] Instead it models in broad-brush strokes the God-desired quality of marriage intimacy. It silently asks this question of its readers, "Don't you want this type of intimacy in your marriage?" As a mirror the Song implicitly requests the reader to evaluate whether or not their marriage reflects the desire of this couple in their own relationship. It silently asks the question of its readers, "Do I have this quality of desire and physical intimacy between my spouse and I in our marriage?" Estes rightly notes, "Instead of merely reporting the experience of the characters, the book, as poetry, endeavors to re-create their experience in the reader."[20] As such the Song does not command obedience; it inspires every wise couple to desire and maintain a relationship that mirrors and models these lovers.

Solomon wrote his best song (SS 1:1) celebrating passion and desire between a heterosexual man and woman within the confines of God-

---

[19] The Song is not as some have claimed a Hebrew or even Christian Kamasutra. Patrick Hunt writes, "The *Song of Songs* is more appropriate to bedside table than coffee table.... It could even be called the Hebrew *Kamasutra*" (*Poetry in the Song of Songs: A Literary Analysis* (New York: Peter Lang Inc., 2008), iv.

[20] Daniel J. Estes, *Handbook on the Wisdom Books and Psalms* (Grand Rapids, MI: Baker, 2005), 401.

ordained marriage. This poem does not narrate the ups and downs of the courtship-marriage-post honeymoon stages of an historical couple. It is an artistic creation that places the two main literary characters into a lush and near perfect environment. In this garden setting the two lovers reveal themselves through their conversation. This sometimes erotically charged dialogue paints on the reader's imagination the pleasure of fulfilled desire and the palpable ache of absence. For this couple longing is only satisfied in the presence of the other. When absent from each other, they yearn for one another and their desire drives them over every obstacle to be one. The movement of the book from her first voiced longing for his kisses to her final wish for his return is achieved by this cyclical progression of absence to presence.[21] For this couple, presence produces shalom; absence is always to be struggled against. No good comes from absence except a desire to be present with the other.[22]

The Song of Songs is an ancient love song about a couple who revel in their strong physical desire for each other. Through the use of intimate

---

[21] Appendix 1 is my outline of the flow of the Song.

[22] What the Song is not: 1. The Song is not about God's love for Israel or Christ's love for the church. This allegorical interpretation was a common view held by the church fathers because of their uncomfortableness with the subject matter and their philosophical foundations. They spiritualized or allegorized the Song. For example, the female lover's breast actually represented a deeper or more spiritual meaning. Since women have two breasts, some commentators said that one breast was the NT and the other was the OT in which the church received her nourishment. Jewish scholars would equate the two breasts with Moses and Aaron who "nourished" the nation of Israel. 2. The Song is not a narrative that traces the love between Solomon and the country lass named the Shulammite. One cannot outline the Song based on their courtship, marriage, and happily-ever-after. The text simply will not sustain such a reading. For examples see the obvious sexual references in 1:2; 1:4; 2:3-6; 2:14; 3:4 which are before the supposed wedding in the later part of chapter 3. Some have surmised that it is a narrative of two male lovers, one being Solomon and the other a rustic shepherd who vie for the affection of the pretty Shulammite whose heart really belongs to the lowly shepherd and not the fabulously wealthy king. Again, the text will not support such a reading.

dialogue this couple shares their desire to be joined when separated and passionately enjoy each other when they are together. For this couple sex/physical oneness is a natural consequence of desire and defeating obstacles to be together. While the garden motif reminds the reader of the garden of Eden, this garden is post-fall and has a number of obstacles the couple must overcome to be one. Through the use of highly charged sexual imagery clothed in Hebrew poetry this fictitious couple invites every couple who is wise to enjoy their own celebration of love within the confines of their marriage.

The Song moves and has its being through the interaction of four (4) main characters or more specifically four (4) voices: the female lover (who speaks the majority of time—approximately sixty-five percent), the male beloved and a chorus of women known as the daughters of Jerusalem.[23] This female chorus functions to let the reader know the inward thoughts of the female lover when the male lover is absent from her. They also act as the near audience for the reader as the female lover shares her exhortation with the daughters, which applies to them.[24] The fourth voice speaks but one full poetic line and it is the narrator's voice who speaks for God (5:1). No other voices are heard in the Song.

---

[23] Interestingly, and not seen in our English translations, the second person pronouns that are used of the "daughters of Jerusalem" are masculine plural in the BHS. This is not a textual issue but a rhetorical device of Solomon to allow both men and women readers to be represented by the "daughters" in the Song and subject to the exhortations of the female lover. See Song of Solomon 2:7, 3:5, 8:4.

[24] Solomon, although the author of the Song, has no voice in his composition. Solomon is directly spoken to only once (8:12). In this instance he acts as the foil for the couple who enjoy only each other while the king has his hordes ("vineyards") of women (Baal-hamon i.e. "master of many" 8:11). Solomon wrote better than he lived. He knew that one mutually exclusive love is better than a harem full of lovely and willing ladies who were bought with wealth (8:7c, d).

GOD'S VOICE ON FEMALE SEXUALITY

One woman muses, "What is right? What is wrong? Can I both be godly and sensuous? I wish I knew how I should think about sex and how You, God, think about sex."[25]

While OT theologian Paul House gets some points right on the Song, he is certainly not helpful when he concludes, "Song of Solomon is artistically and thematically lovely but not particularly theologically enriching."[26] His observation misses badly the opportunity to answer from God's own perspective what God thinks about sex and how divine wisdom should inform women how they should think and act concerning all things sexual. This poem is filled with divinely inspired theology that voices distinctly the proper and good expression of female sexuality.

While we cannot bare all the theology concerning female sexuality based on our present time constraints, allow me to uncover five (5) divine realities that demonstrate 1) that the Song is the foremost voice women need to hear concerning their own sexuality 2) that the Song is the foremost voice that the church needs to proclaim (on Sunday mornings) concerning female sexuality for all her members and 3) that the Song as God's voice provides divine permission for her married female members to celebrate fully his gift of female sexuality in their own marriages.

---

[25] *Intimate Issues*, 3.
[26] Paul House, *Old Testament Theology* (Downers Grove, IVP, 1998), 469.

1. Women Have Divine Permission to Celebrate Physical Intimacy Within Marriage [27]

In the unique opening lines of the Song the female lover pines:[28]

May he kiss me with the kisses of his mouth!
For your love is better than wine (1:2).[29]

Not satisfied she hungers a chapter later:

Sustain me with raisin cakes,
Refresh me with apples,
Because I am lovesick.
Let his left hand be under my head
And his right hand embrace me (2:5-6).

These few poetic lines provide clear evidence of our female protagonist's yearning for multiple kisses, erotic caresses and prolonged lovemaking. Her craving for intimacies is palpable and undeniable. Only the most talented allegorists could cover up what these divine texts so clearly expose—the woman wants sex! While these sample texts are theologically informative, what should not be missed are the subsequent lines. In the following verses 1:3 and 2:7 her erotic desires are not met with divine lightning bolts! There is no divine prohibition, divine sarcasm, or divine censure for this woman's

---

[27] While there is no need to state the obvious boundary markers to these truths to the present audience, to avoid any misunderstandings or applications, all of these theological truths are required by God to be enjoyed within the confines of a heterosexual marriage.

[28] No other book of the Bible begins with a female point of view or voice.

[29] All translations are from the NASB unless otherwise noted.

cravings for physical intimacy in any part of the Song. Only a caution is proffered in the adjuration refrains.[30] This thrice repeated warning challenges the unmarried daughters of Jerusalem not to awaken such "love" (i.e. desires) until the proper time (i.e. marriage). However, for the woman of the Song, there is no similar restraint. She need not abandon or even curtail her fleshly longings since she is already married.[31]

While these verses certainly show God's approval of female sexual desire, it is in 5.1 where his divine affirmation is unmistakable. The section that ends with 5:1 actually began in 3:6 with their separation. Once the couple is together (4:1) the male lover begins an elaborate *wasf* that recounts her exquisite physical beauty (4:1-7).[32] His praise of her body transitions to an invitation for his female lover to overcome unknown and possible dangerous obstacles that separates them (4:8-9). Male desire continues in the next verses and becomes more bodily specific but stays clothed in flora metaphors (4:11-15). His invitation and yearning is answered with her own enticement:

Female lover
Awake, O north *wind*,
And come, *wind of* the south;
Make my garden breathe out *fragrance*,
Let its spices be wafted abroad.
May my beloved come into his garden
And eat its choice fruits! (4:16).

---

[30] Cf. 2:7; 3:5; 8:4.

[31] The Song begins *medias res*. The couple is already married. While a minority of scholars sees the couple as unmarried, (and it is true there is no mention of their marriage in the poem), not being married would contradict the Torah which would have excluded its inclusion in the canon.

[32] *Wasf* is an Arabic term for a physical description.

While dressed in spicy Hebrew images, it is clear that her offer is for lovemaking. The man enthusiastically accepts her invitation with the same metaphorical language that morphs her garden into his garden:

Male lover
I have come into my garden, my sister, *my* bride;
I have gathered my myrrh along with my balsam.
I have eaten my honeycomb and my honey;
I have drunk my wine and my milk (5:1a-d).

Tremper Longman remarks, "He enters the garden and enjoys all of its delights.... The double objects of each of the final three cola indicate the totality of his experience.... He has possessed her completely, a fitting image of sexual intercourse."[33] However, in the midst of such "intimate feasting," an unidentified voice addresses the couple:

Eat, friends;
Drink and imbibe deeply, O lovers (5:1e,f).

While there is discussion among scholars as to the identity of the unknown voice, a legitimate contender is the narrator. Although Amit is writing on Hebrew narrative, she summarizes well the position of the narrator and her words are applicable to this poem: "Both God and the narrator must be trustworthy and hence are the benchmark of trustworthiness for all other personae. Whatever accords with the narrator's statements of God's must be beyond doubt."[34] In this case the narrator's imperatives to continue the

---

[33] Tremper Longman, III, *Song of Songs* (Grand Rapids: Eerdmans, 2001), 159.
[34] Yairah Amit, *Reading Biblical Narratives: Literary Criticism and the Hebrew Bible* (Minneapolis, MN: Fortress Press, 2001), 95.

"feasting" of each other is actually the voice of God.³⁵ Dillow observes, "The poet seems to say this is the voice of God Himself. Only the Lord could pronounce such an affirmation. He, of course, was the most intimate observer of all."³⁶ Since the anonymous voice is God's, the poet is using this short imperative rhetorically to cast his divine favor over the most intimate of human activities between a man and a woman. The point should not be missed that the commands are to both lovers: female and male. The woman is to be "drunk" with their lovemaking just as much as the man. Exum is certainly correct as she observes, "'Eat,' 'drink,' and 'be drunk,' plural forms addressed to both lovers, leave no doubt that eating and drinking in the garden is mutual sexual indulgence and satisfaction."³⁷

Arguably this is the clearest divine voice in all of Scripture proclaiming God's approval, nay his encouragement, for both married females and males to celebrate to the fullest sexual intimacy within marriage. This is the voice sisters in the Lord need to hear (and believe). But if the Song is not rightly proclaimed, how will they hear God's wisdom and how will those unbiblical messages bouncing around their gray matter be countered without God's voice?

---

³⁵ While it is outside the scope of this chapter to pursue, a legitimate question is the absence of the voice of God. "Why not let God speak for himself in the SoS, instead of 'hiding' his voice behind the unnamed narrator?" It may be that since Israel's neighbors were so heavily engaged in various fertility cults that Solomon may have felt the need to keep a respectable distance between God and the act of sex. As Phipps writes, "In Hebrew culture sex had been demythologized; it was considered a proper sphere for man but not for deity." William E. Phipps, "The Plight of the Song of Songs," *JAAR* 42, no 1 (March 1974):83.

³⁶ Joseph C. Dillow, *Solomon on Sex* (Nashville, TN: Nelson Publishers, 1977), 86.

³⁷ J. Cheryl Exum, Song of Songs: A Commentary (Louisville, KY: Westminster John Knox Press, 2005), 183.

2. Women Have Divine Permission to Initiate Sexual Experiences Within Marriage

One area where married women struggle is in the area of initiation of sexual experiences with their husbands. Writing on the top five (5) sexual needs of men and women, the Rosbergs comment, "Of all the sex needs, initiation seems to be the most difficult for many wives to practice."[38] While the reasons for lack of initiation certainly vary among women, it is not an issue for the female lover in the Song.

> I am my beloved's,
> And his desire is for me.
> Come, my beloved, let us go out into the country,
> Let us spend the night in the villages.
> Let us rise early *and go* to the vineyards;
> Let us see whether the vine has budded
> *And its* blossoms have opened,
> *And whether* the pomegranates have bloomed.
> There I will give you my love (7:10-12).

Although her invitation is attired in Hebrew metaphor and figurative language, it does not take a degree in Hebrew to undress her meaning. She is initiating a sexual romp! While the "budding," "opening" and "blooming" may be sexual innuendoes (or flimsy excuses for lovemaking in the vineyard), it is clear that she is enticing him through sensually charged agricultural imagery for a time of lovemaking, and if to be understood literally, outside! Diane Bergant explains, "The word for love is plural in form and, as has been

---

[38] *The 5 Sex Needs*, 136.

the case with its other appearances (1:2, 4:10), is better translated 'lovemaking.'"[39] Hess writes, "The picture is also a metaphor of her body and its fecundity for love. In this verse the drama and journey again lead to the same destination, the place of lovemaking."[40] Longman concurs: The last line "clarifies her intention to explore the vineyard. She will give her love to him; the vineyard again is a place of lovemaking."[41]

The metaphors are not so dense that the reader cannot see that the female is the one expressing sexual desire, planning and initiating the amorous tryst. To understand the theology here one needs to remember how the Song of Solomon teaches. As a model it asks the question: "Don't you want this type of intimacy in your marriage?" And as a mirror it asks, "Do I have this quality of desire and physical intimacy between my spouse and I in our marriage?" In other words it encourages women to ask themselves, "Do I understand that God allows me as a woman to initiate a sensual scenario with my husband?" While many of our married sisters do not live in such an agricultural setting to follow the Shulammite's example line by line (and in some places lovemaking outdoors is illegal—if caught), the verses affirm that women do have God-given approval to be the architect in lovemaking. The modern wise female lover has the divinely approved model to follow in the Shulammite.

---

[39] Dianne Bergant, *The Song of Songs* (Collegeville, MN: The Liturgical Press, 2001), 91.

[40] Richard S. Hess, *Song of Songs* (Grand Rapids, MI: Baker Academic, 2005) 226.

[41] Longman, 201.

3. Women Have Divine Permission to Celebrate Sexual Creativity Within Marriage

Another area where many women feel prohibition is expressing sexual creativity within marriage. Here is a sampling of real questions I have received from women:

"Is role-playing wrong? Does the Bible say anything about it?"

"I don't want anyone to faint so I wanted to text this question. Oral sex, is it wrong, biblical?"

"How can you decide to try new positions?"

"Is it permissible to use toys/devices?"

"A pastor bought his wife some lingerie and wants her to dress like a prostitute in the bedroom. Is this ok in God's eyes? And dance like a stripper for him? What do you think?"

These queries reveal the fact that Christian women wrestle with knowing what is sexually right or wrong in the bedroom…or any other room in the house. And even if some may be erotically adventurous inside or outside the bedroom, there is the morning after. One woman muses, "I blushed when I remember what we had done last night. What would my mother think—what would my pastor think—what did I think?"[42] This is an example of one looking for the divine voice in this vital area.

---

[42] *Intimate Issues*, 210.

The female lover in the Song has no such reservations or doubts. Finishing the section, she began above, not only is there a promise of female initiation of lovemaking, but on her proverbial suggestive menu is a promise of something "old and new" in verse 13.

Female lover

> Come, my beloved, let us go out into the country,
> Let us spend the night in the villages.
> Let us rise early *and go* to the vineyards;
> Let us see whether the vine has budded
> *And its* blossoms have opened,
> *And whether* the pomegranates have bloomed.
> There I will give you my love.
>
> The mandrakes have given forth fragrance;
> And over our doors are all choice *fruits*,
> Both new and old,
> Which I have saved up for you, my beloved (7:11-13).

Verse 13 (14 Hebrew) is somewhat puzzling. What are these "choice *fruits*" that are both "new and old" which the female lover has "saved" for her male lover? In keeping with the double entendre of the previous verses of "budding," "opening" and "blooming" it is safe to assume that there is a sexual connotation associated with this verse. If one consults HALOT and translates כָּל־מְגָדִים as "all delicacies" instead of "choice *fruits*", and recognize that the female lover is the one who has "stored up" "both new and old" "delicacies" for her beloved, it does not take much ingenuity to see her creative use of language as a euphemism for both fresh and "old" favorite sexual activities for them to both to enjoy.[43] Cheryl Exum suggests, "The fruits the woman offers are choice fruits of her garden (4:13, 16). 'New as well as old' includes the whole spectrum of delights, known to lovers who appreciate how new familiar can be."[44] Dianne Bergant sees "new and old" as a merism and writes, "The merism includes the poles and whatever is between them. The woman has already promised to make love (7:13). Here she declares that she has laid up the pleasures of lovemaking for her beloved (*dodi*)."[45] Hess comments, "The expression 'new and old' used of fruit may function as a metaphor for experiences of carnal love that the two have shared. The female promises new delicacies as well as those already favored by her lover."[46]

We are uncertain as to the male lover's response to her creative and not so subtle carnal declaration. But sanctified imagination would guess he said yes. However, it is not his response that is important but her voice, her longing, her desire, her erotic inventiveness that is centered and celebrated in these verses. Her longing meets no divine condemnation, no reprimand, no rebuke. Although the Shulammite's voice is undoubtedly both the model and mirror for females to hear, how will they hear if the church is not proclaiming this theology? Female sexual creativity is to be celebrated within marriage and this truth proclaimed in church.

---

[43] HALOT, 543
[44] Exum, 242.
[45] Bergant, 92.
[46] Hess, 227.

4. Women Have Divine Permission to Celebrate Female Sexual Passion Within Marriage

Leman shares a letter he received from a female Sunday school teacher: "Here's my secret: I really, really love sex. And I'm a woman. (If the other Sunday school teachers could hear me now, I'd be the talk of the church for a year.)"[47] This observation begs the question, why? What are the reasons that a woman who says she loves sex with her husband becomes church news for a year? Isn't this supposed to be the norm? One of the reasons it would be "news" is because women have heard multiple voices announce throughout history (their own personal history and their gender's) that they should not like sex; sex is not for them, or sex is only for procreation. And if they ever discover that they (heaven forbid) actually enjoy sex, they certainly should not acknowledge it! To be a proper Christian woman (they have been told) they must squelch their female sexual passion.

While many have heard these erroneous voices, it was not the voice that governs the female lover of the Song. Listen to a sampling of her voice:

> May he kiss me with the kisses of his mouth!
> For your love is better than wine (1:2).

> Like an apple tree among the trees of the forest,
> So is my beloved among the young men.
> In his shade I took great delight and sat down,
> And his fruit was sweet to my taste.
> He has brought me to *his* banquet hall,
> And his banner over me is love.
> Sustain me with raisin cakes,

---

[47] *Turn Up the Heat*, 232.

Refresh me with apples,
Because I am lovesick.
Let his left hand be under my head
And his right hand embrace me (2:3-6)

My beloved extended his hand through the opening,
And my feelings (*inward parts*)⁴⁸ were aroused for him (5:4).

His mouth is *full of* sweetness.
And he is wholly desirable.
This is my beloved and this is my friend,
O daughters of Jerusalem (5:16).

I would lead you *and* bring you
Into the house of my mother, who used to instruct me;
I would give you spiced wine to drink from the juice of my pomegranates.
Let his left hand be under my head
And his right hand embrace me (8:2-3).

Unless one follows Origen or Bernard of Clairvaux the female voice is unequivocal as it concerns female sexual passion and pleasure. While biology itself teaches that females are designed for sexual pleasure,⁴⁹ here unembarrassed theology needs neither comment nor commentary to demonstrate God's approval of female sexual passion within marriage. The biblical text is clear; the divine voice is clear; her voice is clear. The only voice

---

⁴⁸ HALOT's second definition for מֵעָה "that part of the body through which people come into existence" 609.

⁴⁹ The only function of the female clitoris is to provide sexual pleasure.

104 On Sexual Expression

missing is the church's. The voice of the Song provides a strong theological anchor that allows a woman to have her sexual celebration approved by God and not simply by feelings or the headlines of *Redbook* or *Cosmo*.

5. Women Have Divine Permission to Celebrate Nakedness Within Marriage

Lauren F. Winner observes, "We Christians get embarrassed about our bodies. We are not always sure that God likes them very much. We are not sure whether bodies are good or bad."[50] It is interesting that God designed physical intimacy to be embodied in well, bodies! Without real, corporeal bodies there is no sexual intimacy to be received or given and certainly none to be celebrated.

The first book of the Bible displays for readers that God is not ashamed of bodies, even nude ones. This makes perfect theological sense since God created man and woman bodily (Ge 2:7, 2:21-22) and both without a stitch of clothing (Ge 2:25). While clothing has become a theological necessity after the fall for mankind, in the Song nakedness is unashamedly evident and celebrated between the husband and wife.

The fifth movement of the Song is by far the most erotic stanza of biblical poetry in the canon. The reason for its erotic nature is the detailed *wasf* of the female lover (7:1-9a). What makes this *wasf* so different than the one of chapter four is that here the female lover is nude and possibly dancing. That she is completely uncovered is clearly visible by the body parts that he describes in metaphorical detail:

curves of your hips… (7:1)

---

[50] Lauren F. Winner, *Real Sex: The Naked Truth about Chastity* (Grand Rapids, MI:Brazos Press, 2005), 33.

> your navel is like a round goblet… (7:2)
> your belly is a heap of wheat… (7:2)
> your two breasts are like two fawns… (7:3)
> Your stature is like a palm tree,
> And your breasts are *like its* clusters. (7:7)
> I said, 'I will climb the palm tree,
> I will take hold of its fruit stalks.
> Oh, may your breasts be like clusters of the vine…(7:8)

These physical feminine qualities can only be described in such literary vividness if she is naked. Otherwise these various "parts" would be hidden beneath her garments. While this *wasf* has been the "whipping boy" for feminist scholars against the "male gaze," they do not represent the Shulammite's opinion of his visual contemplation of her body. In response to his thoroughly approving gaze she declares:

> I am my beloved's,
> And his desire is for me (7:10).

Bergant views his gaze and her response to his gaze as "mutual love, not an unequal relationship. It is interesting to note that whenever this formula is appears, it is found in the mouth of the woman. She is clearly desirous of mutual possession."[51] Exum writes, "Whereas Genesis connects the woman's desire to her domination by the man, the Song says desire is mutual."[52] It is clear from her four-word response, וְעָלַי תְּשׁוּקָתוֹ: אֲנִי לְדוֹדִי that the female lover does not shy away from her lover's gaze. While some may argue that the female lover's lack of garments is strictly for his enjoyment, it

---

[51] Bergant, 90.
[52] Exum, 241.

is readily heard in her response that she is not ashamed of her bare physique but embraces and luxuriates in her bodily sensuality with her lover.

While there is ongoing cultural and scholarly discussion concerning how sexually stimulated the modern female gender is by sight, clearly the female lover likes what she sees when she turns her feminine gaze on her nude lover (5:10-16). In this lone female *wasf* in the Song it is clearly evident by the male body parts described that he is naked under her visual scrutiny. While his head, locks, eyes, cheeks, lips and hands would be noticeable if he were clothed, it is her description of his "abdomen" and legs which give physical evidence of his full-frontal nudity.

Female lover
His abdomen is carved ivory
Inlaid with sapphires.

His legs are pillars of alabaster
Set on pedestals of pure gold; (5:14-15).

If he were clothed, neither of these male body parts would be visible to her naked eye. Bergant observes,

> Moving further down his body, the woman marvels at the man's belly. The Hebrew word used [מֵעֶה] usually denotes inner organs, bowels, even womb. The woman would not extol the man's belly unless it was naked, clearly a provocative thought. Although the precious gems probably refer to overlaid decoration, there might also be veiled allusion to the man's genitals. The generous use of double

entendre throughout the poem leaves this reference open to such interpretation.[53]

Uncovering these metaphors Longman proposes, "When one thinks of ivory, one thinks of a tusk of ivory, an object that could easily have erotic connotations. The decoration with lapis, a precious stone blue in color, simply would highlight the object's preciousness. In such an erotic poem, the line at the least is suggestive of, if not explicitly referring to, the man's member."[54] Exum concurs, "There is something sexually suggestive in all these images of hardness—not simply that one or more of these images might be a veiled reference to the man's penis."[55]

While her lover's nudity is clothed under these salacious Hebrew metaphors, her lavish appreciation for his entire body cannot be missed. At the end of her *wasf* she asserts of her naked lover:

His mouth is *full of* sweetness.
And he is wholly desirable.
This is my beloved and this is my friend,
O daughters of Jerusalem (5:16).

As it was in the Garden before the fall, this pair is naked and not ashamed to celebrate it with each other. This female is the model and mirror for all wise women to evaluate their practice and attitude concerning nakedness. The Song (i.e. God) declares that bodies are good and that naked bodies are to be enjoyed within marriage.

---

[53] Bergant, 72.
[54] Longman, 173.
[55] Exum, 207.

CONCLUSION

TO JUDY, HOLLY, JEAN, JASMINE AND OTHER "GOOD GIRLS"

There is an orchestra of voices that the women who stories introduced this chapter can listen to as it concerns their sexuality. However, the Song of Songs has shown that God has not left his daughters without a clear and clarion voice for them to follow in all things sexual. God desires that his daughters understand and follow his voice alone as it concerns their sexuality. While it is certainly not easy to switch off contrary voices, a wise wife will follow the divine voice above all others (Pr 1:5). Women who follow this divine voice inside and outside the bedroom have divine permission to acknowledge and celebrate their sexuality within the confines of their individual heterosexual marriages.[56]

TO THOSE WHO TEACH THE SONG

While much more can be affirmed from the theology of the Song concerning female sexuality, enough theology has been laid bare to allow the women of the church to hear the true and only voice that should guide their sexuality—God's. As Dispensationalists who understand God's word correctly, it is our responsibility to proclaim God's voice distinctly without stammer, stutter or blush concerning female sexuality. At least half of the

---

[56] In this chapter I am not arguing for eliminating the "no" voice to pre-marital sex or sexual immorality. I am arguing for a balanced biblical voice to be heard.

congregation is waiting to see if the church has anything more to say about female sexual pleasure than the negatives.[57]

---

[57] Although hearing this theology in the male voice has its own issues. As one thirty-something female shared, "Without even reading your paper, my first reaction is ugh…another man telling me how to view my sexuality." While such sentiments do not absolve us of our teaching responsibilities, it should sensitize us to how we communicate such theology (cf., Titus 2:3-4).

110 On Sexual Expression

Chapter 6 – On Anxiety

He Has Overcome the World: The Importance of Dispensational Propositions in Addressing the Anxieties of Millennials and Generation Z Related to Salvation, Political Upheaval, and the Environment

C. R. Twombly

INTRODUCTION

Millennials and Generation Z are the most anxious generation on record in American history. Whether it is major media outlets[1] or psychological studies from various research groups,[2] all agree that Millennials and Generation Z are collectively "the anxious generation." And yet, with the rise in anxiety around subjects like environmental crisis, political upheaval and change, and even existential anxiety, there seems to be little that major

---

[1] Karol Markowicz, "'They Can't Even': Why Millennials are the 'Anxious Generation,'" New York Post, NYP Holdings Inc. 2016, https://nypost.com/2016/03/20/they-cant-even-why-millennials-are-the-anxious-generation/. Fagan, Abigail, "Why 90 Percent of Generation Z Says They're Stressed Out," Psychology Today, Sussex Publishers, LLC, https://www.psychologytoday.com/us/blog/the-stressed-years-their-lives/201812/why-90-percent-generation-z-says-theyre-stressed-out.

[2] Richard Scheffler, "Anxiety Disorders in Millennials: Causes and Consequences," Petris Center, Berkeley Institute for the Future of Young Americans, https://petris.org/projects-2/completed-projects-2/anxiety/#:~:text=Anxiety%20is%20a%20growing%20problem,than%20it%20was%20in%202008.

Geoff McMasters, "Millennials and Generation Z Are More Anxious Than Previous Generations," Folio, University of Alberta, https://www.ualberta.ca/folio/2020/01/millennials-and-gen-z-are-more-anxious-than-previous-generations-heres-why.html.

Christian resource outlets have been able to do to slow this major rise. To the contrary, in many cases, conservative Christian resource centers feed into much of the anxiety or provide commentary on these issues which only serves to feed the anxiety of young people around these issues. Many such articles mean well, attempting to provide theological insights into the issues at hand, but lack the Biblical eternal scope for grounding these issues properly. Instead, Christian resource centers either focus on an issue's imminent concerns, only further legitimizing the anxious fixation of young people around these immediate concerns, or instead completely delegitimize these concerns, only serving to build resentment among younger people.

In meeting these concerns, dispensationalism is uniquely positioned as a system with propositions that meet the anxiety of young people within the proper eternal scope without delegitimizing their concern. In particular, dispensationalism's use of a doxological purpose for God's plan, distinct economies in God's unfolding revelation, the Israel-church distinction, and its well-developed premillennial eschatology, each provide accessible Biblical grounding for mitigating Millennial and Generation Z anxieties around the environment, politics, and existential fear, without delegitimizing the concerns of these individuals.

THE MATTER AT HAND: MILLENNIAL AND GENERATION Z ANXIETY

In 2018, the American Psychological Association published its annual "Stress in America" report which found that 91 percent of Generation Z individuals surveyed experienced symptoms of intense stress.[3] Only a year prior, the same survey found that 58 percent of Millennials experience the

---

[3] American Psychological Association (2018), Stress in America: Generation Z, Stress in America™ Survey, 5.

same intense anxiety.⁴ While many think of increases in anxiety as a pandemic related issue, these surveys clearly show there is a generational difference in the level of anxiety irrespective of the pandemic era. In the most recent survey, these metrics have remained fairly consistent through the pandemic era, with Millennials reporting a consistent stress level of 5.7 and Generation Z reporting a consistent stress level of 5.4, out of a total potential stress of 10.⁵ Younger generations are disproportionately anxious about a variety of issues to the point where it is beginning to effect their basic decision making.⁶ When it comes to the locale of their stress, a variety of issues can and have been named; however, three main categories can be discerned: the environment, political upheaval, and existential anxiety.

These different anxieties are also similarly documented. Concerning their political anxieties, in 2019 the Harvard Institute of Politics found that: "the state of our politics is contributing to the mental health challenges millions of young Americans already face."⁷ Their 2019 Youth Poll results found that: "Half of young Americans experience anxiety, and it is correlated with views related to the state of our nation," regardless of their political affiliation or background.⁸ Additionally, 52 percent agreed with the statement that they were particularly "concerned about the moral direction of the country."⁹

---

⁴ American Psychological Association (2017), Stress in America: Generation Z, Stress in America™ Survey, 3.

⁵ American Psychological Association (2021), Stress in America: Generation Z, Stress in America™ Survey, 3.

⁶ American Psychological Association (2021), Stress in America: Generation Z, Stress in America™ Survey, 3.

⁷ "Spring 2019 Harvard IOP Youth Poll Results," Harvard Institute of Politics, Harvard University, 2019, https://iop.harvard.edu/about/newsletter-press-release/spring-2019-harvard-iop-youth-poll-results.

⁸ Ibid.

⁹ Ibid.

Environmental concerns are also rampant among younger generations. In 2021, Pew Research Center reported that 69 percent of Generation Z reported anxiety related to environmental issues.[10] Following quickly behind, 59 percent of Millennials felt the same anxiety surrounding environmental issues.[11] Bath University took a similar survey and found that 59 percent of young people in the U.K. feared for the future of humanity due to environmental concerns.[12] A lead author on the study also noted that these anxieties intersect with political anxieties as well: "This shows eco-anxiety is not just for environmental destruction alone, but inextricably linked to government inaction…"[13] And being that there is a level of mortal anxiety as well, these concerns around the environment are also existential concerns; and likely the same could be said for their concerns surrounding political upheaval.

Existential concerns manifest in a number of ways, from a fear of death to a fear of what comes after death. And surrounding the issue of death, the afterlife, and spirituality, younger people also experience a great amount of

---

[10] Alec Tyson, Brian Kennedy, and Cary Funk, "Gen Z, Millennials Stand Out for Climate Change Activism, Social Media Engagement With Issue," Pew Research Center, 2021, https://www.pewresearch.org/science/2021/05/26/gen-z-millennials-stand-out-for-climate-change-activism-social-media-engagement-with-issue/.

[11] Ibid.

[12] Roger Harrabin, "Climate change: Young people very worried – survey," BBC News, The BBC, https://www.bbc.com/news/world-58549373.

Often anxieties related to the environment are misconstrued as "apocalyptic" or "world-ending"; especially with regard to young people, due to usage of extreme terminology like "fearing for the future of humanity." However, for the vast majority, these concerns are related to what science fiction writers refer to as a "soft apocalypse." In distinction from a global or world-ending apocalypse, a "soft" apocalypse is characterized by an event or events which devastate human civilization such that it is irreversibly changed or lesser in quality. The Bronze Age Collapse, the Fall of Rome, and World War I would all be examples of "soft" apocalypses. This fear then is not that humanity will become extinct, rather that humanity will suffer irreparable harm due to environmental and ecological disasters or mismanagement.

[13] Ibid.

anxiety. In 2017, the Barna Group found that Millennials were twice as likely as previous generations to experience significant spiritual doubt.[14] In his discussion on ministering to Millennials, the Gospel Coalition's Derek Rishmawy crafts his aids around an understanding of the Millennial as one struggling with spiritual doubt of various kinds.[15] And in 2021, the Gospel Coalition, in addressing key questions from Generation Z, addressed issues of salvation specifically.[16] Even NPR ran a story around issues of Millennial spiritual doubt, particularly addressing afterlife doubt/assurance, back in 2013.[17] Ed Springer of Youthworks, an Anglican youth education resource group in the United States, noted that "lack of assurance," is an issue which is constantly plaguing young people today.[18]

And yet, despite both secular and Christian acknowledgement of these issues, attempts to stay the anxieties of young people has done little to dampen the trend, even among Christians. In general, two approaches have been attempted in order to stay the anxieties related to the political, environmental, and existential. The first is to simply dismiss the anxiety as unfounded. And the second is to make the claim that the anxiety is warranted

---

[14] "Two-Thirds of Christians Face Doubt," Barna Group, 2021, https://www.barna.com/research/two-thirds-christians-face-doubt/.
[15] Derek Rishmawy, "Ministering to Millennials," The Gospel Coalition, 2018, https://www.thegospelcoalition.org/article/ministering-to-millennials-in-a-secular-age/.
[16] Josh Butler, "Gen Z's Questions About Salvation and Predestination," The Gospel Coalition, 2021, https://www.thegospelcoalition.org/podcasts/q-a-podcast/gen-z-questions-salvation-predestination/.
[17] David Greene, "On Religion, Some Young People Show Both Doubt And Respect," NPR (National Public Radio), https://www.npr.org/2013/01/17/169450811/on-religion-some-young-people-show-both-doubt-and-respect.
[18] Ed Springer, "How to Build Assurance in Young People," Youthworks, 2021, https://youthworks.net/articles/how-to-build-assurance-in-young-people.

and positive. Both methods can be seen in the writings of non-dispensationalists surrounding these issues.

NON-DISPENSATIONAL APPROACHES: TWO EXTREMES

Politics are by nature divisive. And for that reason, dismissal of political anxieties is an attractive means of avoiding division in a church or church ministry; in addition to being a fairly simple answer to give. In Relevant Magazine's "7 Things Christians Need to Remember About Politics," writer Bryan Roberts makes the sort of dismissals common in Evangelical and Fundamental circles. Roberts writes:

> I balk when pastors tell me the Church should engage in the political process. Why would we do that? The political process is dirty and broken and far from Jesus. Paranoia and vitriol are hardly attractive accessories for the bride of Christ.[19]

The article continues with similar statements about the political process and political concerns. Things like "both parties go to Church," and "those who argue over politics don't love their country more than others."[20] Overall, the goal is to place political issues at a lower order of concern as to mitigate any anxiety and avoid division. In the end though, dismissing the concerns of others does not lead to mitigation of their stress, but instead adds stress as individuals begin to feel distanced, delegitimized, and frustrated at having their very real concerns batted away. After all, "political issues," like the cost

---

[19] Bryan Roberts, "7 Things Christians Need to Remember About Politics," *Relevant Magazine*, Relevant Media Group, 2016, https://relevantmagazine.com/current/7-things-christians-need-remember-about-politics/.
[20] Ibid.

of food, sheltering refugees, adoption, homelessness, judicial corruption, police accountability, and war are not insignificant issues. Therefore, the simple dismissal of "politics are corrupt" alone is insufficient to properly handle these anxieties.

On the other hand, some will instead choose to elevate political issues in the hopes of legitimizing political anxiety as ultimately positive. David G. Kibble for example, makes this statement concerning political activism:

> If evangelism and social justice are not to be identified and conflated together then they must in some sense be separate. The danger here, of course, is that we separate them so much as to make the one more important than the other. It must be emphasized that both are equally important.[21]

Kibble elevated social justice concerns to equality with evangelism, and while he attempts to avoid the conclusions of liberation theologians, it is hard to divorce his own thoughts from that of those he dismisses, like this statement from Gustavo Gutierrez: "to participate in the process of [political] liberation is already, in a certain sense, a salvific work."[22] Kibble's own conclusion is that the kingdom of God being in the hearts of believers necessitates a level of political activism.[23] Trevin Wax makes a similar statement in writing for the Gospel Coalition in 2008: "As Kingdom people, we must be actively spreading God's reign into every segment of society, influencing the world

---

[21] David G. Kibble, "The Kingdom of God and Christian Politics," *themelios*, 1982, https://www.thegospelcoalition.org/themelios/article/the-kingdom-of-god-and-christian-politics/.

[22] Gustavo Gutierrez, *A Theology of Liberation* (London: SCM, 1974), 72.

[23] David G. Kibble, "The Kingdom of God and Christian Politics," *themelios*, 1982, https://www.thegospelcoalition.org/themelios/article/the-kingdom-of-god-and-christian-politics/.

by bringing God's love and grace to all, whether it be through the arts, through business, through politics or through our vocations."[24] Using a non-dispensational theology of a "present" kingdom on earth, Kibble, Wax, and even Gutierrez justify political activism and overt concern—an approach which only further exacerbates feelings of anxiety when the "present" nation does not look like the idealistic kingdom they have conceptualized. By elevating the import of the political to that of the command of God to make disciples, failure or lack of realization to this political goal amounts to not only feelings of anxiety about the absence of godly justice but also feelings of failure before God or disobedience to Him because the supposedly stated command of God for the Christian is not being realized effectively.

The same approaches manifest in non-dispensational perspectives with regard to environmental anxiety. On the side of apathetic dismissal, a rather mixed article from Answers in Genesis writer Avery Foley argues that Christians should not be anxious about the environment; firstly, because God is in control, secondly that "God has commanded us not to be afraid", and then that God has promised that the seasons will continue.[25] Foley continues by arguing that environmental efforts worth supporting should be judged by a metric of their effect on human beings, rather than any environmentally exclusive concern.[26] And while certain aspects of Foley's article may ring true in some sense - like the common assent non-dispensationalists tend to give to the necessity of ambiguous "creation care" measurements derived from Genesis - its dismissal of environmental anxiety as unfounded and disobedient lead to the same anxious ends as dismissals of political anxiety.

---

[24] Trevin Wax, "The Growing Kingdom of God," *TGC* (blog), June 16, 2008, https://www.thegospelcoalition.org/blogs/trevin-wax/the-growing-kingdom-of-god/.

[25] Avery Foley, "Climate Change and the Bible," *Answers in Genesis*, February 20, 2020, https://answersingenesis.org/environmental-science/climate-change/climate-change-and-the-bible/.

[26] Ibid.

Biblical Distinctions Applied   119

Individuals experiencing anxiety over environmental damage, their effects on society, and the animal kingdom, upon being met with this dismissal are given then to frustration or further stress at finding their concerns treated as either unimportant concerns or, at worst, sinful ones.

On the opposite end of the spectrum and, born out of the widespread concern of young Christians, some elevate environmental concerns as fundamentally "gospel" concerns. Christianity Today, for example, published an article in 2016 entitled: "Why Conservation is a Gospel Issue." In it, Peter Harris argues that: "Our worship and work and witness will be incomplete until our responsibility to conserve the glorious, God-given diversity of earth's creatures becomes second nature."[27] Harris' argument is simply that environmental destruction is a sin issue, caused by issues like greed and selfishness, and therefore it is an issue that must be addressed by Christians. This is not only a good thing for Christians to do, but actually a part of ensuring that "our worship… work, and witness" are complete.[28] Geneva College summarizes it this way in their statement on Christians and the environment: "God commissions us to rule over the creation in a way that sustains, protects, and enhances his works so that all creation may fulfill the purposes God intended for it. We must manage the environment not simply for our own benefit but for God's glory."[29] Geneva College, like Christianity Today, builds its argument from Old Testament passages like Genesis 1:28 and Psalm 24:1-2, and gains its specific New Testament commission from

---

[27] Peter Harris, "Why Conservation is a Gospel Issue," *Christianity Today*, September, 8, 2016, https://www.christianitytoday.com/ct/2016/september-web-only/why-does-nature-matter.html.

[28] Ibid.

[29] "Christians and the Environment," Geneva College, https://www.geneva.edu/community/environmental-stewardship/why_care#:~:text=God%20commissions%20us%20to%20rule,but%20for%20God%E2%80%B2s%20glory.

Colossians 1:19-20.[30] Simply put, because God is reconciling all things through Christ, we who are in Christ should reconcile creation to God through creation care. Implicit within this is a presupposition that the entirety of Christ's work is accomplished and that all things should be reconciled to Him *in the present* as much as possible. Once again, this perspective, rather than mitigating environmental anxiety, encourages it, and leads to a deeper anxiety. For as the environment continues to degrade or certain environmental efforts fail, the Christian becomes yet more anxious and discouraged, viewing herself as a failure before God or worse as sinning against God for failing to reconcile the creation.

It is hardly surprising that issues of existential anxiety surrounding death and assurance are addressed using the same theological arguments of either dismissal or elevation such that anxiety is applauded. Dismissal arguments concerning assurance have become far more popular as of recent; most significantly in the form of arguing for an agnosticism about the afterlife and by the removal of hell as an afterlife destination. Peter Enns, for example, popularly argues against the existence of hell in favor of a so-called "kingdom" centered perspective.[31] According to Enns, Christianity's job is to "establish God's Kingdom until Jesus returns to fully restore things," as opposed to offering salvation from any kind of wrath.[32] Arguments like these are meant to stave off existential anxiety by simply removing the cause for anxiety: wrath. Rather than address the actual anxiety related to God, eternal destiny, and the salvation question, Enns and others simply dismiss the question by removing the perceived cause of anxiety. This falters for a number of reasons, chief among them being that there is wrath and justice

---

[30] Ibid.
[31] Peter Enns, "Let's Talk About Hell, Shall We," February, 2019, https://www.youtube.com/watch?v=nR9hc9gAPYM.
[32] Ibid.

Biblical Distinctions Applied

reserved for those who refuse to accept the forgiveness of Christ.[33] Additionally, Enn's argument in application to believers would not lead to further assurance, only further ambiguity, anxiety, and doubt; for by removing hell, God's commission to humanity becomes undefined. While Enns would have his readers and listeners shoot for a philosophic "good life" rather than an eternal destiny and heavenly call, the definition of this "good life" God asks for remains open. Thus further anxiety and confusion will befall those who chase it; never knowing if they have ever arrived. Perhaps it is for this reason that Enns also argues that doubt and uncertainty are ultimately far superior to any form of assurance,[34] once again avoiding the question of assurance by simply dismissing it entirely.

By contrast, some have argued that such lack of assurance is important to a mature Christian life. Joel Beeke, writing for Ligonier, argues that in order to have assurance, one needs to examine their good works which act as proof of salvation.[35] In this sense, Beeke argues, afterlife anxiety encourages the believer to stay "holy". Beeke continues by arguing that God Himself might withhold assurance from a believer so that they "understand how bitter sin is," and "keep us low and humble," as well as to "value assurance even more" and "pursue obedience to God… and give Him glory for our obedience to Him."[36] Jon Bloom, writing for Desiring God, expounds on this point in the following:

---

[33] Matthew 25:41, 2 Thessalonians 1:9, Revelation 20:13-15.

[34] Alan Bean, "The Sin of Certainty: Peter Enn's Journey from Belief to Trust," *Baptist News Global*, April 18, 2016, https://baptistnews.com/article/the-sin-of-certainty-peter-enns-journey-from-belief-to-trust/#.YsiCunbMLrd.

[35] Joel Beeke, "Loss of Assurance," Ligonier Ministries, June 25, 2016. https://www.ligonier.org/learn/articles/loss-assurance.

"We cannot enjoy high levels of genuine assurance in low levels of obedience… loss of assurance shows that sin has serious consequences for the believer…"

[36] Ibid.

> When we see the dross, we can fear that our faith may not be real. And that is what God wants. For when we see the horrible sin in us and feel our own helplessness to get rid of it… it pushes us in desperation to trust Christ's work.[37]

From a non-dispensational perspective, afterlife anxiety is an important part of continuing in proper sanctification. Unfortunately, evaluations of assurance based on works are subjective. How many are enough and how many bad works are too many to prove otherwise, become the continuous refrain as they are with most every salvation issue.[38] This leads only to more of the same anxiety or even despair; or otherwise overwhelming pride. As Alistair Begg noted in his viral sermon on the cross of Christ, to focus upon something other than the cross of Christ in our daily life leads to either a crippling depression at the realization we are incapable or a sort of "gross egotism," believing we are actually quite capable.[39] Therefore, a positive evaluation of afterlife anxiety is ineffective in mitigating these anxieties, leading only to deeper despair, or otherwise the sin of pride.

Many of these issues involve either a lack of understanding surrounding the definitive mission of the church in relation to each of these concerns, a blurred conception of Israel and the church and their distinct commands, and a fundamental misunderstanding of the nature of the kingdom of God.

---

[37] Jon Bloom, "How God Gives Assurance," *Desiring God*, September 4, 2015, https://www.desiringgod.org/articles/how-god-gives-assurance.

[38] Paul's own argument in Galatians would seem to directly contradict any measurement of sanctification by works at all. For, after making his lengthy argument concerning salvation coming through the Spirit by faith, free from obedience to law, Paul delivers, in chapter 5, an exhortation to not only be made alive by the Spirit, but to live by the Spirit and not the law. As he concludes in 5:25: "If we live by the Spirit, let us also walk by the Spirit" (NASB).

[39] Alistair Begg, "The Power and Message of the Cross," November 20, 2019, 34:50-35:00, https://www.youtube.com/watch?v=SL8mJQ39zjw&t=0s.

Further, their concentrations are anthropocentric; whether dealing with politics, the environment, or assurance; and the place of human desires in the Christian life is either dismissed or an indicator of their necessity in our immediate circumstances. Dispensationalism, by contrast, allows for a far more consistent manner by which these anxieties and their locales are addressed. This is because dispensationalism propagates a focus on interpreting progressive revelation through a simple, normal hermeneutic leading to a clear vision for the mission of the church and its members in distinction from the nation of Israel, and a premillennial eschatological conception of the kingdom which is theocentric, doxological, and provides a Christocentric understanding of our desires.

DISPENSATIONAL PROPOSITIONS AND POLITICAL ANXIETY

God clearly cares about politics. This should give at least some level of comfort to the anxious. Historically speaking, we know that it was God Himself who established political orders. In Genesis 9:1-6, God gives an administrative command to Noah to multiply his descendants, spread out, and, "Whoever sheds human blood, by man his blood shall be shed, for in the image of God He made mankind," (Ge 9:7 NASB). By this command to Noah, according to the New Scofield Bible:

> God delegated to him certain areas of His authority, in which he was to obey God through submission to his fellow man. So God instituted a corporate relationship of man to man in human government. The highest function of human government is the

protection of human life, out of which arises the responsibility of capital punishment.[40]

But, as with each dispensation, this administration of God's plan was subject to failure on the part of mankind. C. I. Scofield writes: "The dispensation of human government resulted, upon the plain of Shinar, in the impious attempt to become independent of God…"[41] But one cannot contend with the fact that God cares for the establishment He, Himself brought into existence.

We also know God's plan for government and nations did not end here. Rather, he elected the nation of Israel to function as His own holy nation (Ex 19:6). God related to them through a Covenant which required administrative obedience to governmental laws which were to be enforced (Ex 19:5). While that administration, like the administration previous, ended in failure (Mt 23:37-39), it is notable that God's work at this time was still primarily through the vessel of a law, a government, and a nation of people. And we also know that, one day in future, He intends to work through law, government, and nations for His glory again (Zec 14:9-21). Therefore, if we are to address political anxiety rightly we must understand that a desire for political processes to be just, and thereby glorifying to God, is not an immoral desire. It is a desire very much in line with God's own desire for the nations, which is not an anthropocentric desire for the nations to live in a "ho-hum" harmony, but rather that the nations worship and glorify God together (Zec 14:16).

Mark Saucy, a professor of systematic theology at Kyiv Theological Seminary, offers an important corrective to the views of non-dispensationalists, concerning political desires and anxieties. He writes:

---

[40] E. Shuyler English, "Notes on Genesis," *The New Scofield Study Bible*, NASB, ed. Paul S. Karleen et al., (Oxford, UK: Oxford University Press, 1988), 16.

[41] C. I. Scofield, *Rightly Dividing the Word of Truth* (Independent, 2014), 6.

> I long for justice, peace and prosperity in this world and I long to be part of bringing it. Effectively, and finally, bringing it. I'm sick of evil's deceit and de-humanizing rot, and it is this passion for beauty and good that drives social-justice warriors of all stripes. It's the beautiful picture God made us for and that we all know deep down. And I submit that a Future Israel eschatology satisfies this call to our hearts better than its opposite.[42]

The desire for justice is not wrong. It is an inherent call to the purpose God gave to Adam (Ge 1:28) and the purpose that God intends to restore through Christ (Rev 2:26-27). The desire, though perverted into anxiety, for just and healthy societies is not something to be discouraged, but at its root is a desire which Christ intends to fulfill and satisfy. However, in our attempts to avoid dismissing a desire which is ultimately for Christ and for God's purpose for us, we must be sure not to elevate this purpose beyond its station in the present.

God instituted the church as His steward in the present dispensation. With the closing of the dispensation of the Law, God imparted a specific mission to the church as due worship through a reflection of Christ by pursuing the salvation and sanctification of the world (Mt 28:19-20). And far too often, those who seek to legitimately address their desires, as well as encourage those with the same desire for justice, import commands from previous dispensations which do not have bearing on the present steward simply because they relate to their desires. Most often abused is the Administration of the Law under Israel. The commands of the decalogue given to Moses and the nation of Israel in Exodus 20 are often torn from

---

[42] Mark Saucy, "Why Eschatology Matters," *The Good Book Blog* (blog), May 18, 2020, https://www.biola.edu/blogs/good-book-blog/2020/why-eschatology-matters.

their proper context, and the laws related to them, and applied to our current governments and to the church herself. To this, Scofield offers a correction for application to both problems:

> Instead of pursuing her appointed path of separation from the world and following the Lord in her heavenly calling, she has used the Jewish Scriptures to justify herself lowering her purpose to the civilization of the world..."[43]

The nature of the church, as Scofield points out, is not a national purpose—even as a so-called "redemption" of national governance. This is a degradation of her purpose. Dr. Charles Ryrie notes that the church, in distinction from Israel, is not a national body.[44] Rather, the church is a people made up of all nations (Ac 1:8)! And its aims are notably not legal aims as those of previous dispensations, but aims to promote the grace of God given to all.[45] And rightly so, for it would be immature for the church to go back within the progress of God's revelation and attempt to live in an old framework of ordinance as though the Christ had not died and resurrected, established his church and commissioned them (Heb 6:4-6; 9:1-28). The goals of the church are firmly rooted in evangelism and discipleship as an international-spiritual community. And while both the administrative distinction and the distinction between prior stewards themselves may seem to discourage our desires at first glance, it is just this distinction which saves us from the crippling disappointment and anxiety wrought by attempting to find fulfillment of our political desires within the broken world system.

---

[43] Scofield, *Rightly Dividing the Word of Truth*, 5.
[44] Charles C. Ryrie, *Dispensationalism Today* (Chicago: Moody Press, 1971), 137-138.
[45] Ibid, 63.

For the world system is a tainted one whose ruler is not in favor of the justice which our deep political desires long for. The world system is ruled over by Satan "the prince of this world" who "was within his rights" when he offered up the kingdoms of this world to Jesus in his temptation.[46] John tells us: "We know that we are of God, and that the whole world lies in the power of the evil one," (1Jn 5:19). This transference of the governing nations under his power either came by the failure of Adam as Scofield suggests[47] or at the failure of the Tower of Babel by the abdication of the stewarding nations.[48] Either way, as Scofield says: "The present world system, organized upon the principles of force, greed, selfishness, ambition, and sinful pleasure, is his work…"[49] It is for this precise reason that we cannot place our political expectations upon this present age.[50] Satan has been given it until his appointed time, and so it is characterized by force, greed, selfishness, etc. It is little wonder that young Christians become filled with anxiety as their political desires are thwarted time and time again by the brokenness found in the world system and the outright malevolent influence of Satan.[51]

---

[46] Charles C. Ryrie, "Notes on Matthew," *Ryrie Study Bible* (Chicago: Moody Publishers, 2011), 1159.

[47] C. I. Scofield, "Notes on Revelation," *Scofield Reference Bible* (Oxford: Oxford University Press, 1945), 1350.

[48] A pattern may emerge when considering the reference in Revelation to the Jewish people as "a synagogue of Satan," (Rev 3:9) and to the apostate church as the "whore of Babylon," (Rev 17:5) and of course to the whole of Adamic man as under the power of darkness in Johannine literature. Apostasy of the steward may lead to the institution being placed under Satan's more direct control. However, this is the subject for some future study and cannot be discussed at length in this work.

[49] Scofield, *Scofield Reference Bible*, 1350.

[50] Bruce A. Baker, "Dispensationalism's Evolving Theory of Political Interaction: How Roe v. Wade and Jerry Falwell Brough Dispensationalism from Rejecting Political Action to Embracing It," (paper presented at Council on Dispensational Hermeneutics, 2020), 6-7.

[51] Now, this is not to say that the church in this present age has no place in justice within social arenas. However, it does mean that we address these arenas as the church,

So then, keeping the administrative commands intact and contextualized within the progress of revelation, how does the Christian find satisfaction for these desires for societal justice? If the goals of the church are evangelistic and discipleship oriented, which they most assuredly are, where do our desires for justice and participating in justice find their satisfaction? Here, the dispensational proposition of premillennialism draws our attention to the future dispensation of the kingdom. According to Jesus in his statement to the church at Thyatira:

> Nevertheless what you have, hold fast until I come. He who overcomes, and he who keeps My deeds until the end, TO HIM I WILL GIVE AUTHORITY OVER THE NATIONS; AND HE SHALL RULE THEM WITH A ROD OF IRON, AS THE VESSELS OF THE POTTER ARE BROKEN TO PIECES, as I also have received authority from My Father; and I will give him the morning star (Rev 2:25-28).

From a premillennial dispensational perspective, it is within the future reign of Jesus Christ that our desire for justice finds its fulfillment. But this fulfillment is not a benign extinguishing of our desires, as some may describe. Rather, it is a fulfillment that takes the flames of desire and gives them purpose within the context of our unification with Christ in His reign.

---

not as a national body as Israel once was or as the Noahic Nations once were. Jesus calls for the visiting of the prisoner, whether falsely accused or otherwise, and calls for ministry to those who are poor (Mt 25:36, 40; Lk 6:20, 14:13; 1Jn 3:17). But at no point does Jesus advocate for these things as usurpations or collaborations with political powers (Mk 12:13-17; 1Pe 2:13-14). Rather, the church is called to address these ills within the sphere of their local congregations as expressions of "true religion" (Jas 1:27, 2:1-16). And throughout the New Testament there is no shortage of examples for how this can be done; though the most prominent is that of the establishment of the deacons (Ac 6:1-7).

Though often overlooked, even among dispensationalists, Christ offers the promise of sharing in His rulership. As Paul so harshly expounded to the Corinthians: "Do you not know that we will judge angels? How much more matters of this life?" (1Co 6:3). While other positions, as Saucy notes: "are left trying to answer this human heart cry either in this Age—an epic Non-Starter against the increasing accounts of Christian martyrdom—or with some insipid picture of a rule in or from Heaven,"[52] the dispensational position looks forward to a day when our desires are sanctified and directed toward active participation in justice upon the earth. The dispensational eschatology, "says we get to fulfill our calling against evil in Christ's millennial kingdom where we will rule evil, bring justice, peace, generosity and prosperity to the nations of the world."[53] In the dispensational eschatology, and only in the dispensational eschatology, can the desires of our whole selves, including our political-social selves, find an answer which does not dismiss the desire nor direct it to a flawed presentism.

However, there remains the question of the present longings which we have. While it is important to understand the eschatological fulfillment of our desires, how we handle these desires now remains important. To what do we focus ourselves upon in collaboration with our good desires - such that we do not simply wistfully long for some future day. In what manner do we participate now in the justice we so long to have?

Firstly, we must focus our minds upon the patience of God within the present dispensation. Peter grounds our eschatological longings wholesale when he says: "The Lord is not slow about His promise, as some count slowness, but is patient toward you, not wishing for any to perish but for all to come to repentance." (1Pe 3:9). In the present dispensation, God is extending grace out to all people. The fulfillment of these desires is slow

---

[52] Saucy, "Why Eschatology Matters."
[53] Ibid.

because God is gracious and merciful to those who have not yet heard. And speaking of that same fulfillment as Peter, though concerning the nation of Israel, Paul writes: "For I do not want you, brethren, to be uninformed of this mystery -so that you will not be wise in your own estimation -that a partial hardening has happened to Israel until the fullness of the Gentiles has come in;" (Ro 11:25). And so, if we are to see our desires fulfilled in the reigning Christ at His return, our focus should be on evangelism. And so we arrive back at the very purpose of the church which God has called us to. For while we have no comprehensive idea what a "fullness" of the Gentiles might be, it is not until that fullness enters that the fulfillment of our desires can arrive. Therefore, if we are to claim to take seriously the issues of justice in our time, we must adamantly pursue the purpose of the church in making disciples of all nations. That is our present expression of our desires until our desires can be fulfilled by participation in the reigning Christ.

Through drawing out dispensational propositions we can capably address the anxieties of young people without dismissing their desires or casting them upon a fruitless effort; instead reorienting our desires to both participation in our present mission in the church and our future participation in Christ's reign. Each step is imperative, as are the hermeneutics by which these propositions naturally arise.[54] For this reason, no other perspective but one which is firmly dispensational can properly address the political anxieties of young people. It is necessary to understand the doxological purpose of God in every sphere of the creation, including the political-social sphere. It is also imperative that administrations/stewardships frame our thinking such that we acknowledge God's care for national justice as evidenced in His past dealings and future dealings in which we will participate while avoiding application of our desires to a presentist attempt at God-less-utopia within the fallen world system. Lastly, it is important to

---

[54] Charles C. Ryrie, *Dispensationalism* (Chicago: Moody Press, 1995), 85.

acknowledge the present means by which we progress toward that reality, namely: faithfulness to the present administration of God's plan. With a single piece missing or misunderstood, anxieties are easily fed and established in any heart. Because without an understanding of God's purpose, past dealings, and plan for the church in both the present and future, there can only be anxiety at the hopeless state of present affairs which we can neither wholly repair nor ignore.

DISPENSATIONAL PROPOSITIONS AND THE ENVIRONMENT

Dispensationalism is also unique in its addressing of environmental anxiety in that it confesses God's express purpose for the environment beyond functioning as a backdrop for the "human story." Though some have mishandled or misunderstood God's expressed environmental teleology and therefore addressed the anxieties of young people with dismissal, dispensationalism's proposals provide a distinct role for the environment, not in the story of man, but in the story of God and His plan for the future. God cares about the environment distinctly and not only in its effects on humans. Christopher Cone, in his book *Redacted Dominionism*, explains:

> Yet redacted dominionism results in a doxological rather than an anthropocentric model, recognizing that all things exist to glorify God, and this function is not a responsibility only of humanity. Being doxological and decidedly non-anthropocentric, redacted dominionism asserts that all creatures only have instrumental value as determined by their Creator. As such, human and non-human

beings share the same kind of value, and simply express that valuation within varying roles defined by their Creator.[55]

As dispensationalism centers upon the doxological purpose of God in all things,[56] dispensationalists see the creation within its telos as a fellow worshiper of God through its proper functioning, rather than as a non-expressive entity to be exploited. And with this, Scripture resounds in its truthful proclamation that nature, in its proper functions, glorifies God. Psalm 19, for example, proclaims:

> The heavens are telling of the glory of God; And their expanse is declaring the work of His hands. Day to day pours forth speech, And night to night reveals knowledge. There is no speech, nor are there words; Their voice is not heard. Their line has gone out through all the earth, And their utterances to the end of the world. In them He has placed a tent for the sun, which is as a bridegroom coming out of his chamber; It rejoices as a strong man to run his course. Its rising is from one end of the heavens, And its circuit to the other end of them; And there is nothing hidden from its heat. The law of the LORD is perfect, restoring the soul; The testimony of the LORD is sure, making wise the simple (Ps 19:1-7).

---

[55] Christopher Cone, *Redacted Dominionism: A Biblical Approach to Grounding Environmental Responsibility* (Eugene, OR: Wipf and Stock Publishers, 2012), 26.

Redacted Dominionism represents what I would say is the normative perspective on the dispensation of innocence; that Adam's roles were dispensational in character and following his failure, they were redacted; as opposed to perspectives which would posit a continuous responsibility on the part of human beings to "multiply," "fill the earth," and "subdue it." Ironically, this position *further enables* our care for the environment rather than hindering it.

[56] Ryrie, Dispensationalism *Today*, 46.

Biblical Distinctions Applied   133

Furthermore, Paul's epistle to the Romans echoes out the reflective character of nature by which it proclaims His nature (Ro 1:20). And so if we confess, as any Christian rightly does, that God is most concerned for His own glory, we must confess He is uniquely concerned for His creation.

God shows His unique care for creation throughout the Scriptures; and within the very narrative of the Bible, we can see a unique care for creation shown throughout. God created the earth "good" as a collaborating worshiper under the stewardship of man (Ge 1-2); but when man fell into sin, the creation itself was subject to futility and "slavery to corruption," (Ro 8:20). God however, did not cease looking after creation despite the abrogation of man from his stewardship. God protected the wildlife from the judgment against man through Noah and preserved its biodiversity through selection of every kind of animal (Ge 6:19-20). God also protected the creation in His Law, given to Moses at Mount Sinai. For within the Law was the provision of the sabbath for the land as well as the Year of Jubilee (Lv 25). When Israel did not celebrate these sabbaths and Jubilees, as well as failing to observe God's other commandments, He exiled them from the land: "to fulfill the word of the LORD by the mouth of Jeremiah, until the land had enjoyed its sabbaths. All the days of its desolation it kept sabbath until seventy years were complete." (2Ch 36:21). Therefore, God not only purposed the creation for a specific end but made provision for the land while it suffered under the futility of Adam.

The desires of young people concerning the protection of creation, therefore, are good desires. The desire to see a creation freed from the troubles being brought on by mankind's disobedience and sinfulness is a good desire. It is a desire to see God glorified by the proper functioning of the ecosystems across creation. James Johnson rightly reminds us: "Appreciating and conserving biodiversity as Noah once did makes perfect sense for biblical creationists."[57] If we confess that God created the earth to act as a worshiper through the proper functioning of its ecosystems and natural orders, it is only natural that we would desire for creation to function in that manner. In fact, it is even natural to want to mitigate destructive human factors by which the creation is being subjected to even further torment and futility.[58] However, we must not elevate these desires to levels of priority beyond their current application in our administration.

In the present administration, God has begun a stewardship in the church made up of Jews and Gentiles with the responsibility of making disciples. This administration is distinct from the previous administration under the stewardship of Israel and their responsibilities under the Law. While in the previous administration, God used the Law to mitigate human sinfulness and its effects,[59] which includes environmental and ecological ramifications, in the present administration God has given freedom from the Law and its requirements as they have now served their purpose. The greater purpose of that Law was not permanent nor temporary mitigation, but to show the necessity of Divine intervention in reversing the state into which Adam placed us and the creation (Gal 3:24). In light of the present dispensation and the revelation of redemption through Jesus Christ, we must remember that ecological damages, like all consequences of sin, cannot be legislated away or mitigated out of existence - for this was the very thing the

---

[57] James J. S. Johnson, "Should Creationists Brook Loss of Trout?" *Acts & Facts*, July 30, 2021, https://www.icr.org/article/should-creationists-brook-loss-of-a-trout.
Also see James Johnson's presentation on God's value of biodiversity presented at the 2022 Chafer Theological Seminary Pastors' Conference. Also worth review is the following:
James J. S. Johnson, "God Fitted Habitats for Biodiversity," *Acts & Facts*, February 28, 2013, https://www.icr.org/article/god-fitted-habitats-for-biodiversity.

[58] Johnson, "Should Creationists Brook Loss of Trout?"

[59] Ranald Showers, "Dispensational Theology," lesson 4, lectures on BBN (Bible Broadcasting Network), https://bbn1.bbnradio.org/bbnbienglish/course/29/.

Law proved in Israel (Gal 3:22). Instead, it must be met head on by the One who is capable of reversing the consequences of sin, atoning for all disobedience, and giving resurrected life and restored doxological capability to both man and the created order alike.

However, this does not mean that God's doxological purpose with Creation has simply been set aside. Shawn Lazar rightly reminds us:

> Did you know that salvation is not just about God rescuing individuals but also rescuing creation? The prophets spoke about that. For example, Isaiah looked forward to the time when God would remake heaven and earth (cf. Isa 65:17; 66:22), when the deserts would blossom with flowers (Isa 35:1), and when predators would live in peace with prey (Isa 11:6). The prophets understood that salvation is cosmic.[60]

And to this, the *New Scofield Reference Bible* affirms: "Adam brought down into his ruin the old creation, of which he was lord and head. Christ will bring into moral unity with God, and into eternal life, all of the new creation of which He is Lord and Head (Eph 1:22-23). Even the animal and material creation, cursed for man's sake (Ge 3:17), will be delivered by Christ."[61] This eschatological restoration of the earth as well as mankind is the very Adamic promise - the first promise of the Redeeming Seed - that the futility brought on by Satan's deception would be reversed and the snake himself destroyed (Ge 3:15). And it is this same promise that the creation itself is looking forward to - "For the anxious longing of the creation waits eagerly for the

---

[60] Shawn Lazar, "God Will Save Creation (Romans 8:19-25)," Grace In Focus Blog, Grace Evangelical Society, https://faithalone.org/blog/god-will-save-creation-romans-819-25/.

[61] Schuyler English, "Notes on Romans," *New Scofield Reference Bible*, 1599.

revealing of the sons of God… that the creation itself also will be set free from its slavery to corruption into the freedom of the glory of the children of God," (Ro 8:19; 21).

Premillennialism, and most particularly dispensational premillennialism, is necessary in order to have hope beyond current circumstances to the day when creation will see its restoration. As Charles Ryrie notes: "the glory of the God who is sovereign in human history must be seen in the present heavens and earth… the covenant [Amillennial] view which sees the course of history continuing the present struggle between good and evil until terminated by the beginning of eternity, obviously does not have any goal within temporal history and is therefore pessimistic."[62] The dispensational Christian is encouraged to look forward to the kingdom restoration, which is not the termination of present affairs but the restoration of the present creation and reversal of the curse in time, at the return of our Messiah. This in confirmation of the promise given to Adam that *this present creation* would be restored under the Seed of the Woman, not obliterated for the presentation of an entirely other creation. As Lazar again notes: "God intended humanity to live as physical beings in a physical universe. So to save us, God must also save creation."[63] John Walvoord then further explains:

> The world in general will be delivered from the unproductiveness which characterized great portions of the globe in prior dispensations. Widespread peace and justice, spiritual blessing, and abundance of food will result in a general era of prosperity… the many factors which produce poverty, distress, and unequal distribution of goods will to a great extent be non-existent in the

---

[62] Ryrie, *Dispensationalism*, 18.
[63] Lazar, "God Will Save Creation (Romans 8:19-25)."

> millennium… the curse which creation has endured since Adam's sin will be in part suspended as even animal creation will be changed.[64]

For the desires of so many young people to see creation respected, restored, and the sin-inspired ecological destruction permanently terminated, the Bible points toward the Messiah who is able to reverse environmental disaster as well as restore responsibility and capability to those who subjected the creation through disobedience.

At the present time, however, there remains a work given to the church which does contribute to the restoration of the environment. Though perhaps we do not see it as such, the call to evangelism and discipleship is itself a means by which God, at the present time, is progressively enacting His plan of cosmic restoration. Once again, just a few chapters on from Paul's declaration that the creation "waits eagerly for the revealing of the sons of God," (Ro 8:19), he relates the timing of the restoration of Israel, which coincides with the restoration of the creation (Is 35:1-4). Paul explains that the restoration will not occur until the "fullness of the Gentiles has come in" to salvation (Ro 11:25).[65] Therefore, though the number and nature of this revelation remains difficult to understand, we must be diligently seeking to make disciples of all nations in keeping with the administration given to the church. For by doing so, we continue to move toward our restoration and the restoration of creation for which we long.

The anxieties of young people concerning the environment are not misplaced desires. God desires an innocent environment which functions in accordance with its nature in order to glorify Him. God has preserved the

---

[64] John Walvoord, *The Millennial Kingdom* (Findlay: Dunham Publishing Company, 1968), 318.

[65] Perhaps a parallel expansion of the "revelation of the sons of God" mentioned in 8:19.

natural order throughout Scripture, with the intention of providing a restoration for the environment itself. However, these desires should not become untamed anxieties which elevate our environmental dilemmas to standards of obedience God does not require of our administration. Such elevation only leads to hopelessness or pride, as any observance of law tends toward. The environment remains under the curse and our efforts cannot reverse this futility, but the affairs of the creation are not hopeless. The Scriptures are clear, Christ, at His return, will begin the process of lifting the curse and the environment will have its deliverance alongside God's people. Therefore, in the meantime, our desires should compel us to work toward that end - bringing all people to a knowledge of Christ and discipling them to obey Christ. Only in a dispensational perspective can this environmental hope be maintained.

DISPENSATIONAL PROPOSITIONS AND AFTERLIFE ANXIETY

When addressing issues of afterlife anxiety and assurance, few often understand the theological implications of an assurance-less or assurance minimal position. What we believe about the promise of salvation issued by God and how it operates speaks intimately to how we understand God Himself. Charles Cranfield, speaking of God's promise to Israel in his Romans commentary, draws out this issue well. "The very reliability of God's purpose as the ground for Christian hope is called into question by the exclusion of the majority of Jews. If the truth is that God's purpose with Israel has been frustrated, then what sort of a basis for Christian hope is God's purpose?"[66] If God's promises are frustrated by human failure or only

---

[66] C. E. B. Cranfield, *Romans: A Shorter Commentary* (Grand Rapids: William B. Eerdmans Publishing Company, 1985), 215.

become effective by some other means than their stated means, God becomes impotent. Robert Witmer draws out these implications yet further when speaking of Romans 9:

> Paul here discussed God's sovereign choice because of a practical problem. The Jews gloried in the fact that as Israelites they were God's Chosen People. But now in God's program of salvation in the church, Jewish involvement was decreasing... Had God, then, abandoned the Jewish people?[67]

The problem of assurance thus is double: doubting God's promise either calls into question His sovereign ability to fulfill the promise or His reliability and trustworthiness in fulfilling the promise. A proper view of assurance is therefore vital; any view which calls into question God's promise is one which besmirches God's glorious character.

It is also right that one would desire to have assurance of their afterlife. Hell is a real locale, as is the lake of fire, and the punishments contained within both are terrifying (Rev 9:1-11, 19:20, 20:10). An existential fear of the lake of fire is healthy and natural (Mt 5:29-30). To desire eternal torment outside of fellowship with God would be wholly unnatural and depraved in the deepest sense. Attempts to delegitimize the desire to escape judgment are ridiculous to say the least. All people have an innate knowledge of their lawlessness and proclivity for error (Ro 1:18-19); as well as an understanding that their lawlessness must be met with justice (Jas 2:10). The dismissal of judgment[68] goes against the innate understanding we have concerning law,

---

[67] Robert Witmer, "God's Righteousness Revealed in Sovereign Choice," in *The Bible Knowledge Commentary: New Testament*, ed. John Walvoord and Roy B. Zuck (Wheaton, IL: Victor Books, 1984), 476.

[68] See footnote 31.

punishment, and our own natures. Young people are entirely justified in desiring to be assured that their afterlife experience will not be one of eternal punishment.

Throughout the Scriptures, we see God intentionally interacting with His stewards to provide assurance of His promises to them. Unlike other administrative distinctives, God throughout the Scriptures has consistently acted in the same grace concerning salvation and promises of restoration through the Messiah.[69] One such example of God's continued assurance to His stewards is in His interactions with Abraham. Despite Abraham's continued disobedience, God continuously meets Abraham's failures with restatements that the promise will be fulfilled (Ge 13:14-18; 15:1-21; 17:1-27; 18:10, 17-19; 22:16-18). Abraham's actions have no bearing on the assurance of God's promises to him, rather Abraham's failures and God's faithfulness in response merely magnifies God's glorious character as promise keeper. We see similar interactions throughout the Old Testament, most especially in the writings of the prophets, in which God means to reassure His people of their promises despite their failures and the resulting exile.[70] God clearly desires His people to have assurance in the promises He has made to them; the promise of everlasting life to those who believe is no different (Jn 3:16; 1Jn 5:13; Rev 2:7, 11; 3:5).

The question of many young people, especially Christian young people, is where one looks for assurance. Grant Hawley notes that, in distinction from non-dispensational perspectives, "the belief that assurance should be

---

[69] Ryrie, *Dispensationalism Today*, 123.

[70] Too many examples exist to adequately list them here. A small sample would be: Isaiah 9:1-7, Isaiah 11, Jeremiah 31:1-26, Jeremiah 33, Ezekiel 36 (most especially 22-25), Ezekiel 37:11-28, Ezekiel 40-48, Daniel 12:13, Hosea 11:8-11, Hosea 13:9-14:9, Joel 2:18-27, Zephaniah 3, Zechariah 12:10-14, Zechariah 14.

The prophets contain numerous reaffirmations of the Abrahamic Covenant, the Palestinian ["Moabitic"] Covenant, and the Davidic Covenant.

found in looking to Christ and His promises alone and never to works was nearly universally held among the early Dispensationalists."[71] Hawley points to the writings of several dispensationalists who defend a christocentric assurance, such as James H. Brookes who writes:

> It is my earnest desire and effort to turn your thoughts entirely away from yourself to the Saviour, for it is the most melancholy business that can engage even a redeemed sinner to be probing into his own soul to find some assurance that he is saved. You can never find it there, but only in the word; and, thank God! having once seen it in the word, you can see it every day and every hour, and as often as you read and believe what Jesus says.[72]

The proper response to a lack of assurance is not to attempt to drum up assurance from subjective experience or assessment of goodness; rather, it is in surveying the work of Christ by which the promises are assured to us. This is precisely Paul's argument regarding the promise of everlasting life:

> And if Christ has not been raised, your faith is worthless; you are still in your sins. Then those also who have fallen asleep in Christ have perished. If we have hoped in Christ in this life only, we are of all men most to be pitied. But now Christ has been raised from the dead, the first fruits of those who are asleep. For since by a man came

---

[71] Grant Hawley, "Free Grace and Dispensationalism: Intimately Linked Part 3," *Journal of the Grace Evangelical Society*, Spring 2012, https://faithalone.org/wp-content/uploads/2021/04/Hawley-1.pdf.

[72] James Hall Brookes, *Salvation: The Way Made Plain* (Philadelphia: American Sunday-School Union, 1871), 445, http://books.google.com/books?id=aRgHAAAAQAAJ&pg=PP1#v=onepage&q&f=false.

> death, by a man also came the resurrection of the dead (1Co 15:17-21).

Paul's assurance for the resurrection of the dead into eternal life is the historical fact that Christ has been raised. And conversely, if the dead are not raised then Christ has not been raised and there is no cause for Christian faith at all (1Co 15:16). But upon surveying the work of Christ in His resurrection, a resurrection promised time and time again, we can have assurance that Christ will keep his promise to also resurrect the believer into eternal life. Therefore, assurance is found just as Brooke said: "as you read and believe what Jesus says."[73] For we know from the Scriptures that we ourselves are not sufficient, and so no genuine assurance can be based upon us. Instead, our assurance comes from the resurrection by which we have objective historical evidence of the validity of Christ's promise. This may not seem propositionally dispensational; however, dispensationalism remains distinct from other views in that God's promises are assured in Christ and cannot be thwarted by mankind's insolence.

For example, no view of assurance can rightly reflect God's faithfulness despite our own faithlessness which does not confess the future, literal fulfillment of the promises made to the nation of Israel. As Robert Witmer noted, and even a non-dispensationalist like Charles Cranfield confesses, Israel's promises are linked to our own in that God will certainly not provide more assurance to the present steward than He has to previous stewards. Joseph Parle sums it up this way: "If God did not fulfill or maintain His covenantal promises to Israel, what gives us as the church any confidence

---

[73] Hawley, "Dispensationalism and Free Grace: Intimately Linked Part 3." James Hall Brookes, *Salvation: The Way Made Plain*, 445.

that He will do it for us?"[74] In order for any Christian to have assurance of the promise of God, one must confess God's intention for the nation of Israel is the restoration of the people to the land, to the status of national supremacy, and to an everlasting kingdom under the Messiah. Confessing otherwise leads to a theology in which God is untrustworthy in what He claims, and therefore Christianity itself becomes untenable to maintain. Afterall, Christianity relies on God being trustworthy in what He claims. In order to properly address the afterlife anxiety of young people and provide any real assurance of God's promises, one must confess an assurance of Israel's promise as well.

Another example lies within the uniquely dispensational distinction between the Law and grace. The Law itself served a dispensational purpose, not a salvific or assurance based one (Gal 3:24-26). Scofield writes:

> Christ bore the curse of the law, and redeemed the believer both from the curse and from the dominion of the law. Law neither justifies a sinner nor sanctifies a believer. The believer is both dead to the law and redeemed from it, so that he is "not under the law, but under grace."[75]

Where other views would see the Law functioning as an assuring and sanctifying agent, the dispensational position administratively distinguishes between Law and grace, relieving the believer of association with that Law which has now served its purpose. Any position which postures that the Law remains operative in the life of the believer, especially as a means of

---

[74] Joseph Parle, "Dispensationalism Pt. 1: What is it with Dr. Cone, Dr. Parle, and Dr. Stallard," March 18th, 2021, The Learn the Word Podcast, Audio-Visual, 35:27, https://www.youtube.com/watch?v=SnGs3zpAj4g.

[75] Scofield, "Notes on Galatians," *Scofield Reference Bible*, 1245.

assurance, unsurprisingly results in the person feeling condemnation rather than assurance in keeping with the actual function of the Law. The dispensational position is therefore poised to fully assure the anxious because it delineated between works of the Law and the grace given in salvation on which assurance is built.

Dispensational premillennialism also serves an important role in ensuring this assurance with consistency through a teleology of works as means of fellowship and justification at the judgment seat of Christ in distinction from the faith necessary in final justification at the great white throne. Hawley reminds the reader, "The Judgment Seat of Christ (2 Cor 5:10) as distinct from the Great White Throne Judgment of Rev 20:11-15 is a concept that is unique to Dispensationalism."[76] And it is an important one for centering assurance on the work of Christ and not the work of the believer. Hawley writes: "While every major aspect of Covenant Theology has a significant impact on soteriology, nothing has more of an impact than removing the Judgment Seat of Christ from the equation—a byproduct of kingdom-now millennial views."[77] And he continues:

> When the Millennial Kingdom is removed from the equation—and the Judgment Seat of Christ with it—the non-Dispensationalist is presented with a difficult problem. Passages discussing kingdom inheritance (which is according to works) are equated with passages about the new birth (which is by grace through faith and apart from works).[78]

---

[76] Hawley, "Dispensationalism and Free Grace: Intimately Linked Part 3."

[77] Grant Hawley, "Dispensationalism and Free Grace: Intimately Linked Part 2," *Journal of the Grace Evangelical Society*, Autumn, 2011, https://faithalone.org/wp-content/uploads/2021/04/Hawley.pdf.

[78] Ibid, 94.

The dispensational premillennial position has no problem with such passages however because distinction is kept between the judgment seat of Christ which relates to works and the inheritance of rewards, and the great white throne where justification is freely given to those who believe. The authors of the New Scofield delineate these passages well stating: "In the N.T. Scriptures, God offers the lost, salvation; and the faithful service of the saved, He offers rewards. These passages are clearly distinguished by remembering that salvation is invariably spoken of as a free gift, whereas rewards are earned by works."[79] While other positions elevate works to a factor of assurance, dispensationalism maintains an importance within the theology of good works, while maintaining their distinction from eternal salvation which is by faith. Therefore, assurance of afterlife prosperity can depend wholly upon the work of Christ through faith, rather than on the subjective basis of assessing our own works. When the distinction between the judgments is dissolved, so too is the assurance of the believer as works necessarily enter the salvation equation.

In summary, while faith in Jesus Christ and assurance on the basis of his works and not our own should be considered a simply Christian conviction, it cannot be convincingly maintained outside of the dispensational perspective. Without the various distinctives of dispensationalism, the afterlife anxieties of young people cannot be properly addressed in any consistent manner. One will need to either dismiss their anxieties as unfounded, simply denying the innate sense of coming eschatological condemnation in people, or elevate existential anxiety as a vehicle for gaining some sort of meager assurance through works, resulting in either distress or arrogance. Only within dispensational propositions can the afterlife anxieties of young people be addressed in a manner that affirms God's glorious

---

[79] English, "Notes on 1 Corinthians," *New Scofield Reference Bible*, 1617.

character as a faithful keeper of promises, affirms the desire to be assured, and provides the objective basis in Christ's resurrection by which assurance can be gained and maintained.

CONCLUSIONS: CONCERNING THE ANXIETIES OF YOUNG PEOPLE AND THE PROBLEM OF ACCESSIBILITY

Millennials and Generation Z, whether Christian or unchristian, are the most anxious generation on record; and in order to address these anxieties, we must present a full and whole understanding of God, our desires, and His plan in human history. The desires of young people which pervert themselves into anxiety are not unfounded or carnal wishes of a hapless people. Rather, they are innate longings for political, environmental, and personal restoration under the reign of Christ whether the young person is aware of it or not. And in many ways their anxieties are not unwarranted, as many have not encountered satisfying answers which adequately address these desires—certainly not in the world, but also not within the church. Far too often, these anxieties have either been dismissed or elevated in Christian communities both conservative and liberal. Through use of dispensational propositions however, the desires of young people for political justice, environmental restoration, and afterlife prosperity can be assured and adequately addressed by the introduction of God's doxological purpose; His proven progressive plan toward restoration within history counterbalanced by the distinctions between administrations and stewards within that plan; and through a consistent dispensational premillennialism which sets Christ in His coming as the fulfillment of every desire, promise, and administration. By this means, the young person is called to look upon Christ for fulfillment of their desires as the one who will bring political justice, edenic environmental restoration, and a sure prosperity in the resurrected afterlife.

The concern of this work has been for the one whom Jesus describes as: "the one on whom seed was sown among the thorns, this is the man who hears the word, and the worry of the world and the deceitfulness of wealth choke the word, and it becomes unfruitful," (Mt 13:22). Without a proper understanding of dispensational truth which is accessible and related to present concerns, more and more young people will be like the seed that falls on thorns, "choked out by the worry of the world." If we are to plant and develop fruitful believers on good soil, we must clear the thorns as we are able. Primarily, this is done through explicit evangelism and discipleship which is clear about God's purpose with our world, His unfolding plan throughout every administration, the distinctions therein, and the premillennial restoration which God has revealed in His word.

Secondly, though perhaps lesser in concern, is dissemination of explicitly dispensational materials in public formats. Throughout this work, articles which dismiss or mishandle the anxieties of young people have been referenced which are public, postured by popular resource sites, and easily accessible online; whereas many of the works cited in rebuttal are obscure, older, and no longer easily obtained. Mediums like blog, YouTube video lectures, and podcasting are a few examples of distribution popularly frequented by young people. Publications and other written works, while helpful, are not so accessible to young people who often either do not feel they have the time to read lengthy works, nor the desire to expend monetary resources to obtain them. Online resource distribution is free, openly accessible, and abbreviated such that they appeal to the constraints felt by younger audiences. If we are to properly make disciples of all young people, we must adopt resource distribution methods which have as few barriers between the audience and the truth as possible.

And lastly, we must be sure to make these resources known to our congregations. Many sermons in Bible-believing, even dispensational churches, continue with quotes from a variety of sources without a single dispensationalist in the bunch. If we want to be intentional about relieving the anxieties of young people, we must familiarize them with the resources which stand the best chance of relieving these anxieties as opposed to those who will not. This includes not only those who have passed on to glory, but also most especially those who are currently alive and writing who can be contacted for further clarification on these matters. Congregants will seek out the resources they are familiar with, not those of which they have never heard. Therefore, we need to make sure our people are explicitly introduced to dispensational theologians on these topics.

The problem remains that, for both young people within the church, and young people outside of the church, there is very little access to resources which relate these truths clearly and unambiguously in relation to their desires. So long as dispensational theology remains cloistered among the academics or as a private issue for which debate is not necessary, young people, both saved and unsaved, will continue to be disserviced and resigned to a life of anxious longing. What is necessary is explicit dispensational teaching both evangelistically and as an essential part of our discipleship of new believers which grounds our desires in the imminent coming of our Lord to restore all things in accordance with His promise.

Chapter 7 – On Suffering

On Account of My Name: An Ecclesial Shift Through Righteous Suffering in John 15–16

Cory Marsh

A survey of ancient Jewish literature reveals a significant progression in the theme of righteous suffering. From the Old Testament through Second Temple Judaism, the literature underscores that suffering, while always normative for believers in God, was never a promised consequent for one's faith in God prior to the New Testament. The suffering God's people endured during these eras was on account of their covenant disobedience or was merely an assumed reality with the hope of a future without suffering. Beginning with Jesus in the New Testament, affliction is promised for God's people explicitly as a direct consequence for their obedient faith in God. Such promised righteous suffering finds its most definitive expression in terms of persecution and affliction in the upper room discourse of the Gospel of John.

By surveying the relevant literature and highlighting John 15–16 as a backdrop, this article will demonstrate that Jesus's promise of suffering for Christians is a distinction in the history and literature of God's people.[1] Specifically, it will argue that the phenomenon of suffering, which, out of the four Gospels, is promised on account of Jesus's name only in John 15,

---

[1] While John does not use explicit terms for "promise" (Gk: ἐπαγγέλλω and its cognates), the concept is present. Some may argue that "prediction" is a better word to use since a promise can imply the person making it is also the person who will accomplish it (eg., Romans 4:21). But such implications are not demanded by the word. Thus, the article uses "promise" (ἐπαγγέλλω) as defined by Montanari as, "to announce, declare, proclaim." Franco Montanari, *The Brill Dictionary of Ancient Greek*, edited by Madeleine Goh and Chad Schroeder, (Leiden: Brill, 2015), 733.

suggests an ecclesial shift from the people of God in the OT to the people of God in the NT, as well as from believers living in between the Testaments.² Simply stated, believers in be OT suffered *for their lack of faith* (or disobedience), while believers in the NT are *promised suffering for their obedient faith*. Through the phenomenon of righteous suffering, therefore, a distinction is made between the peoples of God with the church being unique as marked by Jesus's promise of suffering for His namesake during the upper room discourse. The article will conclude by drawing modern day relevance as Christian suffering reveals God's glory and is the natural result for those who have exchanged their life and death for Christ's life and death.

DISCIPLES AS "CHRISTIANS" IN JOHN'S GOSPEL

Though not "Christian" in the technical sense of individual regeneration and corporate baptism after the descent of the Spirit at Pentecost, Jesus's disciples do constitute the Christian church in seed form. Anticipation of the coming Holy Spirit envelopes the narrative in John 14–16, forecasting a new type of assembly previously unknown and comprised of the collective band of Jesus's followers.

In Matthew's account, Jesus would promise to build "my church" (μου τὴν ἐκκλησίαν), thus establishing a new messianic community bearing allegiance to Him (Matthew 16:18).³ In John's account, the narrative uses the

---

² The language of suffering in John 15:21, 16:3, et al. is future tense, it *will* happen, which distinguishes this passage from the Beatitudes in Matthew 5:11, the latter being temporal and aorist. In other words, John is predictive, and Matthew is descriptive.

³ Assuming Jesus's words recorded in Matthew historically predate their publication, this reference to "church/assembly" in Matthew 16:18 is the first instance of the word ἐκκλησία in the NT. By Jesus's use of the pronoun μου, 'ἐκκλησία' takes on

language of "my sheep" (πρόβατά μου) to distinguish a new assembly for God's people belonging to Jesus (Jn 21:16, cf. 10:26–27). In fact, throughout the Fourth Gospel (FG), the disciples individually, as well as corporately, stand for later Christians as the widening of the term "disciple" (μαθητής) develops into what Andreas Köstenberger argued as "one not constrained by boundaries of time and space."[4] Of all the Gospels, the FG uses the most expansive language to describe disciples—both believers present in the narrative as well as forecasting future believers in Jesus. They are "people whom [the Father] gave [Jesus] out of the world" (Jn 17:6), and "Those who *will* believe in [Jesus] through their word" (v. 20).[5] It is therefore proper to refer to these believers in Jesus in the FG as "Christians" or pioneering members of the "church," even if in germinal form, without charge of anachronism. What is especially relevant is that the suffering promised to this nascent church in John 15–16 separates this new community of God's people from previous and future expressions of God's people.

RIGHTEOUS SUFFERING DISTINGUISHES GOD'S PEOPLES

This article defines "righteous suffering" as simply any mental or physical trauma, whether in the form of an event or emotion, endured by those who believe in the biblical God. As an event, the suffering may entail

---

a newer technical meaning not found in the LXX, extending past mere "assembly." It is a *specific* assembly—Jesus's assembly—or in other words, the Christian church.

[4] Andreas J. Köstenberger, *The Mission of Jesus and the Disciples According to the Fourth Gospel: With Implications for the Fourth Gospel's Purpose and the Mission of the Contemporary Church* (Grand Rapids: Eerdmans, 1998), 149.

[5] For the futuristic sense of the present active plural participle πιστευόντων in John 17:20, see Lidija Novakovic, *John 11–21* BHGT (Waco: Baylor University Press, 2020), 207; and Murray J. Harris, *John* EGGNT (Nashville: B&H Academic, 2015), 292.

forms of persecution for a believer in the biblical God, or their family ostracizing them for their faith, or even economical depravation due to the believer's witness for God in Christ. As an emotion, the suffering may include a believer's heartache, grief, or sadness that results from a traumatic event such as family rejection or economic deprivation due to a person's faith. Though they usually go hand in glove, they can each stand alone and be considered "suffering." This is because, as Brian Tabb noted, suffering in the ancient world, as well as today, is broader and more holistic than physical pain. His comparison of suffering in the Second Temple period is especially helpful, as he defines suffering as "the individual or group experience of bearing physical, psychological, economic, and/or social pain, distress, or loss."[6] Many times this includes personal distress or grief; other times it does not. One may experience a form of persecution, for example, but lack personal anguish over the situation. Indeed, they may even count themselves as blessed and rejoice over it, such as the apostles did in Acts 5:41 (cf. 1Pe 4:13). Thus, for this article, "suffering" is thought of as both objective and subjective.[7] But what makes such suffering *righteous*?

As defined earlier, "righteous suffering" is mental or physical trauma in the form of an event or emotion endured by those who believe in the biblical God. They are "righteous" people by virtue of their faith in the true God revealed in Scripture. Beginning with Abram in the OT and throughout the intertestamental period, these were Jewish believers in Yahweh bonded to Him by covenant (Genesis 12:1–3; 15:18; 17:7). It says explicitly of Abram, "And he *believed* the LORD, and he counted it to him as *righteousness*" (Genesis 15:6, emphasis added). In an OT passage quoted three times by NT authors,

---

[6] Brian J. Tabb, *Suffering in Ancient Worldview: Luke, Seneca and 4 Maccabees in Dialogue* LNTS 569 (London: T&T Clark, 2017), 11.

[7] With some variation, see Gerald W. Peterman and Andrew J. Schmutzer, *Between Pain and Grace: A Biblical Theology of Suffering* (Chicago: Moody, 2016), 13–35, who make helpful distinctions between "pain" and "suffering."

God told the prophet Habakkuk, "The *righteous* shall live by *his faith*" (Habakuk 2:4; Romans 1:17; cf. Galatians 3:11; Hebrews 10:38, emphasis added).[8] Paul in the NT picks up this idea as he outlines his gospel theme in Romans for all people, both believing Jews and Gentiles: "For in it [i.e., the gospel], the *righteousness of God is revealed from faith for faith,* as it is written, 'The righteous shall live by faith'" (Romans 1:16, emphasis added). He later says in Romans 5:1, "Therefore, since we have been justified [or made "righteous'] by faith, we have peace with God through our Lord Jesus Christ." As such, it is the concept of righteousness through personal faith that defines God's people and is understood as such in this article vis-à-vis trauma and God's people, or, in other words, "righteous suffering."

In Jesus's final discourse in the FG, promises of affliction underscore a unique distinction previously concealed. Fronted with a first-class condition in John 15:18, Jesus makes plain that "If the world hates you, know that it has hated me before it hated you....Because you are not of the world, but I chose you out of the world, therefore the world hates you." Following these remarks are Jesus's promises of "persecution" (διώκω) for His disciples in verse 21, before elevating future suffering to the extent of being "put out of synagogues" (ἀποσυνάγωγος) and even "physical death" (ἀποκτείνω) for the disciples in 16:2. Finally in 16:33, Jesus delivers the most explicit promise[9] of "affliction" (θλῖψις) with, "I have said these things to you, that in me you may have peace. *In the world you will have tribulation.*" Centered in the middle of these promises of suffering is Jesus's direct statement of reason, in 15:21: "But all these things they will do to you *on account of my name,* because they do not

---

[8] For nuances of the noun אֱמוּנָה ("faith, faithfulness") in Habakkuk 2:4, see Cory M. Marsh, "A Theology of Believer's Repentance in Habakkuk from a Triadic Interpretative Approach," *Evangelical Quarterly* 92 (2021): 201–223.

[9] Or statement of fact, depending on how one translates the present active verb in 16:33, ἔχετε—"you all [will] have."

know him who sent me." With these promises a distinction is made between God's people via the phenomenon of righteous suffering.

In former times, suffering for God's people occurred when they acted in disobedience or disbelief (Psalm 95:7–11; Hebrews 3:16–19). Now, they will suffer for their *obedience* and *belief* in God. Capturing the remarkable distinction suffering makes between the OT and NT, Hugh Stevenson Tigner observes:

> A striking change has taken place in the attitude toward man's sufferings on this earth. Suffering hurts as much as ever, and continues to have its original problem of endurance; but in the New Testament it presents no perplexity to faith; the mortal sufferings of the righteous along with the unrighteous do not embarrass the Christian confidence in God's government. It is now taken for granted that there is no way from man's present situation to the Kingdom of God except through a valley of suffering and a field of trial.[10]

This phenomenon of suffering, which the FG promises on account of Jesus's name only in John 15, demonstrates a subtle, yet significant, ecclesial shift from the people of God in the OT to the people of God in the NT. While suffering was always normative for believers in God, the fact that this section in the FG promises it as a direct consequence for correct faith is a feature reserved exclusively for the NT. Brian J. Tabb suggests a sharp distinction between persecution and suffering by virtue of being a Jesus follower and that of OT saints: "Believers suffer *like* Jesus and *for* his name."

---

[10] Hugh Stevenson Tigner, "The Perspective of Victory: The Problem of Human Suffering in the Old and New Testament," *Interpretation* 2, no. 4 (Oct. 1958): 403.

[11] In other words, it is the notion of suffering *promised* in accordance with their faith in God (e.g., persecution) that separates NT believers apart from believers in the OT as well as believers living in between the Testaments.

In one of the most comprehensive studies offered on Christian suffering by persecution, Scott S. Cunningham outlines six "theological functions" of suffering expressed specifically through Luke-Acts.[12] Enveloped by accurate conclusions such as persecution being divinely ordained under God's providence, its suffering as an integral consequence of following Jesus, and that persecution provides the impetus for the Christian's perseverance, he noted one that lacks further qualification: "The persecuted people of God stand in continuity with God's prophets of old."[13] Though correct that there is a line of continuity by way of persecution and suffering of God's people between the Testaments, OT prophets were never promised such suffering on account of righteousness or Yahweh's name sake (contra. 15:21–25; cf. Matthew 5:10). In other words, while suffering forms a link of continuity specifically between the Old Testament (OT) and the NT, it is only in the latter where such affliction is *promised for righteous behavior*. That is, predictions of suffering in the NT are not due to rebellion or faithlessness but by virtue of faithfulness and obedience to God (cf. Acts 20:23; 1 Thessalonians 3:3–4).[14]

---

[11] Brian J. Tabb, *Suffering in Ancient Worldview*, 217. Emphasis in original.

[12] Scott S. Cunningham, *'Through Many Tribulations': The Theology of Persecution in Luke-Acts*, JSNTSup 142 (Sheffield: Sheffield Academic, 1997).

[13] Cunningham, *'Through Many Tribulations,'* 14.

[14] It bears repeating that what I am arguing is for the *concept* of promises of righteous suffering being unique for NT saints, which extends past a mere word study of "promise." There are exceptions in the OT of afflictions declared or promised for specific saints, for example Jeremiah 1:19, but such was not the norm for God's covenanted people. Instead, suffering for unrighteous behavior or covenantal disloyalty was the norm for the ancient Jews as will be shown.

In fact, a survey of the pertinent literature reveals a significant progression in the theme of righteous suffering beginning in the OT, through the Second Temple Judaism, to its most definitive expressions in the NT. Broadly speaking, suffering occurred among God's people in OT Israel for their covenant infidelity. During Second Temple Judaism, suffering developed into an assumed reality with expectations of a future reversal. Righteous suffering then becomes explicitly promised as a direct consequence for faith in God in the NT (esp. John 15–16). A future age is anticipated through each of the transitions where there will no longer be suffering for God's people. Thus, "Christian suffering," as in righteous suffering ordained for God's people during the present age, is a unique distinction in the history and literature of God's people.

Suffering in OT Israel: Covenant Infidelity

Jeremiah, a remarkably faithful prophet to Yahweh, experienced multiple hardships throughout his thirty-year ministry to Judah. He declared, "O LORD, you know; remember me and visit me, and take vengeance for me on my persecutors. In your forbearance take me not away; know that for your sake [עָלֶיךָ] I bear reproach" (Jeremiah 15:15). Such a lament was surely the appropriate response for enduring his suffering.[15] Though, here and throughout the book, the prophet was never told that he *must* suffer for his righteous faith. He merely reflected on the suffering he endured.

Jeremiah's experiences echo that of David who suffered "reproach" (כְּלִמָּה) both for his inequity and for his faithfulness (Psalm 69:7). Yet David, like the other saints living under the Mosaic economy, was never *promised*

---

[15] See Jill Firth, "Spirituality from Depths: Responding to Crushing Circumstances and Psychological and Spiritual Distress in Jeremiah," in *The Bible and Mental Health: Towards a Biblical Theology of Mental Health*, ed. Christopher C. H. Cook and Isabelle Hamley (Louisville: Westminster John Knox, 2020), 115–127, for traces of the prophet's possible moral injury expressed in lament.

affliction as a direct consequence of his obedience. Rather, when he suffered, it was due to his own sin and rebellion against God's law (e.g., 2 Samuel 12:9–14). Furthermore, the Scripture is clear that the exilic prophet Daniel and his three friends were heavily persecuted as they worshiped Yahweh alone in the midst of pagan Babylon, as did Ezekiel during his twenty-year ministry. Indeed, they endured suffering; but, they were never promised it.

It goes without saying that these noted OT characters suffered incredible afflictions as members of a covenant community. However, they were never *promised* them specifically by virtue of their faithfulness to God's name's sake. That is, unlike the afflictions prescribed for believers in John 15–16, faithful Israelites who suffered in the OT largely did so non-prescriptively. Trauma was not explicitly assured for OT saints *because* of their faithfulness to the covenant or *because* of their witness on behalf of Yahweh. Instead, the general witness of Israel's canonical history is that when believers in Yahweh did suffer afflictions, *they did so as a result of their lack of faith or covenant infidelity, expressed in wicked behavior.*[16] Scholars have documented overwhelming instances of this. Especially in the Pentateuch, suffering, almost without exception, resulted from disobedience.[17]

As for explicit *promises*, the greatest contrast can be seen between "blessings" prescribed for covenant obedience in Deuteronomy 28:1–14 with "curses" prescribed for covenant disobedience in vv. 15–68 (cf. 7:11–15). Faithfulness to the covenant resulted in enjoying Yahweh's love, abundant families and harvests, increased livestock, and protection from sickness and

---

[16] Of course, Job provides a possible exception. But his historical placement within the history of national Israel is disputed. Nevertheless, Job himself was never *promised* his personal suffering as a result of faithfulness. In fact, he was never given an answer to his suffering. Only the reader of Job is privileged with that information.

[17] For a list of examples, see Stephan J. Bramer, "Suffering in the Pentateuch," in *Why O, God? Suffering and Disability in Church*, eds. Larry J. Waters and Roy B. Zuck (Wheaton: Crossway, 2011), 87–97.

enemies. Disobedience, however, resulted in suffering sickness, disease, death, defeat in war, famine, barrenness, and lack of provision. "As with blessing," observes Russell L. Meek, "the curses are conditional upon the people's behavior and come from the hand of Yahweh."[18] Unlike the suffering promised in the FG, suffering in Israel's history was a result not of righteous faith, but of unrighteous faithlessness. Extending past the books of Moses, Israel continued to experience famine, disease, and death due to rebellion throughout her history. As Tigner explains, "The prophets were frequently aggravated to say that it is only through being hammered over the head that Israel will learn any sense, and will be brought to recognize who is the Benefactor and Lord."[19] Along with Habakkuk's prophecy (Habakkuk 1:1–11), the two exiles of national Israel were monumental witnesses to this fact (2Ki 17:7–23).[20]

Suffering in Second Temple Judaism: Future Reversal

Following the canonical witness, a development can be detected within Second Temple literature. Suffering does become more of a reality for righteous faith; though, it still lacks explicit promise or prescription for righteous faith or suffering exclusively on account of Yahweh. The portrayal of suffering believers during this period is most explicit in the warnings and martyrdom portrayed in 2 Maccabees (e.g., 2 Maccabees 6:12–16; 7). Cautiously, like other contemporaneous Hellenized literature, its relevance for NT studies has been questioned.[21] Never considered a sequel to the

---

[18] Russell L. Meek, "Truly God is Good: Suffering in Old Testament Perspective," *Journal of Spiritual Formation and Soul Care* 9, no. 2 (2016): 153–154.

[19] Tigner, "The Perspective of Victory," 402.

[20] See Cory M. Marsh, "A Theology of Believer's Repentance in Habakkuk from a Triadic Interpretative Approach," 215–221, for more on the theme of Israel's wickedness contrasted with the need for righteous faith and personal repentance.

[21] Daniel R. Schwartz, "Maccabees, Second Book of," in *The Eerdmans Dictionary of Early Judaism*, eds. John J. Collins and Daniel C. Harlow (Grand Rapids: Eerdmans,

celebrated 1 Maccabees or even a prequel to 3 Maccabees, it is more akin to the disputed 4 Maccabees, which portrays embellishments of the martyrdom contained in 2 Maccabees, even to the point of containing atoning significance for national Israel.[22]

Nevertheless, 2 Maccabees does paint a stunning portrait of believers in Yahweh who suffer persecution at the hands of Seleucid oppressors on account of their faithfulness to covenant laws.[23] Ultimately, bodily resurrection is the clear hope of the author of 2 Maccabees, providing courage and endurance for faithful martyrs.[24] A theme of *lex talionis* emerges from the book demonstrating that certain events in Jewish history "show God at work caring for his people, rewarding the faithful and punishing the impious."[25]

Though the Jewish believers in 2 Maccabees endure chastisement and barbaric torture while remaining faithful to the law (e.g., 7:1–42), the narrative is more reflective of the OT than the afflictions explicitly promised for believers in John's Gospel. For example, within the very pericope describing a heroic family being severely persecuted, 2 Maccabees explains: "For we suffer thus for our sins. And though the Lord, our God, is angry

---

2010), 905, goes so far as to say, "[2 Maccabees] has no status at all in the Jewish tradition."

[22] Larry R. Heyler, *Exploring Jewish Literature of the Second Temple Period* (Downers Grove: InterVarsity Academic, 2000), 408.

[23] Craig A. Evans, *Ancient Texts for New Testament Studies: A Guide to the Background Literature* (Grand Rapids: Baker Academic, 2005), 22, describes the book as "[t]he greatest example of piety in the face of persecution."

[24] Heyler, *Exploring Jewish Literature*, 164, observes the sporadic impact 2 Maccabees has had on Christians throughout history, specifically for its portrayal of suffering among the faithful to martyrdom.

[25] Harold W. Attridge, "Historiography," in *Jewish Writings of the Second Temple Period: Apocrypha, Pseudepigrapha, Qumran Sectarian Writings, Philo, Josephus*, Compendia Rerum Iudaicarum ad Novum Testamentum, ed. Michael E. Stone (Philadelphia: Fortress, 1984), 2:178.

with us a little while, for our chastisement and correction, yet he will be reconciled again to his servants" (7:32–33; cf. v. 18). The suffering pictured for believers in 2 Maccabees is endured, even acknowledged, but never prescribed as a result for one's faith. Rather, it is more akin to OT thought where suffering is a consequence to sin instead of a reward for faithfulness (e.g., Exodus 34:7). In other words, unlike the FG's witness in John 15, Maccabean believers in Yahweh were never *promised* such afflictions *for* their faith.

Within the sectarian and apocalyptic literary traditions of the second and first century BC, a further development concerning the theme of suffering for believers is noticeable. Two prominent examples are found within the DSS Community Rule 1QS and the Book of Enoch.[26] Discovered in cave one at Qumran in 1947, the Community Rule scroll (also called Manual of Discipline) is the oldest example of "rule literature" genre and focuses much of its contents on communal, ascetic life governed by rigorous rules that function to transform community members into spiritual priests.[27]

One explicit reference of a promise of suffering for the righteous concerns fifteen council members of the community, made up of twelve laymen and three priests: "They shall preserve the faith in the Land with steadfastness and meekness, and shall atone for sin by the practice of justice and by suffering the sorrows of affliction" (1QS 8:1–4). Though certainly a promise of suffering to the faithful, it clearly differs from afflictions promised in John 15–16.

In the latter, afflictions are explicitly assured for one's explicit faith in God and on behalf of His name's sake (cf. 15:21). In 1QS, afflictions are not

---

[26] This section refers to "the Book of Enoch," "Enoch," and "1 Enoch" interchangeably.

[27] See, The Israel Museum, Jerusalem, "The Community Rule," The Digital Dead Sea Scrolls, http://dss.collections.imj.org.il/community.

prescribed for suffering on behalf of Yahweh or merely living according to the Mosaic law.[28] Rather, it is anticipated suffering that extends to all the particular laws designed for this particular council within the particular community. That is, the council was to remain faithful to specific community mandates that pertained to the sectarian group. This included a certain number of years of service, rules for clothing, touching and non-touching of certain communal foods and drink, spitting in the assembly, and even rules against laughing too loudly (6:20–7:25).[29]

Thus, the affliction prescribed for the fifteen-member council was legalistic in nature and tied to extensive law-keeping so much so that their suffering was to have "atoning effects for sin" (1QS 8:4). Nevertheless, though such suffering promised clearly differs from that in John 15–16, a development from the OT in the theme of righteous suffering is present in the sectarian literature—perhaps, most surprisingly, by cryptically forecasting an obedient law-keeper who would indeed atone for sins "by His" suffering.

Like 1QS, a progression in the theme of righteous suffering is detected in the apocalyptic text of 1 Enoch.[30] Among the Jewish apocalypses, Enoch is among the most explicit concerning suffering believers enduring

---

[28] Additional portraits of eschatological suffering are found in 1QS 3:21–23 and 10:16–17. However, in the former, suffering is stated to be caused by a wicked angel's diabolical rule and leading the righteous astray. In the latter, suffering is expressed in a poem reflecting Habakkuk 3, merely assuming the reality of affliction in the world while commending a worshipful response in its midst. Both instances differ from John 15–16, where suffering is explicitly promised as a direct result of their exclusive faith in God (through Christ).

[29] See Reinhard G. Kratz, "Law of Wisdom: Sapiential Traits in the Rule of the Community (1QS 5–7)," in *Hebrew in the Second Period: The Hebrew of the Dead Sea Scrolls and of Other Contemporary Sources*, Studies on the Texts of the Desert of Judah, vol. 108, ed. George J. Brooke and Eibert J. C. Tigchelaar (Leiden: Brill, 2013), 133–145.

[30] For a helpful recent survey of the Enoch collection, see Daniel M. Gurtner, *Introducing the Pseudepigrapha and Second Temple Judaism: Message, Context, and Significance* (Grand Rapids: Baker Academic, 2020), 21–91.

persecution. Particularly, the so-called Book of the Watchers (chs. 6–11) is pervasive with language depicting various afflictions. Though, the work never explicitly identified persecution as the genesis for the book's composition. "Rather," as John J. Collins explains, "it provides a lens through which any crises can be viewed."[31] Because of this, John 15–16 finds its closest ally with 1 Enoch.

While Enoch shares similarities with John's Gospel in that both are written from a Jewish worldview that included apocalyptic thought, their dissimilarities become evident when the distinction of righteous suffering as argued here is recognized. That is, much like other Jewish works predating the NT, Enoch does not explicitly identify suffering as a promised result by virtue of one's faith in Yahweh. Instead, the book is framed by sufferings presented as having to be endured by the righteous while afflictions are poured out on the wicked.

The book initiates with, "The words of the blessing of Enoch, wherewith he blessed the elect and righteous, who will be living in the day of tribulation, when all the wicked and godless are to be removed" (Enoch 1:1–2). Assuming "the elect and righteous" stand for believers in Yahweh, though they are identified as "blessed," they are not promised suffering as a direct consequence of their faith or on account of God (as is promised in John 15–16). Rather, it is the "wicked and godless" who are promised suffering for *their* deeds. While the righteous are anticipated to endure suffering, it is portrayed as a basic assumption living in a world alongside the wicked, particularly during a day of tribulation and retribution against sinners (e.g., Enoch 96:2). Such is the nature of apocalypticism in general, and Enoch, in particular. God's people are to anticipate a future, *sudden reversal of fortunes* where they are delivered from oppression presently suffered and where the

---

[31] John J. Collins, *The Apocalyptic Imagination: An Introduction to Jewish Apocalyptic Literature*, 3rd ed. (Grand Rapids: Eerdmans, 2016), 75.

wicked are punished for their tyranny (cf. Enoch 91:11–13). Though "healing" for afflictions suffered is expressly promised (v. 3), afflictions promised as a direct consequence for righteous faith in Yahweh are not. They are assumed as a present reality.[32]

Doubtless, the Enoch apocalypse is intended to evoke a sense of awe and conviction regarding coming judgment in the eschaton.[33] The book "enables the faithful to cope with the crises of the present and so creates the preconditions for righteous action in the face of adversity."[34] By the end of the book, the faithful are encouraged to be hopeful even though they will experience "shame through ill and affliction" (Enoch 104:2). The final two chapters then present a clear divide between the righteous and the wicked—with elements of suffering acknowledged for both—before closing with warnings to the faithful not to act like the ungodly (104:6–13). Enoch then concludes with a cryptic messianic expectation of "the Son" in 105:2.

The Book of Enoch betrays a clear development in the theme of suffering believers that, like 1QS, begins to separate its contents from its canonical predecessors while anticipating explicit promises of suffering for one's faith in the NT (particularly those in John). Because the work describes suffering that the righteous will endure, even cryptically tying it to a reference to Christ, there is more affinity with its presentation and John's Gospel than with other Jewish literature predating the advent of Jesus. As such, an economical transition by way of righteous suffering is suggested in Enoch

---

[32] Anathea Portier-Young, *Apocalypse against Empire: Theologies of Resistance in Early Judaism* (Grand Rapids: Eerdmans, 2011), 313–335, argues portions of Enoch (e.g., The Apocalypse of Weeks) emerged as literature of resistance against an oppressive Hellenistic imperial rule that was being experienced by its author(s). Thus, descriptions of sufferings for God's people are assumed as a present reality while retribution awaits a future age.

[33] See the overview presented in D. S. Russel, *The Method and Message of Jewish Apocalyptic* (Philadelphia: Westminster Press, 1964), 51–53.

[34] Collins, *The Apocalyptic Imagination*, 75.

164 On Suffering

that will find its fullest revelation in NT writings. Though similarities are present, as the theme of righteous suffering developed, a significant difference remains. The suffering of the righteous in Enoch are described and assumed in the present, while a great reversal of them is clearly expected in the future. In John (particularly, chapters 15–16), righteous suffering is explicitly promised for the present, while any such reversal in the future is assumed. Thus, in the main, righteous suffering in Second Temple Judaism is never explicitly identified or promised to occur exclusively *because* of one's faith in God. That explicit revelation would have to wait until Jesus's statements in the FG, and elsewhere in the NT.

Suffering in the Church: A Promised Consequent

The explicit promises of affliction for Christians "on account of Jesus's name" or *because* of their faith in John 15–16 have already been discussed. What will be developed further here is that the afflictions the FG promises for believers comprising the Christian church, not only separate the current economy from those above governed by Mosaic law, but also from *future* ones where peace and justice will reign supreme (cf. Is 11:6–9, Zec 14:20–21).

In the only other occurrence of θλῖψις ("tribulation, affliction, suffering") in the FG besides that at John 16:33, Jesus drew an illustration comparing the suffering of the disciples to that of a woman in labor (16:21). Much has been written on this passage over the years, from those considering it an allegory representing Christianity replacing Judaism,[35] to those who view it as an enigmatic reference to Mary as the woman in labor and leaning on the crucifixion scene at 19:25–27 as support.[36] Others, such as W. H.

---

[35] Alfred Loisy, *Le Quatrième Èvangile* (Paris: Alphonse Picard, 1903), 785–791.

[36] A. Kerrigan, "John 19, 25–27 in Light of Johannine Theology and the Old Testament," *Antonianum* 35 (1960): 369–416, esp. 380–387.

Brownlee, go so far as to equate the apostles with the woman suffering hardship in the illustration who would give birth to the risen Jesus.[37]

Yet because the operative word for suffering or "tribulation" (θλῖψις) exists only twice in the FG and in the same discourse, it is best to view them as illustrating a single truth with the latter reference in verse 33 advancing the former in verse 21. Though both statements end in encouragement, pain interpreted as suffering is still promised in the pericope and thus an anticipated reality for believers. In his exposition of the passage, Raymond Brown offered insightful implications for the suffering promised in 16:21, 33 and recognized its uniqueness to the Christian church era.

After comparing the uses of θλῖψις throughout the NT, Brown rightly advocated for a "realized" perspective in John that views the suffering promised in chapter 16 with a double focus. The first, verse 21, is the sufferings promised for the disciples brought on by the death of Jesus. The second, verse 33, refers to their continued affliction under persecution as they minster in the world following the death of Jesus.[38] For Brown, Christian affliction is a "suffering which precedes the emergence of the definitive divine dispensation."[39] In other words, affliction promised to the disciples in John underscores not only a unique discontinuity distinguishing Israel's economy from the Christian church but also serves to distinguish the Christian church from the economy of the future eschaton. After all has been said, a transition of dispensations is observable by way of explicit suffering promised for believers throughout the Jewish and Christian literary tradition and finds unambiguous expression in John 15–16.

---

[37] W. H. Brownlee, "Messianic Motifs of Qumran and the New Testament," *New Testament Studies* 3 (1956–1957): 12–30, esp. 29.

[38] Raymond E. Brown, *The Gospel According to John XIII–XXI* (New York: Doubleday, 1970), 733.

[39] Brown, *The Gospel According to John XIII–XXI*.

A REVELATORY PARADIGM OF GLORY THROUGH RIGHTEOUS SUFFERING

The FG's logic of suffering is especially heightened in the upper room discourse of John 14–16. Throughout the narrative, the theme of suffering *promised* for believers elevates from inner angst to physical death. Phrases are used throughout the section depicting suffering as turmoil, grief, and various afflictions anticipated for believers as a community. Though, John's perspective of Jesus's own suffering is enveloped not in misery but in glory. As such, those who suffer as followers of Jesus are to glorify God in their sufferings.

The disciples' mentally troubled state over Jesus's going to the Father initiates the discourse before progressing to promises of both hatred and persecution from nonbelievers due to their faith in Jesus (15:18–21). This theme of *promised* righteous suffering elevates throughout the narrative to assurances of extreme agony involving expulsion from communities and even murder resulting from one's faith in Jesus (16:2–3). An all-too real principle emerges, teaching that because Jesus suffered in both life and death, those in Christ are at times called to suffer in both life and death.

As argued throughout this article, trauma promised to the disciples on behalf of their witness of Jesus Christ is unique in the history of God's people. Yet, it is a continued history in which the church still finds itself. Viewing the disciples as paradigms for later Christians, Jesus's varied promises of tribulation within John 15–16 extends to believers past the first century. Like Jesus's own physical suffering, which the FG presents as real, suffering promised to His followers are real as well—with God's glory as their end for both. Not to be understood as suffering for suffering's sake or in manners of self-inflicted masochism, all the afflictions portrayed in and for believers throughout the FG carry a doxological intention.

Moreover, such trauma is not presented as an exception. Rather, it is the *expectation* of the Christian life. According to John's logic of suffering, which is grounded first in Christ's suffering, there is a necessity for actual, real-life afflictions for believers to experience since a "a servant is not greater than his master" (15:20). The Johannine witness here is clear that Christians are to expect hardship for their faith in Jesus, who experienced it first. As Brown and others have noted, this separates the church from previous and future expressions of God's people.

The suffering Jesus promised for His namesake in John 15 was not restricted to that group or even to those in the first century. Charles E. Hill provides accounts of persecution and harassments suffered by Christians well into the second century. Despite trying to live peaceably within a Greco-Roman culture that hated them, Christians living under the reigns of Marcus Aurelius and Lucius Verus (AD 161–169) were tried and executed for failing to venerate local gods. Later, Christians living in Gaul suffered public harassment, confiscation, arrests, and several brutal executions.[40] Through various accounts, John's Gospel was appealed to by these early Christians for strength, truth, and comfort.

Of course, Christian persecution did not cease in those early centuries. Scholarly volumes have been written that document persecution and martyrdom through the middle ages up to recent times.[41] Alluding to Christian persecution at the hands of militant Islam groups such as ISIS,

---

[40] Charles E. Hill, "Culture," in *How John Works: Storytelling in the Fourth Gospel*, RBS 86, ed. Douglas Estes and Ruth Sheridan (Atlanta: SBL Press, 2016), 267.

[41] Recent, noteworthy examples are, Paul Middleton, ed., *Wiley Blackwell Companion to Christian Martyrdom* (Hoboken: Wiley-Blackwell, 2020), and Christian C. Sahner, *Christian Martyrs Under Islam: Religious Violence and the Making of the Muslim World* (Princeton: Princeton University Press, 2018).

"Recent events in our own day," notes Hill, "offer horrifying reminders that the 'time' is still with us when some believe that the worship of their God justifies or even mandates the killing of Jesus's followers."[42] Christian ministries abound in today's world dedicated to serving the persecuted church, which report estimates exceeding 90,000 Christian deaths per year resulting from severe persecution.[43] Thus, believers in Jesus today should not think of persecution from nonbelievers as suggestive of a faith in error. Rather, as Köstenberger and Patterson state, a believer with a proper faith-filled perspective "will be able to recognize more readily that even adversity and rejection are ultimately ordained by God for his sovereign purposes."[44]

Throughout the Johannine narrative, the disciples as a group were promised they would be persecuted for their faith in Jesus whom the world hates. Yet empowered by Spirit, they were to anticipate it and remain vigilant in their witness regardless of such suffering. Because Christ overcame affliction, so can Christians—guaranteed by Jesus's promise of His return for them and the Holy Spirit's help (14:3, 14–16; cf. 16:33). Contrary to non-Christian ideas of death, the Christian sufferer has real, factual hope. In a recent monograph devoted to early Christian thought and practice concerning death, Jeremiah Mutie details how beginning in the second century, believers differed from surrounding Greco-Roman and even Jewish

---

[42] Hill, "Culture," 267.
[43] Statistics are available from *Center for the Study of Global Christianity* at Gordon-Conwell Theological Seminary, https://www.gordonconwell.edu/center-for-global-christianity/, and *Voice of the Martyrs*, https://www.persecution.com/. The latter is an example of a ministry serving the worldwide persecuted church.
[44] Andreas J. Köstenberger with Richard D. Patterson, *Invitation to Biblical Interpretation: Exploring the Hermeneutical Triad of History, Literature, and Theology* 2nd ed. (Grand Rapids: Kregel Academic, 2021), 590.

cultures. In particular, the Christian's view on dying was "governed more by hope than hopeless despair."[45]

Whether death came naturally or by extreme persecution, Christian treatment of their loved one's death differed substantially precisely because of the hope they had in Christ. As Mutie outlines, unique Christian practices of burying their dead included closing of the eyes as if to picture a restful sleep, the dead believer being placed in a coffin rather than cremated, and the prohibition of outlandish wailings and mourning customary to Jews and pagans. The idea behind the Christian treatment of their dead, as opposed to strict Jewish and pagan cultures, was always to symbolize the hope of the believer's resurrection founded upon Jesus's death and resurrection.[46] For Christians, though there be suffering, there will equally be hope and glory.

The Johannine witness is that followers of Jesus in any age are to testify about Christ while expecting affliction from a world who hates them. They do so knowing that such hatred is really directed toward their Lord.[47] This does not mean that a Christian's faith in Jesus is somehow inauthentic if that believer is lacking the extremities of suffering highlighted in this article. Clearly, not everyone will experience martyrdom or intense forms of trauma because of their faith in Jesus. However, all believers are sure to feel that ancient tension of living for Jesus in a world that hates Him along with "various kinds" of struggles that come as a result (Jn 15:18–19, cf. Jas 1:2–3). As the narrative promises persecution to the group as a whole, no individual Christian should think he suffers persecution alone. It is an affliction experienced by the church locking arms since Jesus's first promises of it in the Upper Room narrative of John 14–16.

---

[45] Jeremiah Mutie, *Death in Second Century Christian Thought: The Meaning of Death in Earliest Christianity* (Cambridge: James Clarke & Co, 2015), 173.

[46] Mutie, *Death*, 156–190.

[47] See Christopher M. Blumhofer, *The Gospel of John and the Future of Israel*, SNTSMS 177 (Cambridge: Cambridge University Press, 2020), 194–204.

Just as Jesus suffered for God's glory, so do those who suffer for His name's sake (15:21). "To follow Jesus," Paul Anderson explains, "is not to escape persecution or even premature death. Just as the 'exaltation' of the cross was Jesus' paradoxical glorification, so will abiding in this knowledge be existential 'nourishment' for disciples undergoing hardship for the sake of their faith."[48] This is "righteous suffering," according to the FG. It is suffering promised to the collective group symbolizing the Christian church and is designed to reveal the glory of God through the world's worst tribulations. Such is the natural result for those who have exchanged their life and death for Christ's life and death.

CONCLUSION

This article has argued that a progression of "righteous suffering" exits in the history and literature of God's people and even serves to underscore differing economies between them. The theme was demonstrated to begin with believers suffering for their covenant infidelity in the OT, developed into Second Temple Judaism with assumed suffering while expecting a future reversal, to the NT explicitly promising suffering as a direct consequent for one's faith in God. Finally, a future age is anticipated through each of the transitions where there will no longer be suffering for God's people. Therefore, suffering as a *promised consequent for faith* in God (through Christ) in the present—as highlighted in John 15—is a feature reserved exclusively for the current Christian era. Such righteous suffering serves as a dramatic avenue for disciples to glorify Christ who suffered on their behalf.

---

[48] Paul N. Anderson, *The Christology of the Fourth Gospel: With a New Introduction, Outlines, and Epilogue* (Eugene: Wipf & Stock, 2010), 259.

Chapter 8 – On Race and Ethnic Diversity
A Dispensational Perspective on Race and Ethnicity
Joseph Parle

The recent deaths of George Floyd, Ahmaud Arbery, and Breonna Taylor brought the topic of race and ethnicity to the forefront of American conversations and hence to the church. While some might be tempted to get their perspective from the media or history, a biblical perspective is critical at this time. This chapter will apply a dispensational methodology to the question of race and ethnicity in order to promote a biblical understanding of the topic.

METHOD AS APPLIED TO CRITICAL RACE THEORY (CRT)

This chapter utilizes Chafer's definition of systematic theology for analyzing this topic. Chafer writes, "Systematic Theology may be defined as the collecting, scientifically arranging, comparing, exhibiting, and defending of all facts from any and every source concerning God and His works. It is *thetic* in that it follows a humanly devised thesis form and presents and verifies truth as *truth*."[1] This definition is critical for determining a dispensational perspective on race and ethnicity. From the outset, I will say I believe Critical Race Theory (CRT) and Cultural Marxism are unbiblical worldviews. The question is whether there is any tangential theological value that can be incorporated into a biblical worldview instead of dismissing everything

---

[1] Lewis Sperry Chafer, *Systematic Theology*, vol. 1 (Grand Rapids, MI: Kregel Publications, 1993), 6. Emphasis his.

related to the systems out of hand. In the social media driven environment of the twenty-first century, sources have become very controversial. Some rely on Fox News while others rely on MSNBC. As people question what is true or fake news from topics ranging from COVID-19 to the 2020 Presidential election, everyone seems to have a favorite authority to quote. The result of this cultural tendency is to focus more on the perceived bias of the source as opposed to the evaluating the positions the source advocates. This is not to say that the philosophical and theological assumptions of the source should not be evaluated. Not all sources are created equal and therefore all must be examined in light of the inspired, authoritative source––the Bible. People with a dispensational theology should be willing to acknowledge and incorporate valid, biblical truth claims from all sources.

This distinction is especially critical on the topic of race. A scholar or pastor who refers to Kendi, Tisby, and/or Emerson might be identified as an advocate of Critical Race Theory or a Cultural Marxist. On the other hand, an individual who quotes Edwards and Whitefield could be identified by some as a racist who is quoting slaveowners. In fact, some might be tempted to reject Dispensationalism as a whole because of Dallas Theological Seminary's former policy of not admitting African Americans and misunderstandings of Scofield's note on the so-called curse of Ham in the *Scofield Reference Bible*.[2] Such conclusions represent the worst label a person of

---

[2] In his article "Towards a Definition of Dispensationalism," Stallard states regarding the note in the *Scofield Reference Bible*, "To Scofield's credit, the Bible editor does not explicitly mention black people in his rather terse note about subjugation: 'A prophetic declaration is made that from Ham will descend an inferior race.' Any allusion to a predicted inferior nature of blacks can only be seen as implicit or perhaps read into the words of Scofield rather than clearly taught. It could be that Scofield believed that the black race was in view, but it is hard to know that from the note itself or in the other writings of Scofield, which this writer has seen. Most scholars see the fulfillment of the subjugation mentioned in the verse in Joshua's conquest of the Canaanites when Israel entered the land after the wilderness wanderings." Mike Stallard, "Toward a Definition of Dispensationalism,"

a particular persuasion can give to another. For liberals, the worst thing to call someone is a racist/bigot and for conservatives the worst thing to call someone is a communist. Hence, people try to diminish the views of the opposing side by connecting those views to what they themselves repudiate. Mislabeling an individual could be a form of slander. When the concept of loving one's neighbor is introduced in Leviticus 19:18, slander is to be avoided (Lv 19:16).

Recently, I watched a debate on Facebook in which individuals were discussing the best references to learn about Critical Race Theory. One of our professors jumped into the conversation and asked if anyone who was discussing Critical Race Theory had actually read primary sources of those who advocate Critical Race Theory. Not a single person in the conversation could cite a primary source they had read on the topic. They instead continued to refer him to various YouTube videos and resources by Neil Shenvi.

A truly dispensational perspective will evaluate any and every type of source in order to determine what truth claims can be incorporated into one's system. And not only that, but a dispensationalist will interpret the views of others literally, according to the author's original intent. The International Conference on Biblical Inerrancy defines literal as, "We affirm the necessity of interpreting the Bible according to its literal, or normal, sense. The literal sense is the grammatical-historical sense, that is, the meaning which the writer expressed. Interpretation according to the literal sense will take account of all figures of speech and literary forms found in the text. We deny the legitimacy of any approach to Scripture that attributes to it meaning which

---

https://dispensationalcouncil.org/wp-content/uploads/2018/07/10_Toward_a_Definition_of_Dispensationalism_Stallard.pdf, 3.

the literal sense does not support."³ Literal interpretation is a sine qua non of the dispensationalism. However, dispensationalists should not only advocate a literal interpretation of the Bible but of all texts. Most traditional dispensationalists would advocate Hirsch's definition of meaning as "that which is represented by a text; it is what the author meant by his use of a particular sign sequence; it is what the signs represent."⁴

The Role of Authorial Intent in Dispensational Discussions on Race

The goal of every dispensationalist should be to portray all sources as the author would intend for them to be portrayed. When I was in my master's program at Dallas Theological Seminary, I stumbled on a dissertation topic that I hoped to purse in my PhD program that will later be a book published by Exegetica Press (if the Lord wills). In researching Jonah 3:4, I had noted how Chisholm used the text to make a distinction between decrees one which God will not change His mind and intentions about which God may change His mind.⁵ Instantly I feared that a professor of Dallas Theological Seminary was slipping into Open Theism and I wrote a paper for a class against his view. My professor Tracy Howard read the paper and gave me a good grade, but he asked me to meet him after class. He asked me if I had considered sending my paper to Dr. Chisholm to ensure I had rightly represented his view. I agreed to do so in hopes that Dr. Chisholm would read my paper and repent of his slippery descent to Open Theism. Much to my surprise, Dr. Chisholm not only read my paper, but he seemed pretty offended by it. He assured me that he did not espouse Open Theism and he simply was trying to wrestle with what the Hebrew says. Seven years later, I finalized my

---

³ Norman L. Geisler, ed., *Inerrancy* (Grand Rapids: Zondervan, 1980), 497.

⁴ E. D. Hirsch, *Validity in Interpretation* (New Haven: Yale University Press, 1967), 4.

⁵ Robert B. Chisholm Jr., "Does God 'Change His Mind'?," *Bibliotheca Sacra* 152, no. 608 (1995): 387–400.

dissertation and acknowledged Dr. Chisholm's role in helping me write it. Although I still disagreed with his view, I found him to be a wealth of information about sources that viewed Jonah's prophecy differently than I did. He would respond to my questions and in the end, I hope I represented his view more fairly.

What role does an author's intended meaning play into these questions of race? In our divided culture, it is very easy to divide evangelical Christianity into us vs. them. An individual can easily portray the opposing view as racist defenders of white supremacy. Alternatively, others portray the side they are opposing as Cultural Marxists. Pastors and scholars are regularly slandered by labels they would never apply to themselves. For me, this is somewhat personal because people I know are sometimes mislabeled. For instance, Dr. Eric Mason, author of *Woke Church*, is a former professor of our college. I attended his Conscious Christianity conference and heard him personally say that he rejects Cultural Marxism. Yet I shook my head when I read a recent dispensationalist who argued that Mason's views were heavily influenced by Marxism. The evidence for the assertion was his views of reparations, his use of the phrase whiteness, and alleged support of Black Lives Matter.[6] Mason himself denies any association with Cultural Marxism. He tweeted, "You can't call someone a Marxist if you haven't read and interacted with his primary sources. When engaging Marxism, you cannot connect social justice

---

[6] After contacting the author (whom I will keep anonymous because my goal in contacting him was to model what I am espousing here), he agreed that he might have misrepresented Mason after he watched a clip of a sermon by Eric Mason titled "What I Mean When I Say Black Lives Matter,"
https://www.youtube.com/watch?v=jPdfBJV1Ys8. At the 30:30 mark Mason explicitly says, "There are things within it [the organization] that I have to part with. When I say 'Black Lives Matter' I'm not supporting the Black Lives Matter organization. I'm supporting Black life."

to communism and socialism and relativism. It's totally embarrassing!"[7] In a February 15, 2019, tweet Mason also favorably cites "'Race' and Racism Pre-Date Karl Marx" by Thabiti Anyabwile which says, "It's not that Marxist thought isn't anywhere to be found in racial discourse. I think it is. Of course, some people are self-consciously Marxist. But most people writing blogs and engaging the subject either are unaware of Marxist influence or are quite aware of having very different influences on their thought. Tossing about the label does nothing for understanding the person you're engaging or improving the discourse. And, in a good many instances, tossing about the labels is simply anachronistic."[8]

As Anyabwile points out, this tendency of guilt by association is not helpful to advancing the discussion on any theological topic. A few years ago, I got an angry call from a professor who was upset that I would not hire him to teach at our school based on his amillennial eschatology. He berated me for allowing something as narrow as eschatology to be a qualifying factor to teach at our school. He was outraged that our institution would reject professors who believed like Jonathan Edwards and George Whitefield whom he mentioned by name. He probably was not too happy when I reminded him that as a school in which a majority of our students are African Americans that there might be other reasons why I would not want to hire Edwards and Whitefield that were referred to earlier in this chapter. I noted that his resume indicated he taught at a reformed graduate school, and I asked him if he thinks that institution would hire a dispensationalist like me as an adjunct. He said that I should not expect to be hired at his reformed institution because they hold to eschatological views that the church has

---

[7] Eric Mason, Twitter post, September 7, 2018, 11:20AM, https://twitter.com/pastoremase/status/1038099769829347329?lang=en

[8] Thabiti Anyabwile, "'Race' and Racism Pre-Date Karl Marx," The Gospel Coalition, April 09, 2018, https://www.thegospelcoalition.org/blogs/thabiti-anyabwile/race-racism-pre-date-karl-marx/).

Biblical Distinctions Applied 177

believed for centuries, and I hold to eschatological views that are characteristic of some cults (never mind that the earliest church fathers were premillennial). This professor hoped to disparage my dispensational eschatology by associating it with something worse. His implied comparison went something like this:

1. Dispensationalists are premillennial.
2. Cults like Jehovah's Witness are premillennial.
3. Therefore, your decision to not hire me based on eschatology is what the cults would do.

The late Ravi Zacharias shows the logical errors of this type of thinking when he states this syllogism:

1. Elephants have ears.
2. I have ears.
3. Therefore, I am an elephant.

One can see a similar logic here:

1. Black Lives Matter is a Marxist Organization.
2. Eric Mason praised Black Lives Matter.
3. Therefore, Eric Mason is a Cultural Marxist.

Or, here is a logic which I have seen among more liberal groups when talking to conservatives:

1. Trump was endorsed by racists through *The Crusader* a KKK newspaper that calls itself "the premier voice of the white resistance."

2. You voted for Trump.
3. Therefore, you are a racist.

These gross oversimplifications illustrate that dispensationalists should be very hesitant to label someone in a way that he or she would not describe himself or herself. This is not the case of the cofounder of the Black Lives Matter movement Patrisse Cullors who admitted she is a trained Marxist. However, saying someone who applauds the phrase "black lives matter" is inherently a cultural Marxist is no different than insinuating that any individual who repeats the phrase "Make America Great Again" adopts every belief that Donald Trump espouses (which is especially concerning for Christians considering his views of sexual purity and his past admission that he does not have anything to ask forgiveness for). Theological positions are often far more nuanced than general labels like Cultural Marxist or racist will allow.

Having said that, does this mean we should never label someone in a way that he or she would not portray himself or herself? I don't think Scripture goes that far. My guess is that the Pharisees would not consider it fair or accurate that Jesus portrayed their theology as Satanic (cf. Jn 8:44) or Peter might feel that Jesus's portrayal of his rebuke as being influenced by Satan in Mark 8:33 and Matthew 16:23 was harsh (even though the Pharisees and Peter were in fact being influenced by Satan at those times). On the other hand, an aspect of love is giving a fellow Christ-follower the benefit of the doubt thereby believing all things best about them as well as hoping all things good for them (cf. 1Co 13:7). This should be applied in cases similar to when individuals like John Piper, Tim Keller, and Al Mohler have been accused of being closet cultural Marxists even when they have written strong theological statements against Critical Race Theory and Cultural Marxism.[9] Avoiding inaccurate labels also applies to comments toward many African Americans who up until recently had little knowledge of Critical Race Theory or Cultural Marxism. Yet, they were accused of espousing them. Eric Mason himself stated that he had to research the phrase that he is so frequently accused of advancing. John Piper quotes Pastor Rasool Berry who mentions a common reaction African Americans have when being accused of espousing Cultural Marxism or Critical Race Theory:

> The brothers and I had not even heard of Critical Race Theory until we were told that, when we said something needs to change when George Floyd is kneeled on, we were being held captive by Critical Race Theory. What are you talking about? I'm just trying to respond to the injustices all around me…I'm being given a label that I don't really want to be talking about. I want to be talking about the death that is in the street, and the disparities like COVID having a disproportionate impact on people of color. We see these disparities across education, health care, economics. I would rather talk about that, but any time you talk about that in Christian circles, you are given this title…More energy is being devoted to the tethering of Critical Race Theory to what we are saying than is being devoted to the problem of racism itself.[10]

---

[9] In my opinion, the best and most balanced critique of Critical Race Theory comes from Tim Keller, "A Biblical Critique of Secular Justice and Critical Theory," Available at https://quarterly.gospelinlife.com/a-biblical-critique-of-secular-justice-and-critical-theory/. See also John Piper, "Critical Race Theory, Part 2: The Problem," https://www.desiringgod.org/interviews/critical-race-theory-part-2. See also Al Mohler, "Karl Marx Meets the Devil: A Conversation with Historian Paul Kengor," https://albertmohler.com/2021/02/10/paul-kengor.

[10] John Piper, "Critical Race Theory, Part 1: The Relationships," https://www.desiringgod.org/interviews/critical-race-theory-part-1.

I sometimes wonder if the arguments of the widespread influence of Critical Race Theory in society is not significantly different than attributing a pre-trib view of the rapture to a fifteen-year-old girl named Margaret MacDonald[11] or arguing that everyone from Ted Cruz to Mike Pence are all influenced by dominion theology. While there may be similarities in these views, we must be careful not to paint too broad of a brush (just because someone has ears like an elephant does not make them an elephant).

Kimberlé Crenshaw: A Primary Source on Critical Race Theory

So what should be said about Critical Race Theory? Perhaps it would be good to consult with one of the more recent adherents (time and space only allow for one) and see how that view relates to Scripture as we develop our systematic theology from any and every source known to the mind of man. As a background, Critical Race Theory was developed in the 1980s by legal scholars who were trying to explain how so much inequality could still exist after the Civil Rights Act of 1964 and other laws that were intended to promote equality. Kimberlé Crenshaw is credited by some as having coined the phrase "Critical Race Theory" while others argue that its origin came from Derrick Bell and Richard Delgado. In her article "Twenty Years of Critical Race Theory: Looking back to Move Forward Commentary: Critical Race Theory: A Commemoration: Lead Article," Crenshaw gives a different historical perspective than what one might find in Voddie T. Baucham Jr.'s *Fault Lines: The Social Justice Movement and Evangelicalism's Looming Catastrophe* or similar resources. Crenshaw does not suggest that Critical Race Theory was invented to topple capitalism but instead it was employed in response to

---

[11] This is a view that was debunked in Thomas Ice, "Is the Pre-Trib Rapture a Satanic Deception?" https://digitalcommons.liberty.edu/cgi/viewcontent.cgi?article=1051&context=pretrib_arch.

fellow liberals who espoused a color-blind philosophy and made hiring decisions based on standards that in her mind advanced the cause of white males at the expense of other minorities.

According to Crenshaw, it started as a legal discussion with Harvard Law School in which African American legal students were protesting the paucity of African American professors and especially those with tenure (after Derrick Bell left in the Spring of 1980, the law school officially had zero tenured minority faculty at the time). In confronting the Dean about this disparity, the Dean mentioned that he was interested in hiring more African American professors but very few met their hiring standards. The students protested that the standards were arbitrary and difficult for females and people of color to achieve based on past inequalities (e.g. law degree from an Ivy league school and significant experience in courts where people of color were rarely hired). The Dean responded to their concerns with this question, "[W]ouldn't you prefer an excellent white professor over a mediocre Black one?"[12] The students responded by presenting a list of thirty black professors that they thought were qualified and a petition of over 500 signatures. In response to the student concerns and protests, the Dean chose to offer a three-week mini-course on civil rights litigation in the January intersession.

For Crenshaw, this situation illustrated how a liberal school that had made great inroads in admitting African American students still supported power structures that prevented African Americans from thriving into positions of power. As a result, the students boycotted the intersession course and hosted an alternative course taught by Derrick Bell that utilized materials from Bell's book *Race, Racism and American Law*. This brief overview shows how Critical Race Theory questioned the popular notion that the law

---

[12] Kimberlé Crenshaw, "Twenty Years of Critical Race Theory: Looking back to Move Forward Commentary: Critical Race Theory: A Commemoration: Lead Article," *Connecticut Law Review* 43, (2011): 1267.

tends to be impartial and objective by emphasizing how the history of how laws were developed in the United States and other countries were designed to disproportionately adversely affect people of color and maintain majority power. The situation with the Dean who tried to give a three-week course while ignoring the larger issues illustrated that tendency. This history lesson may provide an alternative explanation to the origins of the Critical Race Theory. As opposed to being motivated by a desire to overthrow capitalism in America, the motive may have been to rebuke liberals who claimed to support equality in word but failed to do so in deed.[13] Whether this truly is the motive only God knows, but I point this out to encourage scholars to portray the view fairly (even when we disagree with it which I do disagree with it). It is kind of like people who argue that those who believe in a pretribulational rapture do so because they want to avoid suffering. While that may be a motive of some (in the same way that some who espouse Critical Race Theory really do want to overthrow all the capitalistic structures in our country), I hope that those who portray our motives would take us at our word that staying true to what the Bible says about the end times and specifically the need to remove the church to focus on Israel is the true motive. This is not to say that many proponents of Critical Race Theory are not Marxists, as many of them believe that capitalism has caused significant discrimination and inequality. It is just to say that I would prefer to speculate about the development of the concept from those who adhere to it and even contributed to its spreading.

---

[13]For an alternative explanation that racial issues were used to spread Marxism in America see Manning Johnson, *Color, Communism, and Common Sense: A True Story* (Eureka, MT: Lighthouse Trails Publishing, 2021).

Intersectionality

A similar issue is true of the history of the term "intersectionality" which was coined by Crenshaw in her article "Demarginalizing the Intersection of Race and Sex: A Black Feminist Critique of Antidiscrimination Doctrine, Feminist Theory and Antiracist Politics." The title of this article clearly indicates that there are loaded liberal and unbiblical philosophies undergirding the term. Crenshaw coined the term after a legal case of DeGraffenreid v. General Motors. In this case, DeGraffenreid sued General Motors by arguing that African American females were discriminated at the company. General Motors responded by showing how African Americans and females were treated fairly within the organization. Crenshaw's main bone of contention with their evidence was that the African Americans that benefitted most from General Motors were males and the females that benefitted were white. In her opinion, the discriminatory practices were a subset or intersection of both populations: African American females.

In a *Time* interview, Kimberlé Crenshaw defines "intersectionality" as "how certain aspects of who you are will increase your access to the good things or your exposure to the bad things in life."[14] Crenshaw, as the author who coined the term, is careful to distinguish her definition from how it is perceived, "These days, I start with what it's not, because there has been distortion. It's not identity politics on steroids. It is not a mechanism to turn white men into the new pariahs. It's basically a lens, a prism, for seeing the way in which various forms of inequality often operate together and exacerbate each other. We tend to talk about race inequality as separate from inequality based on gender, class, sexuality or immigrant status. What's often missing is how some people are subject to all of these, and the experience is

---

[14] Katy Steinmetz, "Kimberlé Crenshaw on What Intersectionality Means Today," *Time*, February 20, 2020, |PAGE|, https://time.com/5786710/kimberle-crenshaw-intersectionality/.

not just the sum of its parts."[15] For Crenshaw, intersectionality is not a contest to find who is more oppressed that others. It is a perception that the more minority groups one is a part of, the more likely that person will be discriminated against. Her proposed solution for the problem of inequality in America is, "If you see inequality as a 'them' problem or 'unfortunate other' problem, that is a problem. Being able to attend to not just unfair exclusion but also, frankly, unearned inclusion is part of the equality gambit. We've got to be open to looking at all of the ways our systems reproduce these inequalities, and that includes the privileges as well as the harms."[16]

Privilege

This brings me to another controversial term that Crenshaw and many CRT advocates use…the term "privilege." In the previously cited article, she discusses her concept of privilege as follows:

> With the collapse of segregation came the confidence in some quarters that formal equality alone constituted the ultimate realization of racial justice. Yet, this faith in formal equality's triumph over white supremacy was unwarranted; formal equality did little to disrupt ongoing patterns of institutional power and the reproduction of differential privileges and burdens across race. Post-reform struggles such as the battle over integration at Harvard involved efforts to impose an institutional settlement in the name of formal equality that left many dimensions of power and exclusion firmly entrenched. [17]

---

[15] Steinmetz, "Kimberlé Crenshaw."
[16] Steinmetz, "Kimberlé Crenshaw."
[17] Kimberlé Crenshaw, "Twenty Years of Critical Race Theory: Looking back to Move Forward Commentary: Critical Race Theory: A Commemoration: Lead Article," 1312.

There is no doubt that some advocates of CRT have a more extreme version of privilege than what is described here. I once saw a video at a Black Lives Matter protest where white people were asked not to walk on a particular street due to privilege. Such approaches are unbiblical and focused on revenge and white guilt rather than conciliatory.

This concept of privilege seems to be connected with a focus on whiteness which in the CRT world is how Jewish, Polish and Irish individuals were once outcasts but once race was decided by color as opposed to ethnicity these once discriminated groups were elevated as African Americans were considered inferior. CRT advocates tend to argue that while there is formal equality in name, the way the law is applied is often unequal, whether in mass incarceration of African Americans as described in the Netflix documentary 13th or inequality in access to real estate (along with the fact that once a neighborhood becomes majority African American that it becomes less desirable and property values go down or the opposite effect of gentrification in which urban properties become more valuable due to location and minority populations cannot afford the property taxes and other costs to stay in homes they have lived in for a long period of time).[18] CRT advocates use privilege to argue that modern racism is less pronounced and more subtle. Privilege does not mean white people have success only because they are white and did not have it hard. It means that the color of skin wasn't an obstacle to success. In her article, Crenshaw even argues how the reality of an African American president (President Obama) did more to advance a colorblind thinking than produce real change that addressed systemic structures that hurt African Americans.

---

[18] An interesting analysis of how systemic racism still exists in the real estate agency can be found at Elizabeth Korver-Glenn, *Race Brokers Housing Markets and Racial Segregation in 21st Century Urban America* (New York, NY: Oxford University Press, 2022).

This distinction between formal equality and systemic equality are an important distinction for advocates of Critical Race Theory. Imagine that in a country where Christianity was prohibited and Christians were regularly jailed for their faith (e.g. North Korea, current Afghanistan, etc.). The results of these laws were many Christian families were separated from their families due to mass incarceration of Christians. They also lost their property. Over time, Christianity is permitted but the results of incarceration and property loss have long term effects on the poverty rates of Christians in this country. Christianity may now have formal equality in this system but the systemic results of an extended period of time of discrimination have long term effects. And before we as evangelical Christians argue too hard against the possibility of systemic inequalities, it appears that the United States is setting itself up to discriminate against Christians in the present and future. Whether that is removing financial aid for colleges that do not admit homosexuals or forcing bakers that will not make a wedding cake for a homosexual wedding, these are just the beginnings of the persecution that awaits the Christian church. Now someone could say that systemic discrimination of Christians does not exist because there are plenty of rich Christians in the United States and even a Christian could become president but that does not mean that the system could be wired to suppress Christianity (one could equally question whether Antisemitism exists by citing the number of rich Jews and Jews in power –maybe the Egyptians could have pointed to Moses being in Pharaoh's house as evidence that it did not exist during the time of the Exodus -- but we know it exists). It would be most unfortunate if the group that denied that systemic discrimination exists will one day feel the effects of it and have no one to speak for them.

Evaluation of Critical Race Theory

So now that we have discussed what Critical Race Theory is, let us follow the counsel of 1 Thessalonians 5:21-22 (NASB), "Examine everything carefully; hold fast to that which is good; abstain from every form of evil." Regarding this passage, Thomas Constable says, "In view of this danger Christians need to **test** what they hear and read, by comparing it with the Word of God, to determine if it is divine in its origin. This is difficult, but it is possible for a spiritual believer (1Co 2:14). Each Christian has the responsibility and ability to do this, though some have more discernment than others (cf. Ac 17:11; 1 Jn 4:1). What is discovered to be **good** (i.e., in harmony with what has been given by the Holy Spirit in the Word) should be retained."[19] It should be noted that some of the people who reject all the conclusions of Critical Race Theory due to the non-Christian beliefs of the sources have no trouble quoting Ayn Rand, Thomas Sowell, Ben Shapiro, or Candace Owens who do not share conservative evangelical views of the Bible or Jesus Christ.

To begin with, in order to avoid misunderstanding (remember the importance of authorial intent), I will clearly and unequivocally say here that I reject most of the arguments and conclusions of Critical Race Theory and Cultural Marxism. First, as will be mentioned later, I reject Critical Race Theory because it is based on unbiblical distinctions based on the color of skin as opposed to the more biblical concept of ethnicity (i.e. tongue, tribe, and nation). It is important to note that although these distinctions are unbiblical, the color of one's skin has had and still has social consequences in American society today and those consequences should not be ignored. In fact, these distinctions may lump some individuals as offenders when they or

---

[19] Thomas L. Constable, "1 Thessalonians," in *The Bible Knowledge Commentary: An Exposition of the Scriptures*, ed. J. F. Walvoord and R. B. Zuck, vol. 2 (Wheaton, IL: Victor Books, 1985), 709. Emphasis his.

their ancestors were not even in this country when the majority of wrongs are committed (another form of guilt by association). Second, regarding Cultural Marxism, I do not support government control of either the distribution of private property or the attempt for the oppressed to topple all societal structures that could lead to poverty. Thirdly, the system of thought seems more retributive than a grace-oriented approach based on reconciliation after wrongs committed. The solution is not gospel-oriented forgiveness of others as Christ has forgiven us (Eph 4:32) and walking in the Spirit according to that gospel (Gal 2:14-20). Instead, followed to the logical extreme, it can reorient the focus of the Christian from sharing and modeling the gospel to correcting every damaged social structure. Fourth, many advocates of Critical Race Theory reject the Bible as being a homophobic, anti-female book that white males have used to oppress minorities for centuries. This errant view of God's word should be avoided at all costs. CRT further perpetuates what Yancey calls a "white responsibility model"[20] which places the majority of the responsibility for addressing racism at the hand of the majority culture which often alienates rather than motivates attempts at social change. This prevents a mutual responsibility model that Yancey endorses or what Dr. Charles Ware calls "us and us" conversations as opposed to "us and them" conversations.

One piece of advice I frequently give to my students (who often disagree with me) is to "eat the meat and spit out the bones." With so many bones already pointed out on Critical Race Theory, the question is whether there is any meat in Critical Race Theory that could be incorporated into a dispensational theology of race and ethnicity? I personally think there could be some concepts that have potential benefit even though I reject the overall system.

---

[20]George A. Yancey, *Beyond Racial Gridlock: Embracing Mutual Responsibility* (Downers Grove, IL: InterVarsity Press, 2006), 64-74.

Evaluation of Systemic Racism

To begin with, evangelical Christians should be the most suspicious of broken government systems, even in the United States. Blocker has noted that the Bible itself warns Christians about the worldly system, "For all that is in the world, the lust of the flesh and the lust of the eyes and the boastful pride of life, is not from the Father, but is from the world" (1Jn 2:16 NASB). What motivates racism, pride of one's group over another, fleshly desires for self-preservation, and a desire to have what others have. In fact, Dr. Bill Blocker has argued that slavery itself was built on a desire of the early colonists to meet their responsibilities to Britain as well as to ensure their survival in a new land which required cheap, slave labor. In fact, in this chart Dr. Blocker chronicles the history of racism in the United States and how the church responded to it:

Historical Summary Timeline of Racism and the Church's Role

Dr. Bill Blocker

The fact that until less than sixty years ago African Americans were not given equal rights in this country should show us that racism was built into many of the laws and structures we have in this society. The principle of the harvest would indicate that when systems in the United States were sown with racist seeds that one would reap racist structures (Gal. 6:9). A basic understanding of depravity and the world should give us pause in assuming that systemic racism does not exist in the midst of much research that shows that we still live in a racialized society.

Furthermore, a proper view of depravity and the world should also indicate this is not uniquely a white problem as critical race theorists often assert. The genocides in Rwanda or Cambodia by non-white leaders show that prioritizing one ethnicity over another can often have disastrous consequences. In fact, one of the first instances of systemic racism in the Bible can be found in the forced slavery of the Jews and governmentally endorsed attempts to kill male Jewish babies by the Egyptians in Exodus.

One other modern-day example of systemic racism is Planned Parenthood, which was founded by Margaret Sanger who started the Negro Project, spoke to KKK groups, and believed in eugenics. She advocated "the gradual suppression, elimination and eventual extinction, of defective stocks—those human weeds which threaten the blooming of the finest flowers of American civilization."[21] She said regarding her work, "We do not want word to go out that we want to exterminate the Negro population, and the minister is the man who can straighten out that idea if it ever occurs to any of their more rebellious members."[22] These racist seeds she planted have reaped deathly results. Planned Parenthood could argue that despite the views of their founder, they are not racist at all, and they give equal access to all women to abortions. However, the fact that so many Planned Parenthood centers are put in minority neighborhoods and that while African Americans only constitute thirteen percent of the female population but constitute

---

[21] Kristan Hawkins, "Remove Statues of Margaret Sanger, Planned Parenthood Founder Tied to Eugenics and Racism," https://www.usatoday.com/story/opinion/2020/07/23/racism-eugenics-margaret-sanger-deserves-no-honors-column/5480192002/.

[22] Hawkins, "Remove Statues."

thirty-eight percent of abortions (with the help and financing of our government and major donors)[23] should at least cause anyone to admit that, as far as this goes, systemic racism is alive and well in the United States and it has deadly consequences. It also shows that while someone might not be individually racist, he or she can support a system that has racist consequences. There are African Americans who financially support Planned Parenthood who either ignore or do not know the organization's racist origins. Planned Parenthood is an example of how someone can love African American people yet contribute to something that was created for their demise.

An illustration I would suggest for systemic racism is from the movie *The Hunger Games*. In *The Hunger Games*, the people who set up the game had the ability to add obstacles to the game to make it more difficult to survive. In one scene, Katniss Everdeen is too far away from the other players (she is not breaking any of the rules) and the makers of the game are concerned that it will be too easy for her to win if she continues with this strategy. So they add an obstacle for her that they did not give to the other players. They put a forest fire around her so that she has to escape and ends up in the path of the other players who try to kill her. Now with her ingenuity she is able to climb up a tree to save herself by releasing a group of "tracker jackers" but the result was significant injury that hampered her ability to win the game. In the end she won but it would have been best for her and everyone else if the makers of the game had just let the game play out.

What does this have to do with systemic racism? From the founding of this country, a system was built to make it harder for people of color to succeed. And even when they did succeed painful obstacles were put in place to limit the results of their success (for example, Planned Parenthood, the

---

[23] Hawkins, "Remove Statues."

destruction of black wall street in 1921, or the fact that home values go down when high numbers of people of color occupy white neighborhoods so the white people leave those neighborhoods and the people of color lose value on their investment and have less generational wealth to pass down to heirs as a result of past and present discriminatory practices). And even when they do succeed their success is minimized (e.g., President Obama only got elected because he was black or people of color only get certain jobs because of affirmative action). This is not to say each person is not responsible for pursuing their own success. A biblical worldview should advocate a system that reduces the unnecessary obstacles to that success that disproportionately affect people of color.

Evaluation of Privilege

The second item that should be explored is that of privilege. I would like to begin by saying that this concept is often abused. Yancey writes:

> Few actions damage race relations more than playing the race card. It is even more destructive than the racial insensitivity of white Christians because it is an intentional attempt to use one's racial status to escape responsibility and deny one's sin. People of color have taken the good intentions of the majority and squandered their goodwill in order to further our own selfish desires. How are European Americans going to believe our claims of racism when they see us use those claims to get away with sin, to escape our responsibilities and to punish those we do not like? …. When accusations of racism are made only to further the interests of racial minorities, it makes it more difficult for people of color to point out real racism… If we understand the concept of human depravity, we should not be surprised that people play the race card.[24]

---

[24] George Yancey, *Beyond Racial Gridlock*, 101-102.

When some hear the word "privilege" they think of it in these terms, as a manipulation tactic to "play the race card" as Yancey (who incidentally is African American) writes. I can say that in fifteen years of serving as Academic Dean/Provost at the College of Biblical Studies, I have often witnessed this myself. In all my years, I have often been asked to meet with an African American student who accused his or her professor of racism (most of the time the professor is Anglo but occasionally the African American student accused an African American professor of racism). In all the situations, without fail, the professor was invited to a meeting where the professor heard the uncomfortable accusation, pulled out the syllabus, showed how the student's grade was a result of not completing an assignment or cheating/plagiarizing, and I could see no evidence of racism. In my fifteen years, I have yet to have an Anglo student accuse an African American prof of the same thing. I agree with Yancey that for Anglo professors who dedicated their lives to teach at a mostly minority college, this can be a very painful experience.

Having said all that, on the other hand, I do feel a responsibility to listen to the experiences of my brothers and sisters in Christ and mourn with them. In a book club we had several years ago, I was struck by the common experiences many of our African American professors had in being pulled over when they did nothing illegal. In some cases, they were handcuffed or asked to exit the car and were often threatened by law enforcement. Those conversations brought back memories that were buried in the recesses of my mind when I was in high school. My mother is Mexican, and my dad is Irish American. In high school my skin was much darker as I spent most of my summers outside with the marching band or playing baseball with my friends. My mother and I would have tanning contests, and back then I would usually win. During my junior year in high school in 1991, I was dating a very pretty, Polish American girl who lived in a very nice neighborhood. However, I noticed that when I would drive to visit her, I would often be followed by police officers. I mentioned this to my mother, and she had to have "the talk" with me that so many African American parents have with their kids. I made sure that I did not exceed any speed limits, made a complete stop every time, and was cautious to obey every law but the following did not stop. This situation especially got scary on multiple times when police officers pulled me over, yelled at me, asked why I was in the neighborhood, and threatened to arrest me even though I had not committed a crime. After high school, I exchanged the marching band and baseball activities for studying and my skin ever since has begun to look much more like my Irish American father, so much so that very few people who look at me think I am Hispanic at all. What is interesting is ever since that time, I have never had the same experience of being pulled over despite not having committed a crime, being threatened, and asked to produce identification. If anything, every interaction I have had with police officers has been extremely positive.

One common misunderstanding of Critical Race Theory is what former CBS professor Voddie Baucham calls "ethnic gnosticism" which he defines in his book *Faultlines* as "idea that people have special knowledge based solely on their ethnicity."[25] I think the comparison with Gnosticism is unfortunate. Gnosticism emphasized a duality between physical and spiritual that most African Americans are not stating when they say that I as a white man cannot understand their experience. Furthermore, Gnosticism denies that Jesus came in the flesh which Christians do not believe. I think it is a creative philosophical comparison but a major mistake to associate with a historically heretical view.

---

[25] Voddie T. Baucham, *Fault Lines: The Social Justice Movement and Evangelicalisms Looming Catastrophe* (Washington, D.C.: Salem Books, an Imprint of Regnery Publishing, 2021), 92.

Furthermore, the distinction he makes is not biblically accurate. In my Wisdom Literature class, I teach students the difference between knowledge, understanding and wisdom. Knowledge refers to an intellectual comprehension of the truth. Understanding refers to a subjective experience. Wisdom is the union of knowledge and understanding.

An illustration I share is that I used to do premarital counseling before I got married. I had a seminary degree and felt all I needed to do is teach people what the Bible says about marriage. And while God's word will not return void and the premarital counseling was probably positive, my view of marriage completely changed when I got married. Teaching people about spiritual leadership is one thing but being a spiritual leader is quite another. Prior to marriage, I had knowledge, but I lacked understanding.

My point about knowledge versus understanding is that I may know things about the African American experience, but I cannot truly understand what it is like to be in their shoes (and by *their* I am not saying African Americans are a monolithic group because each individual person has different experiences). In the same way, I do not fully understand what it is like to be a white female either. I can empathize for what it is like to be pregnant, but I cannot truly sympathize since I have never experienced pregnancy. Furthermore, Proverbs 14:10 (NASB) says, "The heart knows its own bitterness, And a stranger does not share its joy." Even if someone has experienced something similar, does not mean that they truly feel the same way about that experience as others do. The point I am making is that this is not some gnostic mysterious knowledge but an actual biblical concept that Baucham is misrepresenting.

Prior to trusting in Christ as Savior, I thought Christians had a persecution complex. I saw believers as judgmental jerks that make life miserable. Once I became a Christ-follower and I told unbelievers that Christians are persecuted in America, they laughed and said I was paranoid.

I found this statement hurtful since those who mocked me had not experienced the rejection I had experienced. The point is that we can commit the same mistake when we attempt to explain away the genuine experiences of our fellow African American brothers and sisters in Christ and discount or explain away their experiences with discrimination and racism.

This leads me back to the concept of privilege. In Critical Race Theory, privilege is often used by the person who considers himself or herself to be from a victim group to someone who they consider to be of the oppressor group. This terminology is difficult for achieving any form of racial reconciliation. However, turned the other way, privilege can be a valuable way to understand how to serve our brothers and sisters in Christ. As a point of illustration, many people have probably heard of the winter storms Houston had in February of 2021. Over sixty percent of Texas was without power due to ERCOT shutting it off. Much to my surprise, our home never lost power during the entire event. We had friends, family, and neighbors that were sleeping in houses that were literally less than forty degrees, bundled up near the fireplace and they had no way to warm up food, while we were comfortable at my house. Others had broken pipes from the freeze. I actually felt a certain degree of survivor's guilt. Why was my pastor's wife who has cancer suffering in the cold while I was in the warmth of a heated home with stable pipes? What I did not know was that when I purchased my home it was connected to a hospital grid. That was why our power stayed on even though I had done nothing to deserve it. There were literally people on our neighborhood Facebook page saying that we who had not lost power should have ours cut off and should lose power for an extended period of time just so we would know what it would feel like. I did not feel much sympathy for them, but for everyone else, I felt compelled to share the blessing that I had with them. I called and texted as many people as I knew who lost power begging them to come stay with us. We did not care whether they had large dogs or large families. We just wanted to share our blessing with them.

The reality is that I live a very privileged life (if someone dislikes the term privilege perhaps blessed would be more appropriate). I am blessed to live in a great country with tremendous freedom that most Christians throughout history have never known. While I am not rich by the standards of American society, I have food, clothing, and shelter that is better than what most of the world has ever known. I have rarely experienced the prejudice that many of my African American or Asian brothers and sisters have faced. Privilege does not mean individuals with lighter skin (like myself) achieve success only because of the color of their skin or they did not have it hard. It means that the color of skin was not an obstacle to success. However, the solution to this problem is not to feel guilt for any privilege we have but to use that privilege for the betterment of others, especially those who are in the body of Christ. The verses in 2 Corinthians 8:3-4 (NIV) illustrate this well when speaking of the Macedonians who were not very wealthy, but they used their blessings to benefit others, "For I testify that they gave as much as they were able, and even beyond their ability. Entirely on their own, they urgently pleaded with us for the privilege of sharing in this service to the Lord's people."

Evaluation of Intersectionality

Another item that may be worth exploring is that of intersectionality. As previously mentioned, whereas this term is often represented as a contest to see who is most oppressed, the original intent was to see how different aspects of one's personhood may make them more vulnerable to bad treatment. An interesting biblical example is the Samaritan woman at the well. She had three strikes against her: she was divorced/living with a man, a Samaritan, and a female. Any and all of these reasons were why the disciples were amazed the Jewish, male, pure Jesus would speak with her (Jn 4:27). To be clear, intersectionality is not essential to understanding this passage. This would have been a foreign concept to the original audience and so it should not be imported into the exegetical process. The Samaritan woman at the well does illustrate the concept, however.

What value could the concept of intersectionality bring on the theological level? A few years ago, an African American female faculty member of ours who is married to an African American male faculty of ours mentioned that oftentimes people will acknowledge his doctorate when greeting or introducing him while failing to acknowledge hers. More often than not he is addressed as Dr. Ellen while she is addressed as Venessa even though they both have PhDs from evangelical seminaries. This happened in African American churches as well as Anglo churches. This experience is not unusual as studies have shown this to be common for females in the medical field[26] and for minorities in higher education.[27] Hearing this made me conscientious to make it a point that when I was speaking to or about a professor, especially an African American female professor, to make every effort to call that person doctor even though I may have a personal relationship with her and she may report to me as Provost. Now I will say this is far different from my own personal approach. I was mentored by two men: Dave Anderson and Mike Stallard. Both hold doctorates but even when

---

[26] See Julia A. Files, Anita P. Mayer, Marcia G. Ko, Patricia Friedrich, Marjorie Jenkins, Michael J. Bryan, Suneela Vegunta, Christopher M. Wittich, Melissa A. Lyle, Ryan Melikian, Trevor Duston, Yu-Hui H. Chang, and Sharonne N. Hayes, "Speaker Introductions at Internal Medicine Grand Rounds: Forms of Address Reveal Gender Bias," *Journal of Women's Health* 26, no. 5 (May 2017): 413-419.

[27] Sydney Freeman, Jr and Ty-Ron Douglas, "Put Some Respect on My Name: Navigating the Use of Academic Titles and Personas," *Journal of Underrepresented and Minority Progress* 3, no. 2 (2019) 1-28. This peer reviewed article provides sources of studies that show that ethnic minority faculty are less likely to be called doctor than their Caucasian counterparts. Please note that by citing this article I do not agree with all the recommendations and conclusions of this article.

I was their student, they insisted I call them by their first name. I adopted that practice for myself as I saw it as a sign of humility and brotherly kindness. Of course, in academic circles, it is rare that when someone sees my title of provost that they do not assume I have a doctorate. My experience with some of our African American female faculty is that often they are either assumed not to have a doctorate, or they are treated with such informality that they do not. Does this mean I have become a Cultural Marxist or an advocate of CRT? No, as even Paul recognized individuals by the appropriate title when culturally necessary (cf. Acts 23:3-5). What this familiarity hopefully does is to love my sisters in Christ better and to not act unbecomingly towards them (1Co 13:5).

A BIBLICAL PERSPECTIVE ON RACE AND ETHNICITY

Multiple dispensationalists in the Council on Dispensational Hermeneutics have written on this topic and I commend their work to you.[28] This particular section will focus on the work of dispensationalist Dr. Charles Ware and Ken Ham in the book *One Race One Blood: The Biblical Answer to Racism*[29] as well A Biblical and Theological Rationale for Cultural Diversity Statement that was created by the faculty and board of the College of Biblical Studies where I work.

---

[28] Joel T. Williamson, "Racism and the Torah" (paper presented at the annual meeting of the Council on Dispensational Hermeneutics, Kansas City, MO, 18 September 2020). Thomas Baurain, "The Myth of Racial Reconciliation" (paper presented at the annual meeting of the Council on Dispensational Hermeneutics, Kansas City, MO, 18 September 2020). Christopher Cone, "Every Tribe, Tongue, People, and Nation: The Future of Race Relations and Social Justice Implications for Today" (paper presented at the annual meeting of the Council on Dispensational Hermeneutics, Kansas City, MO, 19 September 2020).

[29] Ken Ham and Charles Ware, *One Race One Blood: The Biblical Answer to Racism* (Green Forest, AR: Master Books, 2017).

One Race One Blood

The title of Ware and Ham's book comes from Acts 17:26 (KJV) which says that humans are all one blood as descendants of Adam and Noah, "And hath made of one blood all nations of men for to dwell on all the face of the earth, and hath determined the times before appointed, and the bounds of their habitation." Furthermore, the Bible speaks of one race—the human race. This is illustrated in James 3:7-8 (NASB), "For every species of beasts and birds, of reptiles and creatures of the sea, is tamed and has been tamed by the human race. But no one can tame the tongue; it is a restless evil and full of deadly poison." Ham further argues that we have far more in common than what differentiates us:

- We're all created by God. *God formed us out of the dust of the ground* (Ge 2:7).
- We're all in God's image. *God said, "Let us make man in Our image"* (Ge 1:26).
- We're all one family. *He [God] has made from our blood every nation"* (Ac 17:26).
- We're all loved by God. *God so loved the world that He gave His only begotten Son* (Jn 3:16).[30]

Not only are we one blood in the sense of our common descent from Adam, but Ham also points out that all tribes, tongues, and nations are purchased by the blood of Jesus Christ, "And they sang a new song, saying, 'Worthy are You to take the book and to break its seals; for You were slain, and purchased for God with Your blood men from every tribe and tongue

---

[30] Ken Ham and Charles Ware, *One Race One Blood: The Biblical Answer to Racism* (Green Forest, AR: 2017), 23.

and people and nation. You have made them to be a kingdom and priests to our God; and they will reign upon the earth'" (Rev 5:9-10 NASB).

God not only made us uniquely different on earth as differing tribe, tongues, and nations but He intends for those distinctions to carry on into heaven. Revelation 7:9-10 (NASB) says, "After these things I looked, and behold, a great multitude which no one could count, from every nation and all tribes and peoples and tongues, standing before the throne and before the Lamb, clothed in white robes, and palm branches were in their hands; and they cry out with a loud voice, saying, 'Salvation to our God who sits on the throne, and to the Lamb.'" God is most glorified when people of various tribe, tongues, and nations from all over the world worship and serve Him (which should lead us to avoid a colorblind perspective). Ware has aptly stated, "This is our future. This is the destiny of the Church – and the Church today can be an earthly preview of this heavenly reality."[31] This ethnic variation in heaven also has the value of fulfilling biblical covenantal promises (cf. Ge 12:3 and Zec 14:16).

Ethnicity vs. Race

As Ware and Ham have pointed out, the Bible speaks of one race which is the human race but multiple ethnicities. One can see this when comparing the following Greek words:

- ἔθνος - Nations, Nationalities, Ethnicity
- γένος - Family, Offspring, Descent

Ware and Ham make the argument that we are all related through Adam (γένος) and there is only one race—the human race. While the Bible makes

---

[31] Ham and Ware, *One Race One Blood*, 120.

distinctions among ethnicities (ἔθνος), distinctions of race by skin color is an unbiblical social construct.

This distinction is especially interesting when it comes to individuals who might be considered black by society based on appearance but Hispanic by ethnicity. I once had a friend who was Puerto Rican with very dark skin, and he became very offended when someone called him black as he was from Puerto Rico and spoke Spanish. I was once lectured about privilege from a white female, and I was told I have no understanding of how privilege works as a white male. I asked her why she thought I was white. She asked me if that was a trick question. I told her that it was not a trick question because my mother is from Mexico. She said I should not call myself Hispanic because I look too white. Following her advice would require me to deny the culture and language in which my mother raised me, which is why when people ask for my background, I call myself a Mexican American. My mother is Mexican, and my father is Irish American. So, for me the term Mexican American best represents both sides of my family. Some have questioned why I do not just call myself an American. To do so would acknowledge my nation, but it would ignore my ethnicity and my dual languages that were a part of my home growing up.

Not only is ethnicity more biblically accurate than race but Ham also argues it is scientifically more accurate as well. Ham quotes Dr. Venter (head of the Celera Genomics Corporation in Rockville, MD) who argues that the human genome experiment found that there is only one race—the human race. Furthermore, Ham cites research from Jorde and Wooding that indicates that the genetic variation within each of the various ethnic groups of Homo sapiens is greater than that between the various ethnic groups.[32] Hence, there is very little biblical or biological reason to make distinctions between the color of one's skin. Ham writes, "We sing 'Jesus loves the little

---

[32] Ham and Ware, *One Race One Blood*, 96-97.

children, all the children of the world. Red and yellow, black and white, they are precious in His sight....' That's a cute song but actually it's really scientifically inaccurate! To be accurate, it should say, 'Jesus loves the little children of the world. Shades of brown from dark to light, all our precious in His sight...' Yes, Jesus loves us all, but believe it or not, all human beings are basically the same color (shades of brown). There are no truly black or white people."[33]

In fact, when skin color was mentioned in the Bible, it often includes a challenging yet redemptive element to it. For instance, the CBS Biblical and Theological Rationale for Cultural Diversity (included later in this chapter) states, "When Miriam and Aaron spoke against Moses's Cushite wife (Nu 12:1), the Lord viewed their ethnic hostility as a rejection of His authority and Moses's leadership, and He judged their rebellion by giving Miriam a skin disease (Nu 12:4-13). Thus, Miriam's attempt to draw 'separation' between a man and his Cushite wife directly led to her 'separation' from her own people (Nu 12:14-15)." Additionally, the Shulammite in Song of Solomon 1:6 (NASB) says, "Do not stare at me because I am swarthy, For the sun has burned me. My mother's sons were angry with me; They made me caretaker of the vineyards, But I have not taken care of my own vineyard." However, the love of Solomon has redeemed that by making her feel black and lovely (1:5). For this reflects the love of God who does not focus on the outward appearance but the heart (1Sa 16:7).

So where did this excessive focus on making distinctions based on the color of one's skin come from? The first and most obvious answer is sin. Sin causes us to focus on our differences than similarities. Beyond that, Ham attributes much of the modern focus on racial distinctions by skin color to evolutionary theory. He quotes the late Stephen J. Gould (not an advocate of

---

[33] Ham and Ware, *One Race One Blood*, 84.

Christianity by any means) as saying, "Biological arguments for racism may have been common before 1859 but they increased by orders of magnitude following the acceptance of evolutionary theory."[34] Ham also points to the original title of Darwin's book: *On the Origin of Species by Means of Natural Selection or the Preservation of Favoured Races in the Struggle for Life*. When man went from being a human created in the image of God to an evolved ape, it was easier to argue that some races of humans were more or less evolved than others. Ham quotes Darwin who wrote in *The Descent of Man*, "At some future point, not very distant as measured by centuries, the civilized races of man will almost certainly exterminate and replace the savage races of the world…The break between man and his nearest allies will then be wider, for it will intervene between man in a more civilized state, as we hope even…than the Caucasian, and some ape as low as a baboon. Instead of now between the negro or Australian and the gorilla."[35]

This Darwinian perspective had destructive effects on the promulgation of racist ideology. Ham says, "In the 1800s before Darwinian Evolution was popularized, most people used the word 'races' to refer to such groups as 'the English race,' 'Irish race,' and so on. However, this all changed in 1859…In *The Descent of Man*, Darwin popularized the idea of different races of people – lower races, higher races, primitive races, advanced races, and so on."[36] He quotes Hunter's *A Civic Biology Presented in Problems* (a popular biology textbook published in 1914) which said, "The Races of Man. At the present time there exist upon the earth five races … the highest of all, the Caucasians,

---

[34] Stephen Jay Gould, *Ontogeny and Phylogeny* (Cambridge, MA: Belknap Press of Harvard University Press, 1977) 127. Cited in Ham and Ware, *One Race One Blood*, 81.

[35] Charles Darwin, *The Descent of Man* (Chicago, IL: William Benton in Great Books of the Western World, 1952) 336. Cited in Ham and Ware, *One Race One Blood*, 56-57.

[36] Ham and Ware, *One Race One Blood*, 80-81.

represented by the civilized white inhabitants of Europe and America."[37] Hence, the focus of a dispensational theology of race and ethnicity should be on ethnicity and not distinctions of race based on the color of one's skin which are neither biblically or scientifically accurate. The focus on ethnicity shows the values God gives to all ethnicities (counteracting the modern tendency towards color blindness) while reducing the likelihood that people will prioritize the color of their skin over their love for their neighbor or even worse see identification with people of similar skin color as more important than identifying with Christ.

In light of these distinctions, how should one approach this issue? George Yancey in his book *Beyond Racial Gridlock: Embracing Mutual Responsibility* divides approaches to the issue of racism into two categories: individualist and structuralist. He defines the individualist definition of racism "holds that racial strife is the result of individuals choosing to act in a racist manner."[38] The individualist perspective often conflates the concepts of prejudice and racism. The CBS faculty committee that designed the Biblical and Theological Rationale for Cultural Diversity for prejudice, "A sinful disposition or attitude toward a particular racial or ethnic group, or individuals within a specific racial or ethnic group, rooted in stereotypes and faulty opinions about the assumed superiority of one group over another." The same committee defined racism as follows, "Intentional or unintentional ideas, individual practices, and established policies rooted in the belief that one group is superior to another. Such ideas, practices, and policies are designed to create, reproduce, and/or maintain a societal hierarchy and therefore power with the express purposes of disadvantaging other ethnicities through social exclusion, political discrimination, economic marginalization, physical and heart level suffering in response to individual

---

[37] Ham and Ware, *One Race One Blood*, 82.
[38] George Yancey, *Beyond Racial Gridlock: Embracing Mutual Responsibility*, 20.

and institutionalized sin. Racism can be expressed overtly and institutionally through a policy or a law. Relatedly, individual racism is an act by one person intended to inflict pain on another person through for example verbal or physical violence." Prejudice typically is an individual perception of groups whereas racism typically has structural elements in which there is an attempt to ensure one ethnicity has superior experiences to another. However, this definition also allows for individual racist tendencies.

In contrast to the individualist view, the structuralist view argues that "society can perpetuate racism even when individuals in society do not intend to be racist."[39] He gives an example of how terrible public schools in poor urban areas are often the result of a property tax system that allows wealthier individuals to pay higher taxes for better schools while schools in poor areas have less access to those funds. He then says, "Personal racism is not to blame for the poor education of people of color; we should blame the social structures by which schools are funded."[40] Yancey rightly attributes the source of racism and solutions for racism to sin. He argues that sin keeps both groups from seeking personal accountability and preferring the system that best protects their interest. He writes, "Defining racism in an individualistic manner can help majority group members maintain their advantages. Thus, the individualism of European Americans is at least somewhat connected to their own sin nature and desire to ignore the plight of people of color. ... Likewise, it is in the interest of people of color to focus on historical and contemporary racism to explain the current state of our society... Concentrating on historical and modern forms of institutional racism can ensure that responsibility for all racial problems will ultimately

---

[39] Yancey, *Beyond Racial Gridlock*, 21-22.
[40] Yancey, *Beyond Racial Gridlock*, 22.

lead to the feet of European Americans. Of course this approach absolves people of color of accountability for their own shortcomings."[41]

In light of these distinctions, Yancey proposes four secular models of racial reconciliation, two individual and two structural:

Individual:

1. Colorblindness – Colorblindness achieves racial reconciliation by ignoring race and forgetting the discriminating of the past while arguing that the best world is one in which no one sees racial or ethnic differences.

2. Anglo-conformity – Racial minorities are encouraged to adopt European American values so that minorities can imitate how whites moved up the economic/social ladder.

Structural:

3. Multiculturalism – Reconciliation occurs by emphasizing the value and worth of minority cultures.

4. White responsibility – White responsibility places the blame for racism at the feet of majority culture and argues that minority cultures cannot be racist because they lack the economic and social power of whites.[42]

Each of these models are inadequate because they do not embrace a mutual responsibility approach in which both majority and minority cultures are encouraged to own and repent of their part in racism. They also tend to focus on what the other group needs to do instead of having what Ware calls "us and us" conversations.[43]

---

[41] Yancey, *Beyond Racial Gridlock*, 25.
[42] Yancey, *Beyond Racial Gridlock*, 27-28.
[43] Ham and Ware, *One Race One Blood*, 139.

Towards a Biblical Theology on Race and Ethnicity

As part of the 2014-2019 strategic plan, the College of Biblical Studies was tasked with Developing a Biblical and Theological Rationale for Cultural Diversity. Our President, Dr. Bill Blocker, met with a committee of faculty and gave them a fresh new challenge of not focusing on external items like social justice or Critical Race Theory but focusing on what the Bible actually says on the topic. The Dallas Statement on Social Justice and the gospel had already come out and the committee felt that it did not define terms like Critical Race Theory and intersectionality well and primarily addressed a straw man view of the issues.[44] Instead, he asked the faculty to summarize what the Bible says about ethnicity and unity. We appreciated Dr. Blocker's counsel and elected to simply start with the Bible and develop our theological framework from there instead of trying to respond to contemporary trends. Dr. Blocker himself was the one who had given me the idea of framing the conversation of systemic racism in terms of the theological concepts of depravity and the world system. He also helped me understand the concept of privilege could possibly be better understood as blessing. With this in mind, the committee worked for several months to develop the statement that is included at the end of this chapter. It does not summarize everything the Bible says about the topic, but it provides a starting point for discussion and understanding. The appendix of this chapter provides the statement that not only the faculty approved but the Board of Directors as well. It includes some of the concepts of ethnicity versus race and provides practical biblical solutions on how to combat racism.

---

[44] For a good evaluation of this statement see Gary Gromacki, "Review on the Statement of Social Justice and the Gospel," (paper presented at the annual meeting of the Council on Dispensational Hermeneutics, Kansas City, MO, 18 September 2020).

SUMMARY

This section attempted to provide a dispensational approach to understanding race and ethnicity. It utilized Chafer's methodology of reviewing any and every source known to the mind of man as part of the development of a biblical and theological perspective on the matter. Furthermore, I focused on the dispensational concept of literal interpretation as the intent of the original author to the original audience. In order understand what CRT advocates believe, I reviewed the work of Kimberlé Crenshaw who is known as one of the original advocates of Critical Race Theory and intersectionality. While the Critical Race Theory system was rejected as being contrary to the Bible some nuggets of truth could be incorporated into a theology of race and ethnicity. Once that process was completed, I reviewed the work of dispensationalist Charles Ware in the book he wrote with Ken Ham called *One Race One Blood: The Biblical Answer to Racism*. This research defended a biblical and biological argument that there is only one race: the human race and distinctions made by the color of one's skin are an unbiblical human construct that is intended to divide rather than unite. In contrast to a model that is largely based on race, an argument was made in support of the mutual responsibility model proposed by Yancey in *Beyond Racial Gridlock: Embracing Mutual Responsibility* as well as to emphasize the more biblical concept of ethnicity (i.e., tribe, tongue, and nation). What follows next is a statement that the board and faculty of the College of Biblical Studies developed in order to help the Body of Christ determine what the Bible says about these matters.

APPENDIX: A BIBLICAL AND THEOLOGICAL RATIONALE FOR CULTURAL DIVERSITY

I. Introduction

The College of Biblical Studies maintains an unwavering commitment to see God glorified, the gospel proclaimed, the Bible affirmed, and the church unified in an environment that welcomes ethnic and cultural diversity. Our dedication to teaching and practicing truth in love, discipling multiethnic Christian servant leaders, and providing transformative instruction for God's glory is undergirded and fueled by our obedience to both the Great Commandments and the Great Commission (Mt 22:36-40, 28:18-20). As we seek to love God and our neighbors well and to make Christian disciples of all nations, the College prayerfully and actively pursues ethnic unity and reconciliation with humility, gentleness, patience, grace, biblical truth, and love (Eph 4:1-4, 15, 32; Col 3:12-15; 4:6).

The College's mission to glorify God by educating and equipping multi-ethnic Christian leaders to impact the world for Christ grounds itself on a biblical and theological worldview in which the Triune God glorifies Himself through unity and diversity. The pursuit of Christian unity in the midst of diversity has its roots within the Triune nature of God. The Scripture declares that there is only one God (Dt 4:35, 6:4; 1Ki 8:60; Ne 9:6; Is 45:21-22), and He exists from eternity in three Persons: Father (Ge 1:1; Ge 17:1; Ex 3:14; Jer 32:17; Eph 1:3; Php 1:2), Son (Jn 1:1, 14; 8:58; 20:28; Ro 9:5; Col 2:9; Heb 1:1-4), and Holy Spirit (Ge 1:2; Jn 6:63; Ac 5:1-10; 2Co 3:17; Ps 139:7-10). Each person of the Trinity is fully God and therefore equal in power, glory, and honor (Is 42:8; Mt 3:13-17; 28:18-20; Jn 17:1-5; 2Co 13:14; Eph 1:20-22; 2Th 2:13-14; Rev 1:8). Thus, the Father is God; the Son is God; the Holy

Biblical Distinctions Applied 211

Spirit is God, yet there are not three gods, but one God.[45] Likewise, the distinction of persons is always maintained within the Godhead. The Father is, from eternity, the Father, never the Son or the Spirit (Is 63:16; Ps 2:7; Mt 3:13-17; Jn 3:16, 12:28; Eph 1:17; 2Th 1:2); likewise, the Son is, from eternity, the Son, never the Father or the Spirit (Jn 1:18, 5:19-23, 20:17; Eph 1:7, 2:18); finally, the Spirit is, from eternity, the Spirit, never the Father or Son (Jn 16:13-15, Ro 8:9, Gal 4:6, 1Co 2:10-11, Eph 1:13-14). This unity of divine essence coupled with the diversity of divine personhood is foundational within the Trinitarian life. Thus, when God chose to create man in His image (Ge 1:26-27) and for His glory (Is 43:6-7; 1Co 10:31; Ps 24:1, 100:2-3), the Lord ensured that His creation reflected both the unity and diversity that characterizes His own divine nature.

The Scripture declares that the Lord is a God of peace, not disorder (Ro 15:33, 1Co 14:33, Phil 4:9). Therefore, unity and diversity can coexist in harmony because it is exemplified within the Triune God (Mt 3:16-17; Jn 14:26-27; 16:5-15; 17:10, 21-22). For example, when the Lord created those who would bear His image (the imago dei), He created one human race comprised of two genders: male and female (Ge 1:26-27), and this the Lord deemed very good (Ge 1:31). An "image" should reflect the character and qualities of that which it represents. Thus, the oneness of humanity and the distinction of the two genders ensured that human beings properly "imaged" the unity and diversity within God.[46]

---

[45] "The Athanasian Creed" from John H. Louth, ed., *Creeds of the Churches: A Reader in Christian Doctrine from the Bible to the Present, 3rd Edition* (Louisville, KY: John Knox Press, 1982), 705. See also "The Definition of Chalcedon" from Louth, *Creeds of the Churches,* 34-36.

[46] While men and women are image bearers, the Lord intentionally created both men and women with God-given, complementary distinctions that not only highlight His unity and diversity but also bring Him great glory. For additional information on the College's position on biblical gender roles, see http://www.cbshouston.edu/gender-roles.

II. Recognizing Human Dignity in light of the *Imago Dei*

God created human beings with material bodies and immaterial spirits, thereby giving them the ability to relate both to God and man (Ge 2:7, 16, 22). As God reigns over creation, He gave man authority to serve as His vice-regents over the earth, and He commands them to "be fruitful, multiply, fill the earth, subdue it, and rule over His creation" (Ge 1:1-2:25, Is 45:18). Having this kind of authority aligns with the likeness of our creator, God. Moreover, the Scripture states that God breathed the breath of life into Adam, thereby establishing a unique connection between God and His image bearer (Ge 2:7). Thus, "to be human is to image God."[47] As our Creator, the Lord also remains intimately involved in the formation of every subsequent human life (Ps 139:1-3, 13-16). God gives human beings unique worth and sets them apart from all other creatures (Ps 8:4-8).

III. Distinguishing Race and Ethnicity

Given the fact that Adam and Eve are the parents of all humans (Ge 1:26-28; 2:7, 21-25; 3:20; Ro 5:12-17, 1Co 15:45), it makes sense that all human beings are also a part of the same species, *Homo Sapiens*, and today, even scientists agree that there is only one biological "race" of humans.[48]

---

[47] Michael S. Heiser, *The Unseen Realm: Recovering the Supernatural Worldview of the Bible*, First Edition. (Bellingham, WA: Lexham Press, 2015), 42–43. Even though God made human beings in His image, an image is never greater than that which it represents. Therefore, image bearers must worship God, and God alone, as their sovereign Lord and Creator (Ex 20:3-6; Dt 6:13-15; Lk 4:8; Ro 1:18-23).

[48] Ken Ham and Charles Ware, *One Race One Blood: A Biblical Answer to Racism* (Green Forest, AZ: Master Books, 2007), 112. Kindle Edition. For additional scholarly statements regarding the opposition to separate "races," see "AAPA Statement on the Biological Aspects of Race," from the American Association of Physical Anthropologists, http://physanth.org/about/position-statements/biological-aspects-race/. See also the "AAA Statement on Race" from the American Anthropological Association,

While the term "race" is often used as a social construct to denote a person's cultural background coupled with other physiological characteristics (such as skin color), the Bible consistently employs the term *ethnos* (Gr. ἔθνος; cf. "ethnic" and "ethnicity") to describe such distinctives.[49] This understanding is often reflected by missionaries who use the term "people groups" to define "a cluster of human beings that are set apart from others because of their language, culture, geography, or religion."[50] Genesis states that from creation to the time of the Flood, humanity "stood in unbroken genetic relation with

---

https://www.americananthro.org/ConnectWithAAA/Content.aspx?ItemNumber=2583.

[49] Τὸ ἔθνος *(ethnos)* is defined as a body of persons united by kinship, culture, and common traditions, *nation, people,* (cf. Ac 8:9; Mt 24:14, 28:19; Mk 11:17, 13:10). The term is also used to denote "people groups foreign to a specific people group, specifically, those who do not belong to groups professing faith in the God of Israel, such as the nations, Gentiles, unbelievers" (Ac 11:1, 18; 14:5; 21:21; 26:17; Ro 3:29; 9:24; 15:10). Finally, the word describes non-Israelite Christians, Gentiles of Christian congregations composed of more than one nationality and not limited to people of Israel (Ro 16:4, Eph 3:1)." See William Arndt et al., *A Greek-English Lexicon of the New Testament and Other Early Christian Literature (BDAG)* (Chicago: University of Chicago Press, 2000), 276-277.

In addition, the Scripture also uses the term ἡ φυλή *(phylē)* to describe different subgroups within a distinct nation, such as the twelve tribes of Israel (Lk 2:36, Php 3:5, Heb 7:13, Rev 7:4). For example, the tribe *(phylē)* of Reuben is a subgroup of the *ethnos* or "nation" of Israel. See William Arndt, *BDAG*, 1069.

The New Testament also uses the word ὁ γένος *(genos)* to describe a "relatively large people group or nation." William Arndt, *BDAG*, 194. It should be noted, however, that the term can have several different connotations in the NT, including "family" (e.g., Ac 7:13), "descent or origin" (e.g., Rev 22:16), "race of people or nation" (e.g., Ac 7:19, 2Co 11:26, Php 3:5), "nationality" (e.g., Mk 7:26, Ac 4:36) or "kind" (e.g., Mt 13:47, Mk 9:29). See Moisés Silva, ed., *New International Dictionary of New Testament Theology and Exegesis* (Grand Rapids, MI: Zondervan, 2014), 556–557.

Of the terms used, τὸ ἔθνος occurs with the most frequency (162 times). See John Kohlenberger III, Edward W. Goodrick, James A. Swanson, *The Exhaustive Concordance of the Greek New Testament* (Grand Rapids, MI: Zondervan Publishing House, 1995), 250-252.

[50] Ham and Ware, *One Race, One Blood*, 115.

the first [human] pair, so that the human race constitutes not only a specific unity, a unity in the sense that all men share the same human nature, but also a genetic or genealogical unity."[51] Thus, Adam and Eve, along with Noah and his descendants (who repopulated the post-diluvian earth, per Ge 9:1-7, 19; 10:32) possessed the same genetic coding for all subsequent human *ethnē* or "ethnicities." Just as God displayed His unity and diversity by creating one human race with two genders, He also reveals the same unity and diversity by creating one human race with various ethnicities. Paul also affirms this in Acts 17:26, when he notes that "God made of *one* [italics mine] every nation [*ethnos*] of man to dwell on all the face of the earth."[52] Despite the fact that "contemporary notion of 'races' is foreign to Scripture, 'ethnicity' more accurately describes the real, observable distinctions of nationality, language, culture, and sometimes religion."[53] Given its alignment with the biblically-used "*ethnos*" rather than the culturally-defined term "race," the word "ethnicity" will be used throughout this statement.

IV. Recounting Sin and Disunity in History

Despite the aforementioned, God-ordained, human unity in the midst of ethnic diversity, the intrusion of sin fractured the God-human (Ge 3:8-11, 22-24; 6:5-6; Is 59:2), man-woman (Ge 3:12, 16), human-world (Ge 3:17-19), human-human relationship (Ge 4:1-16). Sin manifests itself with both a nature (Eph 2:1-3) and behavior that is hostile toward God and others (Ro 1:18-32). With our rebellion, humans traded our once upright, holy nature for a nature that is characterized by death, disorder, and destruction (Ge 6:5-

---

[51] Louis Berkhof, *Systematic Theology* (Grand Rapids, MI: Wm. B. Eerdmans Publishing Company, 1938), 188.

[52] Berkhof, *Systematic Theology*.

[53] Thabiti Anyabwile, "Many Ethnicities, One Race," from the *9Marks Journal*, https://www.9marks.org/article/many-ethnicities-one-race/.

6; Ro 5:12-21). While the *imago dei* is still present within all human beings, it is gravely marred, perverted, and tarnished by sin (Ro 3:23; Jas 3:9-10). Sin is defined as any word, action, and/or desire that violates the word of God and/or conscience and alienates us from the Lord. We sin by actively breaking God's word or by not performing what is commanded of us in God's word. Rather than reflecting divine beauty and peace, our God-given distinctions in personhood, gender, and ethnicity have been sinfully twisted to serve as instruments of division and hostility. This human failure to reflect God's glory rightly and to represent His image accurately assaults the very character of God. Because of His goodness, God simply cannot let false imagers abide (Ps 100:5, 107:1; Hab 1:13; Na 1:2; Ro 1:18; 1Pe 1:14-16).

After sin entered the world (Ge 3:1-24), human beings now have the tendency to affirm either unity or diversity to the exclusion of the other and to use their own preferences for sinful means. For example, at the Tower of Babel, human beings stood united in the common purpose of making a tower that reached to heaven, thereby attempting to make themselves god-like (Ge 11:1-4). For this rebellion, the Lord scattered humanity across the earth and also divided the earth into different languages (Ge 11:5-9). Thus, humans exploited "unity" for idolatrous means. Likewise, Scripture also notes that man will not hesitate to renounce diversity in an attempt to elevate self. For instance, when Miriam and Aaron spoke against Moses's Cushite wife (Nu 12:1), the Lord viewed their ethnic hostility as a rejection of His authority and Moses's leadership, and He judged their rebellion by giving Miriam a skin disease (Nu 12:4-13). Thus, Miriam's attempt to draw "separation" between a man and his Cushite wife directly led to her "separation" from her own people (Nu 12:14-15).[54] In both cases, God judged the exploitation of unity

---

[54] While some have sought to use Scripture to argue against interracial marriage, the Bible issues no such prohibition. The Lord has consistently commanded His people to marry those who worship Him and Him alone (Ex 34:11-16, Dt 7:1-6; Jos

and diversity. Both must be maintained, and both must be used to glorify the Creator, not the created.

Unfortunately, within the history of the church, the Bible has been used as a basis for ethnic prejudice and discrimination. For example, Dutch Reformed Christians used the Bible to sanction apartheid in South Africa during the modern era.[55] Throughout World War II, Hitler and the Third Reich wielded the scriptures in the philosophy and practice of Nazism.[56] Finally, as one of the most blatant historical instances when the Bible has been used in this way, some have used the "curse of Ham" as a biblical justification for slavery and mistreatment of people of African descent.[57] However, the text declares that it was Canaan, Ham's son, who was cursed, not Ham himself (Ge 9:24-27). Later, the text states that Ham fathered "Cush, Mizraim, Put, and Canaan" (Gen 10:6). While Cush, Mizraim, and Put likely correspond to modern Sudan, South Sudan, Ethiopia, Egypt, and Libya, which are in Africa, Canaan became the father of nations that were in

---

23:11-13; 1Ki 11:1-8; Ezr 9:1-3; 1Co 7:39; 2Co 6:14); therefore, inter-faith marriage, not interracial/interethnic marriage, violates divine law. See also John Piper, Did Moses Marry a Black Woman?" https://www.9marks.org/article/did-moses-marry-black-woman/.

[55] Several essay collections feature historical and theological analysis related to South Africa, Christianity, and apartheid. See R. Drew Smith, et. al., *Contesting Post-Racialism: Conflicted Churches in the United States and South Africa* (Jackson: University Press of Mississippi, 2015); R. Drew Smith, ed., *Freedom's Distant Shores: American Protestants and Post-Colonial Alliances with Africa* (Waco: Baylor University Press, 2006); William E. Van Vugt and G. Daan Cloete, *Race and Reconciliation in South Africa* (Lanham, MD: Lexington Books, 2000).

[56] Important studies of this topic include Susannah Heschel, *The Aryan Jesus: Christian Theologians and the Bible in Nazi Germany* (Princeton: Princeton University Press, 2010); Richard Steigman-Gall, *The Holy Reich: Nazi Conceptions of Christianity, 1919-1945* (Cambridge: Cambridge University Press, 2004); Doris L. Bergen, *Twisted Cross: The German Christian Movement in the Third Reich* (Chapel Hill: University of North Carolina Press, 1996).

[57] Colin Kidd, *The Forging of Races: Race and Scripture in the Protestant Atlantic World, 1600-2000*, (Cambridge: Cambridge University Press, 2006).

the vicinity of the current Middle East (Ge 10:15-20).[58] While the "curse of Ham" has often been leveled against blacks, nothing in the text of Scripture states that the Canaanites were dark-skinned. True to Noah's prophecy, God drove the Canaanites out of the land due to their wickedness (Dt 9:4-5). Therefore, the "curse of Canaan" has nothing to do with those of African descent, and its use to justify the African slave trade not only serves as a prime example of poor exegesis, but it also functions as a blatant misuse of Scripture.

V. Envisioning Gospel-Centered Unity

In an attempt to press for unity, many within society and the church have tried to function as if they are "color blind" when it comes to engaging those of different ethnicities. While their efforts may be well-intentioned, they are also misguided. Unity and diversity should not be viewed as an "either-or" but as a "both-and." The Lord created people of different colors, complexions, and ethnicities. We should see and honor His creative work and give glory to the Creator for what He has done. We should see the distinctions and honor them as reflections of divine glory: He creates one human race (thereby establishing the unity of His image bearers) with different ethnicities (thereby cementing the diversity of His creative order).

---

[58] John Piper, *Racial Reconciliation: Unfolding Bethlehem's Fresh Initiative #3, Racial Harmony Sunday*. Sermon Delivered January 14, 1996. https://www.desiringgod.org/messages/racial-reconciliation. See also Gordon J. Wenham, *Genesis 1–15*, vol. 1, *Word Biblical Commentary* (Dallas: Word Incorporated, 1998), 221. In addition, see J. Daniel Hays, *From Every People and Nation: A Biblical Theology of Race*, ed. D. A. Carson, vol. 14, *New Studies in Biblical Theology* (Downers Grove, IL; England: InterVarsity Press; Apollos, 2003), 34. See also Stephen R. Haynes, *Noah's Curse: The Biblical Justification of American Slavery*. New York, NY: Oxford University Press, 2002. Sylvester A. Johnson, *The Myth of Ham in Nineteenth-Century American Christianity: Race, Heathens, and the People of God*. New York, NY: Palgrave Macmillan Publishers, 2004).

The Lord commanded that His people be one as the Triune God is one (Jn 17:11, 20). As each member of Godhead retains His individual personhood while sharing full deity, different groups maintain their ethnic distinctiveness while sharing full humanity. Therefore, unity does not equal uniformity. In fact, the Scripture does not shy away from ethnic diversity but recognizes it openly (Jer 13:23, Jn 4:9, Mk 7:24-29, Ac 8:26-40, Ac 16:1). If the Scripture, the very word of God, recognizes such ethnic distinctions, then the people of God should follow suit. At the same time, solidarity of purpose does not mandate unanimity of action. Brothers and sisters who fully agree on the need for ethnic unity can, and often will, disagree on how to accomplish that unity. Believers must rely upon wisdom, prayer, and love in order to achieve diversity in a way that honors God and promotes peace (Eph 4:1-7, Jas 1:5, Ro 12:9-12; 1Jn 4:11). Since God creates all people in His image, He therefore gives all "ethnic groups the same status and unique value that comes from being His image bearer."[59]

Christ, the great reconciler, is the light of the world (Jn 1:9, 8:12), and He has called a people unto Himself, the church, who reflect His image by serving as lights in the world (Mt 5:14-16).[60] Now, every person can be reconciled to God through the lifesaving blood of Jesus Christ (Gal 3:26-29, Col 1:19-20, 1Jn 2:1-2). As the Lamb of God, Jesus takes away the sins of the world and gave Himself as a ransom for *all* men and women, regardless of ethnicity (Jn 1:29, 1Pe 1:19, 1Ti 2:5-6). The Lord lauded the faith and

---

[59] Hays, *From Every People and Nation: A Biblical Theology of Race*, 202.

[60] The one, holy, catholic, and apostolic church of Jesus Christ is also comprised of different members with distinctive Spirit-given gifts (1Co 12:1-31). Thus, by divine ordination, the bride of Christ also reflects the unity and diversity of the Triune God. Therefore, in His creative work, the Triune God intentionally displays His unity in the creation of one human race and one church; at the same time, He deliberately shows His diversity in the creation of two different, complementary genders; various people groups and ethnicities; and distinctive, edifying gifts among the saints.

righteous acts of Gentiles (Lk 4:24-30, Lk 10:25-37), and he calls His people to proclaim His gospel message to all nations for His glory (Mt 28:18-20). Just as He began the proclamation of the gospel to Gentiles, Samaritans, and people from various nationalities (Mt 4:14-17, Jn 4:1-42), He calls His church to take the gospel to Jerusalem, Judea, Samaria, and the ends of the earth (Ac 1:8). At Pentecost, the Holy Spirit fell on people of many different ethnicities so that all could hear the gospel in their own distinctive languages and take that good news to their countries of origin (Ac 2:1-13). The same Holy Spirit who was present at creation (Ge 1:2), the same Holy Spirit who raised Jesus from the dead (Ro 8:11), is the same Holy Spirit who indwells believers, regardless of ethnicity (1Co 3:16, 6:19; Ac 10:1-48). Empowered by the Holy Spirit whom the Father has sent through Jesus (Jn 14:26), true disciples commit themselves to obeying the Lord and fulfilling His Great Commission. Therefore, it comes as no surprise to see Peter and the apostles proclaiming the good news in Jerusalem (Ac 1-7), Philip preaching the word in Samaria (Ac 8), other leaders announcing the message to Judea (Ac 9-12), and Paul taking the gospel to the ends of the earth (Ac 13-28).

A central aspect of the aforementioned gospel message lies in the fact that salvation is of the Jews (Jn 4:22).[61] While the Lord first took the gospel to the nation of Israel (Mt 10:6, 15:24), it has always been the sovereign plan of God to extend salvation to the Gentiles (Is 49:6, Ro 11:1-36). Because of Jesus Christ's perfect salvific work, anyone who receives His message and ministry through faith is no longer an estranged enemy of God (Ro 10:9-13,

---

[61] Throughout the Scripture, the Lord describes Israel as His treasured possession out of all the other peoples on the earth (Dt 7:6, 14:2, 26:18; Ps 135:4). However, the text also declares that Israel's special status had nothing to do with her own *inherent* worth; on the contrary, Israel's election depended solely upon the sovereign grace and love of the Lord who wills as He chooses (Dt 7:7-8). The Scripture also declares that all have sinned and fallen short of God's glory, regardless of ethnicity (Ro 2:12-29; 3:10, 23; Eph 2:1-3). In Christ, the Father elects and adopts believers of all ethnicities to the praise of His glorious grace (Eph 1:1-6, 2:4-22).

Col 1:21-23). Even though Gentiles have been engrafted into the people of God, this does not allow anyone to overlook the importance of the Jewish nation throughout creative and redemptive history (Ge 12:1-3; Ro 9:1-5, 11:17-24). In His own flesh, Jesus tore down the barrier of the dividing wall between Jew and Gentile and created a new body, from the two, in Himself, thereby establishing peace (Eph 2:11-21). Therefore, the church of God denounces and decries any attempt to rebuild that wall through inclinations towards and acts of anti-Semitism. The head of the church, Jesus Christ, was born a Jew, lived as a Jew, died as a Jew, and was raised from the dead as a Jew.[62] He intercedes for His people, and He will come again, as a Jew, to reign over the millennial kingdom and ultimately, the new heavens and the new earth. Since anti-Semitism, at its core, blasphemes God the Son, it remains wholly rejected by the Son's church.

VI. Practicing Gospel-Centered Unity

In the clearest terms, the College of Biblical Studies emphatically and unequivocally denounces all forms of ethnic supremacy, racism/racialization, ethnic division, and ethnic prejudice (i.e. what Jas 2:1-13 describes as personal favoritism, making distinctions, and partiality) because it portrays a false image of God's Tri-unity, violates the two Great Commandments (Mt 22:36-40), and denigrates His good work of creation. The Christian[63] cannot and

---

[62] Russell Moore, *If You Hate Jews, You Hate Jesus*,
https://www.russellmoore.com/2018/10/28/if-you-hate-jews-you-hate-jesus/.

[63] The Christian (ὁ Χριστιανός) can best be described as "a Christ partisan, one who associates or identifies with Christ" (See *BDAG*, 1090). Therefore, the Christian's primary allegiance belongs to Christ. As His ambassadors, we represent Jesus and His interests, not ourselves or our own interests (2Co 5:20). Therefore, our adherence to Christ must reign supreme and supersede all other relationships, loyalties, or cultural identifiers, including ethnicity and/or land of origin or residence. Christ's commitments must be the Christian's commitments, for we are His (Mt 10:24-25, Lk 6:40, 1Co 3:23, Eph 5:1-2). In His flesh and by His blood, Jesus has created one new

Biblical Distinctions Applied 221

must not be silent in the face of ethnic prejudice. As she proclaims the gospel to all nations (Mk 13:10, Rev 14:6), the church must perform her duty and call sin for what it is: sin. While the Lord has given us ethnic distinctions by His own sovereign choice, He also affirms that our heavenly citizenship dwarfs any other allegiance to country, tribe, or nationality (Php 1:27, 3:20; Mk 11:17). Ethnic supremacy is a moral evil that runs counter to and remains incompatible with biblical Christianity. The gospel serves as the antidote for this evil. Excusing, ignoring, dismissing, or engaging in ethnic prejudice constitutes a break in our adherence to Christ (Gal 3:26-29). Therefore, the sin of ethnic bias and/or economic exploitation/discrimination must be actively addressed, not passively engaged (Ac 6:1-7, Gal 2:11-21). Whether we battle ethnic superiority within our own hearts (the flesh), with the larger culture and societal structures (the world), or against our old foe (the devil) who brings disunity and hatred toward others (Eph 2:1-3), we wage war against sin in a way that brings honor to Christ (Ro 6:6, 11-14, 7:23, 8:12-13; Jas 4:4-10). Like any earthly institution, CBS has missed the mark in its past and continues to grow in its present regarding ethnic reconciliation; nevertheless, we strive toward and labor for a future that is marked by Christian love, peace, unity, and diversity across all ethnicities.

VII. Pursuing Reconciliation, Justice, and Unity

As ambassadors for Christ, we must represent Him faithfully as ministers of reconciliation and press toward godly unity and fellowship with

---

body, the church, which is composed of saints from all ethnicities (Eph 2:11-22; Rev 5:9-10, 7:9). The nations are the Messiah's inheritance (Ps 2:7-8), and since evangelizing and making disciples of those nations remained a clear priority of Jesus Christ (Mt 28:18-20; Ac 1:8, 9:15-16, 22:21, 26:14-18), it should be of the utmost importance to His followers, who only have access to God as a result of Christ's perfect work and by the power of the eternal Spirit (Ro 5:2; Eph 2:18, 3:12; Heb 9:13-14).

brothers and sisters from all backgrounds (1Co 1:10, 2Co 5:18-21, Eph 4:1-6, Gal 3:28, Col 3:11). The pursuit of reconciliation is not easy; it requires sacrifice, suffering, prayer, and toil (Lk 9:23-26, Col 1:24-29, Eph 6:18). It consists in viewing others as more important than ourselves (Php 2:3), serving as a slave to all because we are slaves to Jesus Christ (Ro 6:15-23, 1Co 9:19-23), forgiving one another as Christ has forgiven us (Mk 11:25, Col 3:13), and embracing fellow brothers and sisters of different ethnic or social standings (Phm 1:10-20). Standing united against ethnic animus means submitting to God, recognizing and resisting the devil's scheme to sow disunity by dividing people along ethnic lines (Gal 3:28, Col 3:11, Jas 4:7), confessing individual and corporate sins (Jas 5:16, 1 Jn 1:9), purifying our hearts (Jas 4:8), bearing one another's burdens (Gal 6:2), humbling ourselves (Jas 4:10), outdoing one another in honor (Ro 12:10), and showing affection to each other with brotherly love (Mt 5:23-24; Ro 12:10; 1Jn 2:9; 1Jn 4:7-8, 20). Though we have unity in Christ, this does not necessarily mean that members of God's household will have the same opinions or arrive at the same conclusions. Nevertheless, as brothers and sisters in the Lord, we must be "quick to listen, slow to speak, and slow to become angry" (Jas 1:19), particularly as we engage each other on issues regarding ethnic harmony and diversity. Believers are aliens and sojourners in this world, and our witness should proclaim us as such (1Pe 2:11). Consequently, the unbelieving world should see Christians incarnating the gospel message by loving one another without holding grudges or seeking its own at the expense of others (1Co 13:5). Despite the fact that reconciliation and unity across ethnic lines may be met with hostility (Gal 2:11-14), Christian disciples follow the mandate of the Lord to love one another sacrificially (Jn 15:12-17, 1Jn 4:7-21).

At the final consummation, God will display the beauty and grandeur of His creative and redemptive work. According to Revelation 7:9, the Apostle John sees "a great multitude that no one could number, from every nation, from all tribes and peoples and languages, standing before the throne and before the Lamb." In addition, that multitude cries out with a loud voice, 'Salvation belongs to our God who sits on the throne, and to the Lamb!'" This multitude stands together as one, and the different members openly praise the Lord with "a" loud voice. "When [different ethnic groups] unite in worship to God, the beauty of their praise will echo the depth and greatness of God's beauty far more than if the redeemed were from only a few different people groups."[64] God has therefore sovereignly ordained that unity and diversity typifies heavenly worship. Moreover, the fact that all nations will worship God underscores the fact that He is universally praiseworthy.[65] "The fame, greatness, and worth of an object of beauty increases in proportion to the diversity of those who recognize its beauty. ... Thus the diversity of the source of human admiration will testify to [God's] incomparable glory."[66] Finally, the new Jerusalem boasts the tree of life, the leaves of which serve for the healing of the nations (Rev 22:2). Since Christians serve the Triune Lord and pray for His will to be done on earth as it is in heaven (Mt 6:9-13), both the local and the universal church must strive to value and embrace the unity and diversity of the One whose image we bear (Col 3:10-11).

As Christ adherents, the members of the CBS community strive to live out our heavenly citizenship (Php 1:27, 3:20) by remaining rooted in God's word, focused on God the Son, led by God the Spirit, and committed to God the Father. We seek to value all that Christ values (Mt 6:19-21, 33). God's glory is demonstrated through the proclamation of the gospel among the nations; therefore, CBS remains resolute in its commitment to the pursuit of God's glory by being discipled and making disciples (including faculty, staff,

---

[64] John Piper, *Let the Nations Be Glad: The Supremacy of God in Missions, Third Edition* (Grand Rapids, MI: Baker Academic Publishers, 2010), 222.
[65] Piper, *Let the Nations*.
[66] Piper, *Let the Nations*, 222-223.

students, and board members) who recognize the value of and work toward ethnic reconciliation and unity.

VIII. A Prayer to God

O Triune God, You are the sovereign author and giver of life, and Your very nature reflects perfect unity and diversity. Thank You for creating human beings of different ethnicities, backgrounds, and cultures in Your image, according to Your likeness, and for Your glory.

Father, help us to be honest with You, ourselves, and one another about areas in which we need to grow in our love for You and our neighbors. For the sake of Christian fellowship (*koinonia*), may our commitment to the pursuit of ethnic reconciliation and unity far outweigh any misplaced allegiance to our own comfort and convenience. When we fail to love You and others rightly, convict Your people, by the power of the Holy Spirit, to recognize our error and to call it for what it is: sin. Forgive us, Lord, when we disparage, belittle, or dismiss others on the basis of their ethnicity or race. We repent of this, and we ask for Your forgiveness. Help Your church to be one, as You are one. Give Your sons and daughters sacrificial, other-centered, Spirit-driven agape love for people of every tribe, language, people, and nation. May the world know that we are Yours by a love that is demonstrated as we listen humbly to one another, intercede faithfully for one another, and engage intentionally with one another, across all ethnic lines, for the advancement of the gospel.

Lord, we present this document to You, and we thank You for allowing us to participate in the work of Your ministry. May this work glorify You and strengthen Your church. As ministers of reconciliation and ambassadors for Your Son, use us, in any way that You see fit, as instruments of Your love, justice, truth, righteousness, and peace. Father, bring us shalom and be our shalom through the Prince of Shalom, Jesus Christ. In His name and by Your Spirit we pray. Amen.

Chapter 9 – On Antisemitism
Social Justice, Antisemitism, and Anti-Zionism in Historical and Biblical Perspective
Mike Stallard

INTRODUCTION

Recently, my ministry took me to the country of Poland where I had the opportunity to visit the Nazi concentration and death camp at Auschwitz-Birkenau for the first time. I asked the Polish guide if he knew who Tadeusz Borowski was, and he gladly shared information with me about this famous Polish poet and writer who had lived in the very buildings through which I was walking. My interest in Borowski (1922-1951) goes back to a Ph.D. seminar where I was required to read his collection of autobiographical short stories entitled *This Way for the Gas, Ladies and Gentlemen*.[1] Borowski, a Gentile, was arrested by the Nazis in Warsaw and spent 1943-1945 imprisoned at various places like Auschwitz and Dachau. His fiancé was placed in Birkenau. Due to his youthful, physical strength as well as cunning he was able to survive till the camps were liberated.

---

[1] The short stories comprising this work were written shortly after World War II. The collection of all of his writings was published in 1954, comprising five volumes. The collection in *This Way for the Gas* I assume is a subset of his collected works which was not published in Poland until 1959. It appeared in the United States in 1967. The copy I use is Tadeusz Borowski, *This Way for the Gas, Ladies and Gentlemen* translated by Barbara Vedder (New York: Penguin Books, 1976). In the Introduction, Jan Kott (translated by Michael Kandel) describes the collection as "one of the cruelest of testimonies to what men did to men, and a pitiless verdict that anything can be done to a human being" (12).

Borowski opened his short history "This Way for the Gas" with the words "All of us walk around naked. The delousing is finally over, and our striped suits are back from the tanks of Cyclone B solution, an efficient killer of lice in clothing and of men in gas chambers."[2] The concentration camp was a bundle of contradictions. Things that were helpful – killing lice – were deadly also to humans. One of Borowski's jobs at Auschwitz was to load and help sort through the belongings dumped on the ramp by the trains that brought mostly Jews. The Jews were told that they were going to take a shower and could come back to get their belongings. Instead, most of them – men, women, and children – were gassed and put in the ovens. The volume of belongings – clothes, shoes, hats, meat, sausages, bread, cheese, blankets, coats, briefcases, and drink – was enormous because there were hundreds or thousands on each transport that came in. Those who helped with the large piles of belongings were inmates at Auschwitz. They survived on food they were able to set aside for themselves from the ramp (from the food left behind by the Jews) and which the Nazi guards allowed them to keep. This encouraged them to work hard at their jobs. Borowski records a comment by one of the other helpers: "They can't run out of people, or we'll starve to death in this blasted camp. All of us live on what they bring." Yet they all knew what was going on. In this context, Borowski records asking another one of the prisoners helping at the ramp, "Listen, Henri, are we good people?" While the motivations for suicide may be complicated, one must wonder to what extent Tadeusz was bothered by his conscience over these things. He had survived at the expense of so many who had not. In his small apartment in Warsaw in 1951 (when he was just twenty-nine years old), he

---

[2] Borowski, 29.

turned on the gas and killed himself. Apparently, there were victims of the Holocaust after it was over.³

The Holocaust event has colored theological discussions since that time. Some Jewish people as well as some Gentiles have abandoned belief in God because of what He allowed to take place. Maybe He is not really there; or if He is, he is either finite or possesses diminished love. Some Jewish thinkers attribute the Holocaust to Christianity either mistakenly believing the Nazis to be a movement within Christianity or noting the climate of antisemitism in so-called Christian Germany that allowed National Socialism to be promoted. Moreover, various versions of dual covenant theology have been proposed, some of them part of an ecumenical thrust to find a way to bring Jews and Christians together through theological statements.⁴ The problem of evil in Christian apologetics now has its ultimate historical hurdle to overcome. Consequently, in one of the strangest ironies in history, antisemitism is on the rise in the contemporary world proving once again that sin never seems to allow us to learn from history. An additional irony is that

---

³ In fact, Nazi history is so overpowering, there are twenty-six memorial and education centers in just one northwest section of Germany alone, which is a sampling from the whole country. See Christine Hartung and Ulrike Schrader, eds., *Response to History*, trans. Joseph Swann (Wuppertal-Munster: National Socialist Presbyteries and Memorials, 2015). Out of the voluminous literature on the Holocaust as well as historical research of persecution of Jews in Eastern Europe prior to the Holocaust, two resources that I find useful are Raul Hilberg, *The Destruction of the European Jews* (New York: Holmes & Meier, 1985) and S. M. Dubnow, *History of the Jews in Russia and Poland: From the Earliest Times until the Present Day*, 2 Vols (Philadelphia, PA: The Jewish Publication Society of America, 1916). Dubnow, a Jewish historian, was killed by the Nazis in 1941.

⁴ See Craig A. Blaising, "The Future of Israel as a Theological Question," *JETS* 44 (September 2001): 440-42 and Walter C. Kaiser, *Jewish Christianity: Why Believing Jews and Gentiles Parted Ways in the Early Church* (Silverton, OR: Lampien Press, 2017), 47-48. Dual covenant theology is the view that Jewish people come to God through the Law while Christians come to God through Jesus. There are liberal and conservative expressions of this position.

the Jewish people, especially those who live in Israel, are the ones who are now accused of practicing social injustice and genocide in the world.

WHAT THE HOLOCAUST SHOULD NOT DO

Before we address the upside-down way that social justice is addressed in the Middle East, a few issues need to be discussed to provide a frame to the current historical and theological situation. In particular, I want to organize the discussion around "What the Holocaust Should Not Do." There are several ways in which the Holocaust, as important to history as it is, can cause us to maintain unbalanced and incomplete thinking. Each of these areas needs exploration. The brief introduction provided here should be enough to summarize where our thoughts need to go.

Nazi Killing of Jews More Than Concentration Camps

First, even within Holocaust studies there is often a singular focus on the labor and death camps created by the Nazis to destroy the Jewish people. Certainly these atrocious methods and places deserve a bulk of the attention. However, other avenues in which Jews were killed should not be overlooked. Perhaps the largest and most symbolic example is the massacre of Jewish people in mass at Babyn Yar in the area of Kiev, Ukraine. Naimark laments:

> Regretfully, Western representatives of Holocaust memory often have only the vaguest understanding of the killing of Jews in the east, with the exception of the death camps, Auschwitz being most notable for the sheer power of its symbolism as a "site of memory." The mass shootings of Jews in German-occupied Soviet territory attracted less interest than the horrifying images of the gas chambers and the crematoria. One

Biblical Distinctions Applied   231

could say the same of scholarly examinations in the West of Babyn Yar, which have been strikingly few and relatively recent.[5]

At Babyn Yar, the Germans executed Jewish people mostly by firing-squad beginning on September 29-30, 1941. Around 34,000 were killed on those two days. By the end of the war, 100,000 (mostly Jews) had been killed and buried in mass graves at the ravine called Babyn Yar. Our memory of the Holocaust should not be limited to the death camps, although the numbers there are far greater.

Other Genocides in History

Second, the shadow of the Holocaust should not make any of us forget the other genocides of history. Even in recent times, political leaders "motivated by ideology and immediate gains, are ready to isolate and murder alleged enemies both within their own states and in conquered territories."[6] Most historically aware Christians know about Darfur, Rwanda, Congo, Bosnia, Saddam Hussein's attacks on the Kurds and others, and the tragedy of ISIS persecution of others, especially Christians, in Iraq and Syria. Especially noteworthy for mention is the Turkish genocide of Armenians in the Ottoman Empire during and after World War I. Some estimate that the Turks systematically killed 1.5 million Armenians.[7]

One of the most hypocritical events in history was the presence of Soviets on the panel of judges at the Nuremburg trials following World War II. The Soviet Union under Joseph Stalin had been responsible for the intentional death of millions of people in the two decades leading up to the

---

[5] Norman M. Naimark, "Preface" in *Babyn Yar: History and Memory* edited by Vladyslav Hrynevych and Pau Robert Magocsi (Kiev, Ukraine: Dukh I Litera, 2016), 9.
[6] Ibid., 7.
[7] See Raymond Kévorkian, *The Armenian Genocide: A Complete History* (New York: I. B. Tauris & Co. Ltd., 2011), an exhaustive study of over one thousand pages.

war. Perhaps the most heinous of the government's actions was the premeditated starving of the people of Ukraine, especially in the rural areas of the region, in what has come to be called the "Red Famine" or the Holodomor in 1932-33, although the killing had begun earlier and continued later.[8] Research shows that between 1931 and 1934 more than 3.9 million Ukrainians died of hunger due mostly to Soviet strategy.[9] Although some Jewish people were included in these numbers, the vast majority were from other ethnic backgrounds. This example provides one small portrait within the massive extermination of human beings by communists during the twentieth century, a number cited as high as 100 million souls. As one commentator noted: "the Bolshevik plague that began in Russia was the greatest catastrophe in human history."[10] While Jewish people ended up targets, a wide array of people groups were destroyed as well.[11] A focus on

---

[8] For a definitive, well-documented tragic history of the Soviet regime's attempt to destroy Ukraine for political and economic reasons, see Anne Applebaum, *Red Famine: Stalin's War on Ukraine* (New York: Penguin Books, 2018). The term *Holodomor* comes from the Ukrainian words for "to kill by starvation," or more specifically *holod* (hunger) and *mor* (extermination). See Applebaum, xxiv.

[9] Ibid.

[10] David Satter, "100 Years of Communism—and 100 Million Dead," *The Wall Street Journal*, Online Edition, November 6, 2017.

[11] For an insider view of Stalin's evil, see Roy A. Medvedev, *Let History Judge: The Origins and Consequences of Stalinism* (New York: vintage Books, 1973). Concerning the Jews, Medvedev notes, "After the war Stalin began to exclude all Jews from the Party and government *apparat*, covering his actions with talk about counter-revolutionary activities of international Zionist organizations…" (493). The history of Czarist Russia with its pogroms against Jewish people shows that antisemitism in that part of the world pre-dates the rise of communism. Furthermore, after the breakup of the Soviet Union and the decline of communism, the anti-Semitic tendencies lingered off and on. For a detailed presentation of the relationships in one part of the former Soviet Union, see Paul Robert Magocsi and Yohanan Petrovsky-Shtern, *Jews and Ukrainians: A Millennium of Co-Existence*, 2nd revised ed. (Toronto: University of Toronto Press, 2018). See especially pages 2-3, 55, 83, 151, 188, 248, 276. Although the Jews receive persecution throughout history in Russia or countries near Russia, the history has not been kind to other ethnic groups as well.

the Holocaust should not make us lose sight of other twentieth-century acts of supreme evil.

Antisemitism in Christendom

The most unfortunate discovery, from a Christian point of view, from studying antisemitism over the centuries is the abundant presence of active hatred and antisemitism in Christendom. While an evangelical might take heart in understanding that the largest portion of such developments came through the machinations of the Roman Catholic Church, he will be disappointed when he comes to some of the Reformers and studies what they said about the Jewish people. Three examples are given here as representative of Christendom down through the years. First, the popular church leader John Chrysostom (c. 349-407), Archbishop of Constantinople, who was known as the "golden-mouthed" orator, said the following about the Jews:

> The Jewish people were driven by their drunkenness and plumpness to the ultimate evil; they kicked about, they failed to accept the yoke of Christ, nor did they pull the plow of his teaching. Another prophet hinted at this when he said: "Israel is as obstinate as a stubborn heifer." . . . Although such beasts are unfit for work, they are fit for killing.[12]

While his eight homilies against the Jews contain some valid theological reasoning and use of Scripture, statements such as these provided fodder for Christian attitudes that could never see God as still having a plan for the Jewish people. The harshness of the statements jolts thinking Christians today and certainly offends the Jewish people. In fact, the Nazis used

---

[12] John Chrysostom, *Adversus Judaeos, Homily I*, 5-6.

Chrysostom's teachings to attempt to win the Christians of Germany over to their anti-Semitic agenda:

> These pronouncements became in later centuries a source of inspiration to anti-Semites and also to the Nazis who otherwise had not much patience with Christianity. St. John Chrysostom was frequently quoted and reprinted in the Third Reich as a witness for the prosecution; after the Holocaust, this became an embarrassment for the church and attempts were made to explain their words in the historical context. It was said that the general discourse at the time was aggressive, brutal, and extreme. At a time of struggle for survival and recognition, Christian forgiveness and salvation were not in demand. These anti-Jewish attacks continued and grew even sharper after Christianity had become a state religion in the Roman empire.[13]

Other Church Fathers besides Chrysostom could also be cited as examples of anti-Jewish bias that could feed open hostility, although Chrysostom seems the worst in the early church.

Our second example of antisemitism spawned in Christendom can be found in the Spanish Inquisition initiated by King Ferdinand and Queen Isabella, famous for funding the explorations of Christopher Columbus in the late fifteenth century. In the same year that Columbus sailed the ocean blue (1492), Ferdinand and Isabella expelled the Jews from Spain. Although the Inquisition took on expanded scope over the next three centuries, its early purpose was primarily to deal with the problem of Jewish converts to Christianity. It was thought that some of the converts were just pretending allegiance to the church to prevent persecution or that they had actually

---

[13] Walter Laqueur, *The Changing Face of Antisemitism: From Ancient Times to the Present Day* (New York: Oxford University Press, 2006), 48.

apostasized and gone back to private practice of Judaism.[14] Benzion Netanyahu refutes the usual interpretation that Spain's leaders were attempting to deal with this "religious" problem by removing the Jews from Spain. Instead, at the foundation of the opposition to Jewish converts to Christianity and their descendants, many of whom had been brought up in the church, was *race* and not *religion*:

> Thus we see how, in the midst of a people whose Christian zeal could in no way be doubted, a theory based on racism appeared whose three major articles of faith were: the existence of a *conspiracy* to seize the government of Spain; the ongoing "contamination" of the "blood" of Spanish people; and the need to do away with these frightful dangers through a genocidal solution of the converso problem.[15]

Evidence that race was the driving force and not religious persecution comes from the fact that any religious problem the Jews and/or converted Jews were causing at the time was minor.[16] As a result of the racial fears, Jews were prohibited from intermarriage, forbidden from holding high offices, sometimes tortured, eventually expelled or even worse – even if their families had been Christians for a couple of generations. In short, everything was in place, perhaps for the first time in history, to join virulent antisemitism to a

---

[14] Benzion Netanyahu, *The Origins of the Inquisition in Fifteenth Century Spain* (New York: Random House, 1995), xiii-xiv. The Israeli historian Netanyahu is the father of Benjamin Netanyahu, the current prime minister of Israel as this chapter was written. The book is dedicated to Jonathan Netanyahu who was killed leading the rescue operation at Entebbe on July 4, 1976. The massive tome is almost 1400 pages.
[15] Ibid., 990-91.
[16] Ibid., 1113.

theory of race so as to protect the purity of a peoples' view of themselves.[17] This is before Luther and more than four centuries before Hitler. All of this was done in the name of Christianity.

A third black mark of Christian antisemitism appears in one of evangelicalism's heroes – Martin Luther (1483-1546), the father of the Protestant Reformation. His book *On the Jews and Their Lies* written three years before his death (1543) is the most famous of his anti-Jewish polemical works that uses harsh, vulgar, and murderous language.[18] Luther at that stage in his life came to the conclusion that it was impossible to convert the Jews to the Christian faith.[19] His analysis covers many passages with appropriate interpretation and correct rebuke of some of the views of the Jewish people of his day. He goes overboard, however, into hateful antisemitism on several occasions. He bemoans that the Jews have a "bloodthirsty, vengeful, murderous yearning and hope."[20] At the Nuremberg trials, Nazi war criminal Julius Streicher was asked about prior anti-Semitic literature. He defended himself this way:

> Anti-Semitic publications have existed in Germany for centuries. A book I had, written by Martin Luther, was, for instance, confiscated. Dr. Martin Luther would very probably sit in my place in the defendants' dock today, if this book had been taken into consideration by the Prosecution. In the book *The Jews and Their Lies*, Dr. Martin Luther

---

[17] The inside jacket of my copy of Netanyahu's book summarizes: "This was the first time that extreme anti-Semitism was wedded to a theory of race—a union that would dramatically affect the course of modern history."

[18] One of Luther's books written in the same year (1543) was *On the Holy Name and the Lineage of Christ*, another source of strongly worded anti-Jewish sentiment.

[19] Martin Luther, *On the Jews and Their Lies* translated by Martin H. Bertram (Online edition; AAARGH, 2009), 2.

[20] Ibid., 14.

writes that the Jews are a serpent's brood and one should burn down their synagogues and destroy them.[21]

After the trial, Streicher was executed for his crimes against humanity. Luther, however, was also on trial that day. The Christian looking at this evidence today should not be judged for being perplexed. How can Luther be so right on biblical authority and justification by faith alone, but so wrong on his hatred for the Jews?

I used to say that if Luther had died five years earlier so his anti-Semitic books would not have been published late in his life, the relationship of Jews and Protestants would have been better since that time. I no longer voice this opinion. Last year, I was using Luther's lectures on Isaiah 63:1-6, given as early as 1530, over a decade before his worst books. Isaiah is describing the picture of a victorious Messiah who comes from Edom after judging them in the end-time days. Luther without warrant and using extreme allegorical interpretation identifies Edom as an ungodly synagogue, that is, the Jews. Edom refers to "red Jews" who are "bloodthirsty and murderous." He goes on to say that "every calamity of the Jews is for the sake of Christ." Luther apparently rejoices that the second coming of Jesus will be the final destruction of the Jewish people, contrary to the overall message of Isaiah.[22] Such vitriolic language forces the genuine Christian to ponder the strength of the sin nature when even the greatest of Christians can think this way.[23] It

---

[21] *Trial of the Major War Criminals before the International Military Tribunal: Nuremberg 14 November 1945-1 October 1946*, Vol. 12 (Nuremberg, 1947), 318. The transcripts in English translation can be found online at the Library of Congress website under Military Legal Resources: https://www.loc.gov/rr/frd/Military_Law/ NT_major-war-criminals.html.

[22] Martin Luther, *Lectures on Isaiah*, Vol. 17 edited by Jaroslov Pelikan and Hilton C. Oswald (St. Louis, MO: Concordia, 1969).

[23] Bernard N. Howard, a Jewish Christian, gives three proposals for responding to the Lutheran legacy of antisemitism: 1. Luther's antisemitism should be

is clear that Christian antisemitism cannot hide in the shadows of the Holocaust.[24]

Jewish Persecution of Christians

Another area for which there must be balanced thinking in light of the Holocaust involves Jewish persecution of Christians. It may seem odd to address this in such a context, but a brief review is warranted. The Jewish people certainly have a right to voice the true statement that persecution has gone mostly one way against them. The other side, although historically smaller in volume, is still grievous nonetheless. Virtually every Christian knows that the Jewish leaders of the first century took part in the murder of Jesus outside Jerusalem. Believers should not use this as it has been used in history to label the Jews as the Christ-killers and give them sole blame for the death of Jesus.[25] In the book of Acts, the first Christian martyr (Stephen) was killed by Jewish hands (Ac 7). Jewish persecution of the church at Jerusalem was so great that it displaced most Christians who lived in the city (Ac 8:2). The rest of the book of Acts describes the Jewish efforts to silence the Apostle Paul, but he escapes death. But he stands trial before Roman leaders

---

acknowledged without qualification; 2. Luther's antisemitism should—as far as possible—be understood; 3. Luther's antisemitism should harm his reputation. See "Luther's Jewish Problem," The Gospel Coalition, https://www.thegospelcoalition.or/article/luthers-jewish-problem/.

[24] Other case studies of Christian antisemitism could have been chosen: The history of Czarist Russia with its pogroms against Jewish people shows that antisemitism in that part of the world pre-dates the rise of communism. Furthermore, after the breakup of the Soviet Union and the decline of communism, the anti-Semitic tendencies lingered on. One example would be Ukraine P. 276.

[25] I gave a paper last year at the Pre-Trib Study Group entitled "Why the World Hates the Jews." I propose that Christians should not look at Jewish people as the "Christ-killers" and should instead develop a full-orbed theology of the cross to help explain our views to Jewish people and others. This paper is scheduled to be published in a future edition of the *Journal of Dispensational Theology*.

with the Jews as his accusers. This is similar to what is found in the Apocalypse. Near the end of the first century, Jewish communities were involved in slandering Christians before the pagan Roman authorities at Smyrna (Rev 2:9) and Philadelphia (Rev 3:9). The second century continued the hostility between the two groups leading to the further divide between Jews/Judaism and Christians/Christianity. The martyrdom of Polycarp in AD 155 or 156 is often cited as an instance where Jewish people helped in the indictment and execution of a Christian.[26] However, by the time Christianity emerges as the religion of the Roman Empire in the early fourth century, a robust replacement theology had developed which eliminated any discussion of the role of Israel and the Jewish people in God's sovereign plan of history going forward.[27] The divide was viewed as permanent except for those few Jewish persons who would come into the church on the church's terms. The Jewish communities were now unable to mount persecution of Christians.

Perhaps the biggest change in Jewish perception of Christianity is that the New Testament itself is now viewed as anti-Semitic: "Meanwhile some Jewish, Christian and post-Christian critics have identified the New Testament itself as the source of the problem, seeing the role ascribed to the

---

[26] See *Martyrdom of Polycarp*, XIII. The account of the death of Polycarp is given in *The Encyclical Epistle of the Church at Smyrna: Concerning the Martyrdom of the Holy Polycarp*. This work is part of the Apostolic Fathers collection and is sometimes titled *The Martyrdom of Polycarp*. Scholars are divided over whether the account is a Christian exaggeration and spurious relative to its statements about the Jews; see David E. Aune, *Revelation 1-5*, Word Biblical Commentary, vol. 52A (Dallas, TX: Words Books, 1997), 162.

[27] The history of the development of replacement forms of theology in which the church replaces Israel in God's plan has been well documented. Some sources to consider are Kaiser, *Jewish Christianity*, 21-36; Ronald E. Diprose, *Israel and the Church: The Origins and Effects of Replacement Theology* (Downers Grove, IL: InterVarsity Press, 2000); and Michael J. Vlach, *The Church as a Replacement of Israel: An Analysis of Supersessionism* (New York: Peter Lang, 2009).

Jews in the New Testament as part of a 'culture of contempt' leading directly from John's Gospel to the gas chambers."[28] Of special note would be passages like John 8:44, Revelation 2:9, and Revelation 3:9 where, according to many Jewish interpreters, Jesus describes all Jews as descended from Satan and treats them as a synagogue of Satan.[29] Christian scholars have responded to these charges.[30] However, the believer must understand, in light of all that has happened, how the New Testament would be read by Jewish people, sometimes in an anachronistic way.

One unfortunate fact of post-Holocaust times is that some Jewish people do persecute Messianic believers in Israel.[31] It is quite common for the boycotting of a Jewish businessman who rents or sells property to a church or group of Christians, especially if they are ethnically Jewish. Furthermore, attempted violence takes place on occasion: "A concert for the so-called Messianic Jewish community in Jerusalem two weeks ago turned violent when more than three dozen Jewish and right-wing extremists attacked members of the audience. For seven hours, about 40 right-wing extremists, so-called hilltop youth from the West Bank and members of the self-styled anti-assimilation group Lehava cursed and screamed, sprayed

---

[28] Duncan MacPherson, "Difficult Conversations, *cont'd.*," The Society for Biblical Studies Newsletter, Vol. 12, Issue 2; Online, www.sbsedu.org/L3_e_newsletter30.6.14DifficultConversation2.htm; accessed September 11, 2019. Some respected liberal theologians in Christendom have asserted that John's Gospel sees the Jews as a symbol of evil. See Elaine Pagels, *The Origin of Satan* (New York: Vintage Books, 1996), 104-105.

[29] For example, see Gerald Sigal, "How Does the Book of Revelation Promote Hatred of Jews?," https://jewsforjudaism.org/knowledge/articles/how-does-the-book-of-revelation-promote-hatred-of-jews/.

[30] James D. G. Dunn, "The Question of Anti-semitism in the New Testament Writings of the Period" in *Jews and Christians: The Parting of the Ways A.D. 70 to 135* edited by James D. G. Dunn (Grand Rapids, MI: Eerdmans, 1999), 177-211.

[31] Estimates vary but there may be roughly 20,000 evangelical Messianic believers in Israel today.

pepper spray and tossed live frogs at members of the community."[32] We can only pray that such events will not escalate, and people are not hurt. It would be a tragic testimony for some Jewish people to become persecutors after all that has been done to them. One good sign is that many Jewish leaders seem to be coming forward to defend Christians against persecution around the world.[33] According to a recent British government report, at the present time, Christians are the most persecuted religious group in the world, mostly due to Islamic oppression although not exclusively so.[34] This may provide a way for Jews and Christians to understand each other. Christians are the most persecuted *religious* group while Jewish people have been the most oppressed *ethnic* group in history.

UPSIDE-DOWN SOCIAL JUSTICE IN THE CASE OF ISRAEL

In light of the oppression and misrepresentation of the Jewish people down through the years, it is not surprising that the nation of Israel is today wrongfully considered a colonial and genocidal oppressor who is destroying the Palestinian people. This way of arguing against the Jews of Israel increased after the Six-Day War in 1967 and, in particular, took off in earnest after the 1982 First Lebanon War.[35] Although there have been difficulties

---

[32] Nir Hasson, "'Messianic Jews' Say Police in Jerusalem Didn't Protect Them From Right-wing Mob," Haaretz, June 14, 2019; one of the singers and musicians at the concert is part of the Friends of Israel family and supported by the ministry.

[33] See Tom Wilson, "Jews and the Persecution of Christians," *First Things*, February 13, 2014; https://firstthings.com/web-exclusives/2014/02/jews-and-the-persecution-of-christians.

[34] "Christian Persecution," *Israel My Glory*, 77 (Sep/Oct 2019): 8.

[35] The word *Palestinian* applied to both Jews and Arabs living in the area in the first half of the twentieth century. Since then, especially gaining ground in the 1960s when the PLO was formed, the word was hijacked so that it refers to an ethnic group. As such it is a failed designation. The term was created for political reasons.

from time to time, the military strength of the Israel Defense Forces simply prevents a frontal attack by Arab forces. While terrorist activity continues, the Arab leaders, especially in the Palestinian Authority are expending much energy to convince the world that the Jews in Israel are a Western imposition into the Middle East and have no right to be there. After the invasion of Lebanon in 1982, the Arab mayor of Nablus, Bassam Shaka'a, was asked to describe the response of the people in the so-called occupied territories. His answer expresses the narrative perfectly:

> No one was surprised by the criminal attack on Lebanon. It is a continuation of Israel's policy aimed at exterminating our people, physically and politically. It is a continuation of the battle started by Israel at the very beginning when it considered the land to be its land, and sought to build a "pure" Israel without the inhabitants.[36]

Notice the reversals, the upside-down language mirroring the Holocaust. The Palestinians have been criminally attacked. The goal of Israel is the extermination of the Palestinian Arabs. This is taken to mean elimination by death and not just the end of any self-rule possibilities in the political realm. The real issue is the land which Israel wrongfully considers to belong to the Jewish people. So the Jews have usurped the land belonging to someone else. Israel wants a pure nation with no other ethnic groups like the Palestinian Arabs. The portrait of Nazi Germany is superimposed on the nation of Israel. The nation of Israel, on this view, consistently practices social injustice and does so, apparently, by its own existence as well as its actions. The Arab narrative is somewhat surreal and absolutely false. There are over one million people living in Israel who are not Jewish. Some of them, even Muslims,

---

[36] Cited in the interview article by Ghassan Bishara, "All Palestinians are Living One Battle, Inside and Outside, *Palestinian Journal* 11 (Summer/Fall 1982): 94.

belong to the Israeli Knesset or parliament. Israel does not target Palestinian Arabs for killing like Hitler's storm troopers. Furthermore, it does not target children for indiscriminate killing.[37] The hypocritical nature of the narrative can be seen in the PLO's automatic payment of a stipend to anyone who murders a Jew in Israel.[38]

Two ways in which the Arab narrative about Israel is being advanced in the world are practical political pressure and the promotion of a version of Christian theology that supports the political pressure. In this way, the so-called Palestinian cause seeks to foment Christian opposition to Israel.

Practical Political Pressure: BDS

Here I do not really want to talk about the use made of the United Nations to advance the Palestinian Arab cause, although it is always present. Instead, I want to rehearse briefly the campaign to boycott, divest from, and sanction Israel (known as the BDS movement). One of the leading websites is bdsmovement.net which alleges to promote freedom, justice, and equality. It encourages specific ways in which people can get involved to oppose Israeli apartheid (as the narrative is described). Several articles are posted to advance the narrative. Two of the prominent sources of the published online presentations are the Palestinian BDS National Committee (BNC) and the Palestinian Campaign for Academic and Cultural Boycott of Israel (PACBI).

---

[37] See Alan Dershowitz, *The Case for Israel* (Hoboken, NJ: Wiley & Sons, 2003), 189-96. Dershowitz does a good job of handling the charges from an ethical point of view. Standard histories of modern Israel will also help at least to the point that they were written. For example, see Martin Gilbert, *Israel: A History* (New York: Doubleday, 1998). Gilbert does a good job of letting facts speak for themselves including allowing the critics of Israel, even among Israeli citizens, to be heard. I have not seen that kind of honesty and transparency on the other side.

[38] David Bedein, "Who Says That Crime Does Not Pay?" *Israel Behind the News*, August 22, 2019, https://israelbehindthenews.com/who-says-that-crime-does-not-pay/18944/?utm_medium=email&utm_ campaign=ibn-today.

244 On Antisemitism

To get a flavor of the articles, a snapshot on a recent day showed the following titles (partial listing):³⁹

☐ "Boycott AnyVision: Israel's 'Field-Tested' Facial Recognition Surveillance Company"
☐ "PACBI Welcomes Statement by More than 500 Filmmakers Against 'Close-Up' Initiative Normalizing Israeli Apartheid"
☐ "The BDS Movement Calls to Boycott Three Anti-Palestinian German Clubs"
☐ "Boycott Pop-Kultur Berlin Festival 2019"
☐ "No Impunity for Ethnic Cleansing in Jerusalem – Boycott Israel Now"
☐ "Democratic Socialists of America Commit to National BDS Organizing"
☐ "Human Rights Organizations Based in Israel Voice Concern before Bundestag President over Motion Defining BDS as Antisemitism"

The entire range of boycotting, divesting from, and sanctioning Israel is meant not just to hurt Israel economically (which has not happened yet), but to put the narrative in front of people, especially in the West. Knowing that most people do not know the actual conditions on the ground in Israel and the Palestinian Authority, the presentations hope to produce anti-Israeli thinking while producing sympathy for the Palestinian Arabs. It does not matter if the presentations are true or false.

Besides boycotting the purchase of Israeli products, a most troubling practice of the BDS movement is to attempt to keep Israeli speakers from being heard at various events, especially on college campuses in the United States. Dershowitz points out several examples:

---

³⁹ Snapshot taken on September 13, 2019.

☐ A letter (April 2002) signed by 125 academics was printed in the *Guardian* (Great Britain) calling for a moratorium on support for Israeli academics and universities;

☐ A signatory of the above mentioned letter fired two scholars from an academic journal just because they were Israelis;

☐ A teacher at Oxford University rejected a Ph.D. applicant just because he had served in the Israel Defense Forces.

Such attitudes have also generated discrimination against Jewish students at some prestigious universities. At the 2015 November "Students of Color Conference" (SOCC) at the University of California, two Jewish students from UCLA witnessed the BDS narrative first hand. In response to participation in the conference, one of those Jewish students, Arielle Mokhtarzadeh, made the following observations:

> Over the course of what was probably no longer than an hour, my history was denied, the murder of my people was justified, and a movement whose sole purpose is the destruction of the Jewish homeland was glorified. Statements were made justifying the ruthless murder of innocent Israeli civilians, blatantly denying the Holocaust in which six million Jews were murdered. Why anyone in their right mind would accept these slanders as truths baffles me. But they did. These statements, and others, were met with endless snaps and cheers. I was taken aback.[40]

---

[40] Anthony Berteaux, "In the Safe Spaces on Campus, No Jews Allowed," *The Tower Magazine*, February 2016, www.thetower.org/article/in-the-safe-spaces-on-campus-no-jews-allowed/.

The SOCC meeting taught the absurd idea that the intifadas were peaceful uprisings against Israel. The message was clear: Jewish students who did not get on board with the anti-Israel, anti-Semitic program were not welcome in the progressive movement against racism. There has developed a "dubious bond between the progressive movement and pro-Palestinian activists who often engage in the same racist and discriminatory discourse they claim to fight. As a result of this alliance, progressive Jewish students are often subjected to a double-standard not applied to their peers—an Israel litmus test to prove their loyalties to social justice."[41] In addition, a chapter of Students for Justice in Palestine (SJP) at Northeastern University "was so persistent in their anti-Semitic harassment—from defacing the statue of a Jewish donor to disrupting Holocaust awareness events—that the university was forced to temporarily suspend the organization in 2014."[42]

It is no surprise, in light of such a political climate on many college campuses, that a study of Jews and antisemitism in the ethnic studies or Middle East studies departments are sometimes rejected since so-called Palestinian studies using the Arab narrative predominate and are considered sacrosanct.[43] Therefore, the campus is often not a pleasant place for a pro-Israel student, especially if they are Jewish. In fact, the emphasis on social justice in dealing with Israel has been turned upside-down on its head. This pursuit for social justice is actually leading in our day to a strengthened antisemitism. As one commentator noted, "Social justice ideologues are not interested in issues, resolution or fairness. They mean to win at any cost, even if it means, as in the case of anti-Semitism, promoting the us/them binary

---

[41] Ibid.
[42] Ibid.
[43] Ibid.

code which always and inevitably divides people and prevents them from considering their common humanity."⁴⁴

Theological Pressure: Liberation Theology

Added to the political pressure of the various expressions of the BDS movement, more troubling for the evangelical believer may be the utilization of liberation theology to advance the Arab narrative in the Middle East. Liberation theology developed in the last half of the twentieth century as a theological way of thinking about the oppressed peoples of the world.⁴⁵ Various authors stressed different areas, various parts of the world, and specific people groups, although the original progress was in Latin America within Roman Catholicism. The generalized form sees salvation as political deliverance rather than individual rescue from sin. Specialized forms of liberation theology would be black theology and feminist or womanist theology. Two key passages often sloganized in liberation theology are Jesus's statement "the truth shall make you free" (Jn 8:22) and Moses's demand to Pharaoh "let my people go" (Ex 9:13 et al).

Related to the question of social justice, Israel, and the Palestinian Arabs, one encounters several avenues of liberation theology that converge on the notion that Israel is an apartheid state that should be confronted through BDS and other means. These various elements combine to form what has

---

⁴⁴ Channa Newman, "Pursuit of 'Social Justice' Gives Strength to Anti-Semitism," *The Pittsburgh Jewish Chronicle*, December 2, 2018, https://jewishchronicle.timesofisrael.com/pursuit-of-social-justice-gives-strength-to-anti-semitism/.

⁴⁵ A couple of resources on liberation theology are Ronald Nash, ed., *Liberation Theology* (Milford, MI: Mott Media, 1984) and Deane William Ferm, *Third World Liberation Theologies: An Introductory Survey* (Maryknoll, NY: Orbis Books, 1987). I have sometimes made the comment that liberation theology is Marxism with Bible verses sprinkled on it.

been labeled Christian Palestinianism.[46] At the center of this movement is an Anglican priest named Naim Ateek who could legitimately be called the "father of Christian Palestinianism." He was eleven years old in 1948 and witnessed what he considered unfair treatment of his Christian Arab family, which lost its home as the Israelis moved in. His seminal work *Justice and Only Justice* serves as the foundation document for a Palestinian liberation theology.[47] The dissemination of his views has largely been accomplished through the organization named Sabeel which he founded in 1989. *Sabeel* is the Arabic word for *way, channel,* or *spring*. The stated intention is to promote the liberation of Palestinians by nonviolent methods. There are chapters of Sabeel in many countries including the United Kingdom and the United States.

Wilkinson succinctly describes Naim Ateek and his organization Sabeel in rather strong and broad terms:

> Sabeel's propagation of a Palestinianized version of Roman Catholic liberation theology, its blatant distortion and de-Zionization of God's Word, its monstrous conception of a Marcionite Jesus arrayed in Palestinian robes, its promotion of an interfaith agenda at complete variance with the gospel of Jesus Christ, and its seduction of Western evangelicals already ensnared by replacement theology, have made it a potent and destructive force within the church.[48]

---

[46] Paul R. Wilkinson, *Israel Betrayed, Volume 2 – The Rise of Christian Palestinianism* (San Antonio, TX: Ariel Ministries, 2018), 60. Wilkinson says he calls this movement Christian Palestinianism "because it represents the antithesis of biblical Christian Zionism."

[47] Naim Ateek, *Justice and Only Justice: A Palestinian Theology of Liberation* (Maryknoll, NY: Orbis Books, 1989).

[48] Paul R. Wilkinson, *Israel Betrayed, Volume 2 – The Rise of Christian Palestinianism* (San Antonio, TX: Ariel Ministries, 2018), 69.

To unpack this summary, we start by noticing the respect for the roots of liberation theology and the perception that support from the Catholic Church will be necessary for them to accomplish their agenda. The next two parts, de-Zionization of God's Word and the Marcionite Jesus, stem from the devaluing of the Old Testament in Christian Palestinianism. Ateek notes that among Christian Palestinians a major change took place in how the Old Testament was viewed:

> Before the creation of the State [of Israel], the Old Testament was considered to be an essential part of the Christian Scripture, pointing and witnessing to Jesus. Since the creation of the State, some Jewish and Christian interpreters have read the Old Testament largely as a Zionist text to such an extent that it has become almost repugnant to Palestinian Christians. As a result, the Old Testament has generally fallen into disuse among both clergy and laity, and the Church has been unable to come to terms with its ambiguities, questions, and paradoxes—especially with its direct application to the twentieth-century events in Palestine.[49]

Ateek further commented that "the emergence of the Zionist movement in the twentieth century is a retrogression of the Jewish community into the history of its very distant past, with its most elementary and primitive forms of the concept of God."[50] Ateek sees the Jews as going back to a tribal god. One sees in these words echoes of replacement theology. The Old Testament is downgraded, and the promises to Israel about the land and future of national Israel are thrown away.

---

[49] Ateek, *Justice*, 77.
[50] Ibid., 101.

Part of the equation for Ateek and Christian Palestinianism is the clear statement that they are seeking a special hermeneutic: "Palestinian Christians are looking for a hermeneutic that will help them to identify the authentic Word of *God* in the Bible and to discern the true meaning of those biblical texts that Jewish Zionists and Christian fundamentalists cite to substantiate their subjective claims and prejudices."[51] When reading this, one readily understands that liberation theology is not conservative in orientation. Ateek's teaching is that the plain, literal meaning derived from grammatical-historical interpretation will not work for the Christian Palestinians because it is not what they want to see in Scripture. So they are searching for an alternative. It is they who are subjective and not the Zionists and dispensational fundamentalists who are bringing their prejudices to the text. Do the Christian Palestinians believe they have no prejudices themselves? We must read Scripture as God gave it and follow its lead even if it takes us into territory we were not expecting and do not really like.

The next part of Wilkinson's summary notes that Sabeel is an interfaith organization which really has nothing to do with the gospel of eternal life. The official full name of Sabeel is the Sabeel Ecumenical Liberation Theology Center. As an ecumenical organization it attempts to bring together various groups who share one thing: a dislike for Israel's alleged mistreatment and oppression of the Palestinians. Consequently, support comes mostly from the mainline denominations in the United States and various church groups around the world who are not committed to the literal interpretation of the Bible. Sabeel in this sense would represent a segment of the liberal spectrum in Christendom. One must ask what the end game really is for Christian Palestinianism. What would victory for their cause look like? Is it a nation called Palestine that will be run by the Islamic radicals with Jews living inside of it? That does not match the rhetoric of the PLO and the Palestinian

---

[51] Ibid., 79.

Authority. Is the end game the destruction of the Jews so that only Palestinian Arabs remain? This fits the rhetoric of the PLO but is hardly consistent with Christian teaching. It would be doing to the Jews what they are complaining that the Jews have done to them. Is the end game a two-state solution? The leadership of the Arabs has consistently rejected a two-state solution the many times it has been offered beginning in 1947. It appears that what is really going on is a Christian expression of Palestinian Arab nationalism. Christ and the Bible are not at the center.

The final point in Wilkinson's summary is that Sabeel has been seducing Western evangelicals who hold to replacement theology to the detriment of the church. Evidence of this comes largely from the founding of Christ at the Checkpoint (CATC) in 2010, a conference sponsored every other year by Bethlehem Bible College located in the area under control by the Palestinian Authority. According to Wilkinson, CATC has superseded the more liberal Sabeel due to its evangelicalism. The CATC website affirms, "We feel compelled to address the injustices that have taken place in the ongoing conflict between Israel and Palestine, particularly the Palestinian lands under occupation."[52] One wonders why CATC singles out Israel when so much of the violence in the area is initiated by the Islamic terrorists. Further explanation of what they believe fleshes out the possible reason – their replacement theology.

> We do not condemn the Jewish people and we reject any forms of anti-Semitism. In fact, many of our supporters are Israeli Jews who believe that the present Israeli treatment of the Palestinians does not reflect the deeper moral values of Judaism itself. We simply wish to find a life in the entire Holy Land that is free of discrimination and injustice, where

---

[52] https://christatthecheckpoint.bethbc.edu/about-christ-at-the-checkpoint/.

each person can live without prejudice toward their race or religion. This also means we reject theologies that lead to discrimination or privileges based on ethnicity. Worldviews that promote divine national entitlement or exceptionalism do not promote the values of the Kingdom of God because they place nationalism above Jesus.[53]

Notice the swipe at Zionism and the implied idea that dispensationalists place nationalism in the case of Israel as more important than Jesus. Again, I applaud the notable idea of living without prejudice in political matters, but what is the end game? If they succeed, what will it look like? Both the Jews and the Muslims would have to come to an understanding simultaneously about such things. It will take the second coming of Jesus to make this a reality, but then the land will clearly belong to Israel with no disputes.

CONCLUSION

The Friends of Israel Gospel Ministry, of which I am a part, began as a ministry of social justice to defend the Jewish people. After Kristallnacht on November 9-10, 1938, a pogrom against the Jews by the Nazis, a group of Christian leaders and businessmen met to help with a response to the injustice that was being carried out under the swastika. Among them were Lewis Sperry Chafer, the President of Dallas Theological Seminary, and H. A. Ironside, pastor of Moody Memorial Church in Chicago, both strong dispensationalists. They decided to form The Friends of Israel Refugee Relief Committee to help Jewish people who were fleeing from Nazi tyranny and oppression. They were not wrong to do so. Social justice of these kinds have a place in Christian thinking and action.

---

[53] Ibid.

Biblical Distinctions Applied 253

To close, I want to give some practical recommendations for action, social and spiritual, to respond to perhaps the greatest social justice issue of our time – antisemitism.

1. Consider the commonsense things. Buy Israeli products, books written by Israeli authors, and Jewish magazines and resources. Write letters to the editor when you see anti-Semitism near you. Verbally stand against those who speak evil of the Jews using the old stereotypes.

2. Read and observe widely in various sources so that you are not hypnotized by the charisma of one author or speaker. Part of your studies need to be in Jewish history.

3. Attend a church, if possible, that is pro-Israel and accepts what the Bible says about Israel – past, present, and future. The church should not be afraid of dispensationalism.

4. Study your Bible following a literal understanding and fully embrace dispensationalism; this will lead you to believe that Israel has a right to the land and God has a future for His chosen people. This understanding should increase your love for the Jewish people.

5. Befriend Jewish people where you live. Centuries of persecution and forced conversions make many Jewish people believe that the very act of evangelism is anti-Semitic. They must learn that there are Christians who love them in the name of Jesus. But do not be afraid to share the gospel.

6. Pray for the peace of Jerusalem and your Jewish friends.

7. Make a trip to Israel with a pro-Israel group. Although you cannot see all the facts on the ground through a tour, it will increase your awareness nonetheless.

8. Do not accept all actions of the present Israeli government as right just because it is Israel. Analysis must be done. They must be held to account. However, the interpretation of the facts on the ground should not be done based upon the reporting of *Al Jazeera*.

9. Remember that Jesus is Jewish. How can we not love the Jewish people? The apostle Paul said, "From the standpoint of the gospel they are enemies for your sake, but from the standpoint of God's choice they are beloved for the sake of the fathers" (Ro 11:28).

Chapter 10 – On Sexuality and Gender Identity
Keeping it Classical: A Christian Response to LGBTQ+ Ideology
Mike Dellaperute

INTRODUCTION

In a 2011 Barna research article entitled, "Six Reasons Young Christians Leave the Church,"[1] the authors identify reason three as, "Churches come across as antagonistic to science."[2] Four years later, Sarah Kropp Brown, writing on behalf of the National Association of Evangelicals, confirmed these findings when she observed, "Evangelicals are more than twice as likely as the general public (29 percent vs. 14 percent) to say that science and religion are in conflict and that they are on the side of religion."[3] The anti-science bias of evangelical Christians when addressing cultural issues coincides with the rise in popularity of presuppositional apologetics,[4] defined by Boa and Bowman as grounding, "Reason and fact on the truth of the Christian faith, rather than trying to prove or defend the faith on the basis of

---

[1] "Six Reasons Young Christians Leave Church," (Barna Group, September 27, 2011), https://www.barna.com/research/six-reasons-young-christians-leave-church/.
[2] Ibid.
[3] Sarah Kropp Brown, "Are Evangelicals Anti-Science?" (National Association of Evangelicals, July 14, 2016), https://www.nae.net/evangelicals-anti-science/.
[4] Kenneth Boa and Robert M. Bowman Jr., *Faith Has Its Reasons* (Downers Grove, IVP, 2005), 221.

reason or fact."[5] The tendency to dismiss evidence from science or reason when it appears to conflict with Scripture or personal experience has resulted in a clichéd response to cultural issues, summarized by retired American Baptist minister and USA Today columnist Oliver Thomas as, "The Bible says it … that settles it."[6] However, like many of his contemporaries, with regard to LGBTQ+ ideology Thomas is quick to add, "The church got it wrong."[7] To substantiate his support of LGBTQ+ behavior, Thomas attempts to demonstrate how both science and reason, "Contradict Scripture."[8] If dispensationalists discount science and reason when addressing Sexual Orientation and Gender Identity (SOGI) issues in the culture, the result will be a loss of credibility both with the next generation of believers who already look to the church with skepticism and with the remainder of the culture who embraces LGBTQ+ ideology.

The purpose of this chapter is to illustrate the value of a classical approach to apologetics when addressing SOGI issues in the culture. Boa and Bowman define classical apologetics as, "Logically coherent and supportable by sound arguments."[9] This two-step method for defending the faith begins with science, reason, philosophy or facts in step one and leads to a literal understanding of Scripture in step two.[10] Due to the prevalence of

---

[5] Ibid., 35. It is not the intent of this author to cast a presuppositional approach to apologetics as a whole in a negative light, but rather to demonstrate that, when addressing SOGI issues in the culture at large, a classical approach is beneficial.

[6] Oliver Thomas "American Churches Must Reject Literalism and Admit We Got It Wrong on Gay People," USA Today (Gannett Satellite Information Network, April 29, 2019), https://www.usatoday.com/story/opinion/2019/04/29/american-church-admit-wrong-gays-lesbians-lgbtq-column/3559756002/.

[7] Ibid.

[8] Ibid.

[9] Boa and Bowman, 49. Here a presuppositional epistemology should be distinguished from presuppositional apologetics.

[10] Ibid, 34. A literal approach to Scripture being one of Ryrie's three Sine Qua Non of dispensationalism.

SOGI issues in the culture, this chapter will interact with a wide range of media sources, both popular and scholarly, in order to expose, analyze and respond to the conflicting assertions of LGBTQ+ advocates. The intent of this chapter is not to attack individuals, but rather to challenge the ideas used to justify LGBTQ+ ideology through the evaluation of seven case studies. Although this chapter will primarily focus on contradictions produced by transgender ideology,[11] due to the phenomenon of intersectionality, the entire LGBTQ+ spectrum will be examined in order to demonstrate the scientific, logical, and philosophical inconsistencies within a comprehensive LGBTQ+ system. Rather than pitting biblical teachings on marriage and human sexuality against LGBTQ+ ideology, this chapter will set the contradictory and incoherent assertions of LGBTQ+ advocates against one another in a manner similar to the Paul's appeal to the Pharisees and Sadducees (Ac 23:6-7). Only then will these inconsistencies be contrasted with the consistent and coherent nature of a biblical worldview in order to illustrate the reasonableness of the Christian faith.

In conclusion, this chapter will demonstrate how dispensationalists who intend to address SOGI issues in the culture will realize four distinct benefits by initially appealing to general revelation and common grace in order to expose the fallacies of LGBTQ+ ideology. First, a classical approach will encourage believers to remain informed and active in the culture. Second, a classical approach will help Christians gain confidence when defending a biblical position. Third, this approach will enable evangelicals to gain a hearing in a culture that is growing increasingly hostile toward Christianity.

---

[11] "GLAAD Media Reference Guide - Transgender," (GLAAD, December 7, 2019), https://www.glaad.org/reference/transgender. The acronym GLAAD stands for Gay and Lesbian Alliance Against Defamation. This organization embraces and promotes LGBTQ+ ideology in the culture. Every effort has been made to follow the preferred terminology listed in GLAAD's media reference guide except when said terminology conflicts with science or Scripture, as in the term biology.

Finally, a classical approach will address the anti-science concerns of young believers. Sole reliance on a presuppositional apologetic when interacting with SOGI issues will likely lead to the fulfillment of the prophetic words of Time Magazine's Mary Eberstadt: "Regular Christians are no longer welcome in American culture."[12]

Case 1: The Intersection of Transgender Ideology and Biology

In 2015, an NBC News headline read, "Malisa's Story: Growing up Transgender and a Grandfather's Pride."[13] The story begins by explaining how a prenatal ultrasound revealed that Malisa Philips was as a biological male. However, from a young age, Malisa chose to identify as female. Malisa's tendency to embrace feminine stereotypes, such as dressing and acting like a princess, is the primary evidence used to substantiate Malisa's gender-nonconformity. Next, Malisa's parents point to a transformative moment of self-realization that occurred at the age of six when Malisa donned a wig for the first time. Malisa's parents were then advised to affirm their child's gender identity by allowing Malisa to begin to transition from male to transgender female. Finally, by the age of eight, and with the support of family, teachers, therapists, and pediatric endocrinologists, Malisa formally began gender transition.

---

[12] Mary Eberstadt, "Regular Christians Are No Longer Welcome In American Culture," (Time, June 29, 2016), https://time.com/4385755/faith-in-america/.

[13] "Malisa's Story: Growing up Transgender and a Grandfather's Pride," NBCNews.com (NBCUniversal News Group, May 2, 2019), http://www.nbcnews.com/nightly-news/video/malisa-s-story--growing-up-transgender-and-a-grandfather-s-pride-432490051892. The grandfather referenced in this news article is Representative Mike Honda, a former congressman from California and DNC vice chair. Honda became the subject of an ethics investigation that questioned his use of taxpayer funds in 2015. Honda subsequently lost his seat in 2016 after eight terms in office. The article, dated April 2015, coincides with the investigation conducted by the US House Ethics Committee.

The gender transition process for children like Malisa can be classified into three stages. Stage one involves social transition. In this stage, the child is encouraged to dress and act in a manner that is consistent with their gender identity. The World Professional Association for Transgender Health (WPATH) Standards of Care, 7th Ed., defines gender identity as, "A person's intrinsic sense of being male or female, or an alternate gender."[14] The behaviors associated with social transition include name change, participation in cross-sex activities, and preferred restroom access. After an indeterminate time in stage one,[15] children pursuing gender transition proceed to the chemical stage. This second stage of transition consists of two distinct phases for children like Malisa. Phase one of chemical transition involves the administration of puberty suppressors in order to prevent the undesired physical changes associated with adolescence. Phase two involves cross-sex hormone therapy in order to produce the desired physical characteristics that are surgically enhanced in stage three. Both chemical phases in stage two of gender transition yield permanent results coupled with an array of side effects. Stage three entails surgical transition. Surgical transition involves a

---

[14] E. Coleman et al., "Standards of Care for the Health of Transsexual, Transgender, and Gender Non-conforming People, Version 7," *International Journal of Transgenderism* (13), 96. On their website, WPATH.org, WPATH self-identifies as an, "Interdisciplinary professional and educational organization devoted to transgender health." The claims of evidence-based medicine by an organization that embraces LGBTQ+ ideology has resulted in WPATH becoming the industry standard for gender affirmation treatment of transgender children and adults. Many of the WPATH contributors stand to gain financially from the growing number of gender transitions.

[15] Ibid., 18. WPATH maintains that a children must remain in stage one of gender transition for an extended period of time in order to receive counseling and resolve all comorbid factors. In practice, however, due to the rise of a new condition referred to as, "Rapid Onset Gender Dysphoria," (ROGD), children as young as Malisa are now proceeding to stage two after a single visit to a gender clinic.

myriad of procedures that are also considered irreversible.[16] Due to the graphic, costly, painful, and largely ineffective nature of these surgeries, GLAAD's Media Reference Guide advises, "Journalists should avoid overemphasizing the role of surgeries in the transition process."[17]

When NBC News first posted Malisa's story, Malisa was about to enter puberty. Due to inherent biological factors, if Malisa's parents did not intervene, then Malisa would begin to develop undesired masculine features. However, Malisa's family learned that they could provide their child with puberty suppressors. This initial phase of chemical intervention allows children like Malisa to remain as androgynous as possible until estrogen therapy and a series of complicated surgeries can provide a more convincing visible transition from male to transgender female. Malisa's story illustrates the dominance of the ethical principle of autonomy in contemporary culture.[18] By appealing to autonomy at a young age, children like Malisa are permitted both to self-diagnose and to dictate their preferred course of treatment. Under LGBTQ+ gender affirmation guidelines, the role of medical and psychological experts is primarily to guide children like Malisa through gender transition. Due to the uncontested supremacy of autonomy in contemporary culture, LGBTQ+ advocates deem it unethical to deny a child like Malisa full access to gender transition.

The primary rationale used to support Malisa's transition from male to transgender female is derived from the prevailing presupposition that gender

---

[16] For a more detailed account of social, chemical, and surgical transition, see my article: "The Church and the Transgender Issue," in *The Journal of Ministry and Theology* 20:1 (Spring, 2016), 76-122.

[17] "GLAAD Media Reference Guide - Transgender," (GLAAD, December 7, 2019), https://www.glaad.org/reference/transgender.

[18] Tom Beauchamp and James Childress, *Principles of Biomedical Ethics* (New York: Oxford University Press, 2013), 101. Beauchamp and Childress define autonomy as, "Self-rule that is free from both controlling interference by others and limitations that prevent meaningful choice."

is assigned at birth. This is the premise behind the bourgeoning term "natal gender." Implicit in the term natal gender is the belief that gender is a social construct. Some proponents of LGBTQ+ ideology, such as GLAAD, promote the concept of a fluid and artificial gender spectrum by making a sharp distinction between sex and gender. Sex, according to GLAAD, is, "The classification of a person as male or female. At birth, infants are assigned a sex, usually based on the appearance of their external anatomy."[19] Gender, on the other hand, is understood as a, "Deeply held sense"[20] of being male, female, both, or neither.

Not all LGBTQ+ advocates are willing to exclude biology from the gender conversation. Homosexual apologist and NY Magazine author Andrew Sullivan represents an element within the LGBTQ+ system who is challenging the prevailing transgender narrative on the basis of biology. In his article, "The Nature of Sex."[21] Sullivan observes, "Abolishing clear biological distinctions between men and women is actually a threat to lesbian identity and even existence because it calls into question who is actually a woman."[22] Sullivan further argues that approaching gender as a social construct, "Undermines the fundamental legal groundwork for recognizing and combating sex-based oppression and sex discrimination against women and girls."[23] Sullivan insightfully warns of the brewing internal conflict within the LGBTQ+ system:

---

[19] "GLAAD Media Reference Guide - Transgender," (GLAAD, December 7, 2019), https://www.glaad.org/reference/transgender.
[20] Ibid.
[21] Andrew Sullivan, "The Nature of Sex" (Intelligencer, February 1, 2019), https://nymag.com/intelligencer/2019/02/andrew-sullivan-the-nature-of-sex.html.
[22] Ibid.
[23] Ibid.

> If you abandon biology in the matter of sex and gender altogether, you may help trans people live fuller, less conflicted lives; but you also undermine the very meaning of homosexuality. If you follow the current ideology of gender as entirely fluid, you actually subvert and undermine core arguments in defense of gay rights ... Contemporary transgender ideology is not a complement to gay rights; in some ways it is in active opposition to them.[24]

Sullivan's appeal to biology is borrowed from a biblical understanding of a fixed gender binary of male and female (Ge 1:27). This appeal to a naturally occurring and observable gender binary exposes what Sullivan later admits to be, "Internal tensions and even outright contradictions,"[25] in LGBTQ+ ideology. For if LGBTQ+ advocates continue to exclude biology from the gender conversation, then gender dysphoric children like Malisa will be granted additional autonomous rights. However, as Sullivan also notes, these rights will likely come at the expense of women and others who identify as LGBTQ+.

Evidence of Sullivan's unheeded warning concerning the danger of disregarding biology is presently reverberating throughout the culture. Michael Levenson and Neil Vigdor of the NY Times report on a lawsuit filed by three biological females who challenged the rights of transgender athletes to identify and compete as females.[26] Ryan Mayer of CBS News explains that, by abandoning biology in matters of sex and gender, Connecticut's

---

[24] Ibid.

[25] Ibid.

[26] Michael Levenson and Neil Vigdor, "Inclusion of Transgender Student Athletes Violates Title IX, Trump Administration Says," The New York Times (The New York Times, May 29, 2020), https://www.nytimes.com/2020/05/29/us/connecticut-transgender-student-athletes.html.

Interscholastic Athletic Conference permitted transgender athletes to participate as females, resulting in two male-to-female transgender teens, "Dominating the competition at Connecticut's girls track and field state competitions."[27] The dominance of these transgender athletes came, as Sullivan predicted, at the expense of biological female competitors. If, as GLAAD insists, LGBTQ+ ideology is permitted to continue on its current trajectory, more female athletes, scholars, actresses, coaches, professors and executives can expect to experience similar setbacks for the sake of transgender rights. However if, as Sullivan suggests, the LGBTQ+ community, "Abandons the faddish notion that sex is socially constructed or entirely in the brain, that sex and gender are unconnected, that biology is irrelevant,"[28] then children like Malisa and the Connecticut transgender athletes will be forced to sacrifice their rights for the sake of feminists, lesbians, and gays. This quandary poses a serious internal conflict with potentially devastating implications for LGBTQ+ advocates at the intersection of gender as either biology or social construct.

For many who embrace LGBTQ+ ideology like Levenson and Vigdor, denying the autonomous rights of transgender people like Malisa or the Connecticut athletes constitutes discrimination.[29] This accusation has produced a growing schism in the LGBTQ+ system. Valerie Richardson of the Washington Times explains how these internal inconsistencies have forced lesbian advocates to turn against transgender advocates, as in the case of former outspoken lesbian and tennis great Martina Navratilova.

---

[27] Ryan Mayer, "Transgender Track Athletes Win CT State Championship, Debate Ensues," (CBS New York, June 13, 2018), https://newyork.cbslocal.com/2018/06/13/transgender-track-athletes-win-connecticut-state-championship-debate-ensues/.

[28] Sullivan, "The Nature of Sex."

[29] Levenson and Vigdor, "Inclusion of Transgender Student Athletes Violates Title IX."

Navratilova was, "Stripped of her Athlete Ally Ambassador title ... for calling it 'cheating' to allow transgender females to participate in women's sports."[30] As Sullivan observes, these two competing ideologies cannot coexist in the same comprehensive system without contradiction and, ultimately, conflict. This growing tension over the relationship between biology and gender within the LGBTQ+ community threatens to undermine the entire system, as evidenced in the case of J.K. Rowling.

Case 2: J.K. Rowling's TERF

Although she is best known as the mastermind behind the Harry Potter series, J.K. Rowling is also a self-ascribed liberal feminist and social activist who attempted to gain approval from LGBTQ+ advocacy groups by retroactively labeling one of the central characters in her fictional series as gay in 2007.[31] Recently, however, Rowling has only garnered angst from LGBTQ+ proponents for making Navratilova-esque comments that transgender journalist Grace Robertson of *Vanity Fair* describes as, "Feminist Transphobia."[32] *USA Today's* Charles Trepany reports that Rowling was criticized for coming to the aid of Maya Forstarter, a cisgender female who was fired from a research facility for her controversial statement: "My belief ... is that sex is a biological fact and is immutable. There are two

---

[30] Valerie Richardson, "Martina Navratilova slammed for calling out transgender 'cheating' in women's sports" (AP News, February 20, 2019), https://apnews.com/979971281249864b6ba3ed469e2fbb84.

[31] Kim Renfro, "Why Devoted 'Harry Potter' Fans Feel Betrayed by J.K. Rowling and the 'Fantastic Beasts' Franchise," (Insider, February 2, 2018), https://www.insider.com/fantastic-beasts-jk-rowling-dumbledore-lgbt-backlash-2018-2. Rowling's decision to retroactively assign an LGBTQ+ identity to one of her characters reflects a growing trend in popular media. Other recent retroactive assignments include Lando Calrissian of the *Star Wars* series being labeled "Pansexual" in *Solo* and *Beauty and the Beast's* LeFou being labeled gay in recent adaptations.

[32] Grace Robertson, "Where J.K. Rowling's Transphobia Comes From," Vanity Fair, https://www.vanityfair.com/style/2020/06/jk-rowling-transphobia-feminism.

sexes. Men are male. Women are female. It is impossible to change sex. These were until very recently understood as basic facts of life."[33] By defending Forstarter's appeal to biology, Rowling became the subject of a public-shaming and virtue-signaling campaign that further confirmed Sullivan's suspicions by pitting LGBTQ+ advocate against LGBTQ+ advocate. In the wake of Rowling's comments, GLAAD's head of talent Anthony Ramos released the following statement: "J.K. Rowling, whose books gave kids hope that they could work together to create a better world, has now aligned herself with an anti-science ideology that denies the basic humanity of people who are transgender."[34]

In the process of defending fellow feminist Forstarter and, by extension, the role of biology in determining sex and gender, Rowling had three derogatory labels affixed to her by the LGBTQ+ champions of gender as a social construct. First, like many of her Christian counterparts, GLAAD designated Rowling as anti-science. This demonstrates how an appeal to biology provides common ground for Christians and some LGBTQ+ advocates. Therefore, when addressing SOGI issues in the culture, dispensationalists can begin by deferring to the arguments of Sullivan and Rowling in a manner similar to the way Paul deferred to the Pharisees in order to defend his belief in the resurrection (Ac 23:9). Second, GLAAD interpreted Rowling's support of Forstarter as an attack on the basic humanity of transgender people. With regard to this accusation, Christian apologists who address SOGI issues in the culture must carefully maintain the distinction between ideas and individuals by consistently seasoning their

---

[33] Charles Trepany, "J.K. Rowling Sparks Controversy for Transgender Comments; GLAAD Responds," USA Today (Gannett Satellite Information Network, December 20, 2019), https://www.usatoday.com/story/entertainment/celebrities/2019/12/19/j-k-rowling-transgender-comments-maya-forstater-glaad-response/2701579001/.

[34] Ibid.

response with gentleness and respect (1Pe 3:15). Finally, Rowling's opponents from within the LGBTQ+ community proceeded to brand her as a, "TERF." Sullivan explains that this defamatory acronym stands for, "Trans-Exclusive Radical Feminist ... one minority that is actively not tolerated by the LGBTQ establishment, and often demonized by the gay community."[35] According to Trepany, "The hashtag '#JKRowlingIsATerf' was a top trending topic that day."[36] Sullivan further reveals that radical feminists, including many lesbians, are labeled TERFs if they hold the position that sex is, "Fundamentally biological, and not socially constructed, and that there is a difference between women and trans women that needs to be respected."[37] The angst from the LGBTQ+ community expressed in ad hominem toward one of their own illustrates how Christians who engage SOGI issues must be prepared to face repercussions (1Pe 3:16-17). The internal inconsistencies in LGBTQ+ ideology over biology, feminism, and gender is evident in its selective appeals to biology. The tension created through interactions within the LGBTQ+ spectrum as a whole is further demonstrated in the following relationship scenarios.

Case 3: "B" is for Bisexual and Other Alphabetical Inconsistencies in the LGBTQ+ Relationship Soup

Within the inclusive and affirming LGBTQ+ continuum that is often playfully referred to as "Alphabet Soup,"[38] the letter "B" stands for bisexual. In her historical presentation of the bisexual movement, GLAAD's Miranda Rosenblum explains that bisexual persons have frequently endured oppression at the hands of both the culture at large and an LGBTQ+

---

[35] Sullivan, "The Nature of Sex."
[36] Ibid.
[37] Ibid.
[38] See, for example, California's San Mateo county commission LGBTQ glossary: "LGBPTTQQIIAA+ (Alphabet Soup)" https://lgbtq.smcgov.org/lgbtq-glossary.

subculture that is dominated by exclusively lesbian women and gay men.[39] According to the GSE, a bisexual is, "A person who is romantically, emotionally, physically, and/or sexually attracted to both men and women."[40] While a cursory reading of this definition may appear innocuous, the inherent problem that "B" poses to the remainder of the LGTQ+ system concerns the fact that "Bi," as carefully defined by Rolling Stone's Zachary Zane, "Means two."[41] The existence of the "B" in LGBTQ+ ideology implicitly affirms an innate gender binary with a biological and biblical basis, something that members of the "T" community vehemently deny.

Ironically, the intrinsic acknowledgement of a gender binary that forms the foundation for both bisexuality and a biblical understanding of gender is confirmed explicitly by the GSE definition that restricts the sexual attraction of bisexuals to the two genders of male and female. Therefore, in order to identify as a bisexual in a community where labels matter, an individual who includes males and females in their list of sexual attractions must do so to the exclusion of all other genders on the socially constructed LGBTQ+ spectrum, including transgender persons. For if a bisexual, defined as a person who is attracted to both males and females, is also attracted to someone who claims to be either another gender or transgender, then are they still able to identify as bisexual? While the answer derived from

---

[39] Miranda Rosenblum, "The U.S. Bisexual+ Movement: a #BiWeek History Lesson," (GLAAD, April 10, 2019), https://www.glaad.org/blog/us-bisexual-movement-biweek-history-lesson.

[40] "About," Garden State Equality, https://www.gardenstateequality.org/about. According to their self-description, the Garden State Equality is New Jersey's statewide advocacy and education organization for the lesbian, gay, bisexual, and transgender community. As of this writing, GSE has successfully lobbied for 222 laws that support or promote LGBTQ+ ideology.

[41] Zachary Zane, "What's the Real Difference between Bi- and Pansexual?" (Rolling Stone, October 4, 2019), https://www.rollingstone.com/culture/culture-features/whats-the-real-difference-between-bi-and-pansexual-667087/.

GLAAD's definition and Zane's article is a simple "No;" the problems resulting from that answer trigger complicated inconsistencies to ripple throughout the LGBTQ+ community. Zane reports that many LGBTQ+ individuals are reluctant to surrender their hard-earned titles of "L" or "G" or "B".[42] As a result, the self-proclaimed "inclusive" LGBTQ+ community is now forced to answer the question: Is it necessary for an individual to exclude transgender persons from romantic relationships and sexual attractions in order to maintain the title bisexual, gay, or lesbian?

Psychology Today's Dr. Karen Blair observes that transgender people are in fact being excluded from the dating scene in practice, if not in theory, both in the LGBTQ+ community and among cisgender heterosexuals.[43] This marginalization, according to Tatyana Bellamy-Walker of NBC News, results in emotional trauma for transgender people, including an increase in anxiety and depression.[44] Some, like transgender activist Brynn Tannehill, even suggest that refusing to date a transgender person is transphobia, a form of prejudice and discrimination akin to denying a transgender person access to gender transition or excluding transgender persons from sports competitions.[45] Tannehill even questions whether or not it should be illegal

---

[42] Ibid.

[43] Karen Blair, "Are Trans People Excluded from the World of Dating?" Psychology Today (Sussex Publishers, June 16, 2019), https://www.psychologytoday.com/us/blog/inclusive-insight/201906/are-trans-people-excluded-the-world-dating.

[44] Tatyana Bellamy-Walker, "For Nonbinary People, Struggle for Recognition Extends to Romantic Relationships," (NBCUniversal News Group, August 3, 2019), https://www.nbcnews.com/feature/nbc-out/nonbinary-people-struggle-recognition-extends-romantic-relationships-n1038876.

[45] Brynn Tannehill, "Is Refusing to Date Trans People Transphobic?" (Advocate.com, December 14, 2019), https://www.advocate.com/commentary/2019/12/14/refusing-date-trans-people-transphobic.

to refuse to date a transgender person.⁴⁶ Meanwhile, others within the LGBTQ+ movement disagree with Tannehill. Sullivan insists, "It is not transphobic for a gay man not to be attracted to a trans man."⁴⁷ However, when one considers the long and hard battle that lesbians, gays, and bisexuals fought for identity, recognition and most notably pride in the culture, the question now arises within the LGBTQ+ community: Who would be willing to relinquish their title of lesbian, gay, or bisexual by dating transgender people?

While the preceding question may appear puerile on the surface, a deeper analysis actually creates a great deal of tension within LGBTQ+ ideology. As GLAAD explains, a lesbian is, by definition, "A woman whose enduring physical, romantic, and/or emotional attraction is to other women."⁴⁸ In a similar manner, Sullivan insists, "Gay men are defined by our attraction to our own biological sex. We are men attracted to other men."⁴⁹ Furthermore, according to Live Science's managing editor Tia Ghose, lesbian, gay, and bisexual attractions are inherent and immutable, meaning the individual did not choose and cannot change the object of their sexual attraction.⁵⁰ Evelyn Schlatter and Robert Steinback of the Southern Poverty Law Center (SPLC) support the enduring assertions of Ghose and GLAAD by identifying two of the top ten anti-gay myths as, "No one is born gay … (and) … Gay people can choose to leave homosexuality."⁵¹ LGBTQ+

---

⁴⁶ Ibid
⁴⁷ Sullivan, "The Nature of Sex."
⁴⁸ "GLAAD Media Reference Guide - Lesbian / Gay / Bisexual Glossary of Terms," (GLAAD, October 26, 2016), https://www.glaad.org/reference/lgbtq.
⁴⁹ Sullivan, "The Nature of Sex."
⁵⁰ Tia Ghose, "Being Gay Not a Choice: Science Contradicts Ben Carson," (Livescience, March 6, 2015), https://www.livescience.com/50058-being-gay-not-a-choice.html.
⁵¹ Evelyn Schlatter and Robert Steinback, "10 Anti-Gay Myths Debunked," (Southern Poverty Law Center, February 27, 2011),

apologists like Schlatter and Steinback often cite biological evidence in order to substantiate the claims that sexual attraction is both innate and immutable.[52] However, this supposition raises yet another question concerning internal inconsistencies: Is it appropriate for LGBTQ+ philosophy to appeal to biology in order to validate sexual attraction while simultaneously rejecting biology in matters of gender? Is all biology anti-science?

Concerning biological evidence to support LGBTQ+ ideology, Ghose reluctantly acknowledges, "No studies have found specific gay genes."[53] Furthermore, some LGBTQ+ scientists, like transgender evolutionary biologist Joan Roughgarden, vehemently oppose the notion of gay or transgender genes. Roughgarden fears that the potential discovery of said genes would likely initiate a cisgender-heterosexual-led genocide of LGBTQ+ persons through, "The selective abortion of gay babies."[54] However, lack of biological evidence does not prevent Schlatter and Steinback from asserting, "Modern science cannot state conclusively what causes sexual orientation, but a great many studies suggest that it is the result of both biological and environmental forces, not a personal choice."[55] Nonetheless, LGBTQ+ advocates who appeal to biology for support like Ghose and Roughgarden must rely on actual or perceived LGBTQ+ activity in the animal kingdom in order to provide biological validation for its presence in humanity. Appealing to lesbian, gay, or bisexual activity between animals provides LGBTQ+ advocates with a scientific basis for same-sex

---

https://www.splcenter.org/fighting-hate/intelligence-report/2011/10-anti-gay-myths-debunked.

[52] Ibid.

[53] Ghose, "Being Gay Not a Choice."

[54] Joan Roughgarden, *Evolution's Rainbow*, (Berkeley: University of California Press, 2009), 294.

[55] Schlatter and Steinback, "10 Anti-Gay Myths Debunked."

and bisexual attractions among humans. However, before examining the validity of this claim, it must be acknowledged that this biological assertion still fails to answer the question: If a lesbian is sexually attracted to a transgender person, then is she still a lesbian?

Technically, according to most LGBTQ+ advocates, the answer to the above question is another, "No." As Sullivan explains, "Transgender ideology – including postmodern conceptions of sex and gender – is a threat to homosexuality, because it is a threat to biological sex as a concept."[56] For, if a woman who was at one time sexually attracted to other women becomes romantically involved with a transgender person, then she can no longer claim to be a lesbian. In this scenario, her sexual fluidity has caused her to transition from lesbian to a non-traditional expression of bisexual. Zane explains this conflicting view of fluid sexual attraction in LGBTQ+ ideology as follows: "Fluid, in this case, meaning that sexual attractions have the capacity to change over time and can be dependent on different situations."[57] The implications of Zane's appeal to sexual fluidity in order to defend bisexual activity threaten to undermine the entire LGBTQ+ system by lending support to the much-maligned arguments over reparative/conversion therapy[58] or spiritual transformation (Ro 12:1-2). For, on the one hand, some LGBTQ+ proponents like Zane and Psychology Today's Karen Blair argue in support of sexual fluidity.[59] On the other hand, organizations

---

[56] Sullivan, "The Nature of Sex."

[57] Zane, "What's the Real Difference between Bi- and Pansexual?"

[58] GLAAD, "Conversion Therapy," https://www.glaad.org/conversiontherapy?response_type=embed. GLAAD defines conversion therapy as, "Conversion therapy is any attempt to change a person's sexual orientation, gender identity, or gender expression."

[59] Karen Blair, "4 Ways That Sexuality Can Be Fluid," Psychology Today (Sussex Publishers, December 29, 2019), https://www.psychologytoday.com/us/blog/inclusive-insight/201912/4-ways-sexuality-can-be-fluid.

272 On Sexuality and Gender Identity

like the SPLC and GLAAD insist that sexual attraction cannot be changed or controlled.[60] So the question remains: Can someone's sexual attractions ever change? The coherent answer from a biblical worldview is yes (1Co 6:9-11), and Christians who defend this position would be wise to begin by appealing to sexual fluidity. However, the conflicting answer from within the LGBTQ+ community is hotly contested.

Not only does LGBTQ+ ideology conflict over whether or not gender and sexual attractions are either socially constructed and fluid or biological and fixed, but internal contradictions also prevent a coherent system from developing. Zane, a self-professed bisexual, admits:

> The truth is, however, there's confusion even among members of the LGBTQ community as to what these words mean, particularly when it comes to bisexuality. In fact, the bisexual community doesn't even agree on what it means to be bisexual. The term pansexual was birthed out of the confusion, and to create a definitive and more inclusive label. This has led to in-fighting between members of the community, who are upset that their bisexual identity is being replaced by another label.[61]

As a result of internal inconsistencies surrounding the concept of sexual fluidity, the LGBTQ+ community remains at an impasse over the simple question: If a lesbian is attracted to a transgender person, does that make her bisexual, pansexual, queer, sexually fluid, still a lesbian, or something else? Furthermore, if she is reassigned another title like bisexual, pansexual, or queer, then does this imply that she is a former lesbian? More importantly, can a lesbian ever stop being a lesbian? These are the questions that

---

[60] GLAAD, "Conversion Therapy."
[61] Zane, "What's the Real Difference between Bi- and Pansexual?"

Biblical Distinctions Applied 273

LGBTQ+ ideology fails to resolve satisfactorily. For if, on the one hand, sexual attraction is fluid, as a segment within the LGBTQ+ system clearly maintains, then who can rightly insist that said (former) lesbian who found herself attracted to a transgender person will not someday be attracted to a natal male and live out the rest of her days as a heterosexual female? Philosophically, LGBTQ+ advocates who promote gender and sexual fluidity like Tannehill, Blair, and Zane cannot allow for the possibility of a lesbian sexually transitioning to heterosexual without undermining the entire system. On the other hand, if a lesbian's attraction to other females is inherent and immutable, then back to the initial question: Should lesbians be permitted to date males or transgender people once they identify as lesbian? The solution, implicit in the arguments of Sullivan, GLAAD, and the SPLC is that exclusion is necessary in order to maintain internal consistency. Lesbians need to pursue romantic relationships exclusively with biological women and gays need to pursue romantic relationships exclusively with biological men while the rest need to adopt the inclusive and comprehensive title of "Pansexual" in order to avoid any further inconsistencies. However, not only would this practice force lesbians and gays to discriminate against transgender people, but even the term pansexual has its coherent limitations.

Case 4: Out of the Frying Pansexual

As Zane reports, the term pansexual was conceived by LGBTQ+ advocates in an attempt to create a classification that would resolve the internal conflict surrounding the various sexual identities and attractions highlighted in the preceding section. According to the GSE, a pansexual is, "A person who experiences sexual, romantic, physical, and/or spiritual attraction to members of all genders, identities and/ or expressions."[62] Like

---

[62] "About," Garden State Equality.

"Queer," this umbrella term was originally intended to be broad enough to encompass any past, present, or future addition to the LGBTQ+ spectrum. However, the tensions created by appealing to the all-inclusive claims of pansexuality produce two additional internal inconsistencies for LGBTQ+ advocates, beginning with the law of noncontradiction.

Sproul et al. define the law of noncontradiction as, "'A' cannot be 'A' and 'non-A' at the same time and in the same relationship."[63] This philosophical axiom mandates that pansexuality cannot claim to be inclusive of all sexual attractions, genders, identities, and expressions while simultaneously excluding or condemning some sexual attractions, genders, identities or expressions. The inconsistencies exposed by the law of noncontradiction stem from the fact that, according to LGBTQ+ advocates, there are some sexual attractions, identities, and expressions that no individual or society should ever tolerate. These attractions and behaviors include incest, rape, bestiality, pedophilia, and necrophilia, among others (IRBPN+). With regard to these immoral behaviors, Schlatter and Steinback confirm that the majority of the LGBTQ+ community condemns necrophilia and pedophilia,[64] and the Advocate's Trudy Ring describes any attempt to link bestiality to the LGBTQ+ movement as, "Simply absurd and deeply offensive."[65] However, in the process of deeming some sexual attractions, identities, or expressions on the IRBPN+ spectrum as morally unacceptable or offensive, LGBTQ+ ideology undermines any potential for comprehensive application of the term pansexual. Pansexual must

---

[63] R.C. Sproul, John Gerstner, and Arthur Lindsley, *Classical Apologetics*. (Grand Rapids: Zondervan, 2984), 72.

[64] Schlatter and Steinback, "10 Anti-Gay Myths Debunked."

[65] Trudy Ring, "Right-Wing Pundit Says 'B' in 'LGBTQ' Stands for 'Bestiality'," (Advocate.com, July 18, 2018), https://www.advocate.com/media/2018/7/18/right-wing-pundit-says-b-lgbtq-stands-bestiality.

encompass every sexual attraction, identity, and expression if it is to mean anything.

Philosophy is not the only obstacle that the pansexual solution fails to hurdle. A second inconsistency arises when scientists like Ghose and Roughgarden appeal to the animal kingdom in order to find biological support for LGBTQ+ behavior in human beings. The problem, consistently ignored in LGBTQ+ scientific research and reporting, is that the spectrum of IRBPN+ behaviors frequently occur in nature. In a study focused on non-reproductive sexual behavior in animals, Ina Jane Wundram reports, "A male dolphin carried a dead female for about five hours, copulating with her several times."[66] Greg Palmer documents a myriad of species of insects, birds, fish, reptiles, and primates that engage in forced copulation, evolutionary biology's contemporary euphemism for rape.[67] For some animals like the elephant seal, a creature Roughgarden celebrates in support of LGBTQ+ ideology as, "Exceedingly active in same sex genital behavior,"[68] the fact that forced copulations are so common that they actually constitute normative breeding habits is selectively omitted. Palmer affirms, with regard to the elephant seal's sexual activity, "Rape is by far the most common type of copulation in this species."[69] Furthermore, rape is not the only aberrant sexual behavior witnessed in seals. In several instances, seals have been observed participating in inter-species sexual activity. De Bruyn et al. document instances of forced copulation by fur seals upon king penguins.[70]

---

[66] Ina Jane Wundram, "Nonreproductive Sexual Behavior: Ethological and Cultural Considerations," *American Anthropologist* 81:1 (March 1979), 101.

[67] Greg Palmer, "Rape in Nonhuman Animal Species: Definitions, Evidence, and Implications," *The Journal of Sex Research* 26:3, (August, 1989), 364.

[68] Roughgarden, 141.

[69] Palmer, "Rape in Nonhuman Animal Species: Definitions, Evidence, and Implications," 366.

[70] P. de Bruyn, Cheryl Tosh, and Marthán Bester. "Sexual harassment of a king penguin by an Antarctic fur seal." *Journal of Ethology*, 26:2, (May 2008), 295.

A final act of IRBPN+ sexual activity in nature that is excluded from LGBTQ+ scientific presentations involves the behavior of animals with their own offspring or juveniles of the same species, a form of incest and pedophilia referred to as inbreeding. Among primates, David Lester reports that incest has been documented between mother and son.[71]

LGBTQ+ advocates who selectively appeal to animal behavior as scientific justification for related activities or pansexuality in human beings are confronted with a very complicated epistemological problem. Sexual activity in the animal kingdom, the same biological criteria used to justify LGBTQ+ activity in human beings, can also be used to validate IRBPN+ activity among human beings. Therefore, aside from an appeal to Cyrenaic hedonism, proponents of LGBTQ+ ideology fail to provide any epistemological justification for deferring to some sexual behaviors in the animal kingdom in order to substantiate human sexual behavior while simultaneously disregarding or condemning other sexual behaviors in the animal kingdom as immoral for human beings. By comparison, few Christians would argue with the conclusion that sexual behaviors such as incest (Lev 18:6), rape (Dt 22:25), and bestiality (Ex 22:19) are sinful and immoral. In addition, the principles established from the biblical definition of marriage as one man and one woman (Mt 19:5) coupled with the clear prohibition of sexual activity outside of marriage (Heb 13:4), the grave warning for those who would harm children (Mk 9:42), and the biblical ban on necromancy (Lev 20:27) allow Christians to confidently and consistently defer to Scripture in order to identify pedophilia, necrophilia, and a host of other sexual behaviors as sinful and immoral. LGBTQ+ ideology, on the other hand, must selectively appeal to nature to justify some behaviors while ignoring or condemning others. Furthermore, this inconsistent double

---

[71] Lester, David, "Incest," *The Journal of Sex Research* 8:4 (Nov 1972), 270.

standard does not just exist in LGBTQ+ theory, but also in practice, as evidenced in the case of James Younger.

Case 5: Inconsistency in 3-D... Desistence, Dead-naming, and Double Standards

James Younger was a typical 7-year-old boy who loved super heroes, and pretend sword fights.[72] However, like many children in contemporary culture, James was raised in a broken and dysfunctional home. After his parents divorced, James became the subject of a very bitter, very public custody battle. James's mother, convinced that her son was a female trapped in a male body, began to lead James through the process of social transition. Along with subjecting James to intensive gender-affirmation counseling, James's mother also changed her son's name to Luna. James's situation came to a head in a Dallas courtroom during the summer of 2019 when his mother sued for sole custody so she could begin stage two of gender transition by administering puberty-suppressing hormones to James. A shocked nation watched as a judge initially ruled in her favor. James's father immediately appealed the decision and won. As a result, James was permitted to choose his own gender identity and, as Aaron Feis of the NY Post reports on November 7, 2019, James declared to the world, "I am a boy."[73]

In spite of the fact that James chose to accept and identify as his natal gender, not all LGBTQ+ advocates were as quick to acknowledge his right to autonomy as they were to defend Malisa Philips or the Connecticut transgender athletes. Some, like VOX's openly transgender reporter Katelyn Burns, decried the court's decision to permit James to embrace a cisgender

---

[72] For in-depth commentary on James Younger and gender dysphoria, see my article in The Baptist Bulletin, "Saving James," March/April, 2020.

[73] Aaron Feis, "Texas Child in Gender-Transition Court Battle Attends School as Boy," (New York Post, November 7, 2019), https://nypost.com/2019/11/07/texas-child-in-gender-transition-court-battle-attends-school-as-boy/.

existence in the article, "What the battle over a 7-year-old trans girl could mean for families nationwide."[74] Throughout the commentary, published November 11, 2019, four full days after the NY Post disclosure, Burns insisted on referring to James either as a female named Luna, or with the feminine pronoun "she." Burns's reluctance to affirm James's autonomous gender identity due to its conflict with LGBTQ+ ideology demonstrates that the contradictions within the LGBTQ+ system are not just in theory, but also in practice.

In a 2015 VOX article, senior correspondent German Lopez addressed, "4 Common Mistakes Made about Caitlyn Jenner and transgender people."[75] First, since the concept of a pronoun transcends simple etiquette and encompasses affirmation, Lopez warned, "Don't use a pronoun someone doesn't want you to use."[76] Lopez, writing in defense of Jenner's male-to-female transition, rebuked what he identified as the micro-aggressive tendencies of an element within contemporary culture that either unintentionally or intentionally misgendered Jenner as a "he." Next, Lopez advised, "Avoid using a trans person's deadname."[77] The act of dead-naming, according to Lopez, "Could be taken as an attempt to undermine (their) identity."[78] Therefore, according to the rules of conduct established and practiced by VOX, a person's autonomous rights concerning their individual gender identity should be respected, so long as their beliefs align with

---

[74] Katelyn Burns, "What the Battle over a 7-Year-Old Trans Girl Could Mean for Families Nationwide," (Vox, November 11, 2019), https://www.vox.com/identities/2019/11/11/20955059/luna-younger-transgender-child-custody.

[75] German Lopez, "4 Common Mistakes Made about Caitlyn Jenner and Transgender People," (Vox, June 2, 2015), https://www.vox.com/2015/6/2/8706745/transgender-issues-mistakes.

[76] Ibid.

[77] Ibid.

[78] Ibid.

LGBTQ+ ideology. However, if a child like James Younger experiences a period of gender dysphoria followed by desistence, then, as Burns demonstrates, inconsistent application of these rules by LGBTQ+ proponents is permissible without accusation of micro-aggression, anti-science, denying the basic human rights of the child, or other forms of defamation. The tensions created by the double standard LGBTQ+ advocates apply to dead-naming and pronoun use appear more difficult to resolve than the actual condition of gender dysphoria.[79]

Gender dysphoria, as defined by WPATH, is, "Distress that is caused by the discrepancy between a person's gender identity and that person's assigned sex at birth."[80] This condition is not uncommon in children. Furthermore, by WPATH's own standards, the fact that a child questions their biological gender or even prefers to dress as the opposite gender is not sufficient criteria for a gender dysphoria diagnosis.[81] However, even in cases of actual gender dysphoria, the overwhelming majority of children who experience a period of distress over their biological gender, like Malisa Philips and James Younger, will ultimately desist. Dr. Kenneth Zucker, in his article, "The Myth of Persistence," explains that children who continue to exhibit distress over their natal gender are labeled persisters, while those whose distress resolves are considered desisters.[82] While the statistical data on

---

[79] Mary Jackson, "Fighting to let a boy be a boy," (World Magazine, August 21, 2020), https://world.wng.org/content/fighting_to_let_a_boy_be_a_boy. After this article was initially submitted to the Council on Dispensational Hermeneutics for a September 2020 reading deadline, James's mother took additional legal steps to secure custody of James and reintroduce gender-affirmation treatment with the intent to transition.
[80] E. Coleman et al., "Standards of Care for the Health of Transsexual, Transgender, and Gender Non-conforming People, Version 7," 96.
[81] Ibid.
[82] Zucker, Kenneth, "The Myth of Persistence: Response to 'A Critical Commentary on Follow-up Studies and 'Desistance' Theories About Transgender and

persistence and desistence varies, all parties inside and outside the LGBTQ+ system agree, if gender dysphoric children are not subjected to gender affirmation, then the majority will desist. WPATH recognizes a persistence rate of 6 to 23 percent, indicating an admission by a leading LGBTQ+ science-based organization that gender dysphoric children like Malisa and James will desist as often as 94 percent of the time.[83] Only one contemporary study by radical transgender advocates Temple-Newhook et al. suggests that the desistence rate is consistently lower than 80 percent.[84] This controversial report, which has been challenged by LGBTQ+ advocates and adversaries alike, suggests a desistence rate of 59 percent, which still represents a majority of cases.

Case 6: The Curious Case of Kenneth Zucker

Dr. Kenneth Zucker is a renowned psychologist and transgender activist who has been in the business of transitioning females into transgender males and males into transgender females for decades.[85] According to Jesse Singal, Zucker's accomplishments include holding a leadership position at Toronto's prestigious gender clinic; serving as editor of the Journal Archives of Sexual Behavior; developing the DSM-5 guidelines for gender dysphoria; and

---

Gender Nonconforming Children" by Temple Newhook et al.," *International Journal of Transgenderism* 19:2 (Apr/June 2018), 232.

[83] E. Coleman et al., "Standards of Care for the Health of Transsexual, Transgender, and Gender Non-conforming People, Version 7," 11.

[84] Temple Newhook, Julia, Jake Pyne, Kelley Winters, Stephen Feder, Cindy Holmes, Jemma Tosh, Mari-Lynne Sinnott, Ally Jamieson, and Sarah Pickett, "A Critical Commentary on Follow-up Studies and 'Desistance' Theories about Transgender and Gender-Nonconforming Children," *International Journal of Transgenderism* 19:2, (Apr/June 2018), 212.

[85] Jesse Singal, "How the Fight Over Transgender Kids Got a Leading Sex Researcher Fired," (The Cut, February 8, 2016), https://www.thecut.com/2016/02/fight-over-trans-kids-got-a-researcher-fired.html?mid=twitter-share-scienceofus.

contributing to WPATH's Standards of Care.[86] However, when Zucker was asked to comment on Temple-Newhook's desistence data, he deferred to science and reason in order to conclude, "The 59 percent figure could be interpreted as implying that as many as 41 percent of the potential participants could have been persisters, which is an absurd inference with no empirical basis."[87] Zucker's challenge to the gender affirmation model has caused him to incur the wrath of LGBTQ+ advocates. Singal explains, "Some trans activists … believe that desistence is a transphobic myth."[88] With regard to the presupposition that desistence rarely or never occurs, Singal rightly observes, "While these activists … have tried to poke holes in the consistent findings about gender dysphoria desistance, they just haven't come up with scientifically convincing explanations."[89] Nevertheless, due to the fact that he deferred to empirical data that supported desistence at the expense of the gender affirmation model, Zucker was fired from his position at Toronto's gender clinic. The curious case of Kenneth Zucker demonstrates that the inconsistencies within the LGBTQ+ system do not just set LGB against T, but also run deep enough to create a schism between fellow transgender activists like Zucker and Temple-Newhook. Although LGBTQ+ advocates are quick to label dissenters anti-science, the irony of Zucker's double standard is that, like Rowling and Navratilova, he was ostracized by a movement he helped build based on his appeal to science and reason.

---

[86] Ibid.
[87] Zucker, "The Myth of Persistence," 233.
[88] Singal, "How the Fight Over Transgender Kids Got a Leading Sex Researcher Fired."
[89] Ibid.

Case 7: To Science We Shall Go

A scientific evaluation of puberty suppression reveals the dangerous and damaging consequences of LGBTQ+ ideology on children. When gender dysphoric children like Malisa Philips and James Younger reach the age of puberty, the administration of synthetic puberty-suppressing hormones can repress undesired biological side-effects that naturally accompany adolescence.[90] From a biochemical perspective, Hruz et al. explain how puberty is a three-step process.[91] Step one involves adrenal maturation. Between the ages of six to ten, the adrenal glands begin to secrete androgens in healthy human children. These hormones cause oily skin, acne, body odor, and hair growth, all of which indicates an early stage of puberty. Step two involves gonadal maturation. This phase normally begins between the ages of eight and fourteen with the release of Gonadotropin-releasing hormone (GnRH). The third and final chemical process of puberty involves the secretion of Human Growth Hormone (HGH). This hormone interacts with the hormones present in phases one and two to produce a growth spurt resulting in physical and sexual maturity.[92] Puberty suppressing hormones inhibit the body's natural release of hormones in phase two of puberty.

Gonadal maturation begins in the brain with the hypothalamus and the pituitary gland.[93] When a child begins gonadal maturation, the hypothalamus releases bursts of GnRH. These fluctuating blood levels of GnRH trigger the pituitary gland to release follicle-stimulating hormone (FSH) and luteinizing

---

[90] For a detailed ethical evaluation of puberty suppression, see my book, *The Danger of Puberty Suppression*, (Eugene, Wipf & Stock, 2019).

[91] Paul Hruz, Lawrence Mayer, and Paul McHugh, "Growing Pains: Problems with Puberty Suppression in Treating Gender Dysphoria," New Atlantis: A Journal of Technology & Society 52, (Spring 2017), 8-9.

[92] Ibid.

[93] Fredric H. Martini, William C. Ober, Judi L. Nath, Edwin F. Bartholomew, and Kevin Petti, *Visual Anatomy and Physiology*, 2nd edition (Boston: Pearson, 2015), 594.

hormone (LH) respectively.[94] FSH and LH are trophic hormones. They work together with GnRH and androgens to turn on the gonads. Gonadal maturation ultimately leads to sexual maturity, which results in the masculinization of males and the feminization of females in healthy human beings.[95] However, not everyone experience normative puberty in three successive and complimentary stages.

A rare but serious condition known as precocious puberty occurs when children experience premature gonadal maturation.[96] The long-term effects of premature gonadal maturation include stunted growth, infertility, and shorter lifespans. Puberty suppressors were developed in order to treat precocious puberty. When children are diagnosed with precocious puberty, they are treated with regular doses of synthetic GnRH agonists. These puberty suppressors mask the bursts of GnRH from the hypothalamus by keeping blood levels at a constant high. The constant blood levels of GnRH trick the pituitary gland into shutting down production of FSH and LH, which in turn causes gonadal maturation to slow or cease. Then, when the child reaches normal age for puberty and adrenal maturation begins, administration of synthetic hormones ceases and puberty resumes, thereby enabling children with precocious puberty to lead relatively normal lives.[97]

The problem with puberty suppressors does not lie in their treatment of precocious puberty, but rather in their use for treatment of gender dysphoria. As Dr. Michelle Cretella explains, any study that claims puberty suppressors are safe, reversible, medically necessary, have no know side effects, or are tested and approved is only referring to their use for the treatment of

---

[94] Ibid.
[95] Ibid.
[96] Hruz et al., "Growing Pains," 10.
[97] Ibid., 8-9.

precocious puberty, not gender dysphoria.⁹⁸ The appeal to precocious puberty in order to substantiate the use of puberty suppressors for gender dysphoric children amounts to ethical sleight of hand akin to appealing to some sexual behaviors in animals in order to justify similar behavior in humans. Administering puberty suppressors to gender dysphoric children constitutes an experimental treatment with irreversible results, as the contributors to WPATH readily admit: "There are concerns about negative physical side effects of GnRH analogue use."⁹⁹ Therefore, it is neither medically necessary, nor evidenced-based, nor ethically defensible to treat gender dysphoric children like Malisa Philips or James Younger with puberty suppressors, even on the grounds of autonomy. Not only is this conclusion founded in scientific evidence, but also in ethical principles, such as the Hippocratic Oath.

For nearly three thousand years, nonmaleficence, also known as the Hippocratic Oath, has been the governing principle of medical ethics.¹⁰⁰ Beauchamp and Childress summarize the principle of nonmaleficence as, "First do no harm."¹⁰¹ The origin of this oath, as Nigel de S. Cameron explains, is not from Judeo-Christian values, but rather from Greek pagans.¹⁰² These ancient physicians, imbued with common grace, were able to recognize the intrinsic value of human life and vowed not to injure their patients in the course of medical treatment. Christians can readily adopt the concept of nonmaleficence due to biblical teachings that prohibit harming

---

⁹⁸ Michelle Cretella, "Gender Dysphoria in Children and Suppression of Debate," *Journal of American Physicians and Surgeons* 21:2 (Summer 2016), 52.

⁹⁹ E. Coleman et al., "Standards of Care for the Health of Transsexual, Transgender, and Gender Non-conforming People, Version 7," 20.

¹⁰⁰ Beauchamp and Childress, *Principles of Biomedical Ethics*, 13.

¹⁰¹ Ibid., 150.

¹⁰² Nigel M. de S. Cameron, "Bioethics: The Twilight of Christian Hippocratism." In D.A. Carson and John D. Woodbridge (eds.), *God and Culture* (Grand Rapids, Eerdmans, 1993), 324.

other human beings (Ro 13:10). The administration of puberty suppressors to gender dysphoric children when as many as 94 percent would desist is a clear violation of the most ancient governing ethic that LGBTQ+ advocates attempt to override by appealing to autonomy.

The Conclusion of the Matter

In January 2019, Governor Phil Murphy signed bill C.18A:35-4.35 into law, mandating that all NJ public school curriculum include the contributions of LGBT people beginning September 2020. This controversial decision was lauded by LGBTQ+ advocates, including GSE executive director Christian Fuscarino.[103] By the fall 2019, the GSE began to promote a comprehensive curriculum that would force schools to incorporate LGBTQ+ ideology into all subjects, bypassing any potential parental opt-out. This all-inclusive curriculum was piloted in twelve NJ schools during the spring of 2020. One of the school districts chosen to test the LGBTQ+ pilot curriculum was Pinelands Regional in Little Egg Harbor, NJ, the small Jersey Shore town where I have served as pastor at Calvary Baptist Church for the past twenty years. As Bill Spaeda of NJ101.5 explains, I was unexpectedly placed in a position where I was forced to challenge the intentional indoctrination of Pinelands students with LGBTQ+ ideology.[104] What began as reasoned and respectful opposition to the decision of a local Board of Education has led to opportunities to challenge SOGI issues on both the local and state level,

---

[103] Brooke Sopelsa, "N.J. Governor Signs LGBTQ-Inclusive Curriculum Bill into Law," (NBCUniversal News Group, February 1, 2019), https://www.nbcnews.com/feature/nbc-out/n-j-governor-signs-lgbtq-inclusive-curriculum-bill-law-n965806. Brook Sopelsa is the editorial director of NBC Out, the LGBTQ digital destination of NBC News.

[104] Bill Spadea, "NJ Pastor Fights Back against Forced LGBTQ Curriculum," February 7, 2020, https://nj1015.com/nj-pastor-fights-back-against-forced-lgbtq-curriculum-opinion/.

sometimes as an individual, and other times as part of a larger group. These interactions were only profitable when a classical approach was employed.

Christians who engage the culture over SOGI issues must adopt a classical approach in order to be effective. This involves interacting with culture, science, reason, and philosophy to defend the literal teaching of Scripture. Those who default to an apologetic model that begins with, "The Bible says it," when interacting with LGBTQ+ ideology in the culture will find that their approach falls on deaf, or worse, combative ears. This chapter intended to demonstrate that it is both possible and productive to defend a biblical worldview by appealing to science, philosophy, and reason. Throughout this chapter, seven case studies were presented in order to expose the inconsistencies and internal conflicts within the LGBTQ+ system through an analysis of the culture. In the process, this chapter focused on evaluating the ideas used to support LGBTQ+ ideology, rather than vilifying the individuals who embrace this system. Furthermore, this chapter sought to demonstrate that believers who employ a classical approach will benefit by staying informed, increasing confidence, gaining a hearing in the culture, and addressing the concerns of young Christians. In conclusion, it is the hope of this author that this chapter will encourage other dispensationalists to challenge the dominant but inconsistent and incoherent LGBTQ+ system in the culture with gentleness and respect, beginning with science and reason.

Chapter 11 – On the Environment
Dispensational Kingdom Postponement Theology as a Safeguard for the Edenic Divine Institutions

Paul Miles

The doctrine of kingdom postponement is a watershed for developing and defending a distinctly dispensational worldview. Postponement theology comes from a grammatical-historical approach to progressive revelation, so this article divides the doctrine of postponement into two phases: the kingdom as described in the Old Testament and the kingdom as offered, rejected and postponed in the life of Christ. Both sections feature a non-dispensational trend in theology and a dispensational critique. Two trends have been selected due to the imminent threats that they pose to the divine institutions that were established in the Garden of Eden: Christian ecojustice as a threat to responsible labor shall be handled in relation to Old Testament kingdom descriptions and Christian social justice, specifically relating to feminist and queer theology, as a threat to marriage and family shall be discussed in relation to the kingdom offer. But first, an overview of divine institutions and postponement theology is in order.

DIVINE INSTITUTIONS AND POSTPONEMENT THEOLOGY

Divine Institutions

As one reads Genesis, certain divine institutions emerge that inform the dispensational worldview in light of a postponed kingdom. Charles Clough describes divine institutions as "absolute social structures instituted by God for the entire human race—believers and unbelievers alike."[1] These institutions are designed for the protection and prosperity of mankind. Three divine institutions find their roots in the Garden of Eden as the divine ideal and carry over to the post-fall world. These are responsible labor (Ge 1:26–30, 2:15–17; Ps 8:3–8), marriage (Ge 2:18–24), and, as a result of responsible labor and marriage, family. Sin has rendered each of these institutions dysfunctional.

God established more divine institutions in later chapters of Genesis, but the first three led to the global population and so it could be said that they lay the foundation for the subsequent institutions. After the flood and the Tower of Babel, two divine institutions emerged to restrain evil: these are civil government (Ge 9:5, 6) and national distinction (Ge 10–11). Sin has rendered these institutions necessary. The dispensationalist recognizes two more bodies, though not all dispensationalists would rank them as divine institutions;[2] they are Israel (Ge 12:1–3) and the church (Ac 2:1–4).

This study will focus on the first three institutions (responsible labor, marriage, and family), which are evident the first three chapters of Genesis.

---

[1] Charles A. Clough, *A Biblical Framework for Worship and Obedience in an Age of Global Deception*, II, 39. Available online at https://www.bibleframework.org/images/bfm_documents/1995-BibleFramework-CourseNotes-02.pdf.

[2] Thomas Ice and Charles Clough are excellent dispensationalist theologians who clearly recognize Israel as a blessing to the world, but do not list her as a "divine institution," per se, while Robert Dean is a theologian with similar theology, who does recognize Israel as a divine institution. See Thomas Ice, "The Divine Institutions" available online at https://www.pre-trib.org/articles/all-articles/message/the-divine-institutions; Charles A. Clough, *A Biblical Framework for Worship and Obedience in an Age of Global Deception*, II, 39 Available online at https://www.bibleframework.org/images/bfm_documents/1995-BibleFramework-CourseNotes-02.pdf; Robert Dean, "18 - Divine Institution #6: Israel," available online at https://deanbibleministries.org/conferences/message/018-divine-institution-6-israel-b.

Kingdom postponement has clear implications for government, national distinctions, Israel, and the church as well, but if Satan can confuse the church on these first three, then the church's views on the rest of the divine institutions will crumble soon enough.

Postponement Theology

Postponement theology contends that Jesus offered to Israel the literal, earthly, messianic kingdom, which is described in the Old Testament, but since Israel rejected this kingdom offer, Jesus postponed the literal kingdom to a future day. Among alternative views are those which say that Christ came and, in one way or the other, established the kingdom as a current spiritual reality. Such systems demand a non-literal understanding of the Old Testament terms of the kingdom and an alteration of Christ's intentions while He was on earth.

It is entirely possible to defend exegetically the institutions of responsible labor, marriage, and family without appealing to postponement theology and the dispensationalist, like all conservatives, should be equipped to do so; however, there is an additional argument that is distinctly dispensational, as the errant doctrines that threaten the institutions are often inseparable from kingdom-now eschatology. The question at hand[3] is how to develop a distinctly dispensational worldview, so this chapter will emphasize how a robust theology of kingdom postponement is beneficial to developing and defending a dispensational worldview in light of current Christian compromises on these three divine institutions.

---

[3] This chapter was originally presented to the 2021 meeting of the Council on Dispensational Hermeneutics. The theme of the meeting was "Developing a Dispensational Worldview."

OLD TESTAMENT DESCRIPTIONS OF THE KINGDOM AND THE DIVINE INSTITUTION OF RESPONSIBLE LABOR

Trends in Ecotheology

Current trends in Christian ecojustice[4] are posing threats to the divine institution of responsible labor by distorting the role that man plays in nature and ascribing guilt to Christianity for the industrial use of natural resources. This often comes as a direct attack against the Bible and such attacks are often grounded in misunderstandings. Mark Musser is a dispensationalist who served for several years as a bivocational pastor and farmer. He has done much research on the history of environmentalism and summarizes well that "Environmentalists think that latent within the Biblical commands to subdue and fill the Earth is the concept that people may exploit nature for selfish or even greedy purposes."[5] As conservatives make evident in the term, "*Responsible* Labor," the Bible does not advocate the *irresponsible* use of resources, but first let us consider what Christian ecojustice proponents are saying before providing a dispensationalist response.

Certain unsettling ecothological movements have generally stayed among Christian academia in recent decades, but they could be permeating Christian laity in years to come. For example, the Hodos Institute is an

---

[4] Ecojustice is an odd term. A New Testament word that the NKJV often translates as "justice" is κρίσις (Mt 12:18, 20; 23:23; Lk 11:42; Ac 8:33), which the KJV most frequently translates as "judgment" and occasionally even "damnation" (Mt 23:33, Jn 5:29). Another NKJV word for "justice" is δίκη (Ac 28:4), which the KJV renders as "vengeance." These words have negative connotations in the Greek, likely being related to κρίνω, which deals with separating, judging, and condemning (see Robert Beekes, *Etymological Dictionary of Greek* (Leiden: Brill, 2010), I.780–81, κρίνω). Are ecojustice advocates calling for eco-damnation, eco-judgment, or eco-vengeance? Not necessarily. It seems that ecojustice adopts the buzzword, "justice," which is stripped of its actual meaning, and ecotheologians simply follow the world.

[5] R. Mark Musser, *Nazi Ecology: The Oak Sacrifice of the Judeo-Christian Worldview in the Holocaust* (Taos, NM: Dispensational Publishing House, 2018), 21.

Evangelical academic institution with an agenda to promote its ecotheology among Eastern Orthodox and Evangelical[6] Christians in Ukraine and Russia. Hodos has recently taken a survey and determined that "In general, Christians of both traditions fundamentally shared the belief that the main value of nature and animals was as a resource for satisfying the biological needs of humankind."[7] They clarify:

> For example, one Evangelical interviewee said, "The role of animals is to be our transport (like donkeys, horses), be our 'living canned food,' be materials for experiments. But animals haven't been promised eternal life. They don't have the 'superstructure' of the human spirit". An Orthodox priest put it similarly, "Nature was created for humans. Sun, sea, water, air, the earth that feeds the whole population of the planet,—these are the exceptional providence of God for a human".[8]

This shows that Christians intuitively believe that man is above nature (with the obvious call for responsibility), which is in line with the plain reading of the Biblical text,[9] but the researchers rebuked the interviewees, saying "This

---

[6] "The term 'Evangelicals' is used to denote those who belong to various Russian and Ukrainian Baptist, Pentecostal, and charismatic congregations." Alexander Negrov and Alexander Malov, "Eco-Theology and Environmental Leadership in Orthodox and Evangelical Perspectives in Russia and Ukraine," 18.

[7] Ibid., 8.

[8] Ibid.

[9] The researchers note, "it was noted that in expressing personal theological perspectives on ecology and ecological responsibility, Evangelical interviewees mainly concentrated on the biblical texts and used literal understanding of the Bible, while Orthodox respondents made references to the writings of the Church Fathers and used allegorical (figurative) understanding of biblical passages that they cited." While the Eastern Orthodox use a different hermeneutic, they still seem to arrive at a similar

utilitarian and anthropocentric view has little to do with the Bible and/or Christian tradition and rather is rooted in the modernistic worldview. It is also rotted [sic] in the anthropocentric view of the salvific work of Christ and in the anthropocentric eschatological perspectives."[10] A closer look at the roots of this ecotheological movement will show that the opposite is true, that ecojustice is based on an anti-biblical worldview that is more akin to postmodernism with roots in anti-biblical atheism and anti-biblical Eastern philosophy.[11]

Contemporary Christian ecotheologians borrow much from atheist perspectives on environmentalism. Much of the ecology debate with atheists boils down to the debate between the Biblical worldview, which draws a clear distinction between the Creator and creation, as contrasted to the atheist worldview that sees a continuity of being between nature and a common source. Consider, for example, a quote from the atheist, Niel deGrasse Tyson:

> We are all connected; To each other, biologically, to the earth, chemically, and to the rest of the universe, atomically. That's kinda cool! That makes me smile and I actually feel quite large at the end of that. It's not that we are better than the universe; we're part of the universe. We're in the universe and the universe is in us.[12]

---

conclusion. Alexander Negrov and Alexander Malov, "Eco-Theology and Environmental Leadership in Orthodox and Evangelical Perspectives in Russia and Ukraine," 15–16.

[10] Ibid., 16–17.

[11] On the eastern and western influences of postmodernism, see Philippa Berry, "Postmodernism and post-religion" in *The Cambridge Companion to Postmodernism*, Steven Connor, ed. (Cambridge: Cambridge University Press, 20060), 168–181.

[12] Neil deGrasse Tyson, "We Are Star Stuff - Cosmic Poetry." Available online at https://www.youtube.com/watch?v=QADMMmU6ab8

Notice the continuity. To the atheist, all life shares a common origin in the primordial soup whence life evolved. Moreover, we share origins with all matter since we were together in the Big Bang. This concept has been labeled "Continuity of Being," and is similar to Pagan myths and Eastern philosophy, as opposed to the biblical view of "Creator/Creation Distinction."

The Continuity of Being from evolutionary cosmogony has always been a driving force behind atheist ecology,[13] but the merge with Christianity into modern ecotheology is typically traced to a lecture delivered by a medieval historian named Lynn White Jr. in 1966 at a meeting of the American Association for the Advancement of Science. The text of the lecture was later published as an article entitled, "The Historical Roots of Our Ecologic Crisis."[14] While White identified as "a churchman,"[15] he also accepted the narrative of evolution and concluded that man is not superior to nature. White shames Christianity for their attitudes that "Despite Darwin, we are not, in our hearts, part of the natural process. We are superior to nature, contemptuous of it, willing to use it for our slightest whim."[16] White summarizes his conclusion:

> We would seem to be headed toward conclusions unpalatable to many Christians. Since both science and technology are blessed words in our contemporary vocabulary, some may be happy at the notions, first, that, viewed historically, modern science is an extrapolation of natural theology and, second, that modern

---

[13] A chilling aspect of environmentalist history is the role that Ernst Haeckel, the 19th century German zoologist who even coined the term, "ecology," played in the eventual development and rise of National Socialism. See R. Mark Musser, *Nazi Ecology*, 128 *ff*.

[14] Lynn White Jr., "The Historical Roots of Our Ecologic Crisis" *Science* 155:3767 (March 10, 1967), 1203–1207.

[15] Ibid., 1206.

[16] Ibid.

> technology is at least partly to be explained as an Occidental, voluntarist realization of the Christian dogma of man's transcendence of, and rightful mastery over, nature. But, as we now recognize, somewhat over a century ago science and technology—hitherto quite separate activities—joined to give mankind powers which, to judge by many of the ecologic effects, are out of control. If so, Christianity bears a huge burden of guilt.[17]

White praised the beatniks of those days because they "show a sound instinct in their affinity for Zen Buddhism, which conceives of the man-nature relationship as very nearly the mirror image of the Christian view."[18] It seems that from the beginning of the movement, Christian ecojustice has had roots in atheism and eastern philosophy;[19] indeed, Christian ecotheology has become dominated by panentheism ("God *in* all"),[20] which is softer than pantheism ("God *is* all"), but even non-dispensational Evangelicals[21] have identified this as a problematic doctrine.[22]

---

[17] Ibid.

[18] Ibid.

[19] The Eastern philosophy has emerged to the surface again in a recent call for Asian Christians to participate in interfaith dialogue "for the development of contextual intersectional or liberationist ecotheologies which may redress this inequality" with practitioners of traditional religions, Buddhists, Confucians, and Daoists. See Anna Kirkpatrick-Jung, Tanya Riches, Towards East Asian Ecotheologies of Climate Crisis Religions 11:7 (2020), DOI:10.3390/rel11070341.

[20] As a notable exception, the socio-ecologist, Brian Snyder, modifies some panentheistic ecotheologies for a novel ecotheological perspective from the Creator/creation distinction (which he calls dualism), not in opposition to the former, but as "an alternative means of arriving at the same place." See Brian F. Snyder, "Christian Environmental Ethics and Economic Stasis" *Worldviews* 23 (2019), 154–170.

[21] See, for example, Oliver D. Crisp "Against Mereological Panentheism" *European Journal for Philosophy of Religion* 11:2 (2019), 23–41.

[22] Some ecotheologians would disagree on the importance of an orthodox understanding of God. Laura Ruth Yordy makes the shocking statement, "The anxiety about pantheism, nature-worship, or other sorts of paganism overshadows the concern

Ecojustice crosses several lines of demarcation that dispensational and non-dispensational conservatives alike should be willing to draw, but the dispensationalist has additional grounds for rejecting Christian ecojustice based on the kingdom programs that are prevalent in ecotheological trends. For example, Laura Ruth Yordy considers herself an ecotheology apologist who sees "Christianity as overgrown by weeds that obscure and choke its ecological guidance."[23] Yordy proposes that the Christian life is a witness that demands ecojustice, which she clarifies:

> By witness I mean a particular understanding of discipleship in which the communal lives of the disciples testify, through character, worship, and action, to the Kingdom of God as inaugurated, preached, demonstrated, and promised by Jesus Christ...
>
> The Kingdom is not a generic ideal that Jesus happened to talk about during his ministry, but the realization of his redemption of the world. And redemption is another way of describing "bringing back to God." So Christians witness to Christ and his work of ultimately returning all of creation back to God; that return, or communion, is the Kingdom.... Nonetheless, the Kingdom has only been inaugurated, not fulfilled, so that disciples continue to run the risk of being taunted, threatened, persecuted, or killed. Only when God establishes the Kingdom, when the Reign is fulfilled, will death be vanquished entirely.[24]

---

about creation. But why, in a culture as nature-despising as our own, should nature-worship be of such concern? It is almost as if we hesitate to feed the starving children in Afghanistan lest we make them fat." Laura Ruth Yordy, *Green Witness*, 41.

[23] Laura Ruth Yordy, *Green Witness*, 40.
[24] Ibid., 85–86, 90.

In other words, Yordy recognizes that a fundamental aspect of her ecotheological system is that the Christian life is to declare the kingdom as an already/not yet reality that grows "already" as Christians restore creation, while still anticipating a future, "not yet," establishment of the kingdom.

This treatment of the "already" kingdom is key to many forms of Christian ecojustice. The Red Letter Christian Movement (to be discussed more thoroughly below) is a Christian movement with an ecojustice agenda. One of the founders of the movement has said:

> Jesus said that this peaceable kingdom [of Isaiah 11:6] is already breaking loose in our midst. He said, "The kingdom of God is among you" (Luke 17:21 ISV). I see signs of the kingdom here and now, and I believe that his kingdom is increasing before our eyes. To be a kingdom people is to join God in what he's doing, and to participate with God in rescuing nature from the mess we've made of it.[25]

Notice that he begins with an inaugurated kingdom that is "breaking loose" today. The result is legalism, as instead of accepting God's promises as guarantees that He will fulfill, the promises become mandates that men must fulfill instead. However, if indeed the kingdom is not "already," then it is not currently "breaking loose in our midst." In other words, the theological side of this form of ecojustice falls apart if indeed the kingdom has been postponed.

After starting the Christian ecotheology revolution, Lynn White once remarked that he was amazed at how quickly churches abandoned "the old

---

[25] Shane Claiborne and Tony Campolo, *Red Letter Revolution: What If Jesus Really Meant What He Said?* (Nashville, TN: Thomas Nelson, 2012), 103–104.

scion of Man's Dominion over Nature,"[26] which includes what is referred to here as the divine institution of responsible labor. The issue is a matter of worldview; churches in the 1960s and 1970s simply were not prepared to defend the divine institutions. By no means must one be a dispensationalist to recognize the problems in the emergent trends in Christian environmentalism, but a proper understanding of the kingdom postponement and all that it entails is beneficial to developing a distinctly dispensational worldview that is safeguarded from current trends in ecotheology.

Dispensational Response

On the sixth day, God said, "Let Us make man in Our image, according to Our likeness; let them have dominion over the fish of the sea, over the birds of the air, and over the cattle, over all the earth and over every creeping thing that creeps on the earth" (Ge 1:26). God has put man above the rest of creation to be a responsible laborer. Man is greater than the plants and animals and is free to use them for food (Ge 9:3; Ps 8:6–8). Even the sun, moon, and stars were created for man's service to help him tell time (Ge 1:14). He is also free to use natural resources. Before the fall, gold, bdellium, and onyx stone were available in the land of Havilah (Ge 2:11–12). After the

---

[26] The full quote is: As the inadvertent founder, it would seem, of the Theology of Ecology, I confess amusement at the speed with which the Churches have abandoned the old scion of Man's Dominion over Nature for the equally Biblical position of Man's Trusteeship of Nature. Since the Churches remain, despite some competition, the chief forges for hammering out values, this is important. I feel that before too long, however, they will find themselves going on to the third legitimately Biblical position, that Man is part of a democracy of all God's creatures, organic and inorganic, each praising his Maker according to the law of its being. Quoted by Matthew T. Riley, "A Spiritual Democracy of All God's Creatures: Ecotheology and the Animals of Lynn White Jr." in *Divinanimality: Animal Theory, Creaturely Theology*, Stephen D. Moore, ed. (New York: Fordham University Press, 2014), 241.

fall, there were craftsmen in bronze and iron (Ge 3:22); indeed, Jesus, God incarnate Himself, was a craftsman on earth (Mk 6:3). Abraham was a chosen shepherd whose shepherd descendants served distinct roles in God's plan (Ge 15:1–6). God chose Isaac the shepherd over the wilderness wanderer, Ishmael (Gen. 21), God chose Jacob the shepherd over Esau the hunter (Ge 25–27), and God chose David, who had killed a lion and a bear in defense of his sheep (1Sa 17). The Lord is described as being a shepherd (Ps 23) and Jesus Himself is "the Lamb of God who takes away the sin of the world" (Jn 1:29), which is reminiscent of all of the animals that were sacrificed for man's benefit. The Bible presents responsible labor that uses natural resources as being good and holy.

The sufficiency of Scripture is a basic presupposition to the grammatical-historical hermeneutics of postponement theology, but ecotheologians frequently go beyond the Scriptures and appeal to the voice of nature as a source of revelation. One ecotheologian proposes the "plausibility of reading contemporary environmental concern as a response to the prophetic voices of nonhuman nature, and in that sense as a movement of the Holy Spirit."[27] Another ecotheologian writes in a similar vein, "Reading the Bible ecologically involves reading with suspicion of this bias in order to identify with creation and retrieve its voice, leading to engagement in action on behalf of creation."[28] In his appeal for ecotheologians to get out of this "hermeneutical wilderness," Peet van Dyke, a non-dispensationalist theologian, summarizes the problem:

---

[27] Rachel Muers, "The Holy Spirit, the voices of nature and environmental prophecy" *Scottish Journal of Theology* 67:3 (2014), 323–339.
[28] Jeffrey S. Lamp, "Ecotheology: A people of the Spirit for earth" in *The Routledge Handbook of Pentecostal Theology*, Wolfgang Vondey, ed. (Abingdon, Oxon: Routledge, 2020), 359.

...many eco-theologians (in their over-eagerness to discover something positive in the Bible about nature) have resorted to some serious cherry-picking, wishful-thinking and to what natural scientists would call story-telling. In extreme cases, some eco-theologians have even reverted to a kind of neo-paganist imagery in their desperate attempts to give the earth and its inhabitants a voice. Speaking about "Earth" or "mother earth" in a metaphorical sense, as if she were a conscious being, is not necessarily a problem. However, in some cases the usage of these metaphors borders on a revival of animistic beliefs, where elements of nature (both animate and inanimate) are believed to have indwelling spirits that can "speak" to us or can be addressed by humans.[29]

Christians should recognize that such ecojustice advocates have been taken captive "through philosophy and empty deceit, according to the tradition of men, according to the basic principles of the world, and not according to Christ" (Col 2:8).

The dispensational worldview argues for responsible labor, which includes responsibly subduing the land for human productivity. If a Christian is, as White accuses, "contemptuous" of nature, then he is irresponsible, which is a violation of the divine institution. Ecotheologians seem to miss this point when they write such things as, "Within millennialism it is believed that the faithful would very soon be swept away from earth and the 'obvious correlation is that present earth does not matter, is to be used and even destroyed with impunity.'"[30] Since dispensationalism is based on a holistic

---

[29] Peet van Dyk, "Eco-Theology: In and out of the Wilderness" *Old Testament Essays* 30:3 (2017), 836. He quotes N.H. Creegan, "Theological foundations of the ecological crisis," 31–33.

[30] Peet van Dyk "Challenges in the Search for an Ecotheology," 200. He quotes N.H. Creegan, "Theological foundations of the ecological crisis," 33.

understanding of Scripture, responses to this accusation, and current trends in ecotheology as a whole, can come from the Old Testament, which is silent on the issue of the rapture.

Isaiah 11:6–10 is particularly relevant to the discussion, as it is a passage to which ecotheologians of a kingdom-now perspective frequently appeal:

> "The wolf also shall dwell with the lamb,
> The leopard shall lie down with the young goat,
> The calf and the young lion and the fatling together;
> And a little child shall lead them.
> The cow and the bear shall graze;
> Their young ones shall lie down together;
> And the lion shall eat straw like the ox.
> The nursing child shall play by the cobra's hole,
> And the weaned child shall put his hand in the viper's den.
> They shall not hurt nor destroy in all My holy mountain,
> "For the earth shall be full of the knowledge of the LORD"
> As the waters cover the sea.
> "And in that day there shall be a Root of Jesse,
> Who shall stand as a banner to the people;
> For the Gentiles shall seek Him,
> And His resting place shall be glorious."

Isaiah 11:6–9 describes a renewed environment, followed by verse 10, which attaches that environment to the day when the Root of Jesse "shall stand as a banner to the people." Since dispensationalists see that day as yet future, they see the redacted curse as yet future. Christian ecojustice advocates see the kingdom as already, so they see the redacted curse as already, but with the caveat that the responsibility falls on the church to redact said curse.

A noticeable problem with non-literal approaches is that since Isaiah 11:6–9 is not fulfilled in a plain sense, inaugurated interpreters are left to guess in what sense it is fulfilled. Dwight Pentecost stated a fundamental concept of dispensational interpretation when he wrote, "Inasmuch as God gave the Word of God as a revelation to men, it would be expected that His revelation would be given in such exact and specific terms that His thoughts would be accurately conveyed and understood when interpreted according to the laws of grammar and speech."[31] Among kingdom-now advocates, there is not and cannot be a consensus of Isaiah's meaning, since he cannot be interpreted according to the regular conventions of communication. Eusebius of Caesarea supposed that Isaiah 11:6 is fulfilled by "the church of God, where noble people who have been decorated with worldly honors and awards are gathered together with the poor and the commoners,"[32] while others "understand the wild beasts as referring to the barbarians and Greeks (Eusebius) or Jews (Cyril) transformed by the teachings of Christ."[33] Other commentators have proposed that "a little child shall lead them" is a reference "to Christ, already mentioned in Isaiah 9:6 (Jerome) and frequently described as a shepherd (Henry), but Calvin thinks instead of communities so obedient that their leaders will not need force or violence to restrain them (Calvin: cf. Cyril)."[34] Verse 9 refers to the holy mountain, but this is often spiritualized as well so that the interpretation of "For the earth shall be full of the knowledge of the LORD" is left to the mercy of the interpreter. One historian notes:

---

[31] J. Dwight Pentecost, *Things to Come: A Study in Biblical Eschatology* (Grand Rapids, MI: Dunham Publishing Company, 1958), 10.

[32] Eusebius, *Commentary on Isaiah*, Jonathan J. Armstrong, trans. and Joel C. Elowsky ed. (Downers Grove, IL: InterVarsity Press, 2014), 64.

[33] John F. A. Sawyer, *Isaiah Through The Centuries* (Hoboken, NJ: John Wiley & Sons Ltd, 2018), 84.

[34] Ibid., 85.

> Christian commentators from all ages relate it to New Testament texts about the disciples going forth to all nations (Matt 28:19; cf. John 6:45) (Athanasius, Against the Arians 1.13.8) and predictions that 'at the name of Jesus every knee shall bow' (Phil 2:10) (Cyril). John Wesley's sermon entitled 'The General Spread of the Gospel' (1783) is an exposition of this verse (Sermons 2.481–499).[35]

Several ecotheologians propose that the ecological crisis began in the West with the Industrial Revolution that was founded on Christian ideals. There are scientific and historic problems with this assumption,[36] but regardless, pre-industrial Christian interpreters could not have understood a post-industrial ecological crisis in the text, much less could Isaiah's original audience.

While dispensationalists do not always agree on every detail of Scripture, certain concepts are readily apparent and will certainly surface from a grammatical-historical perspective. The Old Testament description of the coming kingdom as a time when the Edenic curse will be partially restrained is one such concept. Donald Cameron has collected statements from various dispensationalists on the restored animal kingdom:

> Dr Ironside comments: "[Isaiah 11] Verses 6 to 9 are not to be take as symbolic. The actual fulfilment of the conditions of the animal world will be the natural outcome of the presence and authority of Christ." There is a shorter prophecy in Isa 65:25–26 about restored

---

[35] Ibid., 85.
[36] See, for example, S. Fred Singer and Dennis T. Avery, *Unstopable Global Warming Every 1,500 Years*, updated and expanded (Plymouth, UK: Rowman & Littlefield Publishers, 2008), 29–59.

> animal life. Dr Scroggie writes in a similar vein: "In that period, the blessings are material as well as spiritual; the lower creation and nature also participate in the new order of things, which certainly is not true of the Christian Age". William Kelly puts these matters into perspective: "Indeed the mighty and blessed transformation which the Lord will cause for the lower creation is but part of the still grander prospect which the reconciliation of all things opens (Col 1:20); when the things in the heavens and the things on the earth, even the universe, shall be headed up in the Christ, the heir of all things" (Eph 1:10). Evolution will play no part—were there to be evolution—a purely hypothetical situation. To be consistent, this would make the carnivorous even more efficient raptors rather than peace loving! Only He who imposed the curse can and will remove it.[37]

Such statements align with a plain reading of the text that accepts the kingdom as a literal reality that was postponed until a future date, but it is also noteworthy that even non-dispensationalists recognize the plain meaning of the text, even if they disagree with dispensationalism.

A glaring example would be the bulk of Jewish commentators who see Isaiah 11:6–9 as a reference to the future messianic kingdom while rejecting the legitimacy of Jesus Christ altogether.[38] J. M. M. Roberts has written a

---

[37] Donald CB Cameron, *The Millennium: Restoration after Retribution* (Kilmarnock, Scotland: John Ritchie Ltd., 2014), 156–157. He cites HA Ironside, *The Prophet Isaiah* (London: Pickering & Inglis, 1952), 50; W Graham Scroggie, *Prophecy and History* (London & Edinburgh, Marshall, Morgan & Scott, nd), 98–99; and William Kelly, *An Exposition of the Book of Isaiah* (Oak Park, IL: Bible Truth Publishers, 1975 reprint), 274.

[38] See Andor Kelenhegyi, "The Beast Between Us: The Construction of Identity and Alterity through Animal Symbolism in Late Antique Jewish and Christian Tradition" PhD Dissertation, Central European University, Budapest, 2017, 219–220; cf. Mekhilta de Rabbi Ishmael Pisha 12:1; Sifra Hukkotai 1. Interestingly, Samuel

commentary on Isaiah from a theologically liberal perspective, wherein he rightly notes a connection to the pre-fallen world, but unfortunately writes off the Genesis account as a myth, such that the reliability of Isaiah and other biblical authors[39] are diminished. This is in clear contradiction to the grammatical-historicist's insistence on biblical inerrancy,[40] but then Roberts recognizes that from the original audience's perspective, "the expectation of a return to that mythological golden age of peace and security between humans and animals under the messianic rule of God's ideal king is not surprising."[41] A key disagreement between the dispensationalist's and Roberts' perspectives is that while they agree with what the author meant, the dispensationalist *agrees with the biblical author* while Roberts diminishes it to a similar status as other Ancient Near Eastern texts.[42]

A more condemning quote comes from within the Christian ecojustice movement itself. Gene Tucker, who generally agrees with Lynn White,[43] brings out some natural conclusions, with which he disagrees, to a plain interpretation of Isaiah 11:6–9:

White's commentary from 1709, which claims to approach Isaiah literally, mocking contains, "The *Jews* are so simple as to ground their Hopes of their Imaginary Messiah, still to come, upon this and other such like Expressions, the literal Completion of which they still expect." Samuel White, *A commentary on the prophet Isaiah, wherein the literal sense of his prophecy's is briefly explain'd* (London: Arthur Collins, 1709), 89.

[39] Roberts mentions Leviticus 26:6, Ezekiel 34:25–26, and Hosea 2:18. J. J. M. Roberts, *First Isaiah*, Peter Machinist, ed. (Minneapolis: 1517 Media, 2015), 180. doi:10.2307/j.ctvgs0919.21.

[40] Paul Lee Tan, *The Interpretation of Prophecy* (Dallas: Bible Communications, Inc., 2010), 275–277.

[41] J. J. M. Roberts, *First Isaiah*, 180.

[42] Ibid., 180–182.

[43] Gene M. Tucker, "Rain on a Land Where No One Lives: The Hebrew Bible on the Environment" *Journal of Biblical Literature* 116:1 (Spring, 1997), 3–6.

> In the context of the announcement of a new Davidic king (11:1–5), these verses proclaim a transformation in the natural, cosmic sphere. Natural enemies in the animal world will live together in peace, even changing their diets. On the one hand, as so frequently in the prophetic literature, the poem stresses the relationship between justice, mercy, peace, and harmony in the natural order (cf. also Hos 1:18 and Ezek 34:25). Who does not long for a world without fear and violence? But on the other hand, the lines suggest that the world may have been created good, even very good, but not quite good enough. The text presumes a negative evaluation of the world as it is, filled with predators and prey, violence and death. One message of the passage, to put it bluntly, is that there will come a time when the world will be made safe for domestic animals and for children.
>
> It is a serious problem for the affirmation of a good creation. Such visions, wonderful as they are, when linked with the sense of a fallen humanity and an earth that is cursed, pave the way for the apocalyptic rejection of this world as it is. So, does creation need to be redeemed?[44]

Notice Tucker's apparent agreement with dispensationalists over the original intention of Isaiah 11:1–5 (cf. Hos 1:18, Eze 34:25). The thrust of the disagreement is not over what the text of Isaiah seems to say, but rather it is over whether or not one should accept the plain meaning. An underlying disagreement is that Tucker argues that the ground was not corrupted at the fall, but instead that humanity's relationship to nature became detached and

---

[44] Ibid., 11–12.

ambiguous.⁴⁵ His article never offers a reconciliation of Isaiah 11 with his ecotheology, but seems to brush the issue under a rug.⁴⁶ This passage is troublesome for the ecojustice perspectives on the past (what happened at the fall), the present (the current state of nature), and the future (whether a curse will be reduced), but it fits perfectly within the dispensational framework of history.

The curse will be partially redacted in the days of the messianic kingdom such that natural enemies from the animal kingdom can dwell in peace. This promise is stated quite plainly in Isaiah 11 and elsewhere. The defense of responsible labor on the grounds of kingdom postponement is a particularly dispensational aspect of worldview, since other theologians spiritualize, allegorize, or mythologize the promises of a redacted curse.

THE KINGDOM OFFER AND THE DIVINE INSTITUTIONS OF MARRIAGE AND FAMILY

Trends in Critical Theology

Current trends in critical theology, specifically related to feminist liberation theology and queer theology undermine heterosexual complementarianism, which is a Biblical restriction of gender, gender roles, and sexuality that serves as the basis of the divine institutions of marriage and family. The Christian versions of these trends will tend to read Jesus as establishing a spiritual kingdom of social justice on earth, which comes with a Church Age mandate for Christians to endorse that which the world deems as "social justice," thereby leaving the church vulnerable to views that are in

---

⁴⁵ Ibid., 6–9. His conclusion is based on a division of the text into a Priestly and a Yahwist source, which tends to be another point of contention with dispensationalism's high view of Scripture.

⁴⁶ Ibid., 16.

clear contradiction to the biblical text. Several of these systems collapse, however, if one starts with the presupposition that Jesus offered a literal kingdom that was rejected and that He therefore postponed the kingdom to a future day.

Modern evangelical liberation theologians tend to read Jesus as spiritualizing and inaugurating the kingdom, such that the church's current mission is to do likewise. Often the liberation theologian's starting point is similar to the dispensationalist's. For example, the liberation theologian, David Gushee, recounts his work with Glen Stassen:

> Kingdom hope intensified, we suggest, whenever real-world Jewish realities worsened. The destruction of Jerusalem and the Temple in 587–586 BC, the Exile, the loss of Jewish sovereignty under a succession of world powers, and, in the time of Jesus, the miseries and offenses of pagan Roman occupation, sharpened and even more deeply politicized Kingdom hope—which became the hope of Israel being delivered from foreign oppressors, and sometimes broadened to the hope of a world transformed. Kingdom hope was never otherworldly, though sometimes it sounds somewhat dreamy with lions and lambs lying down in peace together. It was certainly a social hope; a this-worldly hope; a Jewish hope. Its themes are entirely alien to the classical world of Greece and Rome.
>
> It is this account of this particular species of apocalyptic, messianic, Jewish eschatology that we offered as the theological frame within which Jesus of Nazareth, Messiah of Israel and Lord of the Church and the world, offered his moral teachings.[47]

---

[47] David P. Gushee and Cori D. Norred, "The Kingdom of God, Hope and Christian Ethics" *Studies in Christian Ethics* 31:1 (2018), 5–6.

It seems from this quote that Gushee and Stassen recognize the plain description of the kingdom according to the Old Testament prophets. The great divide occurs over their understanding of how Jesus used the Old Testament and what He did while He was on earth. Rather than seeing Jesus as offering to establish this literal kingdom, they see Jesus as redefining the prophetic tradition and making the kingdom of God into a current reality of social justice that carries over as a mandate for the church:

> Through the exegetical work that Glen Stassen primarily undertook, we became convinced that Jesus drew most heavily for his version of 'Kingdom of God' on materials in Isaiah, especially the redemptive/restorationist themes of Isaiah 40–66. In choosing to anchor his preaching mainly in this part of Isaiah, Jesus was authentically connected to his Jewish roots but, perhaps like all prophets, selectively appropriated those aspects of the tradition that he wanted to highlight…
>
> Stassen and I identified seven 'marks' of the Kingdom of God in Jesus' preaching, citing passages in the Synoptic Gospels that allude to, cite or parallel passages in Isaiah. These seven purported marks of the Kingdom are deliverance (salvation), justice, peace, healing, restoration of community, the experience of God's active redeeming presence, and joyful human response…
>
> To the extent that we practice his peace-making, justice-making, community-restoring, relationship-healing teachings, we participate in the inaugurated Kingdom of God. This is what it

means to be a follower, or disciple, of Jesus Christ. This is also the primary task of the Christian Church.[48]

Their evangelical liberation theology became manifest in gender issues, which resulted in them leaving their roles at Southern Baptist Theological Seminary in 1996.[49]

Gushee and Stassen recognize "a patriarchal strand [i.e. complementarianism] and an egalitarian strand in the New Testament, in Paul and beyond Paul," but they write it off as a "deeply ingrained patriarchalism of the ancient world," preferring that "egalitarianism certainly fits the characteristics of our own ethical method much more adequately."[50] This fluid approach to biblical inerrancy is common in egalitarianism.[51] Phyllis Trible is a feminist who writes more bluntly:

> A feminist who loves the Bible produces, in the thinking of many, an oxymoron. Perhaps clever as rhetoric, the description offers no possibility for existential integrity. After all, if no man can serve two masters, no woman can serve two authorities, a master called scripture and a mistress called feminism.[52]

---

[48] Ibid., 6.
[49] David P. Gushee and Glen H. Stassen, *Kingdom Ethics*, 235.
[50] Ibid., 240.
[51] See Carlos Montoya, "How Egalitarianism Attacks Inerrancy in the Latin American Church," in *God's Perfect Word: The Implications of Inerrancy for the Global Church*, Mark Tatlock, ed. (Sun Valley, CA: The Master's Academy International, 2015), 64–76.
[52] Phyllis Trible, quoted by Mary A. Kassian, *The Feminist Gospel: The Movement to Unite Feminism With the Church* (Wheaton, IL: Crossway Books, 1992), 109.

The call to feminism is a call to abandon the objective meaning of the Biblical text; indeed, the related doctrine of the social gospel typically rests on liberal theology, as Earl Radmacher explains:

> The leading concept among leading liberal theologians was that the church is a spiritual society with the task of spreading the "social gospel," which act paves the way for the coming kingdom… Because of their blind optimism as to the essential goodness of man and his possibility of progress, they saw little need for the local churches, which simply impeded this progress by feverishly clinging to their ecclesiastical dogmas and traditions.[53]

While the dispensationalist explains the church's mandate in terms of evangelism and discipleship,[54] systems that advocate a liberation, a social gospel, or the like (whether they are liberal or conservative), typically blur the church's vision into growing a spiritual kingdom on earth[55] through charitable works to usher in the eschaton.[56] This view is incompatible with dispensationalism for several reasons,[57] but one key reason is that

---

[53] Earl D. Radmacher, *The Nature of the Church* (Hayesville, NC: Schoettle Publishing Co., 1996), 92.

[54] Bret Nazworth, "God's Grace in Missions, Evangelism, and Disciple-Making" in *Freely By His Grace: Classical Grace Theology*, J.B. Hixon, Rick Whitmore, and Roy Zuck, eds. (Duluth, MN: Grace Gospel Press, 2012), 553–580.

[55] The postmillennialist version of this is presented well in David Chilton, *Paradise Restored*, 71.

[56] John MacArthur and Richard Mayhue, eds., *Biblical Doctrine: A Systematic Summary of Bible Truth* (Wheaton, IL: Crossway, 2017), 886–888.

[57] Thomas Ice was a Christian Reconstructionist who was a dispensationalist from 1974 to 1986. The system eventually collapsed as it was too contradictory. His testimony is recommended and available in Thomas Ice and Hershel Wayne House, *Dominion Theology: Blessing or Curse* (Portland: Multnomah, 1988), 7 *ff*.

dispensationalism sees the kingdom as postponed as opposed to an inaugurated, growing spiritual reality.

Another hermeneutical key to feminist liberation philosophy is the worldview lens that sees the world as being run by patriarchy that oppresses women. Elisabeth Schüssler Fiorenza exemplifies this aspect of critical feminist liberation theology when she writes regarding the woman with the spirit of infirmity who was bent over in Luke 13:10–17, "Recognizing ourselves in the story of the wo/man bent double, we wo/men must identify ourselves *as wo/men* deformed and exploited by societal and ecclesiastical kyriarchy."[58] Schüssler Fiorenza expounds further:

> In short, a critical feminist the*logy of liberation names the*logically the kyriarchal bondage of wo/men in Western society and church. Kyriarchy inculcates and perpetrates not only sexism but also racism and property-class relationships as basic structures of wo/men's oppression. In a kyriarchal society or religion all wo/men are bound into a system of male privilege and domination, but impoverished third-world wo/men constitute the bottom of the oppressive kyriarchal pyramid. Kyriarchy cannot be toppled except when the basis or bottom of the kyriarchal pyramid—which consists of the exploitation of multiply oppressed wo/men—becomes liberated.[59]

We are socialized into gender roles as soon as we are born. Every culture gives different symbolic significance and derives different social roles from the human biological capacities of sexual intercourse, childbearing, and lactation. Sexual dimorphism and strictly defined gender roles are products of a kyriarchal culture,

---

[58] Elisabeth Schüssler Fiorenza, *Changing Horizons: Expolorations in Feminist Interpretation* (Minneapolis: Fortress Press, 2013), 247.
[59] Ibid., 247.

which maintain and legitimize structures of control and domination, that is, the exploitation of wo/men by men.[60]

This lens depicts males negatively and raises the question of the reliability of a male Christ, and so a need arises for unique feminist Christologies:

> As the early proponents of feminist theology strove to understand the exclusion of women and women's experience in church practice and theological reflection, they were increasingly faced with the realization that it may be the very fabric of Christianity that caused the exclusion. Traditional belief held that Christ's incarnation and subsequent death and descent into hell were to enable the divine to experience all and therefore redeem all. If Christ could not experience being female, then the question arose as to whether the female state could be redeemed.[61]

Christian feminism often reframes the doctrine of Christ so that Christology becomes "a political practice, aiming not only at personal change, but also at structural change."[62] The redirecting of attention to overthrowing the patriarchy distracts the feminist from the biblical teaching of redemption, as "Redemption, then, within feminist christology is about liberation. Therefore it involves struggle against oppression as well as struggle for personal integrity and human freedom; it is about wholeness and transformation."[63]

---

[60] Ibid., 250–251.
[61] Lisa Isherwood, "Feminist Christologies" in *The Blackwell Companion to Jesus*, Delbert Burkett, ed. (West Sussex, UK: Blackwell Publishing Ltd., 2011), 428.
[62] Ibid., 432.
[63] Ibid.

Biblical Distinctions Applied 313

Feminist theologies quickly fall into Christological fallacies, which are too numerous to list here, but several of the more liberal errors that are relevant to the current discussion can be boiled down to a Christology of embodiment in place of a metaphysical Christology. The notion, in so many words, is that since God became human, the Bible is not the best source of Christology, but rather people should turn to their own bodies to understand Christ. The feminist theologian, Rita Nakashima Brock, has called the more Scriptural approach to Christology, "the broken heart of patriarchy, as we have been encouraged to rip ourselves away from what is dear to us: feeling, the earth, others, ourselves."[64] The result is a Christology that associates Christ with "erotic power." Lisa Isherwood is another feminist Christologist who summarizes this school of thought:

> Carter Heyward and Rita Brock are two feminist theologians associated with the notion of Christ as erotic power. Brock believes that when speaking of Jesus as powerful, we have to be quite clear about what type of power we are speaking of, and for her it is erotic power. This understanding leaves us in no doubt about where the source of this power lies. It is not an abstract concept but is deeply embedded in our very being and is part of our nature, residing there as our innate desire to relate with each other, not just for the benefit of the individual self, but for the justice and growth of the whole cosmos. This kind of power is wild and cannot be controlled, and living at this level saves us from sterility that comes from living by the head alone. Christianity has always encouraged agape, a type of love that Brock sees as heady and objective and therefore not as

---

[64] Rita Nakashima Brock, *Journeys by Heart: A Christology of Erotic Power* (New York: Crossroad, 1988), cited by Lisa Isherwood, "Feminist Christologies," 435.

> something that will change the world. Eros on the other hand will engage us and so can change the world. Brock is convinced that erotic power redeems both the world and Christ.[65]

The abandonment of the "heady and objective" approach to knowing Christ in favor of an embodiment leaves the interpretation to the subjective whims of the interpreter's erotic leanings. Not everyone has heterosexual erotic leanings, so it follows that for feminist Christology to be sustainable, there must be room for a related queer theology. In her book entitled, *The Carnal Knowledge of God*, Rebecca Voelkel argues for an embodied theology that affirms her complexities as a cisgender lesbian. She begins her case from a panentheistic perspective:

> One way to describe this connection, this shared essence, this real relationship is that God has "carnal knowledge" of humanity. God, in the act of creation, draws from God's own essence and places part of God's self within creation. God knows intimately creation's embodiment. God understands and is in deep relationship with our flesh and bones. God creates in order to be in passionate relationship with creation. "Let us make humankind in our image, according to our likeness," is one way God expresses this carnal relationship. And, in a related way, humanity has carnal knowledge of God—for how could we not, being embodied? We can have some understanding of God's body, God's longings, God's desires because of how God created us.[66]

---

[65] Lisa Isherwood, "Feminist Christologies," 435.
[66] Rebecca M. M. Voelkel, *Carnal Knowledge of God: Embodied Love and the Movement for Justice* (Minneapolis: Fortress Press, 2017), 7.

This is the root of feminist and queer theological understandings of God, but the topic at hand is eschatology and specifically how kingdom postponement protects dispensational congregants. Voelkel recognizes her theology's dependence on an already/not yet view of the kingdom:

> Any constructive theological project that takes seriously women's and genderqueer people's bodies and sexualities is deeply eschatological. That is to say, the vision of how and what the world ought to be and how and what God's future holds forms the basis and inspiration for much of liberated, feminist, queered embodiment. Especially in a colonized context, an eschatological vision is necessary to discern what liberation, decolonization, and hope might look like.
>
> ... Eschatology has traditionally been focused on the "last things." But many Christians recognize that eschatology is more properly about the promised reign of God in all human experience and in all creation. It has powerful implications for both the individual and the community. Eschatology is not primarily concerned with what lies beyond death and outside of history. Eschatology is a practical and vital hope for the world as it is right now and in which we are all participating.
>
> This "here and now" eschatology fits well with a liberation, feminist, and queer understanding of eschatology. It roots our Christian hope in what God is doing to create a more just and liberated world. Nevertheless, precisely because justice is a major part of what we are hoping for, a sense of the timing and pacing of the eschaton is key.
>
> Here, I am aligning myself with a tradition that celebrates an inaugurated eschatology as contrasted with a "realized" or

"sapiential" eschatology on the one hand and "futuristic" or "apocalyptic" eschatology on the other.⁶⁷

Several liberation and queer theologians would disagree with Voelkel's future kingdom, but the future aspect of her eschatology does not conflict with her main contention. Rather, she seems to be demonstrating that it is the "already" aspect of the kingdom that her queer theology depends on, so allowing for a future kingdom does not contradict liberation theology so long as there is still a current spiritual kingdom to rely upon.⁶⁸ Postponement theology rejects this foundational aspect of Voelkel's system.

Another way to view Queer Theology and Feminist Theology is to see them as the theological sides of Queer Theory and Feminist Theory, which in turn are fields of Critical Theory.⁶⁹ Modern Critical Theory is inseparable from "intersectionality," which is a term that Kimberlé Williams Crenshaw coined in 1989 to address legal challenges for Black women,⁷⁰ but has since proven to be a constant work-in-progress, a global academic movement to identify and engulf new critical groups.⁷¹ The queer theologian, Chris Greenough, illustrates:

---

⁶⁷ Ibid., 79–80.

⁶⁸ Social gospel sentiments have also infiltrated progressive dispensationalism, which has a similar already/not yet approach to the kingdom. See the discussion on progressive dispensationalism and related issues in Andrew Woods, *The Coming Kingdom*, 345–347.

⁶⁹ Chris Greenough traces the development of queer theology from its roots in liberation theology to feminist theology to queer theology, which is the inevitable result of what came previously in Chris Greenough, *Queer Theologies* (Abingdon, Oxon: Routledge, 2020), 8–32.

⁷⁰ Kimberlé Williams Crenshaw, "Demarginalizing the Intersection of Race and Sex: A Black Feminist Critique of Antidiscrimination Doctrine, Feminist Theory and Antiracist Politics" *University of Chicago Legal Forum* 1989, 139–167.

⁷¹ For a history of significant developments through 2013, see Devon W. Carbado, Kimberlé Williams Crenshaw, Vickie M. Mays, Barbara Tomlinson,

> Intersectionality shows how systems of oppression and discrimination are multiple. The most marginalised people, therefore, fall under multiple minority groups. Writings from feminist and womanist thinkers were critical in the development of thinking (contesting categories of identity and exploring issues of marginalisation) which later came to characterise queer theory.[72]

Critical Race Theory is another discipline of Critical Theory, which one would imagine is separate from Queer Theology and Feminist Theology, but since they are under the umbrella of Critical Theory, they are intertwined through intersectionality. Another queer theologian has observed "that questions of sex and questions of race are always inextricably related."[73]

Racism is sin. It is anti-biblical as are the aberrant views of gender roles and sexuality that Queer Theory and Feminist Theory promote, but queer and feminist theologies have managed to infiltrate mainstream Christianity in recent years through their attachment to Black theology. As one "African American queer lesbian womanist scholar" puts it, "The disenfranchisement of women intersects with the disenfranchisement of Black men, of poor people, etc.; the disenfranchisement of Black lesbian women intersects with the disenfranchisement of transgender women, and so on."[74] Well-intended evangelicals have become entangled with some views that undermine the

---

"Intersectionality: Mapping the Movements of a Theory," *Du Bois Review* 10:2 (Fall 2013), 405-424.

[72] Chris Greenough, *Queer Theologies*, 24.

[73] Susannah Cornwall, *Controversies in Queer Theology* (London, SCM Press, 2011), 104.

[74] Pamela R. Lightsey, *Our Lives Matter: A Womanist Queer Theology* (Eugene, OR: Pickwick Publications, 2015), xx.

divine institutions of marriage and family by accepting certain fronts of anti-racism that are accompanied by critical theology.⁷⁵

The hashtag #blacklivesmatter emerged in 2013 after the acquittal of George Zimmerman, and a movement grew, which led to the establishment of Black Lives Matter Global Network (BLM) to serve as a loose network of activists in the Black Lives Matter Movement.⁷⁶ It has been estimated that "about half of the United States' Protestant clergy (both Black and White) were engaged by BLM, sensing its possibility for racial justice,"⁷⁷ so it seems that BLM perspectives could be integrating into a significant portion of the American Protestant worldview. At first, this may sound like good news for

---

⁷⁵ Similarities that predate Crenshaw's intersectionality can be seen in the example of Martin Luther King Jr., who did much good for America, but whose low view of Scripture led to a rejection of the divine sonship of Jesus, the virgin birth, and the bodily resurrection and therefore a spiritualization of the second coming of Christ, the day of judgment, immortality, and the kingdom of God. King's theology has gone essentially unnoticed by evangelicals, who rightfully praise the good that he did, but fail to examine the underlying presuppositions. King is rightly declared a heretic, yet he is hailed as an icon of Christian social justice by atheists and Christians alike.

For an example of King's low view of Scripture, see Martin Luther King Jr. "Light on the Old Testament from the Ancient Near East" in *The Papers of Martin Luther King, Jr. Volume I: Called to Serve, January 1929-June 1951* Clayborne Carson, Ralph Luker, and Penny A. Russell, eds. (Los Angeles: University of California Press at Berkley, 1992), 162–180.

For King's rejection of the divine sonship of Jesus, the virgin birth, and the bodily resurrection, see Martin Luther King Jr. "What Experiences of Christians Living in the Early Christian Century Led to the Christian Doctrines of the Divine Sonship of Jesus, the Virgin Birth, and the Bodily Resurrection" in *The Papers of Martin Luther King, Jr. Volume I*, 225–230.

For King's spiritualization of the second coming of Christ, the day of judgment, immortality, and the Kingdom of God, see Martin Luther King Jr. "The Christian Pertinence of Eschatological Hope" in *The Papers of Martin Luther King, Jr. Volume I*, 268–273.

⁷⁶ Adam Szetela (2020) Black Lives Matter at five: limits and possibilities, Ethnic and Racial Studies, 43:8, 1358-1383, DOI: 10.1080/01419870.2019.1638955

⁷⁷ Melissa M. Matthes, *When Sorrow Comes: The Power of Sermons from Pearl Harbor to Black Lives Matter* (Cambridge: Harvard University Press, 2021), 312.

Biblical Distinctions Applied 319

dispensationalists, who want to reach people of all races, but BLM actually promotes a worldview that undermines the divine institutions of marriage and family.

The BLM website featured a "What We Believe" page, which has since been withdrawn, though the original version is archived on the University of Central Arkansas website.[78] This statement put BLM's intentions in clear terms, and is worth resurfacing here since there has been no indication that BLM has changed views. The statement includes:

> We see ourselves as part of the global Black family, and we are aware of the different ways we are impacted or privileged as Black people who exist in different parts of the world.
>
> We are guided by the fact that all Black lives matter, regardless of actual or perceived sexual identity, gender identity, gender expression, economic status, ability, disability, religious beliefs or disbeliefs, immigration status, or location.
>
> We make space for transgender brothers and sisters to participate and lead.
>
> We are self-reflexive and do the work required to dismantle cisgender privilege and uplift Black trans folk, especially Black trans women who continue to be disproportionately impacted by trans-antagonistic violence...
>
> We disrupt the Western-prescribed nuclear family structure requirement by supporting each other as extended families and "villages" that collectively care for one another, especially our

---

[78] Available online at https://uca.edu/training/files/2020/09/black-Lives-Matter-Handout.pdf.

children, to the degree that mothers, parents, and children are comfortable.

We foster a queer-affirming network. When we gather, we do so with the intention of freeing ourselves from the tight grip of heteronormative thinking, or rather, the belief that all in the world are heterosexual (unless s/he or they disclose otherwise)...

We embody and practice justice, liberation, and peace in our engagements with one another.[79]

Of particular interest to this discussion is the explicit assault on the divine institutions of marriage and family. All spiritually healthy Christians want to help trans people—though there is disagreement over methodology—a difference with BLM is on the treatment of those who are cisgender; in addition to uplifting Black trans folk, whatever that means, BLM specifically wants to dismantle cisgender privilege. In the BLM worldview, it is preferable to be queer rather than heterosexual and families should be blurred into wider villages.

The Black Lives Matters movement does not claim to be Christian, though Christians are accepting the cause and ideology. Cru is a large Evangelical parachurch organization that is generally reflective of the state of Evangelicalism. Cru has been drifting into Critical Theory for several years now, and the events of 2020 increased the tensions within the organization, thus prompting several staff members to write a 174-page document entitled, *Seeking Clarity and Unity*[80] in November 2020. The document circulated internally before being released to the public in May 2021. Cru has since then

---

[79] Ibid.

[80] Scott Pendleton, et al., *Seeking Clarity and Unity* (Cru, 2020). Available online at https://languagendreligion.files.wordpress.com/2021/05/seeking-clarity-and-unity.pdf.

withdrawn the document from its website.[81] While, according to the document, Critical Race Theory is the bulk of the concern within CRU, it is inseparable from Queer Theory, which involves topics that are recurring in the document as well.[82] As circles within Cru accept the BLM agenda,[83] one is left wondering if this Evangelical mega-organization is now, in accordance with BLM's purpose, trying to "disrupt the Western-prescribed nuclear family structure."

Perhaps a more consistent example of a critical theology movement that claims to be Christian is the Red Letter Christian movement. The movement's co-founder, Tony Campolo, describes the term: "By calling ourselves Red Letter Christians, we are alluding to those old versions of the Bible wherein the words of Jesus are printed in red. In adopting the name, we are saying that we are committed to living out the things that Jesus taught."[84] Campolo believes the entire Bible to be inspired, but sees a contrast rather than continuity throughout, as "Those black letters that make up the words of the Old Testament are the record of those mighty acts in which we see God revealed," whereas in "the red letters of the Gospels, Jesus spells out for us specific directives for how his followers should relate to others and what sacrifices are required of them if they are to be citizens of his kingdom."[85] Since Jesus spoke much about the kingdom, and since Red

---

[81] In the *Christianity Today* article, "Cru Divided Over Emphasis on Race" (published on June 3, 2021), Curtis Yee gives the history of the document and links to a page on the Cru website that is not functional, presumably because the document has been withdrawn. It is still available online elsewhere. See Yee's article at https://www.christianitytoday.com/news/2021/june/cru-divided-over-emphasis-on-race.html.

[82] Scott Pendleton, et al., *Seeking Clarity and Unity* (Cru, 2020), 4, 12, 24, 35, 40, 45, 47, 50, 56, 59, 73, 74, 75, 92, 93, 95, 97, 98, 101, 103, 104, 110, 122.

[83] Ibid., 4, 6, 9, 29, 40, 41.

[84] Tony Campolo, *Red Letter Christians* (Grand Rapids: Regal Books, 2008), 20–21.

[85] Shane Claiborne and Tony Campolo, *Red Letter Revolution: What If Jesus Really Meant What He Said?* (Nashville, TN: Thomas Nelson, 2012), 8.

Letter Christians understand Jesus's words as commanding the church to advocate social justice, it comes as no surprise that much of the Red Letter justice agenda is inseparable from a kingdom-now eschatology.

On the surface, it may seem that Red Letter Christians have a high regard for Jesus and the Bible, but the Red Letter Christians website is more telling. The website has a blog with categories such as Creation & Environment, Interfaith, Race, Women, and LGBTQ+, each featuring blog posts from their perspective, which has plenty of examples of critical theologians appealing to non-biblical and even anti-biblical sources[86] and cherry-picking[87] the biblical evidence when they do use the Bible. Red Letter Christians redefine Christ's kingdom teaching into a current spiritual kingdom of social justice as is apparent in the "Red Letter Christian Pledge," which is as follows:

> I dedicate my life to Jesus, and commit to live as if Jesus meant the things he said in the "red letters" of Scripture.

---

[86] For example, a blog post from the Red Letter Christians website includes: "As recently as 2013, you could catch me making Christian apologetic arguments against same-sex marriage. But the more I've consumed content by artists like Lil Nas X, the more I realize the church and some of the puritanical standards I parroted end up creating a special kind of hell on earth for those on the receiving end of that condemnation. And for that I am sorry." Bauer, Mark Bauer, "What Lil Nas X is Telling Us About the Hell We Create," Red Letter Christians, April 7, 2021, https://www.redletterchristians.org/what-lil-nas-x-is-telling-us-about-the-hell-we-create/.

[87] For example, another blog post on the Red Letter Christians website has: "…where is our sexual ethic to be found? In Biblical principle, not precedent. Jesus tells us to love our neighbor and to do to others what we want done to us. Is cheating on my partner wrong? Yes, because it is not how I would wish to be treated, and it is not loving toward my partner. It has nothing to do with my or my potential bedmate's genitals." Hugh Hollowell, "Open and Affirming Because of the Bible," Red Letter Christians, November 30, 2011, https://www.redletterchristians.org/open-and-affirming-because-of-the-bible/.

I will allow Jesus and his teaching to shape my decisions and priorities.

I denounce belief-only Christianity and refuse to allow my faith to be a ticket into heaven and an excuse to ignore the suffering world around me.

I will seek first the Kingdom of God – on earth as it is in heaven – and live in a way that moves the world towards God's dream, where the first are last and the last are first, where the poor are blessed and the peacemakers are the children of God, working towards a society where all are treated equally and resources shared equitably.

I recognize that I will fall short in my attempts to follow Jesus, and I trust in God's grace and the community to catch me when I do.

I know that I cannot do this alone, so I commit to share this journey with others who are walking in the way of Jesus. I will surround myself with people who remind me of Jesus, help me become more like him and hold me accountable for my actions and words.

I will share Jesus with the world, with my words and with my deeds. Like Jesus, I will interrupt injustice, and stand up for the life and dignity of all. I will allow my life to point towards Christ, everywhere I go.[88]

There are several points of contention between the Red Letter Christians Movement and orthodox Christianity, but to the extent that Red Letter

---

[88] Red Letter Christians, "Red Letter Christian Pledge" Available online at https://www.redletterchristians.org/pledge/.

Christians try to apply the Bible, they do so from a position that cannot endure being separated from a kingdom-now perspective.

The divine institutions of marriage and family have been under attack since Genesis. Current threats within Christendom to God's plan for these institutions are found in Critical Theology, which combines feminist theology, queer theology, and other critical theology agendas that seem at first to have good intentions. These intentions may be attractive to well-meaning Christians, especially on the topic of racism, but Critical Theory has a way of combining these issues in an anti-biblical manner. The dispensationalist sees Jesus as offering to establish a literal kingdom on earth, but theologians who hold to liberal critical theologies will typically see Jesus as building a spiritual kingdom of social justice, which is a work that continues today through a mandate to build a social justice spiritual kingdom now. On the grounds of postponement theology, dispensationalists have a unique aspect to protect their worldview from current trends in critical theology.

Dispensationalist Response

Dispensationalists are not the only ones who see problems in liberal critical theologies and theories. In her critique of Christian feminism, Mary A. Kassian does well to summarize a key presupposition to the feminist hermeneutic:

> Biblical feminists have as a basic premise the idea that truth is relative; there is no absolute right or wrong and no ultimate standard. According to Biblical feminists, even the truth in the Bible is subject to alteration. This attitude is well-disguised; however, if one

examines Biblical feminist literature closely, one can find numerous examples of it.[89]

Conservative Christians agree that the Bible has objective meaning. They may disagree with each other, and perhaps even contradict themselves on certain issues, but they recognize that the relativism of feminism is not biblically sustainable.

Anyone with internet access should be able to tell that wherever Judeo-Christian worldviews thrive, so do women. Elisabeth Schüssler Fiorenza, on the other hand, accuses the complementarian view of marriage of being a Western kyriarchy that is based on paganism, not Christianity,[90] insisting that women are "deformed and exploited by societal and ecclesiastical kyriarchy."[91] While conservatives recognize that there is exploitation within churches, such activity is contrary to conservative biblicism, not because of it. MacArthur and Mayhue summarize the biblical position well:

> The teaching in 1 Timothy 2 shows that women in the church are not permitted to hold the office of a pastor or teacher (cf. Acts 13:1; 1 Cor. 12:28; Eph. 4:11). However, this would not preclude a woman from teaching in other appropriate contexts, such as teaching other women (Titus 2:3–4) or teaching children (2 Tim. 1:5; 3:14–15). The Bible clearly indicates that women are spiritual equals with men and that the ministry of women is essential to the body of Christ.

---

[89] Mary A. Kassian, *Women, Creation and the Fall* (Westchester, IL: Crossway Books, 1990), 147.

[90] Elisabeth Schüssler Fiorenza, *Changing Horizons: Expolorations in Feminist Interpretation* (Minneapolis: Fortress Press, 2013), 248–249.

[91] Ibid., 247.

> Nonetheless, by God's design, women are excluded from leadership over men in the church.[92]

Accusations that complementarianism is a paganistic kyriarchy that needs to be overthrown simply fail to represent the position.

Moreover, any conservative Christian should be grieved by the plight of racism in America, including White on Black racist attitudes and actions. Dismantling Black American families will not make the situation better, so any Christian who is willing to defend the divine institution of family should be ready to stand against Black Lives Matter for their anti-family agenda.

Christian attacks on the institution of marriage even include accusations that Jesus was gay.[93] Postponement theology comes from a holistic reading of the Bible, which recognizes homosexual behavior as a sin that extends beyond Jewish taboo as it is a corruption of God's intention for marriage that carries through the dispensations, but by no means does it take a postponement theologian to recognize this sinful behavior.

Accusations of Western kyriarchy, attempts to destroy black families, theories that Jesus was gay, etc.: these are all false teachings from the more liberal critical theologians, but this is not to say that every flaw in critical theology is easily identifiable. Regarding transgender people, Gushee and Stassen write:

> Transgender people need to be recipients of Christ's delivering, compassionate love and need to be offered welcome in community.

---

[92] John MacArthur and Richard Mayhue, eds., *Biblical Doctrine: A Systematic Summary of Bible Truth* (Wheaton, IL: Crossway, 2017), 764.

[93] See, for example, Theodore W. Jennings Fr., "The 'Gay' Jesus" in *The Blackwell Companion to Jesus*, Delbert Burkett, ed. (West Sussex, UK: Blackwell Publishing, 2011), 443–457; EL Kornegay, Jr., *A Queering of Black Theology: James Baldwin's Blues Project and Gospel Prose* (New York: Palgrave Macmillan, 2013), 114–118.

> They need justice and an end to domination violence, economic discrimination, and exclusion from community. They need to be treated as sacred persons in God's sight.[94]

A conservative Christian may like to agree with the *words* of this statement, but the *underlying sentiment* is corrupted. Nobody in the discussion wants the transgendered to face violence, economic hardship, or exclusion from society, but the first and greatest need that all people have—queer and cisgender alike—is the gospel of salvation. Hopefully, Gushee and Stassen would agree. Hopefully, they would also agree that sacred persons in God's sight should conform to His vision for them. The disagreement is not over whether or not people should love transgender people, but rather the argument is over what God wants for them. Those who defend the divine institutions of marriage and family have a different understanding of God's intentions from those who do not.

These and many other points of contention with critical theology are readily available to any conservative Christian, but the dispensationalist has a framework of kingdom postponement that he can draw from for additional defenses against these threats to marriage and family. Jesus's earthly ministry is source material for much of the social justice reading of Scripture. To recount Gushee's earlier comment, "To the extent that we practice his peace-making, justice-making, community-restoring, relationship-healing teachings, we participate in the inaugurated Kingdom of God. This is what it means to be a follower, or disciple, of Jesus Christ." The Red Letter Pledge has, "Like Jesus, I will interrupt injustice, and stand up for the life and dignity of all." The Bible says that Jesus performed miracles and unfortunate people benefitted. The social justice reading seems to indicate that Jesus's healing

---

[94] David P. Gushee and Glen H. Stassen, *Kingdom Ethics*, 250.

ministry was a "justice-making" ministry with the purposes to "interrupt injustice." The kingdom postponement reading has that Jesus, like other prophets, used miracles to support the authenticity of His claims, with one of these claims being the authentic offer of a literal, earthly, messianic kingdom.

For example, Matthew 9:1–8 records an instance of Jesus healing a paralytic wherein Jesus stated His purpose for the miracle. He did not heal the man for the man's sake. Some scribes were present who accused Jesus of blasphemy (Mt 9:3), so He healed the man, telling the scribes, "But that you may know that the Son of Man has power on earth to forgive sin" (Mt 9:6). The paralytic certainly benefitted, but the miracle was to verify the Messiah for the scribes' sake. From there, Jesus went to Matthew's house, where He dined with the tax collectors (Mt 9:9–13), and this was a stumbling block for the Pharisees who ultimately rejected Christ. Likewise, it should be a stumbling block for the Red Letter Christians, as their worldview, if applied consistently, should have them side with the Pharisees in this situation, after all, the tax collectors were the first-century bourgeoisie who oppressed the proletariats (cf. Lk 3:12–13).

Jesus did send out His disciples to perform miracles, but that does not mean that this particular sending carries over to the church. The sending of the twelve in Matthew 10 came with the message, "The kingdom of heaven is at hand" (Mt 10:7). The dispensationalist, Stanley Toussaint, comments, "To authenticate their message concerning the nearness of the kingdom, the Lord gave them power to perform signs. These miracles were not to be used merely to instill awe, but to show that the kingdom was at hand (Matthew 12:28)."[95]

---

[95] Stanley Toussaint, *Behold the King: A Study of Matthew* (Portland, OR: Multnomah Press, 1981), 139.

After Israel's utter rejection of the Messiah and messianic kingdom at the blasphemy of the Holy Spirit (Mt 12:22–50), Jesus revealed that there would be an interval before the coming tribulation and subsequent kingdom. Even after the shift, Jesus's ministry remained focused on Israel. Matthew 15:21–28 tells of a Canaanite woman who came to Jesus for a miracle, but Jesus initially refused because this was not His mission, but when she recognizes her separation from Jesus's initial ministry, He does help her. Stanley Toussaint comments:

> When she comes to Him as a Gentile outside the pale of Jewish blessings, she is helped. She sees that she has no right to their blessings, but turns to Him in faith alone. On the basis of her great faith, not because of her relationship to the covenant people, her request is granted.
>
> In this miracle of mercy there is a clear foreview of Gentile blessing which fits the pattern established in Matthew 1:1 and Romans 15:8–9. The actions of Christ show that He was a minister of the circumcision for the truth of God for confirmation of the promises made unto the fathers and that the Gentiles might glorify God for His mercy.[96]

Jesus loves Gentiles, but the notion that Jesus came and established a kingdom of justice on earth simply fails to recognize the entire narrative. The messianic kingdom will be of a thoroughly Jewish nature[97] and Jesus offered it to the Jews. When God's attention shifted to the Gentiles during the postponement's resulting interim, the use of miracles went through a shift as well. Miracles initially confirmed the dispensational shift to the Church Age

---

[96] Stanley Toussaint, *Behold the King*, 196.

[97] Arnold Fruchtenbaum, *The Footsteps of the Messiah: A Study of the Sequence of Prophetic Events*, revised ed. (San Antonio, TX: Ariel Ministries, 2018), 403–484.

and the human agents that God selected for ministering the transition. Once the shift was accomplished, God withdrew the miraculous gifts, as is evidenced by Paul leaving Epaphroditus and Trophimus sick (Php 2:25–27, 2Ti 4:20) and Paul's and James' instruction for Christians to resort to medicine rather than miraculous healing (1Ti 5:23, Jas 5:10–15).[98] If the insistence on social justice comes from Christ's kingdom offer and postponement, then it would follow that social justice should have ceased when the miracles ceased.

As noted, Rebecca Voelkel holds to inaugurated eschatology with a future kingdom. This is a fitting framework for her queer liberation theology. What is particularly interesting is that she utilizes kingdom offer language in reference to Jesus's preaching, but unfortunately her version of the offer skews the kingdom. She writes of Christ's ministry that the "kin-dom is already 'on offer' for anyone who is willing to accept it (Luke 19:11–27)."[99] Rather than seeing Jesus offer a national kingdom to national Israel, she sees Jesus as redefining the kingdom into a present spiritual reality for individuals who accept it. This difference brings vastly different results; while the dispensationalist has evangelism and discipleship on his agenda, Voelkel's current task is to build a movement of lovers who are "guided by an embodied and sexual eschatological vision of liberation and decolonization… practicing revolutionary patience even as they are prepared for and awaiting the inbreaking of the kin-dom."[100] To accept postponement theology is to reject the very foundations of critical theology.

---

[98] For an excellent treatment of this topic from a dispensational perspective, see Moses Onwubiko, *Signs and Wonders: A Biblical Reply to the Claims of Modern Day Miracle Workers* (Nashville, TN: Grace Evangelistic Ministries, 2009), 60–61, 74.

[99] Rebecca M. M. Voelkel, *Carnal Knowledge of God: Embodied Love and the Movement for Justice* (Minneapolis: Fortress Press, 2017), 79–81.

[100] Ibid., 131–132.

As a final word on the matter, it is worth mentioning that dispensationalism's most famous doctrine, the pretribulational rapture, is frequently critiqued for distracting Christians from social justice. One critic writes, "This doctrine [the rapture], when combined with dispensational theology, had much to do with the 'great reversal' of evangelicals from their earlier commitments to civil rights and equality."[101] In reality, the direct opposite is true. The imminent rapture is a source of urgency for the dispensationalist.[102] The same critic disregards dispensationalist soteriology, since "their teaching specifically states that eternal security is reserved solely for those who have been saved from their sins through the atoning blood of Jesus Christ, God's Son – his provision for their sins."[103] The stakes are high. Perhaps there is a degree of temporal comfort in conforming to the world, but the message of salvation offers a comfort that is far beyond any discomfort in this life. By no means does a person need to be a dispensationalist to believe in Christ alone for eternal life, but the doctrine of kingdom postponement, especially when combined with the imminent rapture, has done far more good for promoting the salvific Gospel than any movements for the social gospel ever could.

CONCLUSION

This article has discussed three divine institutions which are apparent in the Garden of Eden: responsible labor, marriage, and family. These institutions are foundational to any decent society, but they are under attack

---

[101] L.B. Gallien, Jr., "American Evangelicalism's Struggle Over Civil Rights" in *The Wiley-Blackwell Companion to Religion and Social Justice*, Michael D. Palmer and Stanley M. Burgess, eds. (Chichester, West Sussex: Wiley-Blackwell, 2012), 526.

[102] For a discussion on this and other benefits of understanding the rapture, see Mark Hitchcock, *The End*, 3–21.

[103] L.B. Gallien, Jr., "American Evangelicalism's Struggle Over Civil Rights," 526.

from worldly ideologies that are infiltrating Christendom. It does not take a dispensationalist to defend the divine institutions, but there are uniquely dispensational responses that are available through the doctrine of kingdom postponement. Christian forms of errant ecotheology and social justice are constantly evolving and updating, so a reactive approach to the doctrines will prove to be a tedious task in the years to come. However, these errors are usually built on frameworks of kingdom-now theology, so the dispensationalist can construct a proactive defense against institutional compromises by being well versed in postponement theology, both through an appreciation of Old Testament descriptions of the kingdom, as well as through an understanding of Christ's ministry of the kingdom offer and postponement.

Chapter 12 – On Diversity and Inclusion
Every Tribe, Tongue, People, and Nation: The Future of Race Relations and Social Justice Implications for Today[1]
Christopher Cone

> *"But the one who hates his brother is in the darkness and walks in the darkness, and does not know where he is going because the darkness has blinded his eyes."*[2]

INTRODUCTION

Jesus's presentation of the kingdom of the heavens in Matthew 5-7 was particularly intended for first-century Jewish people to understand that internal righteousness and not simply external adherence to moral code was necessary to enter that kingdom. In addition to demonstrating this key deficiency on the part of His listeners, His Sermon on the Mount further offers a model for the character of kingdom members and the culture of the kingdom, and thus has contemporary applications, since believers in Jesus during the church age have been transferred (positionally) to His kingdom.[3] While that kingdom currently has no (other) earthly expression in this age, it

---

[1] Presented to the Council on Dispensational Hermeneutics at Calvary University, Kansas City, Missouri, September 19, 2019, subsequently published in Christopher Cone, *Authentic Social Justice* (Lees Summit, MO: Exegetica Publishing, 2020), 139-174.

[2] *New American Standard Bible: 1995 Update* (La Habra, CA: The Lockman Foundation, 1995), 1 John 2:11.

[3] Colossians 1:13.

will one day come to earth in literal fulfillment of God's kingdom promises in physical manifestation (hence, Matthew's term "kingdom of the heavens"), thus the applicability of the Sermon for the present day is strengthened by the future certainty of kingdom-promise fulfillment. If it is appropriate to understand the Sermon on the Mount as having contemporary implications for character and ethics in general (because of the kingdom citizenship component of church-age believers), then future aspects of the kingdom and of the two intertwining destinies (heavenly and earthly) show a model of God's design for the future of human relations.

This study (a) introduces several ideological diagnoses of social injustice with their respective prescriptions, (b) illustrates the extent of the problem as expressed in racial disunity, (c) outlines the solution expressed in Biblical eschatology, and (d) examines the hermeneutic legitimacy of contemporary application of the Sermon on the Mount, and of its future aspects and the destinies implied for its citizens, especially in light of the "every tribe" inclusiveness found in passages like Genesis 12:3b, Revelation 5:9, 7:9, 10:11, 11:9, 13:7, 14:6, 16:10, and 17:15. The resulting focus on human relationships and ethnic diversity in the kingdom helps us consider the implications of that diversity for the present-day church and its interactions with society, particularly on the topics of race and unity, with a view to candid and robust dialogue as we together pursue God's design for His church.

THREE IDEOLOGICAL MODELS FOR SOCIAL JUSTICE

An oft-repeated description of social justice suggests that it "entails a 'redistribution' of resources from those who have "unjustly" gained them to those who justly deserve them..."⁴ Some might accept a less specific attribution, that "[s]ocial justice is really the capacity to organize with others to accomplish ends that benefit the whole community."⁵ Still, in popular usage the term seems to most generally imply, "among other things, equality of the burdens, the advantages, and the opportunities of citizenship...social justice is intimately related to the concept of equality, and that the violation of it is intimately related to the concept of inequality."⁶

Model 1 – An Ecclesiastical Approach:
The Amillennial Economic Mean Between Individualism and Collectivism

Probably first coined by Jesuit philosopher Luigi Taparelli d'Azeglio in 1843,⁷ the term *social justice* for him represented the "constitutional justice of a society, the justice that defends right order in the constitutional arrangements of the society. Its task at that juncture of history, he believed, was to defend the inherited rights of the existing powers, the Church and the aristocracy, against the rising tide of democratic equality."⁸ Taparelli opposed the capitalism of John Locke and Adam Smith because "he saw liberalism as a product of the Protestant Reformation, which exalted private judgment over the divine authority of the Roman Catholic Church and thereby replaced

---

⁴ Joe R. Feagin, "Social Justice and Sociology: Agendas for the Twenty-First Century" in *Critical Strategies for Social Research*, ed. William K. Carroll (Toronto: Canadian Scholars' Press, 2004), 32.

⁵ Michael Novak, "Social Justice: Not What You Think It Is" *The Heritage Foundation*, December 29, 2009, https://www.heritage.org/poverty-and-inequality/report/social-justice-not-what-you-think-it.

⁶ G. J. Papageorgiou, "Social Values and Social Justice," *Economic Geography*, 56, no. 2 (April 1980): 110-19.

⁷ Thomas Patrick Burke, "The Origins of Social Justice: Taparelli d'Azeglio" in *Modern Age*, (Spring 2019): 98, referred to by Luigi Taparelli d'Azeglio in Saggio teoretico di dritto naturale appoggiato sul fatto, 5 volumes (Palermo, 1843).

⁸ Ibid., 105.

the Catholic sense of community with an emphasis on the self-interest of the isolated individual."[9] Still, Taparelli's was not an economic core.

Though building on Taparelli's foundation, Pope Pius XI focused almost exclusively on the economic aspects of social justice, a term which soon came to represent "a new kind of virtue (or habit) necessary for post-agrarian societies…"[10] From within this anti-individualistic stream of economic theory, Pius XI's 1931 encyclical *Quadragesimo Anno*[11] epitomized the social justice mandate for the Roman Catholic Church. The encyclical sought to address "that difficult problem of human relations called 'the social question,'"[12] and along with Leo XIII's 1891 encyclical, *On the Condition of Workers,* proposed "a true Catholic social science."[13] Quoting Leo XIII, Pius XI reaffirms that, the Church "strives not only to instruct the mind, but to regulate by her precepts the life and morals of individuals, and that ameliorates the condition of the workers through her numerous and beneficent institutions."[14]

Pius XI combats the "twin rocks of shipwreck,"[15] namely *individualism*, which he suggests is fostered when the social and collective aspects of property ownership are ignored, and *collectivism*, on the other hand, which thrives when personal property rights are minimized. To strike the necessary balance, he reminds the reader that, "there resides in Us the right and duty to pronounce with supreme authority upon social and economic matters."[16]

---

[9] Ibid., 104.
[10] Novak, Ibid.
[11] Penned by Oswald von Nell-Bruening SJ.
[12] Pope Pius XI, "*Quadragisimo Anno,*" May 15, 1931, 2, http://w2.vatican.va/content/pius-xi/en/encyclicals/documents/hf_p-xi_enc_19310515_quadragesimo-anno.html.
[13] Pope Pius XI, "*Quadragisimo Anno,* 20.
[14] Pope Pius XI, "*Quadragisimo Anno,* 17.
[15] Ibid., 46.
[16] Ibid., 41.

In this Pius XI distinguishes the Catholic doctrine of social justice from its secular counterpart (socialism): because "man is older than the State,"[17] the state doesn't have the right to define or infringe upon property rights. Rather those authorities reside with the Church. Pius XI emphasizes that, "the deposit of truth that God committed to Us and the grave duty of disseminating and interpreting the whole moral law, and of urging it in season and out of season, *bring under and subject to Our supreme jurisdiction not only social order but economic activities themselves* [emphasis mine]."[18] The Church, by virtue of the cultural mandate, has jurisdiction beyond that of the state.

Pius XI asserted that not only was the state insufficient for handling such challenges, but the free market also lacked the capacity to properly regulate society, as he made clear in stating that "right ordering of economic life cannot be left to a free competition of forces. For from this source, as from a poisoned spring, have originated and spread all the errors of individualist economic teaching."[19] On the basis of natural law, then, neither the state, nor an entirely free market were fitted to govern society, but only the Church had divinely appropriated access and the mandate to provide the hermeneutic underpinnings necessary for the proper economic ordering of society." Christian social philosophy, must be kept in mind regarding ownership and labor and their association together, and must be put into actual practice."[20]

This practice and right ordering avoid the two great errors of individualism and the capitalism that fosters it, and collectivism and the brand of socialism leading to communism that solidifies it. Pius XI prescribes a kinder gentler sort of socialism that "inclines toward and in a certain

---

[17] Ibid., 49.
[18] Ibid., 41.
[19] Pope Pius XI, "*Quadragisimo Anno*, 88.
[20] Ibid., 110.

measure approaches the truths which Christian tradition has always held sacred"[21] But he is careful not to prescribe socialism in its pure sense, warning that, "Socialism, if it remains truly Socialism, even after it has yielded to truth and justice on the points which we have mentioned, cannot be reconciled with the teachings of the Catholic Church because its concept of society itself is utterly foreign to Christian truth.[22] Specifically, the deficiency is evident in that socialism "affirms that human association has been instituted for the sake of material advantage alone,"[23] consequently, Pius XI concludes that "no one can be at the same time a good Catholic and a true socialist,"[24] and exhorts readers not to "permit the children of this world to appear wiser in their generation than we who by the Divine Goodness are the children of the light."[25] The solution for inequality and oppression is to be found not in either economic system of capitalism nor socialism/communism, but in Christian truth as disseminated and interpreted by the Catholic Church.

Model 2 – The Statist Approach:
Collectivist Abolition of Free Trade as the Economic Messiah

In the Preface to the 1888 English edition of *The Manifesto of the Communist Party*, Frederick Engels introduces the fundamental proposition of communism as follows:

> That in every historical epoch, the prevailing mode of economic production and exchange, and the social organization necessarily following from it, form the basis upon which it is built up, and from that which alone can be explained the political and intellectual history

---

[21] Ibid., 113.
[22] Ibid., 117.
[23] Ibid., 118.
[24] Ibid., 120.
[25] Pope Pius XI, "*Quadragisimo Anno*, 146.

of that epoch; that consequently the whole history of mankind (since the dissolution of primitive tribal society, holding land in common ownership) has been a history of class struggles, contests between exploiting and exploited, ruling and oppressed classes; That the history of these class struggles forms a series of evolutions in which, nowadays, a stage has been reached where the exploited and oppressed class – the proletariat – cannot attain its emancipation from the sway of the exploiting and ruling class – the bourgeoisie – without, at the same time, and once and for all, emancipating society at large from all exploitation, oppression, class distinction, and class struggles.[26]

For Marx and Engels, social justice (even though they do not use the term in the document, as it had not yet come into vogue) hinged on resolving class struggle, which meant reforming the economic engines of inequality, primarily, by eliminating distinctions through the implemented communist ideal. While socialism was not philosophically dissimilar from Marx' and Engels' communism, they viewed socialism as a middle-class enterprise and communism as a working-class effort. Thus, communism would be more efficacious in actually bringing about change.[27]

Economics, and capitalism specifically, is asserted to be a catalyst for destructive societal forces. Marx and Engels posit a better economic model as the solution. Karl Polanyi asserted that "To allow the market mechanism to be sole director of the fate of human beings and the natural environment, indeed, even of the amount and use of purchasing power, would result in the

---

[26] Karl Marx and Frederick Engels, Preface to the 1888 English Edition, *Manifesto of the Communist Party*, (From *Marx/Engels Selected Works*, vol. 1, [Progress Publishers, Moscow, 1969], 98-137), 8.

[27] Ibid.

demolition of society."[28] Feagin expresses four significant deficiencies in capitalist economies and societies.[29] Problem 1: Capitalism transfers wealth from the poor and working classes to the rich and affluent social classes: "in most countries great income and wealth inequalities create major related injustices, including shar differentials in hunger, housing, life satisfaction, life expectancy, and political power."[30] Problem 2: Capitalism (through the exploitation of transnational corporations) brings disruption and marginalization to many. Problem 3: Capitalism takes a heavy toll on the environment. Problem 4: Capitalism fosters racial and ethnic inequality and oppression, homophobia, and other inequities. Racial divides are perceived as an economic problem, with economic solutions as the cure.

The specific problem diagnosed in the *Manifesto* is the systematic bourgeoisie abuse of the working class (proletariat) in "shameless, direct, brutal exploitation"[31] primarily through the "single unconscionable freedom – Free Trade."[32] Only the proletariat has the capability to end the ongoing economic cycle through revolution. The other classes – like the lower middle class – "decay and finally disappear in the face of Modern Industry."[33] Marx and Engels viewed the lower middle class not as revolutionary enough to bring lasting change, but rather motivated in their own fight against the bourgeoisie, "to save from extinction their existence as fractions of the middle class. They are therefore not revolutionary, but conservative… reactionary, for they try to roll back the wheel of history."[34] Only the proletariat has the capacity for effective revolution, for it is their labor that

---

[28] Feagin, 29.
[29] Ibid., 30-32.
[30] Feagin, 30.
[31] Marx and Engels., 16.
[32] Ibid.
[33] Ibid., 20.
[34] Ibid.

has been commodified as the capital which greases the economic wheels of a free market that benefits the bourgeoisie to the detriment of all else. As Marx and Engels seek to inspire the working class to revolution and a new economic model (communism), they prophecy that, "the bourgeoisie therefore produces, above all, are its own grave-diggers. Its fall and the victory of the proletariat are equally inevitable."[35]

One critical means for the resolution of class struggle is the abolition of private property, for communism "deprives no man of the power to appropriate the products of society; all that it does is to deprive him of the power to subjugate the labour of others by means of such appropriations."[36] In short, if anyone can own property it will be the bourgeoisie, and the bourgeoisie have always oppressed the proletariat by capitalizing the labor of the proletariat in order to get property. Since the proletariat rarely ever get property anyway, if there is no ownership of property at all, then the bourgeoisie can't oppress the proletariat, and the proletariat haven't lost anything, plus then they would be free from oppression.

Beyond the abolition of property, Marx and Engels want to abolish the family by replacing "home education with social."[37] The refined educational model "seek[s] to alter the character of that intervention, and to rescue education from the influence of the ruling class."[38] Ultimately, this protects proletariat children from being "transformed into simple articles of commerce and instruments of labour."[39] Further developments of communism include the abolition of national differences and nationalism (in favor of the partisanship of communism),[40] in seeking to eliminate

---

[35] Marx and Engels., 21.
[36] Ibid., 24.
[37] Ibid.
[38] Ibid.
[39] Ibid., 25.
[40] Ibid.

oppression of the ruling class through ideas, religion is abolished – "The Communist revolution is the most radical rupture with traditional property relations; no wonder that its development involved the most radical rupture with traditional ideas."[41] Eternal truths, religion, and morality are traded in as part of traditional, patriarchal, ruling class societal norms that must be removed if there is to be revolution suitable for installing lasting equality. Thus, if the working class unite (in the communist ideal), as prescribed, then "In place of the old bourgeois society, with its classes and class antagonisms, we shall have an association, in which the free development of each is the condition for the free development of all."[42]

Marx' and Engels' prescription of communism as the economic remedy for inequality and oppression demands that the state set boundaries and ultimately manage the ownership of property, effectually eliminating individualism. The Catholic response to that concept, from Leo XIII and Pius XI, is the assertion that the state could claim no right to take such sweeping oversight. Both the secular and the ecclesiastical, however, agreed that individualism was not a viable solution, and was in fact a common enemy. These two models – Marx' and Engels' secular and the Catholic non-secular models, while sharing a mutual distaste for individualism, are rooted in competing views of human nature and of authority itself, have pursued, to date, mutually exclusive political power in order to exact the kinds of societal evolution necessary to achieve their respective ends. The paths to social justice for these two models scarcely intersect, but they are remarkably intertwined in iterations of Liberation Theology.

---

[41] Marx and Engels., 26.
[42] Ibid., 27.

Model 3 – The Liberation Theology Synthesis:
Postmillennial Dominionism

Gustavo Gutiérrez is credited with originating the term Liberation Theology, in his 1971 publication, *Teología de la liberación*. Gutiérrez defines theology as "a critical reflection on the Church's presence and activity in the world, in the light of revelation,"[43] adding that "Theology is reflection, a critical attitude. First comes the commitment to charity, to service. Theology comes "later." It is second. *The Church's pastoral action is not arrived at as a conclusion from theological premises.* Theology does not lead to pastoral activity but is rather a reflection on it. [emphasis mine]"[44] For Gutiérrez, theology is not the product of exegetical analysis, but rather is much more broadly construed – this is in part reflects a logical expression of the Catholic hermeneutic of interpreting the Bible according to the tradition of the Church.[45] Theology is active, and a "variable understanding,"[46] addressing the needs of the moment.

In Gutiérrez' estimation liberation has three components: "the political liberation of oppressed peoples and social classes; man's liberation in the course of history; and liberation from sin as condition of a life of communion of all men with the Lord."[47] The mandate for liberation of the oppressed is rooted in a theological extrapolation of redemption by way of the Catholic Church-tradition hermeneutic. The "redemptive work embraces every

---

[43] Gustavo Gutiérrez, "Notes For a Theology of Liberation" in Theological Studies (Lima, Peru), 244, http://cdn.theologicalstudies.net/31/31.2/31.2.1.pdf.

[44] Ibid., 244-245.

[45] *Catechism of the Catholic Church*, 113, http://www.vatican.va/archive/ccc_css/archive/catechism/p1s1c2a3.htm.

[46] Gutiérrez, 244.

[47] Ibid., 248.

dimension of human existence."[48] Consequently, liberation becomes *part* of theology, with an "eschatological hope"[49] of social revolution.

The dominionist premise provides the means for achieving that eschatological hope, as Gutiérrez posits, "Mastering the earth, as Genesis bids him do, is a work of salvation, meant to produce its plenitude. To work, to transform this world, is to save…it means participating fully in the salvific process that affects the whole man."[50] Not only is Christ "the Saviour who, by liberating us from sin, liberates us from the very root of social injustice,"[51] but humanity, by way of the dominion mandate is co-participant in that salvific enterprise.

Inadequacy of the Three Models

Tracing these three streams through the lenses of Leo XIII and Pius XI, Marx and Engels, and Gutiérrez certainly constitutes no comprehensive analysis of the history of social justice (that would be far beyond the scope of this present work), but merely an *introduction of context for opposing foundations* of social justice in the contemporary western mind. Further, this context-setting provides the helpful backdrop for the consideration of contemporary application of the Sermon on the Mount – a central theme of this project.

Still, these streams and their advocates were focused on equality in relation to economic underpinnings as governed either by the church, the state, or some combination of both. But each of these streams to date have proved deficient in their economic and political prescriptions, as they have not sufficiently addressed the root cause of the symptoms. Each of the three models diagnosed symptoms and prescribed solutions. The RCC asserted the

---

[48] Gutiérrez, 255.
[49] Ibid., 253.
[50] Ibid., 256.
[51] Ibid., 257.

faults of the extremes of individualism and collectivism, and prescribed an Aristotelian golden economic mean insured by the church. Marxism asserted the evils of class struggle resulting from free trade and sought a statist economic control to extinguish any hint of oppression-inciting free trade. Liberation theology pinpointed the problem as failing to fulfill the dominion mandate and synthesized the RCC and Marxist prescriptions to seek a church-driven political revolution that would complete the liberation of the whole man. To this point, while encountering varying degrees of success, each of these prescriptions has failed to accomplish its stated goal, at least in part because the problems diagnosed were symptomatic and not causative. The root cause of injustice and oppression is neither economic nor political, but rather was rooted simply *in the devaluation of human life that naturally results from the spiritually bankrupt devaluing of the Creator.* With good reason Solomon asserted that "the fear of the Lord is the beginning of wisdom, and the knowledge of the Holy One is understanding."[52]

The Biblical record inextricably links the proper valuation of human life to the right perspective of and response to the Creator. Genesis 1:26-27 sets the linkage as the created origin of humanity and the image of God in humanity. Genesis 9:5-6 underscores the sacredness of human life based on that linkage. Romans 5:12 asserts the universal need and traces it back to Adam's sin and the hereditary consequence for all of subsequent humanity, while 5:18 describes how God likewise provided for the resolution of that problem for all of humanity. John 3:16 and 12:32 explain how God has reached out to all humanity. God's intention of delivering all of humanity is expressed in 1 Timothy 2:4, and the universal accessibility to that deliverance is pronounced in Titus 2:11. Because of the love of God expressed and executed through His redemptive plan, we have a new ontological unity in

---

[52] Proverbs 9:10.

Christ, explained in Ephesians 2:14-18. Consequently, as Galatians 6:10 expresses, believers are to prioritize brothers and sisters in Christ, and *to do good to all.* That same love that God demonstrated for His created beings, we are to show toward one another, as Philippians 2:1-11 indicates. Humanity is created in God's image, valued based on God's image in us, saved because of God's grace, and expected to do good to one another as expressive and illustrative of His grace. Titus 3:1-7 lays out an application of this progression of thought: there is (1) an ethical expectation (including showing consideration for all humanity), (2) because once we were in need, (3) and because of God's love for all, (4) He saved us through Jesus Christ, (5) making us heirs of eternal life, (6) thus, there is an expectation based on our relationship to Him, and (7) because it is good for others:

> 1 Remind them to be subject to rulers, to authorities, to be obedient, to be ready for every good deed, 2 to malign no one, to be peaceable, gentle, showing every consideration for all men. 3 For we also once were foolish ourselves, disobedient, deceived, enslaved to various lusts and pleasures, spending our life in malice and envy, hateful, hating one another. 4 But when the kindness of God our Savior and *His* love for mankind appeared, 5 He saved us, not on the basis of deeds which we have done in righteousness, but according to His mercy, by the washing of regeneration and renewing by the Holy Spirit, 6 whom He poured out upon us richly through Jesus Christ our Savior, 7 so that being justified by His grace we would be made heirs according to *the* hope of eternal life. 8 This is a trustworthy statement; and concerning these things I want you to speak confidently, so that those who have believed God will be careful to

engage in good deeds. These things are good and profitable for men.[53]

These passages are emblematic of the univocal Biblical perspective that proper valuation of human life is rooted in proper valuation of the Creator, and that proper expression of that valuation in action cannot be unlinked from the epistemological premise that God has the right as the Creator to define reality and valuation itself – and that He has done so. Nor can orthodox expression of valuation in practice be unlinked from the metaphysical realities that God has revealed in Scripture. As John succinctly puts it, "If someone says, "I love God," and hates his brother, he is a liar; for the one who does not love his brother whom he has seen, cannot love God whom he has not seen."[54] *Position undergirds practice, and where there is faulty practice, there is neglect of positional truths.*

A CASE STUDY IN FAILURE: POST-CIVIL WAR AMERICA AND THE FREEDMEN'S BUREAU

For any who might opine that there is no contemporary need for resolution of events more than a century past, William Dubois' observations help to clarify the heartbreaking prominence of the "color line" especially immediately following the Civil War. Dubois characterizes the era as representative of an ever-unasked question, "How does it feel to be a problem?"[55] Dubois recognizes that during and from this time there was external perspective by those outside the black community that there was a

---

[53] Titus 3:1–8.
[54] 1 John 4:20.
[55] W. E. B. Dubois, *The Souls of Black Folk* (Oxford, UK: Oxford University Press, 2007), 7.

problem to be resolved. Likewise, and perhaps consequently, there was internal perspective of individuals within the community that there was indeed a problem, and that problem, according to Dubois would create a painful rift for these men and women: "The history of the American Negro is the history of this strife – this longing to attain self-conscious manhood, to merge his double self into a better and truer self. In this merging he wishes neither of the older selves to be lost. He would not Africanize America, for America has too much to teach the world and Africa. He would not bleach his Negro soul in a flood of white Americanism, for he knows that Negro blood has a message for the world. He simply wishes to make it possible for a man to be both a Negro and an American, without being cursed and spit upon by his fellows, without having the doors of Opportunity closed roughly in his face."[56] "This, then, is the end of his striving: to be a co-worker in the kingdom of culture, to escape both death and isolation, to husband and use his best powers and his latent genius.[57]

Dubois understood this duality of oppositional cultures to create an unworkable situation in practice: "The double-aimed struggle of the black artisan—on the one hand to escape white contempt for a nation of mere hewers of wood and drawers of water, and on the other hand to plough and nail and dig for a poverty-stricken horde— could only result in making him a poor craftsman, for he had but half a heart in either cause... this seeking to satisfy two unreconciled ideals, has wrought sad havoc with the courage and faith and deeds of ten thousand thousand people,—has sent them often wooing false gods and invoking false means of salvation, and at times has even seemed about to make them ashamed of themselves."[58] Dubois measures this difficulty not as a momentary response to contemporary

---

[56] Dubois, 9.
[57] Dubois.
[58] Ibid., 10.

Biblical Distinctions Applied 349

events, but rather as a deep seated consequence of a long enduring system of injustice and oppression. He observes in particular implications of the abuse of black women on the culture, "The red stain of bastardy, which two centuries of systematic legal defilement of Negro women had stamped upon his race, meant not only the loss of ancient African chastity, but also the hereditary weight of a mass of corruption from white adulterers, threatening almost the obliteration of the Negro home."[59]

While the conditions that Dubois recounts were not swiftly developed, their contemporary import was undeniable, and cut right to the very valuation of the black person in America. On the one hand, those outside the community viewed them as half-human, and thus undeserving of the privileges of personhood, and on the other hand, having no hope within the community, there was little to strive for. Dubois echoes the painful cries, "Lo! we are diseased and dying, cried the dark hosts; we cannot write, our voting is vain; what need of education, since we must always cook and serve? And the Nation echoed and enforced this self-criticism, saying: Be content to be servants, and nothing more; what need of higher culture for half-men? Away with the black man's ballot, by force or fraud, – and behold the suicide of a race! "Nevertheless, out of the evil came something of good, – the more careful adjustment of education to real life, the clearer perception of the Negroes' social responsibilities, and the sobering realization of the meaning of progress."[60] While Dubois commendably finds some solace in that the pain of those times would help shape an approach to impacting culture, from a Biblical perspective the wounds were simply abhorrent and incompatible with the Divine expression of human valuation. It was not merely men and women who were violated – it was also their Creator.

---

[59] Ibid., 12.
[60] Dubois,13.

Dubois further suggests that the "problem of the twentieth century is the problem of the color-line, – the relation of the darker to the lighter races of men in Asia and Africa, in America and the islands of the sea. It was a phase of this problem that caused the Civil War; and however much they who marched South and North in 1861 may have fixed on the technical points of union and local autonomy as a shibboleth, all nevertheless knew, as we know, that the question of Negro slavery was the real cause of the conflict."[61] The valuation problem that had caused rift between brothers and sisters had manifest unsurprisingly in a national rift that shipwrecked a country and its people.

But once that conflict formally ended, there were great questions to be answered. Dubois retold history from the perspective of those who now had no place in society, were not yet fully treated as fully human, but were no longer either treated simply as property. What should be done with thousands of newly emancipated people? Dubois describes the governmental process of dealing with the "problem:" "Thus did the United States government definitely assume charge of the emancipated Negro as the ward of the nation. It was a tremendous undertaking. Here at a stroke of the pen was erected a government of millions of men, – and not ordinary men either, but black men emasculated by a peculiarly complete system of slavery, centuries old; and now, suddenly, violently, they come into a new birthright, at a time of war and passion, in the midst of the stricken and embittered population of their former masters."[62] This new cultural birth was traumatic, and did not bring with it the resolution of the valuation problem.

Lincoln's 1863 Emancipation Proclamation did not immediately provide its intended benefit. Dubois describes how the canyon grew between black and white post-Civil War, and how the government's efforts to

---

[61] Ibid., 15.
[62] Dubois, 20-21.

establish and administer the Freedmen's Bureau was neither able to resolve some most basic problems, nor to ultimately quell enduring and growing racial tensions. As Dubois explains, the Bureau could do nothing other than fail: "In a time of perfect calm, amid willing neighbors and streaming wealth, the social uplifting of four million slaves to an assured and self-sustaining place in the body politic and economic would have been a herculean task; but when to the inherent difficulties of so delicate and nice a social operation were added the spite and hate of conflict, the hell of war; when suspicion and cruelty were rife, and gaunt Hunger wept beside Bereavement, – in such a case, the work of any instrument of social regeneration was in large part foredoomed to failure."[63] Dubois' concluding comment here is illustrative of the bigger reality in view – in the conditions symptomatic of a cursed and fallen creation, where the proper valuation of the Creator is not in view, and consequently *there is no remaining basis for the proper valuation of human life*, it is unsurprising that any instrument of social regeneration would be met with failure.

It is evident that the momentous progress that was made with the Proclamation had been engaged, at least by Lincoln's words as "an act of justice, warranted by the Constitution, upon military necessity…the considerate judgment of mankind, and the gracious favor of Almighty God."[64] That step of cultural progress was undertaken with the perspective of God as the Supreme Valuer, and thus the freeing of those He created *was* an act of justice. Still, that ontological acknowledgment did not change the hearts of men, nor their own individual perspectives on valuation. Dubois laments that "Slavery "classed the black man and the ox together. And the

---

[63] Dubois, 25.
[64] Abraham Lincoln, "A Proclamation" January 1, 1863, https://www.archives.gov/exhibits/featured-documents/emancipation-proclamation/transcript.html.

Negro knew full well that, whatever their deeper convictions may have been, Southern men had fought with desperate energy to perpetuate this slavery under which the black masses, with half-articulate thought, had writhed and shivered."[65] "So the cleft between the white and black South grew…it never should have been; it was as inevitable as its results were pitiable."[66]

Dubois reminds the reader that this wasn't merely a cultural phenomenon, *it was intensely personal.* Those that endured these times encountered dehumanizing torment to an incredible degree. Dubois reveals his own emotion at recounting the horrors, and explains with vivid clarity how both man and woman were scarred who lived through them:

> it is doubly difficult to write of this period calmly, so intense was the feeling, so mighty the human passions that swayed and blinded men. Amid it all, two figures ever stand to typify that day to coming ages, – the one, a gray-haired gentleman, whose fathers had quit themselves like men, whose sons lay in nameless graves; who bowed to the evil of slavery because its abolition threatened untold ill to all; who stood at last, in the evening of life, a blighted, ruined form, with hate in his eyes; – and the other, a form hovering dark and mother-like, her awful face black with the mists of centuries, had aforetime quailed at that white master's command, had bent in love over the cradles of his sons and daughters, and closed in death the sunken eyes of his wife, – aye, too, at his behest had laid herself low to his lust, and borne a tawny man-child to the world, only to see her dark boy's limbs scattered to the winds by midnight marauders riding after "cursed Niggers." These were the saddest sights of that woful [sic] day; and no man clasped the hands of these two passing figures of

---

[65] Dubois, 25.
[66] Ibid., 25.

the present-past; but, hating, they went to their long home, and, hating, their children's children live today.[67]

While Dubois recognizes that the Freedmen's Bureau saw success in the area of making education accessible (a victory that would have lasting impact), the Bureau was powerless to heal the scars Dubois exposes. Among other failures, the Bureau "failed to begin the establishment of good-will between ex-masters and freedmen, to guard its work wholly from paternalistic methods which discouraged self-reliance, and to carry out to any considerable extent its implied promises to furnish the freedmen with land."[68] "Its successes were the result of hard work, supplemented by the aid of philanthropists and the eager striving of black men. Its failures were the result of bad local agents, the inherent difficulties of the work, and national neglect."[69] Dubois identifies particular failures as if they might one day be remedied for future efforts. But the Biblicist might diagnose that those failures emanated from the same causative failures of every other economic and political enterprise designed to offset the symptoms of the spiritually dead human heart: *while the policies changed, the hearts of men had not.*

Despite its few successes, the numerous inadequacies of the Freedmen's Bureau illustrate the inherent deficiencies of governmental efforts to resolve deep-seated human problems. Whereas Leo XIII and Pius XI, Marx and Engels, and Gutiérrez proposed economic solutions that as of yet have not resolved the problem, post-Civil War conditions in America showed that governments simply aren't equipped to address the issues that lead to the economic conditions that foster oppression. The problem is neither simply

---

[67] Dubois, 26.
[68] Ibid., 29.
[69] Ibid., 29.

economic nor related to governance. The ongoing strife that Dubois exposed *is rooted simply in how individuals view their Creator, themselves, and others.*

In 1953 Dubois recognized that the color-line was symptomatic of an even greater problem: "I still think today as yesterday that the color-line is a great problem of this century. But today I see more clearly than yesterday that back of the problem of race and color, lies a greater problem which both obscures and implements it: and *that is the fact that so many civilized persons are willing to live in comfort even if the price of this is poverty, ignorance and disease of the majority of their fellowmen; that to maintain this privilege men have waged war until today war tends to become universal and continuous, and the excuse for this war continues largely to be color and race* [emphasis mine].[70]

While Dubois doesn't diagnose the problem as related directly to valuation, when considering this tragic episode of history, interlocutors would benefit from seeing through the Biblical lens, that all men being created equal is not the mere rhetoric of political calls to revolution, *but is representative of the Divine valuation of all human life as originating in God and thus constituting only one race*,[71] as bearing the image of God and thus bearing God-defined value,[72] as being reinforced in the prophetic hope of universal blessing covenanted by God to Abraham,[73] and in the eschatological assurance that God would purchase those to be blessed from every tribe, tongue, people, and nation.[74]

---

[70] Dubois, 208.
[71] Genesis 1:27, 31.
[72] 1:26-27, 9:6.
[73] Genesis 12:3b.
[74] Revelation 5:9.

MODEL 4 – THE MATTHEW 5-7 MODEL AND "EVERY TRIBE" INCLUSIVENESS

As Jesus began the public aspect of His earthly ministry, Matthew records Him as proclaiming and saying, "Repent for the kingdom of the heavens is at hand."[75] He traveled throughout the cities and villages and proclaimed "the gospel of the kingdom,"[76] and was healing many, demonstrating the validity of His messianic claim.[77] He acknowledges that part of His purpose for His sending was to accomplish that announcing of the kingdom.[78] The Sermon on the Mount offers in ten sections principles related to the coming kingdom. In this message Jesus (1) outlines the coming rewards (beatitudes) of the kingdom in 5:1-12, (2) describes how one enters the kingdom in 5:13-20, (3) contrasts authentic, internal righteousness with insufficient external righteousness in 5:21-47, (4) underscores the standard – the perfection of God the Father in 5:48, (5) distinguishes between the pursuit and temporal rewards of external righteousness and the pursuit and eternal rewards of kingdom-quality righteousness in 6:1-18, (6) exhorts the pursuit of eternal rewards in 6:19-24, (7) encourages in 6:25-34 that in the pursuit of eternal reward there is present provision, (8) exposits in 7:1-14 the present character of kingdom-quality righteousness, (9) warns in 7:15-23 of the dangers of false fruit, and (10) illustrates in 7:24-29 by contrast the wisdom of building on solid foundation versus building on sand. In this Sermon is found a central and early portrait of the kingdom, and in this episode, Matthew records eight or nine direct mentions by Jesus of the

---

[75] Matthew 4:17.
[76] 9:35.
[77] Luke 4:14-21.
[78] 4:43.

kingdom, found in 5:3, 5:10, 5:19 (twice), 5:20, 6:10, 6:13 (in a textual variant), 6:33, and 7:21.

The 5:19 references relate to the abiding value of the Law, with future implications extending to the eschatological messianic kingdom: "Whoever then annuls one of the least of these commandments, and teaches others *to do* the same, shall be called least in the kingdom of heaven; but whoever keeps and teaches *them,* he shall be called great in the kingdom of heaven."[79] In 5:20, Jesus first draws the explicit contrast between inauthentic appearances of righteousness and the internal righteousness that is necessary for entrance into the kingdom: "For I say to you that unless your righteousness surpasses *that* of the scribes and Pharisees, you will not enter the kingdom of heaven."[80] In 6:10, Jesus teaches the disciples to pray, specifically to request that the kingdom of the heavens would come to earth as prophesied – a clear indication that it hadn't yet come: "Your kingdom come. Your will be done, On earth as it is in heaven."[81] In a textual variant[82] in the concluding portion of that same prayer, Jesus models the request in 6:13, "And do not lead us into temptation, but deliver us from evil. [For Yours is the kingdom and the power and the glory forever. Amen.]"[83] If authentic, this kingdom reference

---

[79] Matthew 5:19.

[80] 5:20.

[81] 6:10.

[82] "Several late manuscripts (157 225 418) append a trinitarian ascription, "for thine is the kingdom and the power and the glory of the Father and of the Son and of the Holy Spirit for ever. Amen." The same expansion occurs also at the close of the Lord's Prayer in the liturgy that is traditionally ascribed to St. John Chrysostom. The absence of any ascription [is evident] in early and important representatives of the Alexandrian (א B), the Western (D and most of the Old Latin), and other (*f*) types of text..." (Bruce Manning Metzger, United Bible Societies, *A Textual Commentary on the Greek New Testament,* second edition, *A Companion Volume to the United Bible Societies' Greek New Testament* [4th rev. ed.] [London; New York: United Bible Societies, 1994], 14.)

[83] Matthew 6:13.

speaks of a present tense kingdom but adds no earthly geographic implications to the revelation.

While the aforementioned passages (5:19, 5:20, 6:10, and 6:13) give no specific indicators beyond a general futuristic idea of a coming earthly kingdom, the beatitudes-preamble of 5:3-12 is explicitly eschatological with only three exceptions. Six of the nine identify future blessings associated with current conditional responsibilities. They include being comforted,[84] inheriting the earth,[85] being satisfied,[86] receiving mercy,[87] seeing God,[88] and being called sons of God.[89] The final of the beatitudes uses no verb, though it is still future looking, indicating the greatness of reward in heaven.

The first of the beatitudes, on the other hand, in 5:3, speaks of a presently held blessing: "Blessed are the poor in spirit, for theirs is (ἐστιν) the kingdom of heaven."[90] The penultimate beatitude likewise uses the same present tense phrasing in 5:10, "Blessed are those who have been persecuted for the sake of righteousness, for theirs is (ἐστιν) the kingdom of heaven."[91] While Jesus was proclaiming the kingdom as *being near* (ἤγγικεν),[92] He presented its possession *as a current reality*. How one understands the Author's usage of the present tense impacts the reader's understanding of social implications of the Sermon on the Mount.

---

[84] 5:4.
[85] 5:5.
[86] 5:6.
[87] 5:7.
[88] 5:8.
[89] 5:9.
[90] 5:3.
[91] Matthew 5:10.
[92] 4:17.

On this context, Chafer illustrates what Hullinger refers to as the *kingdom view* interpretation of the Sermon:[93] "In this manifesto the King declares the essential character of the kingdom, the conduct which will be required in the kingdom, and the directions of entrance into the kingdom…when His kingdom was rejected and its realization delayed until the return of the King, the application of all Scripture which conditions life in the kingdom was delayed as well."[94] While through this lens the Sermon has secondary applications for today, the conditions are all future looking. In favor of a *disciple ethic* interpretation of the Sermon, Hullinger suggests "it could be successfully argued that the invitation at the end of the sermon regarding the narrow road is not an invitation to salvation as it is often presented, but rather, an invitation to Jesus' disciples to embrace the ethic he has expounded."[95] Hullinger's assertion is not incompatible with Chafer's future-fulfillment understanding and it complements Ryrie's assertion that all of the Sermon "has relevance for today."[96] While the future-looking beatitudes are evidence that Chafer is on the right theological track, the two that specifically address the kingdom in present tense terms indicate that there is more in view than simply the future physical arrival of the King in His kingdom.

George Eldon Ladd draws a similar conclusion in his assertion that "The Word of God *does* say that the Kingdom of God is a present spiritual reality,"[97] but Ladd goes too far in assigning geography to that present reality as "an inner spiritual redemptive blessing…present and at work in the

---

[93] Jerry Hullinger, "Is There a "Dispensational" Approach to the Sermon on the Mount?" *1024 Project,* 2/17/2014, https://1024project.com/2014/02/17/is-there-a-dispensational-approach-to-the-sermon-on-the-mount/.

[94] Lewis Sperry Chafer, *Systematic Theology,* 8 volumes (Dallas, TX: Dallas Seminary Press, 1948), 4:177-178.

[95] Hullinger, Ibid.

[96] Charles Ryrie, *Dispensationalism Today* (Chicago, IL: Moody Press, 1969), 108.

[97] George Eldon Ladd, *The Gospel of the Kingdom* (Grand Rapids, MI: Eerdmans, 1959), 16.

world"[98] Ladd's already-not-yet theology is grounded in a geographically present (even if spiritual) manifestation of the kingdom within each believing individual. By contrast, Paul's instruction on the kingdom in the current age explicitly indicates different geographic parameters, as he reveals that God has "transferred *us* to the kingdom of His beloved Son."[99] It is evident that the kingdom doesn't change its location to the inner man, but rather the new creature is positionally transferred to the kingdom, hence, Paul's exhortation to "...keep seeking the things above, where Christ is, seated at the right hand of God. Set your mind on the things above, not on the things that are on earth. For you have died and your life is hidden with Christ in God. When Christ, who is our life, is revealed, then you also will be revealed with Him in glory."[100]

D. Martin Lloyd Jones takes Ladd's geographical leap to its logical conclusion when he asserts that "the kingdom of God is in every true Christian. He reigns in the Church when she acknowledges Him truly. The kingdom has come, the kingdom is coming, the kingdom is yet to come. Now we must always bear that in mind. Whenever Christ is enthroned as King, the kingdom of God is come, so that, while we cannot say that He is ruling over all in the world at the present time, He is certainly ruling in that way in the hearts and lives of all His people"[101] If Christ is presently ruling on the throne, as is asserted by already-not-yet, amillennial, and postmillennial models, then the kingdom is here and should be expected to generate kingdom results.

---

[98] Ladd, 18-19.
[99] Colossians 1:17.
[100] *New American Standard Bible: 1995 Update* (La Habra, CA: The Lockman Foundation, 1995), Colossians 3:1–4.
[101] D. Martin Lloyd Jones, *Studies in the Sermon on the Mount* (Grand Rapids, MI: Eerdmans, 1984), 16.

Gentry and Wellum directly connect the Biblical covenants to God's plan for kingdom results in the form of social justice, characterizing Israel, "As a community in covenant relationship to Yahweh, they are called to mirror to the world the character of Yahweh in terms of social justice and to be a vehicle of blessing and salvation to the nations."[102] After Israel's failure to fulfill that calling, "The Lord will establish Zion as the people/place where all nations will seek his instruction for social justice."[103] Yet even after return from exile, "the failure to practice social justice remains a central problem."[104] Despite these failings, "Both social justice and faithful loyal love are expressions of the character of Yahweh and of conduct expected in the covenant community where Yahweh is king,"[105] and thus "A coming Davidic king…will perfectly represent the Lord by implementing social justice…"[106] That kingdom is manifest in the current church: "The *newness* of the church is a redemptive-historical newness, rooted in the coming of Christ and the inauguration of the new covenant. In him, all of the previous covenants, which in type, shadow and prophetic announcement anticipated and foreshadowed him have now come to their *telos*."[107]

The assertions by Gentry and Wellum underscore the practical appeal of already-not-yet, postmillennial, and amillennial interpretations of the Sermon. The ethical implications are further illustrated by David Jones' kingdom-now assertion that, "As the kingdom of God grows, then the gospel gradually counteracts and corrects the effects of sin in the world through the process of restoration and reconciliation…the gospel is no less

---

[102] Peter Gentry and Stephen Wellum, *Kingdom Through Covenant: A Biblical Theological Understanding of the Covenants,* 2nd Edition (Wheaton, IL: Crossway, 2018), 436.
[103] Gentry and Wellum, 437.
[104] Ibid., 438.
[105] Gentry and Wellum, 582.
[106] Ibid., 643.
[107] Ibid., 685.

comprehensive than the fall…"¹⁰⁸ The realized eschatology interpretations of the Sermon on the Mount, with kingdom present both in time and space provide a compelling ethical foundation for contemporary social justice engagement and lend support to the economic and political ideologies espoused by Leo XIII and Pius XI, and Gutiérrez, and even Marx and Engels (atheism not withstanding).

On the other hand, reading the Sermon and other kingdom passages of Matthew through the normative literal grammatical historical hermeneutic (LGH) helps the reader understand as did Toussaint, that, "The kingdom exists in the intercalation only in the sense that the sons of the kingdom are present. But strictly speaking the kingdom of the heavens…refers to the prophesied and coming kingdom on earth."¹⁰⁹ The exhortation of 6:33 is an important echo of 5:3 and 5:10, to that end: "But seek first His kingdom and His righteousness, and all these things will be added to you."¹¹⁰ While there is a future tense promise (προστεθήσεται), there is a present tense responsibility (ζητεῖτε). This supports the model Chafer and Ryrie advocated, and brings to focus an important principle: *there is no theological necessity for realized eschatology in order to justify a vibrant sense of contemporary responsibility.* The mandate to seek first the kingdom and its righteousness has nothing whatsoever with the timing of the actual coming of the kingdom. Jesus's listeners were to be seeking that kingdom and its characteristic righteousness *even when the kingdom wasn't present in any fulfillment sense.* Likewise, the Sermon's final kingdom reference in 7:21 emphasizes the present tense responsibility (ποιῶν) for a future entering into (εἰσελεύσεται) the kingdom: "Not everyone who says to Me, 'Lord, Lord,' will enter the kingdom of heaven, but he who

---

[108] David Jones, *Introduction to Biblical Ethics* (Nashville: TN, B&H Academic, 2013), 64.
[109] Stanley Toussaint, *Behold the King: A Study of Matthew* (Portland, OR: Multnomah, 1980), 172.
[110] Matthew 6:33.

does the will of My Father who is in heaven *will enter*."[111] The one doing His will in the present will enter the kingdom at some future point in time.

CONCLUSION

While realized eschatology models offer easy motivation for social justice because of their integral assertions that the kingdom is already here, the LGH derived understanding that eschatology has not been realized does not at all minimize present responsibility. In fact, such a perspective makes the responsibility perhaps even clearer. Rather than asserting some mystery form of the kingdom and claiming a tangible manifestation when there simply isn't any, the mere fact that believers are actually citizens of a not-yet-here kingdom and that they are *told* to seek first the righteousness of that kingdom provides an explicit higher-order mandate.

When that kingdom is physically relocated to earth, then the promise of universal blessing through Abraham, given in Genesis 12:3b will be tangible reality. When that kingdom is physically relocated to earth, we will behold "a great multitude which no one could count, from every nation and *all* tribes and peoples and tongues,"[112] While this is a heavenly multitude in Revelation 7:9, their geography changes in Revelation 19. God's original promise to Abraham, and His covenant program expressed through the subsequent covenants is brought to fruition in the reign of Jesus Christ at the arrival of His kingdom of the heavens *on earth* (hence, Matthew's verbiage), and the ushering in of eternity that soon follows.

If that certain kingdom future reflects an enduring unity of nation, tribe, people, and tongue, then in the present seeking the kingdom and its righteousness, we are building houses on the rock – a present activity with

---

[111] Matthew 7:21.
[112] Revelation 7:9.

enduring result. If one enduring condition (even though not in any way brought on by our efforts) includes the unity of nation, tribe, people, and tongue, then our present activity should be characterized by things that reflect that eschatological progress. Biblical ethics in the church age corroborate this concept as we are to honor all people,[113] treating others as worthy of more honor than ourselves.[114] We are to do good to all, not only of the household of faith, though especially to those of the household of faith.[115] We are "to malign no one, to be peaceable, gentle, showing every consideration for all men."[116]

It is worth noting that among the reasons Paul offers for that last mandate, is that *we too were formerly enslaved*.[117] Certainly, the enslavement to which Paul refers is not the kind which Dubois laments, but enslavement of any human derivation keeps us from living as our Creator designed. Should we not demonstrate the newness of thinking exemplified by Paul when he referred to Onesimus as no longer a slave, but a beloved brother?[118] Paul expresses present-tense kingdom love when he exhorts Philemon to "accept [Onesimus] as me,"[119] and in so doing Philemon would be refreshing Paul's heart in Christ.[120]

If believers are *"willing to live in comfort even if the price of this is poverty, ignorance and disease of the majority of their fellowmen,"*[121] even continually waging war "to maintain this privilege,"[122] as Dubois asserts, then how can we claim

---

[113] 1 Peter 2:17.
[114] Philippians 2:1-11.
[115] Galatians 6:10.
[116] Titus 3:2.
[117] 3:3.
[118] Philemon 16.
[119] 17.
[120] 20.
[121] Dubois, 208.
[122] Ibid.

to be imitating Paul as he imitates Christ?[123] Are such injustices capable of being met with the ideologies of Marx and Engels, Leo XIII and Pius XI, and Gutiérrez? Or might we recognize that Christ mandated, in the Sermon on the Mount, *a future-looking perspective that had clear present-day applications*? Might we fix our gaze on what Paul highlights, in Philippians 2:1-11 – the example of Jesus Christ as modeling both the future-focus and the right-now striving? We don't need to manipulate hermeneutic methods, contrive theological fictions, nor seek economic and political saviors in order to advocate for a strong commitment to social justice (as defined by the Creator). While the particulars of *how* to best express and apply that commitment might be open to debate, that *the Bible requires such a commitment in this present age of those who would follow Jesus* is not.

---

[123] 1 Corinthians 4:16, 11:1.

Chapter 13 – On Social Justice
Towards a Theology of Justice: Contributions of the Old Testament to Concepts of Biblical Justice
Joseph Parle

Throughout church history, the church has developed orthodox positions often by evaluating two extreme (often false) positions. The church came to affirm the dual nature of Jesus Christ (fully God and fully man) as well as the Trinity (three eternally coexistent persons with one divine essence) in response to the Arian controversy which emphasized the humanity of Christ at the expense of His deity while also responding to the docetist and gnostic views that emphasized the deity of Christ at the expense of His humanity. The formation of the canon was in response to Marcionism which diminished the value of the Old Testament and several Gospels (i.e. Matthew, Mark and John) as well as the General Epistles while the authors of the gnostic and pseudepigraphal writings that claimed inspiration for their works. In a more contemporary sense, the modern debate over social justice seems to pit historical extremes of the church in which some argued against getting involved in social matters because it is pointless to clean a sinking ship (as an illustration of why one should not focus on earthly matters since the world will be destroyed)[1] against the liberation theology and social gospel advocates who diminish the eternal value of the gospel in an effort to focus on current issues affecting the oppressed. A biblical assessment of the Old

---

[1] For specific examples of abuses of the Bible to avoid involvement in social issues like slavery and segregation see Michael D. Emerson, *Divided By Faith* (New York, Oxford University Press, 2000), 21-49.

Testament and New Testament will show that God is very concerned with justice on earth but such concerns should be for His glory and for the end of bringing the lost to a saving knowledge of Jesus Christ. This chapter will evaluate the Old Testament and New Testament concepts of justice with a desire to demonstrate how the church should get involved in societal issues of our day.

METHOD

This chapter will utilize Mike Stallard's traditional dispensational model for developing a concise theology of biblical justice. In his article entitled "Literal Interpretation, Theological Method, and the Essence of Dispensationalism," he describes this traditional dispensational approach as follows:

1	The recognition of one's own preunderstanding
2	The formulation of a biblical theology from the Old Testament based upon literal interpretation (grammatical-historical method of interpretation) of the Old Testament text
3	The formulation of a biblical theology from the New Testament based upon literal interpretation (the grammatical-historical method of interpretation) of the New Testament text, which method includes the backgrounds arrived at via point 2 above

| 4 | The production of a systematic theology by harmonizing all inputs to theology including points 2 and 3 above[2] |

With respect to my preunderstanding, I acknowledge that I work at a primarily African American Bible College and have a Mexican mother as well as an Irish American father so my personal experiences with minorities has affected my approach to this issue. From a theological perspective, I am an evangelical traditional/classical/essentialist dispensationalist[3] who believes in the inerrancy of the original autographa of the Scripture, a literal approach to interpretation, a moderate Calvinist who believes that the good news of the gospel requires one to acknowledge he or she is a sinner who cannot save himself or herself, that Jesus died on the cross to pay the penalty for those sins and rose again to prove His victory over sin and death, and that salvation is completely by grace through faith in trusting Jesus's finished work on the cross as payment for the person's sin for eternal life. From a political perspective, I consider myself to be a compassionate conservative that typically votes Republican. I believe that capitalism is a better and more biblical economic system than socialism. I fully acknowledge that my preunderstanding can affect the conclusions I reach in this chapter and will try to avoid reading my assumptions into the passages I evaluate.

The second step will be to evaluate verses related to justice in the Old Testament from a literal perspective through the lens of the original Israelite

---

[2]Mike Stallard, "Literal Interpretation, Theological Method, and the Essence of Dispensationalism," *Journal of Ministry and Theology*, 1, no. 1 (Spring 1997): 29.

[3]Some have recently seemed to portray the dispensationalist system as though it were at odds with a passion for social justice issues. See, for example, Bryan Loritts, *Insider Outsider: My Journey As a Stranger in White Evangelicalism and My Hope for Us All* (Grand Rapids, MI, Zondervan, 2018), 42-53. However, I think a literal dispensational reading of the Bible should lead to concern about social justice issues.

audience. The third step will be to see how the New Testament describes justice with the Old Testament as background material. The fourth step will be to harmonize the data from the Old Testament and New Testament to help develop a theology of biblical justice. The final step will be to determine how these concepts apply to modern situations.[4]

The last step of application will utilize a model that I presented in a paper for the Council of Dispensational Hermeneutics.[5] In that paper, I argued that a dispensational approach effectively contributes to accurate expository preaching because dispensationalists rightly recognize the process of beginning with the exegesis of the text, moving to the identification of the timeless theological truth, and then identifying the homiletical application to the contemporary audience (see Figure 1 below).[6] Hence, this chapter will determine what aspects of justice are timeless as indicated by the text itself as occurring in the future or in the immutable character of God.

---

[4]Time and space do not permit an exhaustive evaluation of justice in the Old Testament and New Testament or how these concepts apply to all situations where justice may be involved.

[5]Joseph Parle, "Overcoming the Myth that Dispensationalists Do Not Believe the Old Testament Applies to Modern Contexts," (paper presented at the annual meeting of the Council on Dispensational Hermeneutics, Houston, Texas, 4 October 2012), 3.

[6]This process is described in Timothy S. Warren, "The Theological Process in Sermon Preparation," *Bibliotheca Sacra* 156, no. 623: 336–356.

Sermon Preparation Process

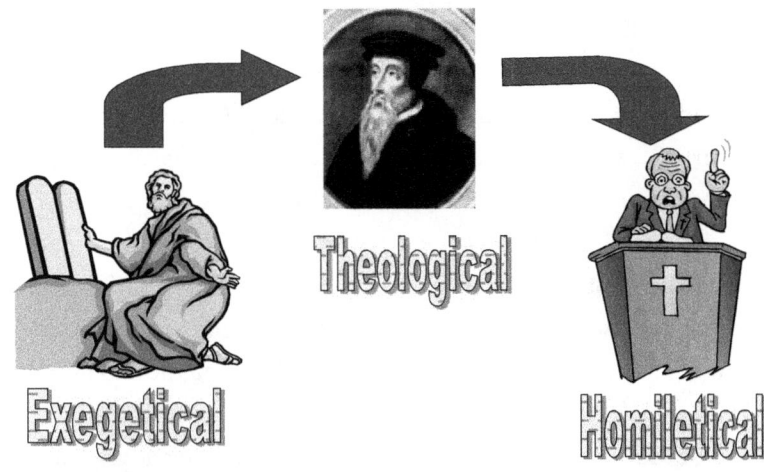

Figure One: Expository Preaching Lesson Preparation Process

TERMINOLOGY

Prior to evaluating the Old Testament and New Testament verses that deal with justice, a discussion of terms may be in order. This chapter hesitantly uses the phrase "biblical justice" instead of social justice because of the baggage that the phrase "social justice" has in conservative theological circles. The phrase "social justice warriors" is often used disparagingly of evangelicals and others who advocate for social justice. Part of the criticism is due to the fact that liberals have co-opted the phrase to refer to distribution of wealth. For instance, Finn and Jacobson in a blog for Oxford University Press state that some define it this way when they write, "Discussions of social justice in the context of social work generally address the differing philosophical approaches used to inform societal decisions about the distribution or allocation of resources. These discussions refer to three dominant theories of resource distribution: Utilitarian, libertarian, and egalitarian."[7] The Center for Economic and Social Justice provides the following definitions:

> Social justice encompasses economic justice. Social justice is the virtue which guides us in creating those organized human interactions we call institutions. In turn, social institutions, when justly organized, provide us with access to what is good for the person, both individually and in our associations with others. Social justice also imposes on each of us a personal responsibility to collaborate with others, at whatever level of the "Common Good" in which we participate, to design and continually perfect our institutions as tools for personal and social development…
>
> Economic justice, which touches the individual person as well as the social order, encompasses the moral principles which guide us in designing our economic institutions. These institutions determine how each person earns a living, enters into contracts, exchanges goods and services with others and otherwise produces an independent material foundation for his or her economic sustenance. The ultimate purpose of economic justice is to free each person to engage creatively in the unlimited work beyond economics, that of the mind and the spirit.[8]

---

[7] Janet L. Finn and Maxine Jacobson, "What is social justice?" Available at https://blog.oup.com/2017/03/what-is-social-justice/.

[8] Center for Economic and Social Justice, "Defining Economic and Social Justice," Available at https://www.cesj.org/learn/definitions/defining-economic-justice-and-social-justice/.

The frequent connection between social justice and the redistribution of wealth (which is not how I personally would use the term) may warrant a better term.

However, I hesitate in doing so because of the history of the phrase "social justice."[9] The origin of the phrase social justice dates back to Luigi Taparelli d'Azeglio in 1843. He used the term differently than those who desire to redistribute wealth use it today:

> Taparelli discusses justice and social justice against the background of the French Revolution of 1789 with its cry of equality and brutal treatment of kings and aristocracies, and also of the revolution of 1830 that installed Louis Philippe. The question at issue for him, although Taparelli does not formulate it precisely in these terms, is something like this: how should a society treat its traditional rulers? Is the existence of an aristocracy unjust? For 'distributive justice governs public administrators in the distribution of the offices (funzioni) of the society.' His answer is that social justice requires us to accept inequality. Justice, he argues, is the habitual inclination to level or balance accounts. Distributive justice equalizes proportions in the common good. Social justice is justice between man and man. But what proportions exist between man and man? Considering man in the abstract endowed solely with the qualities of human nature, between man and man the relationship that exists is one of complete equality, for "man and man" signifies here nothing other than humanity replicated twice.

---

[9] For more on the history of the phrase see Christopher Cone, "Every Tribe, Tongue, People, and Nation: The Future of Race Relations and Social Justice Implications for Today," (paper presented at the annual meeting of the Council on Dispensational Hermeneutics, Kansas City, MO, 19 September 2020), 2-7.

What proportionate equality could be greater? Social justice should therefore level all men in regard to the rights given with their humanity, since the Creator has equalized them by nature; man fulfills the intentions of his Maker by acting according to the norm of this justice…The consequence is that justice has very different requirements for private goods and common or social goods. In the one case it requires a quantitative equality, but not in the other…

From this brief account certain important things should be clear about Taparelli's conception of social justice. Unlike the conception of social justice generally accepted in our society at the present time, which is socialist and difficult, if not impossible, to harmonize with our ordinary conception of justice, Taparelli's conception 1) is simply the ordinary and traditional conception of justice applied in a new area, namely the constitutional arrangements of society, 2) does not apply to states of affairs in society that could exist independently of human actions, 3) constitutes a defense of societal inequality, and 4) is conservative.[10]

The co-opting of the term for economic purposes seems to be a relatively recent phenomenon. Either way, to argue that social justice has its origin in Cultural Marxism is anachronistic since the term was developed before Karl Marx published any of his ideas about Marxism.

Since some people are concerned about the current correlation between social justice and the coercive redistribution of wealth, some use the phrase "generous justice"[11] while others prefer "biblical justice." Carter discusses

---

[10] Thomas Patrick Burke, "The Origins of Social Justice: Taparelli d'Azeglio," Available at https://isi.org/intercollegiate-review/the-origins-of-social-justice-taparelli-dazeglio/.

[11] Timothy Keller, *Generous Justice: How God's Grace Makes Us Just* (New York: Penguin Books, 2016).

biblical justice when he quotes Tim Keller's statements regarding two Hebrew words that are commonly used for justice: *mishpat* and *tzadeqah*. Keller says:

> The Hebrew word for 'justice,' *mishpat,* occurs in its various forms more than 200 times in the Hebrew Old Testament. Its most basic meaning is to treat people equitably. It means acquitting or punishing every person on the merits of the case, regardless of race or social status. Anyone who does the same wrong should be given the same penalty.
>
> But *mishpat* means more than just the punishment of wrongdoing. It also means giving people their rights. Deuteronomy 18 directs that the priests of the tabernacle should be supported by a certain percentage of the people's income. This support is described as 'the priests' *mishpat*,' which means their due or their right. *Mishpat*, then, is giving people what they are due, whether punishment or protection or care. …
>
> We get more insight when we consider a second Hebrew word that can be translated as 'being just,' though it usually translated as 'being righteous.' The word is *tzadeqah*, and it refers to a life of right relationships.
>
> When most modern people see the word 'righteousness' in the Bible, they tend to think of it in terms of private morality, such as sexual chastity or diligence in prayer and Bible study. But in the Bible, *tzadeqah* refers to day-to-day living in which a person conducts all relationships in family and society with fairness, generosity and equity. It is not surprising, then, to discover that *tzadeqah* and *mishpat* are brought together scores of times in the Bible.

> These two words roughly correspond to what some have called 'primary' and 'rectifying justice.' Rectifying justice is *mishpat*. It means punishing wrongdoers and caring for the victims of unjust treatment. Primary justice, or *tzadeqah*, is behavior that, if it was prevalent in the world, would render rectifying justice unnecessary, because everyone would be living in right relationship to everyone else. Therefore, though *tzadeqah* is primarily about being in a right relationship with God, the righteous life that results is profoundly social.[12]

Carter then concludes:

> As Keller says, when the two Hebrew words *tzadeqah* and *mishpat* are tied together—as they are more than three dozen times—the English expression that best conveys the meaning is 'social justice.' Social justice, then, would be not only a biblical concept, but also a subset of biblical justice.
>
> Claiming that we need only 'biblical justice' and not 'social justice' is a category error (i.e., a semantic or ontological error in which things belonging to a particular category are presented as if they belong to a different category). Biblical justice includes all forms of God-ordained justice, including the rectifying justice that belongs to the government (what we'd call public or legal justice) as well as justice between individuals (what could be called inter-individual

---

[12] Joe Carter, "The FAQs: What Christians Should Know About Social Justice," https://www.thegospelcoalition.org/article/faqs-christians-know-social-justice/. For additional analysis on these two terms see Steven W. Boyd, "The Biblical Case Against Counter-Social Justice: YHWH's Demand for Justice and Righteousness," (paper presented at the annual meeting of the Council on Dispensational Hermeneutics, Kansas City, MO, September 2020).

justice) and justice involving organizations and groups (what we'd call social justice).[13]

While I agree with Carter that biblical justice includes social justice, I hesitantly prefer to use the phrase biblical justice because of the baggage that social justice now has with it. However, I completely agree with Carter when he writes, "Social justice, as a biblical concept, is not a term we should abandon without a fight. To paraphrase Colson, we should not shrink from the term nor allow the secular world to distort its biblical meaning."[14]

My preferred definition of social justice is as follows:

> Perhaps it would be helpful to add that we use the term 'social justice' in the same way that Chuck Colson, Marvin Olasky, Albert Mohler, and many other conservative, biblically grounded Christians have used it. We don't understand it in terms of government-mandated redistribution of wealth. On the contrary, we see it as a matter of the church rolling up its sleeves and becoming the hands and feet of Jesus. As Christians, we have a responsibility to redress those social factors that conspire to keep entire segments of our population mired in hopelessness and despair. What's more, we need to approach this task primarily from a *relational* perspective. As we understand it, 'social justice' means nothing more than 'doing right by one's neighbor.' As you know, that's an idea that figures significantly in the words of Jesus.[15]

---

[13]Carter, "The FAQs."
[14]Carter, "The FAQs."
[15]Focus on the Family, "What the Bible Says About Human Rights and Social Justice," Available at https://www.focusonthefamily.com/family-qa/what-the-bible-says-about-human-rights-and-social-justice/. Emphasis his.

The definition above provides a more biblical perspective of the concept.

OLD TESTAMENT THEOLOGY OF JUSTICE

While this is not a comprehensive Old Testament theology on justice, this section of the chapter will attempt to summarize some of the salient points about justice. This section will focus on how the Old Testament portrays God as a God of justice who predicts a future full of justice and requires mankind to participate in acts of justice.

Portrayal of God as a God of Justice

The Old Testament repeatedly portrays God as a God of justice. Justice is an inherent part of God's character. For instance, Deuteronomy 32:4 (NASB) says, "The Rock! His work is perfect, For all His ways are just; A God of faithfulness and without injustice, Righteous and upright is He." Multiple times in the Old Testament God's character is associated with justice (Is 30:18, Jer 4:1-2, Mal 2:17, Ps 89:14). In Isaiah 30:18 both God's covenantal name of Yahweh and the name Elohim are associated with His justice (כִּי־אֱלֹהֵי מִשְׁפָּט יְהוָה). Isaiah 61:8 (ESV) proclaims that God loves justice, "For I the LORD love justice; I hate robbery and wrong; I will faithfully give them their recompense, and I will make an everlasting covenant with them." Jeremiah 9:24 (ESV) declares that the Lord delights in justice, "I am the LORD who practices steadfast love, justice, and righteousness in the earth. For in these things I delight, declares the LORD." Isaiah 33:5-6 (ESV) predicts a time when God will fill Zion with justice and righteousness. "The LORD is exalted, for he dwells on high; he will fill Zion with justice and righteousness, and he will be the stability of your times, abundance of salvation, wisdom, and knowledge; the fear of the LORD is Zion's treasure."

Portrayal of Future of Justice

Several passages point to a future in which justice reigns, which would seem to indicate that God's desire for justice is not just limited to Old Testament Israel. For instance, Isaiah 28:17 (ESV) says, "And I will make justice the line, and righteousness the plumb line; and hail will sweep away the refuge of lies, and waters will overwhelm the shelter." Isaiah 9:7 predicts a messianic kingdom full of justice while Isaiah 42:4 states that the Messiah will not faint or become discouraged until He establishes justice in the earth (see also Jeremiah 23:5 and Jeremiah 33:15). Isaiah 32:15-16 predicts that once the Holy Spirit comes upon Israel that God will establish justice in the wilderness while Isaiah 51:4 predicts that God will set His justice as a light for the nations.

God Demands Justice

In multiple instances God commands justice. Genesis 18:19 (NASB) says that God chose Abraham "so that he may command his children and his household after him to keep the way of the LORD by doing righteousness and justice." Micah 6:8 (ESV), "He has told you, O man, what is good; and what does the LORD require of you but to do justice, and to love kindness, and to walk humbly with your God?" Jeremiah 21:12 (ESV) says, "O house of David! Thus says the LORD: 'Execute justice in the morning, and deliver from the hand of the oppressor him who has been robbed, lest my wrath go forth like fire, and burn with none to quench it, because of your evil deeds.'" It appears that the Davidic kings were responsible for delivering people from oppressors who rob from others. Barclay states, "The reference is clearly to the judicial system. TEV renders 'Protect the person who is being cheated from the one who is cheating him.' The verb *has been robbed* is used elsewhere in Jeremiah only in 22:3. It may have the meaning of 'robbed' (Jdg 9:25), but it may also be used in the sense of depriving someone of their rights (Is 10:2). Note that although the text has **him**, 'the person' or 'people' would be better, since the reference is not to males alone."[16]

Many of God's commands regarding justice were protecting the most vulnerable. Zechariah 7:9-10 (NASB), "Thus has the LORD of hosts said, 'Dispense true justice and practice kindness and compassion each to his brother; and do not oppress the widow or the orphan, the stranger or the poor; and do not devise evil in your hearts against one another.'" The widow does not have a husband to look out for her; the orphan lacks parents; the stranger lacks the standing in the government for protection while the poor do not have the resources to secure their own protection. Each of these were worthy of justice in the eyes of God for His glory. Ralph Smith adds:

> 7:7–10 provides one of the finest summaries of the teaching of the former prophets. It has a strong emphasis on social justice. But it is not social justice for social justice's sake. Social justice is God's requirement. 'Thus says Yahweh of hosts' (7:9). They refused to hearken to the words of Yahweh that he gave by his spirit through the former prophets (7:12). God requires social justice between brothers (7:10) and toward the disadvantaged (widows, orphans, aliens, and poor 7:10). The verbs are imperatives שפטו 'judge' and עשו 'do, or act.' They are commands from Yahweh."[17]

---

[16] Barclay M. Newman Jr. and Philip C. Stine, *A Handbook on Jeremiah*, UBS Handbook Series (New York: United Bible Societies, 2003), 469.

[17] Ralph L. Smith, *Micah-Malachi*, vol. 32, Word Biblical Commentary (Dallas: Word, Incorporated, 1984), 225.

Hosea 12:7 rebukes rich people for oppressing the poor with false balances (see also Micah 6:11). Amos 5:11 rebukes those who trample on the poor and exact grain taxes on them. Ezekiel 18:7-8 commends a person who "does not oppress anyone, but restores to the debtor his pledge, commits no robbery, gives his bread to the hungry and covers the naked with a garment, does not lend at interest or take any profit, withholds his hand from injustice, executes true justice between man and man." Several passages argue that Israel was supposed to defend the rights of the poor (Ex 23:6; Dt 10:19, 17:19, 27:19; Ps 82:3-4, 140:12; Pr 31:4-5, Is 1:17, 10:2; Jer 7:6, 22:16; and Eze 22:29).

The Old Testament does not only discuss justice but also injustice. Deuteronomy 16:19-20 (ESV) includes some themes that are commonly found in Old Testament justice passages, "You shall not pervert justice. You shall not show partiality, and you shall not accept a bribe, for a bribe blinds the eyes of the wise and subverts the cause of the righteous. Justice, and only justice, you shall follow, that you may live and inherit the land that the LORD your God is giving you." This Hebrew phrase translated pervert justice (תַטֶּה מִשְׁפָּט) is often used of accepting bribes (1Sa 8:13, Pr 17:23, etc.) or denying the needy of the justice that they are due (Ex 23:6; Dt 24:17, 27:19; and Is 10:2). Hence, God had a concern about ensuring that the most vulnerable people's rights were preserved without duplicity or greed.

Another common Old Testament phrase is "justice and equity" or "justice and righteousness" that translates the same Hebrew phrase (מִשְׁפָּט וּצְדָקָה). 2 Samuel 8:15 (ESV) says, "So David reigned over all Israel. And David administered justice and equity to all his people." The concept of equity in the eyes of the law seems to be an essential element to Old Testament justice. The Queen of Sheba acknowledged God's role in making David a king that would "execute justice and righteousness" (1Ki 10:9 ESV). Psalm 99:4 (ESV) includes all the elements of equity, justice and righteousness, "The King in his might loves justice. You have established equity; you have executed justice and righteousness in Jacob." Proverbs 2:9 also declares these elements are a result of wise living. These same concepts of justice and righteousness describe the Lord in the Old Testament (cf. Jer 9:24) as well as His Anointed Messiah Son (Jer 23:5 and 33:15). God commands His people to model justice and righteousness (Jeremiah 22:33 and Amos 5:24), encourages those who do not to repent and model it (Eze 18:27 and 33:14-19), and rebukes those who do not (Am 5:7).

SUMMARY

A review of the Old Testament description of justice demonstrated that justice is presented as an essential part of God the Father and God the Son's character. God predicts a future full of justice and commands His people to show justice even to the most helpless of society, namely the poor, widow, orphan, and alien. God demands His leaders show justice, equity, and righteousness in their dealings as opposed to perverting justice and accepting bribes.

SYNTHESIS WITH THE NEW TESTAMENT

This section will review the concept of justice in the New Testament in order to assess continuity or discontinuity from the New Testament concepts. Based on that assessment, an argument will be made to evaluate how Old Testament and New Testament concepts of justice apply to modern contexts.

A review of New Testament discussions of justice seems to validate some of the concepts discussed in the review of the Old Testament. God's character requires justice as described in Jesus's quotation of Isaiah 42:1-4 in

Matthew 12:18-21. Similarly, Jesus quotes Isaiah 61:1 in Luke 4:17-18. Regarding these quotations, Keller writes, "These are the words Jesus read in the synagogue in Nazareth when he announced the beginning of his ministry. He identified himself as the 'Servant of the Lord,' prophesied by Isaiah, who would bring 'justice' to the world (Is 42:1-7). Most people know that Jesus came to bring forgiveness and grace. Less well known in the biblical teaching that a true experience of the grace of Jesus Christ inevitably motivates a man or woman to seek justice in the world."[18]

The New Testament also seems to have a great deal of concern for the poor. In Matthew 11:4 Jesus proclaims to John the Baptist that the poor have the good news preached to them as a sign of His messianic identity. Paul says in Galatians 2:9-10 (ESV), "And when James and Cephas and John, who seemed to be pillars, perceived the grace that was given to me, they gave the right hand of fellowship to Barnabas and me, that we should go to the Gentiles and they to the circumcised. Only, they asked us to remember the poor, the very thing I was eager to do." A frequent refrain from those who criticize the so called social justice warriors is that if one just preaches the gospel that should be enough. In this passage, it seems as though preaching the gospel to the Gentiles was not enough for the pillars of the early church. They also wanted for Paul to dedicate himself to caring for the poor. James 1:27 expresses a similar concern for widows and orphans as an essential element of godly religion when James says. "Religion that is pure and undefiled before God the Father is this: to visit orphans and widows in their affliction, and to keep oneself unstained from the world" (Jam 1:27 ESV). James continues that with an admonition against a partiality that favors rich visitors to the church over poor ones (2:1) and he speaks out against the rich employers who fraudulently withheld wages from their laborers (5:1-6). John

---

[18] Tim Keller, *Generous Justice*, xiii.

says in 1 John 3:17-18 (ESV), "But if anyone has the world's goods and sees his brother in need, yet closes his heart against him, how does God's love abide in him? Little children, let us not love in word or talk but in deed and in truth." Colossians 4:1-2 emphasizes equity for slaves when masters are encouraged to treat their slaves with justice and fairness.

As in the Old Testament, God rebukes His people when they do not operate justly. Jesus says in Matthew 23:23-24 (NASB), "Woe to you, scribes and Pharisees, hypocrites! For you tithe mint and dill and cummin, and have neglected the weightier provisions of the law: justice and mercy and faithfulness; but these are the things you should have done without neglecting the others. You blind guides, who strain out a gnat and swallow a camel!" In this passage, Jesus declares that justice, mercy, and faithfulness are the weightier provisions of the law and he criticizes the Pharisees for not giving those the attention they deserve while trying to legalistically obey some of the less weighty aspects of the law. Mason says:

> The Lord Jesus calls justice a weighty matter in Scripture. Jesus is using a play on words by contrasting the naturally light weight of the mint, dill, and cumin with the weight and expanse of the deeper matters of the law. According to R.T. France, 'There is no suggestion that the scribes and Pharisees were opposed in principle to justice, mercy, and faithfulness. The problem is they did not devote the same care to working out the practical implications of these basic principles as they did to the minutiae of tithing herbs.' ... What minutiae are we engaging in to show our dedication to exegesis, historical theology, biblical theology, systematic theology, Old Testament, New Testament, Bible exposition, hermeneutics, pastoral theology, etc. while we miss some of the key opportunities

for fleshing out and communicating a commitment to the heart of God?[19]

Galatians 2:11-14 also involves a situation in which Paul confronted Peter for not acting consistently with the truth of the gospel. In neglecting to eat with the Gentiles in the presence of the Jews, Paul confronted Peter for acting hypocritically and not treating the Gentiles with the equity that the gospel demands. Regarding this passage, Hendriksen and Simon J. Kistemaker write:

> Paul saw that Peter and all those who followed his example "were not straight-footing *toward*, or in *accordance with*, the truth of the gospel," thus literally. In the New Testament the verb *they are straight-footings* occurs only here. The meaning is probably either that, as Paul saw it, these people were not advancing *toward*, i.e., *in the direction of*, the gospel-truth, or that they were not pursuing a straight course *in accordance with* that truth.[20]

Acting unjustly and righteously to the exclusion of others is not walking in accordance with the truth of the gospel and should be called out as Paul did here. While some argue that Christians should focus on the gospel and not get entangled with social issues, Paul rebukes Peter for not living in light of the truth of the gospel by seeking the approval of the Jews at the expense of the Gentiles. And even those who preached the gospel faithfully did not always do not always act responsibly when it comes to ensuring justice for all

---

[19] Eric Mason, *Woke Church* (Chicago, IL, Moody Publishers, 2018), 48.
[20] William Hendriksen and Simon J. Kistemaker, *Exposition of Galatians*, vol. 8, New Testament Commentary (Grand Rapids: Baker Book House, 1953–2001), 95.

(e.g. Jonathan Edwards and George Whitefield were slave owners and Whitefield in particular openly lobbied for and advocated for slavery).

Furthermore, Galatians 6:10 (NASB) says, "So then, while we have opportunity, let us do good to all people, and especially to those who are of the household of the faith." As Christians, we should be focused on doing good for all, especially Christians. This likely means mourning when our fellow brothers and sisters locally and globally suffer and trying to address that pain rather than deny it. Cone, quoting Dubois, paints a good picture of what this should look like:

> If believers are "willing to live in comfort even if the price of this is poverty, ignorance and disease of the majority of their fellowmen," even continually waging war "to maintain this privilege," as Dubois asserts, then how can we claim to be imitating Paul as he imitates Christ? Are such injustices capable of being met with the ideologies of Marx and Engels, Leo XIII and Pius XI, and Gutiérrez? Or might we recognize that Christ mandated, in the Sermon on the Mount, a future-looking perspective that had clear present-day applications? Might we fix our gaze on what Paul highlights, in Philippians 2:1-11 – the example of Jesus Christ as modeling both the future-focus and the right-now striving? We don't need to manipulate hermeneutic methods, contrive theological fictions, nor seek economic and political saviors in order to advocate for a strong commitment to social justice (as defined by the Creator). While the particulars of how to best express and apply that commitment might be open to debate, that the Bible requires such a commitment in this present age of those who would follow Jesus is not.[21]

---

[21] Christopher Cone, *Authentic Social Justice* (Independence, MO: Exegetica Publishing: 2020), 173.

Biblical Distinctions Applied 385

Paul modeled this compassion well in appealing to Philemon for the release of Onesimus. [22]

The New Testament does add a dynamic to justice that is not found as frequently in the Old Testament. Luke 18 includes some of these concepts. Luke 18:7-8 (ESV) says, "And will not God give justice to his elect, who cry to him day and night? Will he delay long over them? I tell you, he will give justice to them speedily. Nevertheless, when the Son of Man comes, will he find faith on earth?" This passage describes how God as a just judge (in comparison to the unjust judge in the previous parable) will respond to the cries for justice on the part of His followers. He then proceeds to contrast a self-righteous Pharisee with a tax collector who begs God for forgiveness before concluding in Luke 18:14 (ESV), "I tell you, this man went down to his house justified, rather than the other. For everyone who exalts himself will be humbled, but the one who humbles himself will be exalted." Romans 3:26 (ESV) makes a similar statement when it says, "It was to show his righteousness at the present time, so that he might be just and the justifier of the one who has faith in Jesus." This New Testament concept of God's justice being preserved through the finished work of Christ is based on Old Testament concepts (Ge 15:6, Hab 2:4) but the New Testament lends greater clarity to how God's justice and mercy would be preserved. Hence, this New Testament concept of justice does not show discontinuity with the Old Testament but instead expands on concepts already present in the Old Testament.

---

[22] For more on the history of the phrase see Elliott E. Johnson, "Does Philemon Provide a Sufficient Perspective to Address Social Justice?" (aper presented at the annual meeting of the Council on Dispensational Hermeneutics, Kansas City, MO, 19 September 2020), 2-7.

WHAT IS DISPENSATIONAL ABOUT THIS APPROACH

Upon reading this chapter, one might wonder what is uniquely dispensational about this approach. After all, many evangelicals speaking out about social justice with some exceptions are doing so from an approach outside of Dispensationalism. I would assert that the method and the underlying eschatological assumptions of this chapter are uniquely dispensational.

As was previously mentioned, this chapter employed Stallard's approach which begins with a recognition of preunderstanding followed by literal interpretation of the Old Testament, then a literal interpretation of the New Testament followed by a synthesis of the results in which the Old Testament informs the understanding of the New Testament. Those outside of the dispensationalist camp may come to the text with a preunderstanding that either man or the election/salvation/ deliverance of man is the focal point of the Bible and interpret these texts in that light. Additionally, there is a tendency at least among Covenant theologians to allow the meaning of the New Testament or Old Testament to trump or provide a spiritual application for verses addressed to Israel as the church. Instead, this chapter attempted to follow Warren's process of identifying the exegetical meaning of the original Old Testament text as written by the original author to the original audience (often Israel) and then identifying the timeless transdispensational theological truth about God and/or His expectations of mankind that could be applied to the modern day audience. Hence, while one most recognize that many of the commands are given to Israel which rules theocratically as a representative of God, these commands to seek justice are also rooted in His character and the expectations for just rule extended past Israel to Gentile nations as well as detailed by Amos and other prophets. Additionally, commands to seek justice and the needs of the poor and vulnerable were repeated in the New Testament to Gentile (e.g. see previous citations from Galatians and Philemon) and Jewish Christians (James 2) alike.

Additionally, the eschatological assumptions of the nature of the Davidic kingdom would be different in a traditional dispensational approach from other approaches. Whereas some might be motivated to get involved with social justice matters to usher in the kingdom of Christ or out of a belief that the kingdom is already present, traditional dispensationalists would point to a future kingdom which does not have a timing connected to involvement in social justice. In fact, the time that precedes the kingdom, the tribulation, is the most unjust period of all. The traditional dispensational perspective on the kingdom is more clearly linked to a desire to literally apply what the Bible commands and to reflect the holiness and character of God.

APPLICATION

Thus far, the chapter has focused on the exegetical analysis of what the Old Testament and New Testament texts would have meant to the original audience in an effort to compose a theology of biblical justice. As part of the process for determining how one should apply those texts to contemporary situations, one must identify the timeless truths. Because the Old Testament and New Testament concepts of biblical justice are connected to the character of God, it is fair to assume that those concepts are timeless. Furthermore, in both the Old Testament and New Testament, God requires His people to advocate justice for all people, especially those who cannot speak for themselves. This includes but is not limited to the orphan, widow, alien, and the poor. It would be a consistent application of this theological principle to include the unborn, those who are trafficked, persecuted Christians domestically as well as internationally, Jews, and other oppressed people.

Additionally, the biblical concept of justice emphasizes equity and avoiding partiality. Justice should not be bought by bribes and access to legal justice should not be disproportionately based on income. As a church, we should welcome the rich and poor alike into our fellowship. We should also fight all forms of racial injustice in which individuals are discriminated against based on race. God's concern for the alien and equity should cause Christians to advocate submission to governing authorities according to Romans 13, not only for illegal aliens but the companies and industries that rely on their inexpensive labor. We should pursue legal avenues like a guest worker program that would allow more legal immigration while providing inexpensive labor to those businesses and industries that desperately need it.

Furthermore, while the New Testament expands on the justice of God when viewed through the lens of the gospel and the finished work of Jesus Christ on the cross, one should not see that as the only remedy to address society's injustices. While Paul was sent to share the gospel to the gentiles, he was still encouraged to remember the poor. When Paul confronted Peter for his hypocritical actions towards the gentiles while trying to impress his Jewish friends, he did so in light of the gospel. As Jesus's statements to the Pharisees, we as Christians should be more concerned with the weightier issues of God's word like sharing the gospel with the unreached, care for the poor, deliverance for the oppressed, and equity than things like the right to bear arms which comes from a valid application of Luke 22:36-37 but certainly does not appear to be as central to a scriptural understanding of Scripture that some conservative evangelicals make it out to be. It seems unusual that as Christians we would rightly speak out about the rights of the unborn yet act as though advocating for someone else who cannot speak for himself or herself is a form of Cultural Marxism.[23] These statements are not intended to

---

[23]To be clear, I wholeheartedly support the right to bear arms as being necessary for protecting one's family and preserving a free society. I also support the rights of the

agree with social gospel advocates who convert the gospel from an eternal salvation/deliverance to earthly deliverance. Instead, because of the glory of God and His gospel, we advocate for justice because of the grace the gospel has provided in us. Eric Mason writes:

> In Western theology, we tend to lack a comprehensive view of God's perfections, particularly righteousness/ justice and even our understanding of justification. Justification is a huge greenhouse of truth that extends beyond 'being declared righteous'! Justified isn't merely a position but a practice! Christ's righteousness being imputed to us by faith leads our being right with God as well as our making things right on earth – knowing that Jesus will return and bring to completion the work He has been doing through his people.[24]

CONCLUSION

This chapter analyzed some verses in the Old Testament and New Testament related to justice. I utilized Stallard's traditional dispensational method for analyzing the passages to develop a theology of justice based on the biblical data. This involves acknowledging presuppositions, then interpreting the Old Testament literally, followed by the New Testament literally with the Old Testament as a background, with the final step of synchronizing results. After implementing this process, I utilized Warren's

---

unborn. My point is simply that the Bible says less about these issues, but they often are the central focus of Christian conservatives who remain relatively silent about other matters the Bible speaks about far more frequently. And even when we discuss abortion, very little attention is given to fertilized embryos that are destroyed at fertility clinics and other similar issues that have the same effect as an abortion but are more likely remedies a rich person would use as opposed to a poor person. If Christians used the same vigor to oppose segregation, slavery, and other racial injustices as they have guns, our society would be very different.

[24]Eric Mason, *Woke Church*, 45.

process of identifying the timeless truth in order to get specific applications. I made the argument that social justice (defined as loving one's neighbor) is a biblical concept in both the Old Testament and New Testament and the biblical principles of seeking justice for all (especially those who cannot pursue justice for themselves) is an applicable principle in the current dispensation. Perhaps, rather than appealing to the phrase "social justice warrior" as a derogatory term, the bride of Christ can see those who speak out for those who cannot speak for themselves in more of a positive light.

Chapter 14 – On Outreach and Mission
Integral Mission: Is Social Action Part of the Gospel?
Paul Barreca

INTRODUCTION

Integral Mission is producing missionaries and mission movements that incorporate socio-economic engagement as an essential component of the gospel. This chapter will evaluate the origin of Integral Mission and argue that the gospel is being re-defined to require socio-economic engagement, something beyond its biblical definition. A review of Acts and the Epistles of the New Testament demonstrates that although socio-economic injustices were widespread in first-century Rome, the early church did not establish programs to address social needs as a method for evangelism. Although societal changes may have been brought about by people whose lives were transformed by the gospel, societal change was not the reason that Christians shared the gospel. This chapter seeks to elevate the biblical gospel because of its inherent power to change lives, while keeping it separate from human programs and social action, which, although important, are different endeavors.[1]

---

[1] As the director of a missionary agency rooted in classical dispensationalism, this author supervises missionaries around the world who, among other ministries, feed and educate the poor, care for refugees and provide many types of humanitarian and disaster-relief services. In every setting, they and thousands of other Christian missionaries are helping the world's most needy communities while maintaining the centrality of the gospel of Christ as the only power sufficient to change lives.

CALLED TO COMPASSION

Jesus exemplified compassion. While Christians may differ regarding the integration of social engagement into the gospel, there should be no debate concerning the compassion that Jesus demonstrated toward the poor and needy, nor the expectation that Christians today should act with compassion toward those in need.

English New Testaments have translated "compassion" from the Greek root word σπλαγχνον, which is used frequently in the Gospels to describe Christ's attitude toward various individuals and groups of people. He showed compassion on the multitudes needing a shepherd (Mt 9:36), the mourning widow (Lk 7:31), the large crowd at the feeding of the 5,000 (Mt 14:14, 15:32; Mk 6:34), the large crowd at the feeding of the 4,000 (Mk 8:2), the boy with the evil spirit (Mk 9:22), and the two blind men as he was leaving Jericho (Mt 20:34). Volumes have been written on the meekness, gentleness and love demonstrated by Jesus. As Christians are being transformed by the Holy Spirit into the likeness of Jesus, they will develop a heart of compassion and begin to act with compassion toward others, following John's exhortation that, *"whoever says he abides in him ought to walk in the same way in which he walked"* (1Jn 2:6; see also Ro 8:29, 12:2, 13:14; 2Co 3:18, 5:17; Col 3:10-12).

Regardless of one's position concerning Integral Mission, every Christian should stand in agreement that the transformational character of Christ within a believer's life should result in a heart of compassion. In a book that challenges the shift toward a social justice gospel, Gary Gilley points out that all Christians should agree about compassion for the needy. "Make no mistake: that the people of God should be concerned about injustice and social issues that plague our world at large, and they should be model citizens who do good to those around them, is not in question and is not the issue."[2]

The purpose of this chapter is not to debate the necessity of compassion from believers toward the poor and needy nor is it to cast doubt on the intentions, godliness or effectiveness of the large number of theologians, missionaries, and Christian institutions advancing the Integral Mission concept today. The question at hand is one of definition and the consequences of modifying our definition of the gospel to include the popular themes of social justice in contemporary culture.

Denny Spitters and Matthew Ellison expressed this concern in *"When Everything is Missions:"*

> Yet we are concerned that an uncritical use of words, and in particular a lack of shared definition for the words mission, missions, missionary, and missional, has led to a distortion of Jesus' biblical mandate, ushered in an everything-is-missions paradigm, and moved missions from the initiation and oversight of local churches to make it the domain of individual believers responding to individualized callings.[3]

History is filled with excellent examples of Christians feeding the hungry, clothing the poor, building hospitals, and demonstrating the compassion of Jesus to a needy world. These practices are not in question, but rather, the question at hand is if there is support from the Bible or early

---

[2] Gary Gilley, *The Social Justice Primer: In Search of the Message and Mission of the Church* (Springfield, IL: Think on These Things Ministries, 2019), Kindle location 1238.
[3] Denny Ellision and Matthew Spitters, *When Everything is Missions* (Pioneers, 2017), 22.

church practice to consider the gospel a blend of the spoken message about Christ and the acts of compassion demonstrated by ministers of the gospel.

A BRIEF INTRODUCTION TO INTEGRAL MISSION

Integral Mission(s) also referred to as "Holistic Mission(s)," emphasizes the incorporation of social action as an essential component of gospel proclamation. The Lausanne Movement posts the following definition of Integral Mission on their website: "Integral Mission can be defined as the task of bringing the whole of life under the lordship of Jesus Christ, and includes the affirmation that there is no biblical dichotomy between evangelistic and social responsibility."[4] The Oxford dictionary defines dichotomy as 'a division or contrast between two things that are or are represented as being opposed or entirely different.'[5] The Lausanne definition of Integral Mission therefore considers evangelism and social action to be synonymous. If *evangelistic responsibility* means 'sharing the gospel message' then equating it to *social responsibility* gives it a new meaning.

The terms "Integral Mission(s)" or "Holistic Mission(s)" are not always used to describe the contemporary emphasis on social action themes within the missions community. However, the influence of this philosophy is pronounced. Books advocating the integration of social action/social responsibility with gospel proclamation include *The Hole in our Gospel* (Richard Stearns, W Publishing: Nashville, 2009), *Scatter* (Andrew Scott, Moody: Chicago, 2016), *The Local Church, Agent of Transformation: An Ecclesiology for Integral Mission* (Rene Padilla, Ediciones Kairos, 2004), *Simply Good News* (N.

---

[4] Ravi Jayakaran, *About Integral Mission*, Lausanne Movement, www.lausanne.org/networks/issues/integral-mission.

[5] Oxford English Dictionary, s.v. "dichotomy," https://www.lexico.com/en/definition/dichotomy.

T. Wright, Harper One, 2017), *Creation Care and the Gospel: Reconsidering the Mission of the Church* (Robert S. White and Colin Bell, Hendrickson Pub, 2016) as well as books and articles by Shane Claiborne, Rick Warren, Jim Wallis and Ruth Padilla DeBorst. The endorsement lists for these books include many well-known influencers, speakers and personalities within the evangelical community including David Platt and Louie Giglio (*Scatter*), Bill Hybels, Luci Swindol, Max Lucado, T.D. Jakes, Chuck Colson, John Ortberg, Tony Campolo and Eugene Peterson (*The Hole in Our Gospel*).

The Lausanne conferences and the covenants that they produced were highly influential and advanced the concept of Integral Mission. Writing about the first Lausanne conference called by Billy Graham in 1974, John Mark Terry and Robert L. Gallagher note, "the needs of the poor and the social implications of the gospel attracted much attention and comment at the conference."[6] One of the seven key issues agreed upon at the conference was "the relationship of evangelism and social concern."[7] This was a new concept from leaders who had previously been focused exclusively on world evangelization through the proclamation of the biblical gospel alone.

Integral Mission has its roots in the Liberation Theology of the Roman Catholic Church in Central and South America. Ron Sider, who wrote *Rich Christians in an Age of Hunger*, (London: Hodder & Stoughton, 1997), was an early link between Latin American Liberation Theology of the 1970s and Evangelicalism in America. Gilley writes, "What Sider was advocating in the 1980s has become commonplace now, that is, many believe the gospel has both spiritual and social dimensions which are of equal importance."[8]

---

[6] John Mark Terry and Robert L. Gallagher, *Encountering the History of Missions from the Early Church to Today* (Grand Rapids: Baker Academics, 2017), 309.

[7] Terry and Gallagher.

[8] Gilley, Kindle location 1036.

Integral Mission proponents have a wide platform in many theologically conservative institutions involved in training and sending missionaries. Dallas Theological Seminary's "World Evangelization Conference" featured Ruth Padilla DeBorst as the key-note speaker (March 5-8, 2019). DeBorst is a leading advocate for Integral Mission and contributed the view "An Integral Transformational Approach" in *The Mission of the Church–Five Views in Conversation,* edited by Craig Ott.[9]

Lancaster Bible College featured Dr Michael Young-Suk Oh, Global Executive Director/CEO of the Lausanne Movement as the main speaker for the Lancaster Bible College Missions Conference, February 11-15, 2019.[10]

Jim Wallis, founder and president of Sojourners and a leading proponent for Christian engagement in social justice causes, has been a frequent guest speaker at prominent evangelical schools and events. Mary Danielsen provides the following analysis of Jim Wallis' popularity in evangelical circles:

> Lest any think that Jim Wallis and his social gospel are not being warmly embraced by many within Protestant/evangelical Christianity, some of the places that have invited Jim Wallis to speak of the last half a decade or so include Wheaton College, the Mennonite Church USA, Cedarville University, and Willow Creek to name a few. What's more, his books are found in countless Christian bookstores including the Southern Baptist Convention Resource branch, LifeWay; and his books are frequently used in Christian seminary and college courses. In addition, at least three traditional

---

[9] DeBorst, Ruth Padilla, "An Integral Transformational Approach," in *The Mission of the Church - Five Views in Conversation,* General Editor Craig Ott (Grand Rapids: Baker Academics, 2016), 41-67.

[10] "2019 Missions Conference Registration," received by the author, December 21, 2018.

Christian publishing houses-Baker Books, InterVarsity Press, and Zondervan-publish his books.[11]

IS INTEGRAL MISSION REDEFINING THE GOSPEL?

Whether Scripture defines the gospel as an integration of the message about Jesus and action to alleviate social injustices will be discussed later. However, before offering a critique, the assertion that Integral Mission proponents are re-defining the gospel needs to be established.

Richard Stearns "The Hole in Our Gospel"

Integral Mission advocates say that including social action as part of the gospel is a return to the true gospel proclaimed and modeled by Jesus. They put forward the idea that the gospel is incomplete when it is reduced to a proclamation of the truth about Jesus without associated action to remedy human suffering and injustices. Richard Sterns is critical of a message-only version of the gospel. He writes:

> More and more, our view of the gospel has been narrowed to a simple transaction, marked by checking a box on a bingo card at some prayer breakfast, registering a decision for Christ, or coming forward during an altar call. I have to admit that my own view of evangelism, based on the Great Commission, amounted to just that for many years. It was about saving as many people from hell as possible-for the *next* life (italics his). It minimized any concern for those same people in *this* (italics his) life. It wasn't as important that

---

[11] Mary Danielsen, *The Dangerous Truth about the Social Justice Gospel,* lighthousetrailsresearch.com/blog, September 18, 2018, https://www.lighthousetrailsresearch.com/blog/?p=28830.

> they were poor or hungry or persecuted, or perhaps rich, greedy, and arrogant: we just had to get them to pray the "sinner's prayer," and then we'd move on the next potential convert… There is a real problem with this limited view of the kingdom of God: it is not the whole gospel.[12]

According to Stearns, the "whole gospel" includes something more than the proclamation leading to a "simple transaction." Most would agree with his complaint against the type of ministry he describes and admits to having practiced. People are not born again because they pray "the sinner's prayer," unless that prayer reflects that they understand their own sinfulness and have placed their faith in Jesus Christ, his death and resurrection, as the remedy for their sin. Stearns has identified some real problems, namely manipulative and incomplete presentations of the gospel and evangelism without discipleship. The solution, however, is not to incorporate social action into the gospel but rather to return to the genuine gospel, a message sufficiently powerful to change lives without emotional manipulation. Stearns advocates for a "whole gospel" that includes both the words of the gospel and works of humanitarianism. He rightly says that Christians who practice hit-and-run evangelism need to be exhorted to proclaim Christ clearly and to love their neighbor (Mt 5:43, 19:19, 22:39), serve those in need (Mt 10:43), and care for orphans and widows (Jas 1:27). However, Stearns goes much further than such exhortations. He adds a works component to the proclamation of the gospel itself that is not contained in the Bible.

---

[12] Richard Stearns, *The Hole in Our Gospel* (Nashville: W Publishing, 2009), 5.

Lausanne Movement, The Manila Manifesto, 1989

The second Lausanne conference held in Manila in 1989 produced the Manila Manifesto. Under the heading, "The Whole Gospel" is found the sub-point "The Gospel and Social Responsibility." Part of that statement reads:

> Yet Jesus not only proclaimed the kingdom of God, he also demonstrated its arrival by works of mercy and power. We are called today to a similar integration of words and deeds. In a spirit of humility, we are to preach and teach, minister to the sick, feed the hungry, care for prisoners, help the disadvantaged and handicapped, and deliver the oppressed.[13]

The statement on "The Gospel and Social Responsibility" in the Manila Manifesto reflects a shift within the global community of evangelical leaders. Since the Manila Manifesto was published, Christian witness has been expanding from the proclamation of the gospel message to include socio-economic action in combination with that message. To be a part of the "Whole Gospel," one is called to "minister to the sick, feed the hungry and care for prisoners, help the disadvantaged and handicapped and deliver the oppressed." Gary Gilley describes this as the "two pronged" gospel. "...A two-prong gospel has arisen composed of both the Great Commission and the so-called Cultural Mandate."[14] Historically, evangelism has been understood to be the proclamation of the gospel message itself. As Gilley writes,

---

[13] Lausanne Movement, *The Manila Manifesto,* 1989, https://www.lausanne.org/content/manifesto/the-manila-manifesto.

[14] Gilley, Kindle location 43.

Everywhere true Christianity has gone it has benefited the society which it has touched. But historically, conservative Christianity has always seen social improvement as taking a backseat to the church's true calling of proclaiming the gospel and making disciples. It has never seen the social agenda as an end in itself—until now.[15]

The Micah Network, the Micah Declaration, 2001

The Micah Network set out in 2001 to advance Integral Mission. Based on Micah 6:8, the group's objective is stated as follows:

> Our definition of Integral Mission is taken from a consultation [1] held in Oxford, United Kingdom, in September 2001, which resulted in The Micah Declaration on Integral Mission being produced. The introductory extract outlines the summarized definition of Integral Mission as follows:
> Integral Mission or holistic transformation is the proclamation and demonstration of the gospel. It is not simply that evangelism and social involvement are to be done alongside each other. Rather, in Integral Mission our proclamation has social consequences as we call people to love and repentance in all areas of life. And our social involvement has evangelistic consequences as we bear witness to the transforming grace of Jesus Christ.[16]

The phrase "social involvement has evangelistic consequences" is significant and will be discussed in greater detail.

---

[15] Gilley, Kindle location 206.
[16] Micah Network, "Integral Mission," 2019, https://www.micahnetwork.org/integral-mission.

Lausanne Movement: The Cape Town Commitment, 2010

A central phrase from the Micah Declaration (2001) was incorporated into the most recent Lausanne covenant produced in Cape Town in 2010. Article 10, "We Love the Mission of God" states the following:

> Evangelism itself is the proclamation of the historical, biblical Christ as Savior and Lord, with a view to persuading people to come to him personally and so be reconciled to God....The results of evangelism include obedience to Christ, incorporation into his Church and responsible service in the world.... We affirm that evangelism and socio-political involvement are both part of our Christian duty. For both are necessary expressions of our doctrines of God and humankind, our love for our neighbor and our obedience to Jesus Christ....The salvation we proclaim should be transforming us in the totality of our personal and social responsibilities. Faith without works is dead.'[54] Integral Mission is the proclamation and demonstration of the gospel. It is not simply that evangelism and social involvement are to be done alongside each other. Rather, in Integral Mission our proclamation has social consequences as we call people to love and repentance in all areas of life. And our social involvement has evangelistic consequences as we bear witness to the transforming grace of Jesus Christ. If we ignore the world, we betray the Word of God which sends us out to serve the world. If we ignore the Word of God, we have nothing to bring to the world.[17]

---

[17] Lausanne Movement, *The Cape Town Commitment,* 2010, https://www.lausanne.org/content/ctc/ctcommitment#_ftnref55.

402 On Outreach and Mission

The Cape Town Commitment is built around a strong call to evangelism and engagement with all communities and people groups. Such a call is needed and commendable. However, it is at this point that the document takes a turn toward contemporary social engagement. After good theological development about the gospel, "socio-political involvement" is introduced without biblical example or instruction. While the key phrase, "our proclamation has social consequences… and our social involvement has evangelistic consequences," is carefully worded, little attempt is made to demonstrate the biblical connection in uniting social action and evangelism. The Cape Town Commitment is more correct when it emphasizes that compassion is the believer's duty. The NT does not confuse compassion or social involvement with the proclamation of the message, other than to urge believers that our behavior should be exemplary among the Gentiles (Titus 2:8, 1Ti 5:14, 1Pe 2:12, 15, 3:16).

The Integral Mission perspective mistakes the command for personal compassion and good works for a mandate that the mission of the church is to develop social action programs. It is not that these things are wrong for a church to do, it is simply that there is no New Testament mandate for the local church to fulfill these duties in a corporate sense.

Cru19 Connection Weekend

This shift in how the gospel is presented in evangelical missions conversations can be found in the workshop topics at the Cru19 Connection Weekend. Several workshop topics and general sessions centered on social justice themes.[18] In a general session, Sandra Van Opstal focused on social justice themes in the United States such as the disproportionate prison

---

[18] Cru19 Workshops, July 20, 2019, https://www.cru.org/cru19/workshops/. Workshops included "The Roots of Injustice," "Soul Care in a Racially Complex Society," and "Justice and Jesus."

population of African American men, white supremacy, and the detaining and return of illegal immigrants. She condemned the church's refusal to intervene on behalf of immigrants (presumably those who arrived in the United States illegally) by saying, "I cannot come to you today Cru and not speak where I stand. Watching the church sing their songs in stadiums all across the country, raise a banner for Jesus, and stay silent while we experience another holocaust, stay silent while churches send their mission trips to Guatemala and Honduras, to the very places where these people are coming from, and then stay silent when they show up in your neighborhood."[19] It is beyond the scope of this chapter to address the legal, political, and humanitarian complexities associated with immigration waves entering the southern border of the U.S. Opstal does not address these complexities either, except to condemn all who fail to embrace her point-of-view. In a speech loosely connected to the book of Amos, Van Opstal said near the close of her speech, "We will disciple you and form you to be Christian activists."[20] The connection between becoming a mature disciple and a Christian activist was not established in her speech.

MOPS admonition concerning the gospel

Another example of a change in the way evangelical leaders speak about the gospel is MOPS CEO, Mandy Arioto, on an all-leader call, June 22, 2016.[21] She explained the gospel in the following way: "We are people who are reclaiming the good news, who are walking out among the way of the one we follow, a man named Jesus, and bringing good news to hurting people. Eight million people are leaving the church every year and so we are taking

---

[19] Sandra Van Opstal, Cru 19 General Session Address, July 20, 2019, https://www.cru.org/cru19/archive/general-sessions/07-20-sandra-van-opstal/ approximate location minute 21.

[20] Van Opstal.

[21] MOPS is an acronym for "Mothers of Preschoolers," a community outreach ministry supporting mothers and frequently hosted at churches.

serious responsibility for the fact that we need to be people who come bearing the good news, reclaiming the good news. And what is good news? **Good news is friends when you are lonely, it is food when you are hungry, it is kindness with no strings attached, it is food when your baby is sick.** Good news is Jesus. And it is the embarrassingly extravagant love of God"[22] (emphasis added).

Summary

These examples illustrate the way some leaders in well-known Christian mission and outreach organizations are talking about the gospel. In books, articles and conference sessions, the Integral Mission concept is being presented on a wide scale. Christians are being taught that social action is a part of what it means to proclaim the gospel.

DECLINING EFFORTS IN GLOBAL EVANGELISM AND DISCIPLESHIP

Is the Integral Mission approach as reflected in the books, articles and organizations mentioned here a cause or an effect? Has this approach arisen *because of* general trends toward social justice among evangelicals, or has Integral Mission *created* a trend moving evangelical Christians toward social engagement themes? Although both are likely true, the result is that the evangelical church is widely embracing social engagement themes while at the same time reducing the emphasis on proclaiming the message of the cross.

---

[22] Mary Arioto, "All Leader Call with Mandy," *MOPS International*, vimeo.com/179370370/9ac450e4b8?cjevent=405a5c48c29d11e983e201e50a24060c, minute 7.

One source indicates a shift in missionary emphasis away from evangelism and discipleship and toward relief/development, and education/training covering a span from 1998 to 2016. This shift corresponds to the time during which Christian leaders have promoted the Integral Mission concept. Using data from the North American Mission Handbook, Missio Nexus compiled the following charts:[23]

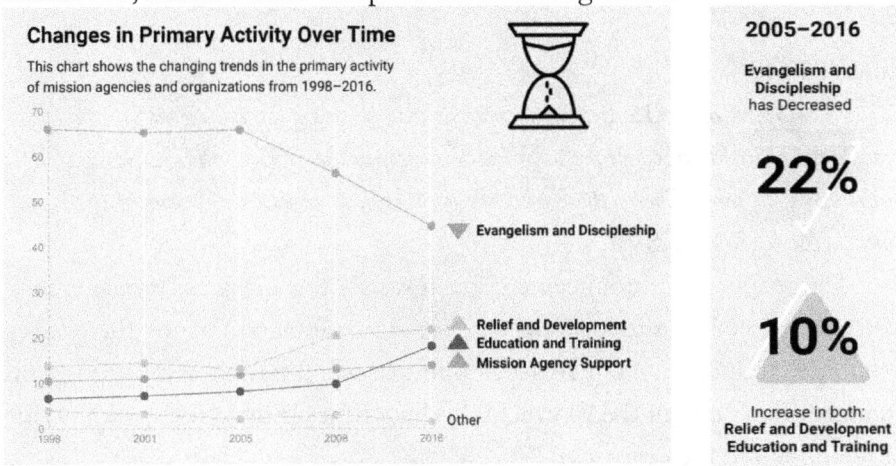

Used by Permission. Missio Nexus

The shift is notable for several reasons. First, the shift begins in 2005, shortly after the Micah Declaration (2001). Second, the shift is away from *evangelism/discipleship* and towards *education/training,* and *relief/development.* Third, the trend has not levelled off, at least through 2016. If this trend continues, it portends a tremendous decline in missionary efforts to proclaim the gospel, make disciples and plant churches.

---

[23] Missio Nexus. *Missiographics,* "Primary Activities of Mission Agencies-USA and Canada," 2017. Used by Permission.

WAS SOCIAL ACTION INTEGRATED INTO THE GOSPEL BY JESUS?

An examination of some of the passages frequently referenced by Integral Mission proponents demonstrates that Jesus did not advocate the kind of social action promoted by many today.

Luke 4:18-19

"The Spirit of the Lord is upon me, because he has anointed me to proclaim good news to the poor. He has sent me to proclaim liberty to the captives and recovering of sight to the blind, to set at liberty those who are oppressed, to proclaim the year of the Lord's favor." (Lk 4:18-19, ESV)

The inaugural announcement by Jesus in the Nazareth synagogue is often referenced to support social action as an integral part of the gospel. Ron Sider includes Luke 4:18-19 as one of several passages supporting his argument that "one of the central biblical doctrines is that God is on the side of the poor and the oppressed."[24]

Richard Stearns includes an appeal from this passage under the heading "Jesus Had a Mission Statement."[25] He writes:

> Proclaiming the whole gospel then, means much more than evangelism in the hopes that people will hear and respond to the good news of salvation by faith in Christ. It also encompasses tangible compassion for the sick and the poor, as well as biblical

---

[24] Ronald J Sider, "An Evangelical Theology of Liberation," *Perspectives on Evangelical Theology* (1980): 130-32.

[25] Stearns, 8.

justice, efforts to right the wrongs that are so prevalent in our world.[26]

Stearns and Sider were early influencers of today's social action proponents. Sider's article is helpful where he points out errors in Liberation Theology, even though he embraces many of its ideas. Stearns calls the church to consider the poor and to provide physical assistance alongside of gospel proclamation, something historically practiced in the Christian missions movement and strongly needed today. But Sider and Stearns both use Luke 4:18-19 as a mandate that the **mission** of the church is to care for the poor because that was Christ's mission. Such a position is without exegetical support.

Christ's public miracles provided sight for the blind, healing for the sick and even resurrection from the dead, but the miracles themselves were not his ultimate purpose. As wonderful as they were to those who were blessed, their primary purpose was to validate Christ's identity as the Son of God and Messiah of Israel in order to gain a hearing for His message. If the purpose of Christ's incarnation was to heal the sick, then his mission was a failure, for there were many who were sick even after his resurrection. Those who were healed eventually succumbed to some later physical illness and died.

To claim that Christ was sent to reduce human physical suffering and that the mission of the church is to do the same misses the main point of this remarkable passage. Jesus's miracles proved that he was the Son of God. He made this clear when the disciples of John came to ask if he was indeed the Messiah. "Now when John heard in prison about the deeds of the Christ, he

---

[26] Stearns, 9. There are many aspects of Stearn's book that are commendable. It is beyond the intention of this chapter to provide a full analysis of *The Hole in Our Gospel*. Michael Stallard provides such an analysis in his fair and thoughtful review in "Gospel Centeredness, Jesus, and Social Ethics," *The Journal of Ministry and Theology* 15 (Fall 2011): 5-24.

sent word by his disciples and said to him, "Are you the one who is to come, or shall we look for another?" And Jesus answered them, "Go and tell John what you hear and see: the blind receive their sight and the lame walk, lepers are cleansed and the deaf hear, and the dead are raised up, and the poor have good news preached to them" (Mt 11:2-5, ESV).

Jesus explains that his miracles served to bear witness that he was sent by God the Father. "But the testimony that I have is greater than that of John. For the works that the Father has given me to accomplish, the very works that I am doing, bear witness about me that the Father has sent me," (Jn 5:36, ESV).

The author of Hebrews also clarifies that the signs and wonders performed by Jesus bore witness to the truth of his message. "How shall we escape if we neglect such a great salvation? It was declared at first by the Lord, and it was attested to us by those who heard, "while God also bore witness by signs and wonders and various miracles and by gifts of the Holy Spirit distributed according to his will" (Heb 2:3-4, ESV).

Christ was compassionate toward the poor. His compassion provides an example for Christians to follow. But the greatest thing that Jesus did for the sick and the poor was to deliver them from their sins. His physical healing demonstrated that he had the power to do this as he made clear when he said, "But **that you may know that the Son of Man has authority on earth to forgive sins,**" he then said to the paralytic, "Rise, pick up your bed and go home" (Mt 9:6, ESV).

The Commissioning of the Twelve, Matthew 10:5-42

"These twelve Jesus sent out, instructing them, "Go nowhere among the Gentiles and enter no town of the Samaritans, but go rather to the lost sheep of the house of Israel. And proclaim as you go, saying, 'The kingdom of heaven is at hand.' Heal the sick, raise the dead, cleanse lepers, cast out demons. You received without paying; give without pay" (Mt 10:5-8, ESV).

The Twelve were commissioned to invite Israel to receive Jesus as their Messiah. The commissioning strategy established by Jesus in this passage is not in force today. Jesus was offering the Kingdom (verse 7), an offer that will ultimately be fulfilled when the righteous remnant of Israel welcome Jesus as their King at the end of the Great Tribulation (Zec 12:10, Rev 20:4). In Matthew 10, the Twelve were instructed to "proclaim the kingdom of heaven is at hand." (ESV) "Proclaim" is translated from the Greek κηρύσσω, "announce, make known" by a herald.[27] This is the same word used frequently in the epistles to exhort Christians to "preach the gospel" (Ac 8:25, Ro 1:15). The New Testament epistles speak about preaching Christ (Ac 8:5, 1Co 1:23), preaching the gospel (Col 1:23) and preaching the word (2Ti 2:4), among other commands. It is only in the Gospels and Acts where we find reference to preaching the kingdom of God.

This passage is not a call to believers today to raise the dead and heal the sick, nor should it be taken as an appeal to social action. Craig Bloomberg writes, "Verse 8 has regularly been taken as support for modern medical missions as well; appropriate as these may be, they are not what Jesus envisions here."[28]

---

[27] William Arndt et al., *A Greek-English Lexicon of the New Testament and Other Early Christian Literature : A Translation and Adaption of the Fourth Revised and Augmented Edition of Walter Bauer's Griechisch-Deutsches Worterbuch Zu Den Schrift En Des Neuen Testaments Und Der Ubrigen Urchristlichen Literatur* (Chicago: University of Chicago Press, 1979), 431.

[28] Craig Blomberg, *Matthew*, vol. 22, The New American Commentary (Nashville: Broadman & Holman Publishers, 1992), 171.

The Good Samaritan, Luke 10:25-37

This parable is often cited to support the integration of social action into the gospel. Jesus shares this parable in answer to the question, "Who is my neighbor?" (Lk 10:29). The lesson strikes directly at the heart of Jewish prejudice against the Samaritans. Here we find the story of a victim—a man assaulted by robbers and left for dead. The example of the Samaritan is vitally important for us to follow today, but not in the way some social action apologists interpret this passage.

There is continuity in the parable of the Good Samaritan and Paul's exhortation to do good to everyone "as we have opportunity" (Gal 6:10). There is no indication in the text that the Samaritan went out looking for someone to help. That was not the point of Jesus's parable. Just as Paul instructs Christians in Galatians 6:10, the Samaritan was presented with an opportunity to "do good" (Gal 6:10). He did what we all should do when we see a need and have the means to meet it. He went into action while others passed by. The fact that he was a Samaritan only reinforced that we are all called to compassion without prejudice. As powerful and familiar as this parable is to us, it should not be interpreted as a call to churches to establish programs to address community needs. There is nothing wrong with such programs, as they may be a part of a church or an individual Christian or even a Christian organization responding to real community needs locally or internationally. But they should not be construed as something commanded in this text.

Many passages in the Gospels speak of Christ's healing and compassion. These passages provide insight into Christ's character. They testify to his authority and genuineness as the Son of God, but they do not characterize the essence of the gospel as including a combination of the gospel message and social action.

WAS SOCIAL ACTION INTEGRATED INTO THE GOSPEL BY THE APOSTOLIC CHURCH?

The Apostolic church does not provide an example of a church engaged in social action causes. Despite living during a time of great injustice, there is no evidence in the New Testament that the Apostolic church practiced anything resembling the type of social action suggested by Integral Mission proponents. Noting this absence of New Testament examples, Kevin DeYoung and Greg Gilbert write, "If you are looking for a picture of the early church giving itself to creation care, plans for societal renewal, and strategies to serve the community in Jesus's name, you won't find them in Acts"[29]

There is much attention today to the "mission of the church." DeYoung and Gilbert address this in their book, *What is the Mission of the Church*. "It used to be that *mission* (emphasis in original) referred pretty narrowly to Christians sent out cross-culturally to convert non-Christians and plant churches. But now *mission* is understood much more broadly. Environmental stewardship is mission. Community renewal is mission. Blessing our neighbors is mission. Mission is here. Mission is there. Mission is everywhere. We are all missionaries."[30]

Whatever difficulty there may be in defining "mission," there should be little debate concerning the definition and usage of "gospel," as the Greek ευαγγελιον is used seventy-six times in the New Testament. None of those references include a description of social action or suggest that compassion should be shown to non-believers as a component of the gospel.

---

[29] Kevin DeYoung and Greg Gilbert, *What is the Mission of the Church? Making Sense of Social Justice, Shalom and the Great Commission* (Wheaton: Crossway, 2011), 49.

[30] DeYoung and Gilbert, 18.

Rather than a broad definition of the gospel encompassing social action, community projects, health care, and other noble causes, the New Testament usage of ευαγγελιον is narrow. The definition of the gospel is not elastic but specific and contained.

1 Corinthians 15:1-3

"Now I would remind you, brothers, of the gospel I preached to you, which you received, in which you stand.... For I delivered to you as of first importance what I also received: that Christ died for our sins in accordance with the Scriptures" (1 Corinthians 15:1, 3, ESV).

After numerous warnings to the Corinthians about divisions in the church (chapter 3), sexual immorality (chapter 5), lawsuits against fellow Christians (chapter 6), and the abuse of the Lord's Table (chapter 11), Paul addresses perhaps the most consequential matter facing the troubled church. Some in Corinth were denying the resurrection, the cornerstone of the gospel message (15:12-19). He begins his correction of the Corinthian error by clearly elaborating the content of the gospel:

1. Jesus died for our sins (15:3).
2. He was buried (15:4).
3. He was raised from the dead (15:4).
4. He appeared to others (15:5-9).

This passage provides a minimalist picture of the content of the gospel message. If social action is a part of the gospel, Paul withholds that information from the most straight-forward explanation of the gospel in the New Testament.

Acts 15:7

"And after there had been much debate, Peter stood up and said to them, "Brothers, you know that in the early days God made a choice among you, that by my mouth the Gentiles should hear the **word of the gospel** and believe" (Ac 15:7, ESV).

The expansion of the gospel through Paul's missionary activity raised a question among the Jewish church in Jerusalem concerning the core of the gospel message. At issue was whether the Gentiles needed to follow the commands of the Law. The church council in Jerusalem was a significant event for clarification of the gospel message.

Peter delivers the council's decision concerning the importance of the gospel message, unattached to any human effort. The phrase, "the word of the gospel," indicates a spoken message that Peter faithfully declared to both Jews and Gentiles. The Jerusalem Council could have included any number of social action programs as a means by which to satisfy the desires of the new Gentile believers or the established Jewish church, but they did not. Instead, they validated that the gospel is a word to be preached so that both Jew and Gentile could be saved.

Galatians 1:11-3:1

The Galatian Christians were quickly moving away from the gospel (1:6-9). Paul brings them back to the truth of the gospel, using the root word ευαγγελιον fifteen times in this epistle. Paul explains that the gospel has not come from human origin (1:11-12) and rehearses his presentation of the gospel to the church's leaders in Jerusalem (2:14). He declares that the gospel brings about justification by faith (3:8). Indeed, it was the gospel that brought about Abraham's justification. Paul's gospel to the Gentiles is the same gospel Peter proclaimed as the Apostle to the Jews (2:7-9).

Paul speaks much about the gospel in Galatians, but he does not include anything about social action. One statement about the poor is found in Galatians 2:10. "Only, they asked us to remember the poor, the very thing I was eager to do" (Galatians 2:10, ESV). This was not a request from the

414 On Outreach and Mission

Jerusalem council that Paul establish humanitarian works among the Gentiles. This related exclusively to the needs of the saints in Jerusalem, a request Paul faithfully carried out by collecting a gift from the Macedonian churches to be brought to Jerusalem (2Co 8-9, Ro 15:25-26). Timothy George explains the context of this request:

> Paul and Barnabas were asked to remember "the poor," a shorthand expression for "the poor among the saints in Jerusalem" (Rom 15:26). From its earliest days the Jerusalem church faced a condition of grinding poverty, as can be seen from the dispute over widows receiving sufficient food and the practice of sharing all things in common to care for the needy (Ac 4:32–35, 6:1–4).[31]

The extensive treatment of the gospel contained in Galatians does not include social action as a component that gospel.

Summary

While numerous injustices existed in the first century, Paul did not address them or begin efforts to eradicate them.[32] As Gary Gilley writes, "there are no examples of early Christians attempting to transform or create culture or influence the political system in a direct way. Nor do we find them organizing programs to feed the hungry of the world or to right social

---

[31] Timothy George, *Galatians*, vol. 30, The New American Commentary (Nashville: Broadman & Holman Publishers, 1994), 165.

[32] In Paul's instruction to Philemon, he urges him to receive his runaway slave Onesimus back *"no longer as a bondservant but more than a bondservant, as a beloved brother— especially to me, but how much more to you, both in the flesh and in the Lord."* (Philemon 16, ESV) Paul's advocacy on behalf of Onesimus was astoundingly counter-cultural, but it falls short of a full treatise against slavery. Later generations of Christians would boldly speak out against the injustice of slavery, bringing about its end in Europe and America.

injustices. Almost all of their attention was on evangelizing the lost as well as the spiritual life and physical needs of the believing community."[33] The idea that speaking about and participating in social causes was used to woo sinners to the gospel is not found in Scripture.

PRACTICAL CONSIDERATIONS ABOUT THE SOCIAL ACTION GOSPEL

It has been established that integrating social action into what it means to proclaim the gospel is not supported in Scripture. Christians are commanded to love their neighbor (Mt 5:43, 19:19, 22:39; Ro 13:9; Gal 5:14), practice compassion (Col 3:12), practice justice (Mic 6:8), and do good to all men (Gal 6:10). However, the compassion that we are commanded to show to all people is nowhere equated in Scripture with what it means to preach the gospel. The following practical considerations demonstrate the weakness of integrating social action as a part of what it means to proclaim the gospel.

Non-Christians Also Practice Social Action

If "our proclamation has social consequences… and our social involvement has evangelistic consequences,"[34] it has these consequences for Muslims, Jehovah's Witnesses, Jews and atheists. The argument cuts both ways, making a case that in general, kindness and generosity reflect positively on all who practice these actions. Christians can and should respond to human needs both on a personal and corporate level, but compassion is not restricted to Christians, nor would anyone expect that it should be. The idea that people will be compelled to respond to the gospel because Christians

---

[33] Gilley, Kindle location 620.
[34] Micah Network, "Integral Mission," 2019 and Lausanne Movement, *The Cape Town Commitment,* 2010.

have been kind ties the effectiveness of evangelism to the good works of a believer rather than to the power of the gospel itself.

A Christian's Civic Responsibility

It is right that all people should care about poverty, homelessness, disease and injustice, both Christians and non-Christians. Many of the appeals put forth by Christian social action proponents should be embraced by all. As fellow human beings, Christians and non-Christians have a common interest in helping those who are disadvantaged. Who would not be moved with compassion for an ill child, a starving nation, or women captured as sex-slaves? There is no objection to showing compassion in any of these circumstances. Christians should stand up with all others to speak out and act with meaningful intervention because it is a part of our Christian duty as good citizens. Failure to do so is a violation of the Lord's command and gives the unsaved an opportunity to bring accusation against Jesus and his followers. In 1 Peter, the Apostle urges Christians that living as the "people of God" requires them to maintain a good and honorable testimony in front of their non-believing neighbors. *"Keep your conduct among the Gentiles honorable, so that when they speak against you as evildoers, they may see your good deeds and glorify God on the day of visitation."* (1Pe 2:12, ESV). See also Matthew 5:16, Romans 13:1-4, Titus 2:8, 1 Peter 3:16.

Theology Or Political Ideology?

Some of today's social justice themes are driven by leftist political ideology. Ron Sider, an early promoter, advocated themes originating from Liberation Theology, as noted earlier. Gary Gilley points out the extent of Sider's influence. "Sider has long been a bridge between Liberation Theology and evangelicalism. While not endorsing the darker sides of Liberation Theology, such as bloody revolutions and overthrowing of governments, he has accepted the socialistic features of the movement and has attempted to integrate them into the evangelical church in the West."[35] Its connection with Liberation Theology brings many left-leaning themes into evangelical churches, colleges, and seminaries. Environmentalism, immigration policy, racial reconciliation, racial imbalance in the prison population, worker's rights, and other themes that have been prevalent in the American Left are now becoming mainstream in the evangelical social justice movement, as well.

Revealing Omissions

Injustices not in line with left-leaning politics are seldom mentioned by evangelical social justice advocates. Injustices such as abortion, anti-Semitism, and the persecution of Christians take a back seat to the environment, sex-trafficking, water and food scarcity, AIDS, and other medical needs. As mentioned above, Who is not moved with compassion by these things? Certainly, Christian should engage in helping in these situations, as should all people. However, such engagement is not the same as proclaiming the gospel. Ministries of compassion might possibly become a platform for presenting the gospel, but they do not themselves communicate the gospel. While compassion work could potentially open doors for evangelistic communication of the gospel message, the gospel itself must be preached. It is the gospel that liberates, not human endeavors.

It Is Easier to Dig Wells Than It Is to Share the Gospel

Social action tends to be much easier than evangelism because those who walk in darkness are opposed to the light of the gospel (2Co 4:4, Jn 12:40, Mt 10:22, 2Ti 3:12). A Muslim community is unlikely to be offended

---

[35] Gilley, Kindle location 1030.

by Christians who provide safe drinking water. But that same community may be greatly offended by Christians who share the gospel. The concern of this writer is that over time, Christians will resort to the path of least resistance, leading to what could be called "The Social Gospel 2.0." Under the goal that "our social involvement has evangelistic consequences," Christians are finding it very easy to omit the "proclamation" part and just trust social involvement to take care of the "evangelistic consequences."

The Lost Will Not Be Saved Because Christians Do Good Deeds

Duane Litfin expresses the following thought:

> The belief that we can "preach the gospel" with our actions alone represents muddled thinking. However important our actions may be (and they are very important indeed), and whatever else they may be doing (they serve a range of crucial functions), they are not "preaching the Gospel." The Gospel is inherently verbal, and preaching it is inherently verbal behavior.[36]

Speaking directly to the question of Integral Mission he also writes,

> Few would deny that the holistic mission of the church is the best possible platform for our verbal witness, and that our jaded generation will be more inclined to give us a hearing if we are living it out. (Indeed, the longest section of my new book, *Word versus Deed*,

---

[36] Duane Litfin, "Works and Words: Why You Can't Preach the Gospel with Deeds," *Christianity Today*, May 30, 2012, 40. See his book on the same subject, Duane Litfin, *Word versus Deed: Resetting the Scales to a Biblical Balance*, (Crossway, 2012).

is devoted to the crucial role of our deeds.) But this does not permit us to hold the Gospel hostage to our shortcomings.[37]

Christians must not allow the truth of the gospel to be minimized or even lost simply because our post-modern generation is more moved by image and intention than by precise words explaining the vital historical facts of Jesus, and the necessity of faith in him alone.

The Gospel Is Powerful Even When the Messengers Are Weak

Christians are called to compassion, justice and selfless love for others. Failure to follow these commands is pure disobedience. But can the gospel be believed when its messengers themselves are unjust oppressors? If the gospel is sufficiently powerful to provide all that is needed for a sinner to understand Christ's work on his or her behalf and turn in faith to him, the answer is, "yes." This is not an excuse for Christians to disobey the Lord but rather a reminder that the power is in the gospel message itself, not in the messenger (Ro 1:16-17, Mt 16:18). This paradox is demonstrated by African slaves who in large numbers became devoted Christians during the American nineteenth century. Enslaving another human is one of the most violent examples of injustice. Professing Christians not only engaged in this wicked atrocity, they attempted to justify it with the Bible. Yet despite the appalling injustices committed against slaves, many of them saw the true Christ and turned to him for spiritual deliverance. Eric Lincoln writes, "The black Christians who formed the historic black churches also knew implicitly that their understanding of Christianity, which was premised on the rock of

---

[37] Litfin.

antiracial discrimination, was more authentic than the Christianity practiced in white churches."[38]

Only Jesus Can Establish His Kingdom

Social gospel advocates often use the vague and biblically imprecise statement that by practicing justice, we are "building the kingdom." Though there are many things that Christians and churches should do to please and honor our Savior, they cannot build his kingdom. There is little room here to discuss an issue so broad, other than to say that the future kingdom belongs to Jesus and only he can establish it. Integral Mission advocates proclaim that by improving society, we can see the kingdom of God come to earth. Richard Stearns writes, "The whole Gospel is a vision for ushering in God's kingdom–now, not in some future time, and here, on earth, not in some distant heaven."[39] Ruth Padilla Deborst writes,

> The good news of God's reconciling purposes will reach into our world, mired as it is in corruption, injustice, violence, poverty, and the plunder of creation, if and when the followers of the wounded King allow the Spirit to weave them into a community of such radical discipleship that in all they are, all they do, and all they say they witness to God's integral transformation until the kingdom comes in full.[40]

Even the most utopian, crime-free, justice-focused human community on earth cannot compare to the glories of Christ's future kingdom. Instead of ushering in Christ's kingdom, believers should see their activity in this world

---

[38] C. Eric Lincoln, *The Black Church in the African American Experience* (Duke University Press: 2002), Kindle Edition, location 332.
[39] Sterns, xxii.
[40] Deborst, 64.

as filling Christ-like character while we walk in this world, "that you may be blameless and innocent, children of God without blemish in the midst of a crooked and twisted generation, among whom you shine as lights in the world" (Php 2:15, ESV). "For at one time you were darkness, but now you are light in the Lord. Walk as children of light" (Eph 5:8, ESV).

Dispensationalists understand that the church will not bring about Christ's kingdom. As good citizens, Christians participate in society because God has ordained human government and because until our redemption is complete, we are both citizens of heaven and citizens of earth (Php 3:20, 2Co 5:1, Eph 2:19).

God's plan does not culminate with the glorious triumph of the church over injustice. It culminates with Jesus executing justice upon a world in rebellion, as he invites his redeemed ones to share authority with him in his righteous kingdom.

AN APPEAL FOR COMPASSION WITHOUT REDEFINING THE GOSPEL

It was stated at the outset that Christians are called to follow the example of Jesus and demonstrate compassion to those in need. But the demonstration of that compassion is not the same thing as proclaiming the gospel which is the message of the life, death and resurrection of Jesus. The Integral Mission movement is redefining what it means to proclaim the gospel, something that should cause great concern for truth-loving Christians. The fact that many of its principles are drawn from the political left should be carefully evaluated so that Christians are not swept up by the philosophies of the day (Col 2:8).

This objection to redefining the gospel should not be interpreted as opposition to Christian compassion or efforts to speak against injustice or help those in need. The outworking of Christian compassion is powerful and beautifully diverse, just as diverse as the body of Christ. Galatians 6:10 provides an outline of how that compassion is focused.

"So then, as we have opportunity…" Wherever Christians see a need, they should seek to meet that need. Compassion is connected to the needs we encounter while living in a fallen world. Individual Christians, local churches and mission movements may be drawn to serve a variety of needs. This world will present no shortage of opportunities for Christians to selflessly love and serve others. Let the church do this with dedication and enthusiasm, but let the church proclaim the gospel.

"Let us do good to everyone…" There is no prejudice in how believers demonstrate compassion. Goodness should be shown to everyone regardless of their spiritual condition. Where there is a human need, Christians are called to respond.

"And especially to those who are of the household of faith." The primary recipients of Christian kindness are other Christians. Brothers and sisters in Christ who are in need should receive generous concern, prayer and action from other portions of the body capable of rendering assistance. The first place to practice compassion is on behalf of fellow Christians suffering injustice, poverty and persecution.

In a recent graduation lecture to the students at Bethlehem College and Seminary, John Piper gave a passionate and clear example of what it means to talk with biblical accuracy and deep tenderness about social involvement and the Christian's responsibility to the world in which we live. His message, "What Do Christians Care About (Most)?" [41] emphasized that Christians should think about social action and injustice differently than non-Christians

---

[41] John Piper, "What Do Christians Care about (Most)?" Commencement address at Bethlehem College & Seminary, May 17, 2019, Minneapolis, www.desiringgod.org/messages/what-do-christians-care-about-most.

because Christians are ultimately concerned with the injustices that we all have committed against God. He said,

> Millions of Christians including many missionaries have convinced themselves that they are loving lost people by caring mostly about their suffering in this world and little about how they will spend eternity. It is unfortunate that some missionaries, who are deeply committed to loving and helping people, are leaving out the most important part of Christian compassion—compassion for the eternal destiny of the people to whom they minister.

Three additional quotes from this address are worth considering. Piper continues,

> Christians care about all injustice, especially injustice against God... The word "all" is intended to **prick the conscience of Christians,** who because of self-indulgence or fear, have dulled the capacity of their hearts to care about the injustices of the world and all the countless ways that people all over the world are treated by other people worse than they deserve.

> If you don't care about all injustice, you're striving in your heart against God.

> Christians care about all injustice, especially... injustice against God. The word "all" especially is intended to **call out unbelief among Christians.** It's intended to call out practical unbelief of Christians for whom the injustices against humans ignite more passion in their

hearts, in their mouths, than the global tragedy of injustice against God. (Italics added to demonstrate Piper's emphasis in his address).

While it has been shown that Integral Mission proponents equate social action with the proclamation of the gospel, Piper is more precise when he says, "If you don't care about all injustice, you're striving in your heart against God." This is true and provides all the motivation that Christians need to "*do justice, and to love kindness, and to walk humbly with your God.*" (Mic 6:8, ESV) Christians do not need to redefine the gospel in order to practice justice, kindness and humility in our world. They simply need to obey God.

In efforts to speak out against injustice and help a world in need, Christians must remember that it is the gospel that liberates. The following scriptures remind Christians of this power, and should be kept in clear focus, so that evangelism relies fully on the power of God and not the efforts of humans.

"For I am not ashamed of the gospel, for it is the power of God for salvation to everyone who believes, to the Jew first and also to the Greek" (Ro 1:16, ESV).

"For Christ did not send me to baptize but to preach the gospel, and not with words of eloquent wisdom, lest the cross of Christ be emptied of its power" (1Co 1:17, ESV).

"and my speech and my message were not in plausible words of wisdom, but in demonstration of the Spirit and of power, so that your faith might not rest in the wisdom of men but in the power of God" (1Co 2:4–5, ESV).

"But we have this treasure in jars of clay, to show that the surpassing power belongs to God and not to us" (2Co 4:7, ESV).

Chapter 15 – On American Government
The Biblical Basis of the United States Constitution[1]
Mike Stallard

INTRODUCTION

Surprisingly perhaps, the United States Constitution never uses the word *God*. Such a state of affairs is totally different than the Declaration of Independence which appeals to God as a major part of its argument on three occasions. First, the Declaration opens with an appeal to "the separate and equal Station to which the Laws of Nature and of Nature's God entitle them." Second, one can note the most famous line of the document: "We hold these Truths to be self-evident, that all Men are created equal, that they are endowed by their Creator with certain inalienable Rights, that among

---

[1] The only book level treatments of this topic that this author has seen to date is the older work Dan Gilbert, *The Biblical Basis of the Constitution* (Grand Rapids: Zondervan, 1936) and the more recent work, Douglas Anderson and Mark A. Beliles, *Contending for the Constitution: Recalling the Christian Influence on the Writing of the Constitution and the Biblical Basis of American Law and Liberty* (Charlottesville, VA: Providence Foundation, 2005). Gilbert's work argues primarily from the moral quality of the content of the Constitution to a basis in similar biblical teaching especially in the Ten Commandments. The latter work of Anderson and Beliles is more comprehensive of various issues and more targeted in its critique of modern abuses of the Constitution. Yet it still argues somewhat from analogy. My presentation here, while not dismissing these two approaches, is in a different direction but with similar conclusions. This article was originally given as a Faculty Forum chapel presentation at Baptist Bible Seminary in Clarks Summit, Pennsylvania. It was then published as Mike Stallard, "The Biblical Basis of the United States Constitution," *The Journal of Ministry and Theology* 16 (Fall 2012): 5-23.

these are Life, Liberty, and the Pursuit of Happiness." These first two references to God appeal to God's design of nature and of men to justify the existence of an equality that does not come from those who govern. Instead it comes from the Creator God and is revealed in the work of his design. By using such language the Framers are raising the bar so to speak. To violate these divine designs is a serious charge indeed. Third, the Declaration closes with a statement of faith in God: "And for the support of this Declaration, with a firm Reliance on the Protection of divine Providence, we mutually pledge to each other our Lives, our Fortunes, and our sacred Honor." Here it is clear that the Framers believed in the immanence of God. God is a God of history who governs the affairs of men. There can never be any harmony between these words and a full-blown deistic outlook. God is active in the world now. He is not on the sidelines watching what men do. In such ways, the human authors of the Declaration made major foundational appeals to God and His creation.[2]

In light of this truth in 1776, the obvious question is why the Constitution does not use similar language just eleven years later in 1787. One could point at the outset to the different purposes of the two documents as a place to start one's explanation. The Constitution is a pragmatic text which answers the "how" question. It is intended simply to give the structure of how the government is to operate. On the other hand, the Declaration answers a "why" question. Consequently, it is more philosophical. Furthermore, the young nation is defending its decision for independence in the eyes of a Western world steeped in Judeo-Christian ethics during the

---

[2] Later on a brief look will be given to influences upon the Founders that came from outside the Bible or beyond strictly Judeo-Christian thought. Interesting debates emerge about whether the Founders were more influenced by Locke, Leibniz, or Montesquieu along with a host of other writers and thinkers contemporary and ancient. Even if influence is found, such dependence would not negate the Founders use of the Bible and the Judeo-Christian worldview of which they were a part.

Biblical Distinctions Applied 427

Enlightenment with its own twists and turns. Legally and morally, the need to appeal to God should not be a surprise.

Yet the oddity remains. Why is God not referenced in the United States Constitution?[3] One might expect such a reference in the Preamble—the union established with the help of God would fit nicely. However, no direct appeal to God is made there, although one might see the purpose of securing the "Blessings of Liberty" as hearkening back to the Declaration and its pronouncements. There are some indirect references to God perhaps as seen in the need for Senators to be "on Oath or Affirmation" when trying a president for impeachment.[4] The overwhelming majority of oaths in those days, as in this day in our land, were done with an oath to God. Thus, George Washington at the first inauguration added the words "So help me, God" to the constitutionally established words in Article II, Section 1.[5] The word *Lord*

---

[3] One interesting exercise would be to compare the appeals to God in the Articles of Confederation, the document used to govern the new nation starting in 1781 (although the document was approved by the Continental Congress in 1777) until the U. S. Constitution was established. The Preamble to that document refers to the Lord in the standard expression for dates: "on the fifteenth day of November in the Year of our Lord One Thousand Seven Hundred and Seventy seven." Like the Constitution there are indirect appeals to God by mentioning oaths (Article IX). However, the Articles of Confederation have one appeal to God in the closing section of the document that is similar to the Declaration and not the Constitution: "And Whereas it hath pleased the *Great Governor of the World* to incline the hearts of the legislatures we respectively represent in Congress, to approve of, and to authorize us to ratify the said articles of confederation and perpetual union" (emphasis supplied). In spite of this reference, the Articles seem to fall short of the Declaration in statements about God.

[4] U. S. Constitution, Article I, Section 3.

[5] Peter A., Lillback and Jerry Newcombe, *George Washington's Sacred Fire* (Bryn Mawr, PA: Providence Forum Press, 2006), 224. The actual wording of the Presidential Oath in Article II, Section 1 is "I do solemnly swear (or affirm) that I will faithfully execute the Office of President of the United States, and will to the best of my Ability, preserve, protect and defend the Constitution of the United States." In 2009 at the inauguration of Barack Obama, the words were not said quite right. Later Chief Justice Roberts visited the White House and administered the Oath again. Technically, President Obama was not President until that later moment. The adding of the words

is used in the final statement giving the date of the document: "in the Year of our Lord." However, the Constitution is clear that no religious test can be applied as a "Qualification to any Office or public Trust under the United States."[6] This last point is often misused by those who reject Christian influence in the country and wish to see the founding as secular in orientation.[7]

So, what is to be made of the diminished God-language in the U. S. Constitution? Does it reflect a world view of the Founders that downplays biblical heritage and Christian teaching? What follows is a presentation that answers this question in the negative and shows a measured amount of affinity between biblical teaching and the content of the Constitution. However, before continuing some cautions need to be voiced.

CAUTION: THE NEED FOR BALANCE

Cultures and subcultures almost always rewrite some of their historical traditions in their own image. From the young secular man that once told this author with apparent glee that Benjamin Franklin had over twenty illegitimate children to the staunch evangelical Christian who sees a copy of a Bible verse tucked in the pocket of every Founding Father, the predictable portrait emerges to justify the current position.[8] They – the Founding Fathers

---

"So help me God" is a tradition started by Washington and carried on by each following President.

[6] U. S. Constitution, Article VI.

[7] For example, see Austin Cline, "Godless Constitution: Constitutional Law without Gods or Religion," http://atheism.about.com/od/godlessliberals/p/Constitution.htm.

[8] This author cannot remember the person's name who said this or the occasion. The discussion of Benjamin Franklin's moral life has been a major point of examination by scholars. There is no question that he did not practice the sexual morality taught in the Bible although he called it weakness rather than strength in a person's character. At least one illegitimate son is clearly known. There is no hard

— were like "us." Typically. in such cases the truth is somewhere between the extremes.

The Christian must admit that the Founding Fathers were not perfect, evangelical believers. For example, much is rightly made of the refusal of the Founders to eliminate slavery in the young nation.[9] This was their great sin which they left the nation and which was only solved by the bloodletting of a Civil War. One might be hard pressed to praise men who had the power to end slavery but chose not to do so (many actually owned slaves). Evangelical Christians who like the religious, even evangelical, tone of the statements of the Founders must be honest about these indisputable historical details.

On the other hand, there has been in our nation a growing trend, especially since the 1960s, to accuse the Founding Fathers of being deists rather than more traditional Christians. While it is true that men like Thomas Jefferson and Benjamin Franklin toyed with mild forms of deistic thought, neither was a full-blown deist since they both believed in prayer and the involvement of the deity in the affairs of nations. One example to discuss is *the* Founding Father, George Washington, the first president of the United States. Due largely to Paul Boller's influential *George Washington and Religion* (1963) it has become fashionable during a time of intensified secularization to insist that Washington was at best a nominal Christian and most likely a deist.[10] This false historical image has been so strong that even fairly conservative and accurate historians on the contemporary scene have been

---

evidence for any others although there is abundant recorded evidence of the flirtatious nature of this particular Founding Father. For more information, see H. W. Brands, *The First American: The Life and Times of Benjamin Franklin* (New York: Doubleday, 2000).

[9] A study of the biblical view of slavery cannot be made here. However, the assumption is made that New Testament principles lead in the direction that forcing other human beings into unwilling servitude is a serious and heinous sin.

[10] See Paul F. Boller, Jr., *George Washington and Religion* (Dallas: Southern Methodist University, 1963).

taken in by the ruse.[11] However, the stellar and thoroughly documented work *George Washington's Sacred Fire* by Peter Lillback has proven with more than a thousand pages of argumentation that the Father of our country was deeply evangelical in his convictions.[12] Secularists must honestly face such an avalanche of evidence.

DEPRAVITY AND THE CONSTITUTION

Perhaps the most remarkable evidence of a biblical worldview in the Constitution is the underlying belief in the depravity of men and women. This is in stark contrast with the French Revolution of 1789. Americans emphasized a freedom with responsibility while many French emphasized a liberty with limited responsibility. Americans started from the premise that men were basically evil and that absolute power corrupts absolutely. The French started from the premise that men were basically good. What resulted immediately from each revolution may be instructive. In America, a dynamic nation emerges with a limited government including checks and balances on the evil tendencies of men. France immediately goes through a reign of terror followed by the despotism of Napoleon.

Most American Founders were horrified at what was happening in France during the French revolutionary period. John Adams found the French somewhat immoral and irreligious in everyday living.[13] This was contrasted to the moral uprightness, in his view, of Americans in general (although not all as Franklin's example showed) for whom the system of

---

[11] Michael Allen and Larry Schweikart, *A Patriot's History of the United States* (New York: Sentinel, 2004), 130. The authors state that "Like Franklin, Washington tended toward Deism…"

[12] Peter A. Lillback and Jerry Newcombe, *George Washington's Sacred Fire* (Bryn Mawr, PA: Providence Forum Press, 2006).

[13] Cited in Brands, *The First American*, 552ff.

government was appropriate. George Washington at a human level was hostile to the radical revolutionaries for many reasons including their harsh treatment of Marquis de Lafayette, a beloved figure in the American Revolution.[14] However, the major concern was that the French Revolution was demonstrating what the depravity of man could accomplish if left unchecked. Washington noted that "the blessed religion revealed in the Word of God will remain an eternal and awful monument to prove that the best Institutions may be abused by human depravity." [15] Lillback captures the intent of Washington and by extension that of many other Founders:

> Washington's religion manifested itself precisely at this point in the constitutional debate. The ideas he expressed by terms such as "limited power," "the separation of powers," "the rule of the people," "checks and balances," and the "need for amendment," all existed for one simple reason—people abuse power. The idea of abuse of power and political depravity were openly admitted at the Constitutional Convention, and also seriously pondered by Washington. Political depravity is a theological concept that flows from the doctrine of human sinfulness—a basic postulate of Christian teaching. In fact, Washington asserted that human depravity could ultimately destroy the Constitution, even with the checks and balances it possessed. In his proposed Address to Congress in April 1789, he described how the Constitution, with all

---

[14] Lafayette became a tragic figure due to the French Revolution. He seemed to cause animosity on both sides, the rebels and the loyalists. He escaped the guillotine and eventually went to the Southern Netherlands in an attempt to gather his family and go to the United States. Instead, he ended up in prison for a few years at the hands of a counter-revolutionary force. Washington demonstrates great relief in a letter to Lafayette when he was finally released. See Lillback, *Sacred Fire*, 783.

[15] Cited in Lillback, *Sacred Fire*, 58.

of its wisdom, could ultimately come to naught by the depravity of the people and those who govern them, since the Constitution in the hands of a corrupt people was a mere "wall of words" or a "mound of parchment."[16]

In Lillback's analysis, the connection between the design of the Constitution and a belief in human depravity is obvious, especially in Washington. Thus, it is not surprising to see Alexis de Tocqueville some years later note that Americans viewed their Christian religion, even when they did not take it seriously at the personal level, as "indispensable to the maintenance of republican institutions."[17] However, perhaps the clearest statement of the Founders on the issue of depravity is found in the *Federalist* No. 51:

> But what is government itself but the greatest of all reflections on human nature? If men were angels, no government would be necessary. If angels were to govern men, neither external nor internal controls on government would be necessary. In framing a government which is to be administered by men over men, the great difficulty lies in this: You must first enable the government to control the governed; and in the next place, oblige it to control itself.[18]

---

[16] Ibid., 220.

[17] Alexis de Tocqueville, *Democracy in America* (reprint ed., New York: Vintage Books, 1945). This work was originally published in 1835 translated by Henry Reeve into English. A retranslation by Francis Bowen occurred in 1862. There have been numerous printings of this popular document.

[18] Alexander Hamilton, John Jay, and James Madison, *The Federalist: A Commentary on the Constitution of the United States Being a Collection of Essays written in Support of the Constitution agreed upon September 17, 1787, by the Federal Convention,* Introduction by Edward Meade Earle (reprint ed., New York: Random House, n.d.), 337. The so-called Federalist Papers were circulated initially as individually published essays but eventually

The writer goes on to mention that such an understanding is obvious by looking at experience. The observation of nature thus goes hand in hand with biblical teaching on depravity.

That depravity is a concern in the biblical text appears in passages like Ephesians 2:1-7 and Romans 3:9-18. While evangelicals debate the extent of depravity in each man and what specific work of God erases or ameliorates such depravity, the tendency of evangelicals generally is to believe a doctrine of man's depravity. Man is a sinner. He must be saved. The sinful nature of a man, among negative implications, leads to problems in political governance.

One should not be astonished to view the Founders as interested in the Bible in such a way. Eidsmoe claims that "Washington, Hamilton, Jay, Madison, and Witherspoon are more typical of the Founding Fathers as a whole than are Jefferson and Franklin. Their religious convictions earnestly sought to establish a government that would reflect and promote the ideals they revered."[19] If Madison is the author of *Federalist* No. 51 mentioned above, it can be said of his words that he "learned this concept at the feet of the man he respectfully called 'the old Doctor,' the Rev. Witherspoon."[20] The Founders for the most part did not fear Christianity. Instead, they allowed it to keep them grounded solidly in a biblical understanding of depravity.

---

collected in one volume. The Federalist Paper here is generally thought to be written by Hamilton or Madison.

[19] John Eidsmoe, "The Judeo-Christian Roots of the Constitution" in *Restoring the Constitution* edited by H. Wayne House (Dallas, TX: Probe Books, 1987), 94.

[20] Ibid., 98.

"SEPARATION OF POWERS" AND "CHECKS AND BALANCES"

Consequently, the Framers developed a system of Constitutional checks and balances within the Federal Government. First of all, there are three separate branches of government: legislative (Article I), executive (Article II), and judicial (Article III). This prevents the consolidation of power in the hands of one man (potentially tyrannical monarchy) or in the hands of a group of men (an oligarchy or aristocracy running over the other factions in the nation). Furthermore, the duties of each intrude upon the duties of those in other branches of government to deepen the checks and balances. For example, the President appoints ambassadors and Supreme Court justices, but the Congress must approve such appointments.[21] The President and his executive branch handle foreign affairs including the execution of war. [22] He is the commander in chief of the military. However, only Congress can declare war.[23] The President can make treaties with foreign powers, but they do not get implemented without ratification by the Senate.[24]

Similarly, the legislative branch makes laws.[25] However, the President can veto the laws made by the legislature.[26] The Congress can override the veto.[27] Moreover, the legislature is bicameral. That is, there are two houses, a lower house of Representatives and an upper house of Senators. Bills must be passed by both houses not just one.[28] The give and take involved in all of this makes it more difficult for any one person or group of legislators to

---

[21] U. S. Constitution, Article II, Section 2.
[22] Ibid.
[23] U. S. Constitution, Article I, Section 8.
[24] U. S. Constitution, Article II, Section 2.
[25] See especially U. S. Constitution, Article I, Sections 7 and 8.
[26] Ibid.
[27] Ibid.
[28] Ibid.

consolidate power. For the legislature (and for the President), terms are specified that are not lifetime terms. Each person must face the people for re-election.

Finally, for the judicial branch, the President appoints its members, not the judges themselves. That is, the Court is not a self-perpetuating body. However, appointments are approved by the Senate (as stated earlier). The justices decide disputes about the law between parties. Countermanding that to some extent is the fact that the Congress can decide the limits of the jurisdiction of the Supreme Court and all Federal Courts it creates. In these ways and others, the appropriate balance of power is maintained between three branches of government with additional checks and balances to prevent the consolidation of power. Depravity in the form of abuse of power thus has a chance to be checked and prevented. The result of this approach to government has been successful enough that many other nations have copied the same general framework for how they operate in their government. The major goal is to maintain individual liberty in balance with personal responsibility.

One must also note that the biblical doctrine of depravity does not stand alone in the Framers' minds when they developed this approach to government. The Founders knew about the Greek City-States and the Roman Republic. They also knew the history of the British Empire with its Common Law and the checks and balances and liberties involved in that developing governance. In a general sense, all of these elements factor into the development of the American founding.

However, one person stands out for special mention. He is quoted more often by the Framers than anyone else other than the biblical authors although he is little known.[29] His name is Charles de Montesquieu (1689-

---

[29] Eidsmoe, "The Judeo-Christian Roots of the Constitution," 79-80.

1755), a Frenchman who studied and wrote political philosophy that attracted many of the American Founding Fathers. His major work is *The Spirit of the Laws* published in 1748. He was an expert in Roman history and Greek philosophy, although he saw their systems overall as insufficient for implementation in the modern context. Nonetheless, many of the features of the ancient political systems can easily inform modern developments. Furthermore, one cannot evaluate Montesquieu as a child of Continental Europe in general or France in particular. He lived for several months in England and seems to have the greatest praise for English political traditions. Thus, there are many things to say in analyzing Montesquieu and the influences upon him which cannot be covered completely in this forum.

However, there are two major points whose absence would cause an inadequate view to be obtained relative to the topic at hand. First, Montesquieu argues from human nature or experience that some form of republicanism might be preferred to help maintain the balance or tension between an individual's security and freedom.[30] Such concerns stem from the difficulties that seem to be inherent in the social structure of humanity. While not espousing a view of depravity, one might come to the same place as Scripture by noting that such social structure needs protection if any lasting good is going to come from the governmental forms that it takes.

Second, Montesquieu proposes a separation of powers, partly through study of the English system. However, it is also true that separation of power ideas hearken back to the Greek and Roman days. However, Pangle's commentary on Montesquieu attempts to put things in the proper place:

---

[30] Charles de Montesquieu, *The Spirit of the Laws*, Great Books of the Western World, vol. 38, Edited by Robert Hutchins (Chicago: Encyclopedia Britannica, 1952), 9-13. See also Thomas Pangle, *Montesquieu's Philosophy of Liberalism: A Commentary on* The Spirit of the Letters (Chicago: University of Chicago Press, 1973), 20-47.

This understanding of the true nature of the English system emerges clearly enough in Montesquieu's description of the principles of the English constitution. The idea of preventing oppression in a republic by balancing selfish competitive factions was of course not invented in Montesquieu's England. Nor is the scheme of institutionalizing this balance through a division of governmental power an innovation. But in the English system as described by Montesquieu these ideas take on a radically new form. In addition Montesquieu's new principle of "separation of powers" goes beyond the classical aim of stabilizing the balance of competing factions and tries to create out of the competition of selfish interests a new guarantee for personal security and the rule of law.[31]

Hence, Montesquieu's use of balance of power ideas in government actually forges creatively to new heights. The Founders were able to think along the trajectory and extrapolate to their situation with the details filled in. Along the way, the American Fathers would have easily seen the affinity of Montesquieu's approach to the biblical worldview that they imbibed from the religiosity of Colonial America and its recent Great Awakening.

FEDERAL GOVERNMENT VERSUS STATE GOVERNMENTS

A second major way in which the Framers helped to put chains on depravity and thereby preserve liberty was to limit the Federal Government in such a way so that the various states retained more responsibilities. This sets up a kind of tension between Federal and State governments which diffuses power and provides further checks on the Federal Government than

---

[31] Pangle, *Montesquieu's Philosophy of Liberalism*, 117.

the internal checks and balances. The principles for this overall understanding are grounded in the Ninth and Tenth Amendments to the Constitution:

Ninth Amendment: The enumeration in the Constitution, of certain rights, shall not be construed to deny or disparage others retained by the people.

Tenth Amendment: The powers not delegated to the United States by the Constitution, nor prohibited by it to the States, are reserved to the States respectively, or to the people.[32]

The Ninth Amendment denies a regulative principle in the Constitution in determining the rights of individuals. The rights the people have are more than are listed in the actual document. The enumerated lists do not limit the people's rights. They limit the Federal Government. The Tenth Amendment may be even stronger. The Federal Government has only those powers listed in the Constitution. Any powers not specifically cited to belong to the Federal Government are automatically assumed to be powers belonging to the States or to individuals. This focus on "States' Rights" was designed to prevent the development of a centralized despotic government. Thus, de Tocqueville noted that the "government of the states is the rule, the Federal government the exception."[33]

One might be tempted to look at the Framers' design to attempt to hold off the depravity of man as producing an inefficient system of government. Such an assessment is accurate. In the balance between security and freedom, there must be enough security to allow people to live without fear. However, there must be enough obstacles in the way of the government to allow for the maximum amount of freedom. Thus, Americans prosper without the

---

[32] These two amendments are among the most disobeyed statements of the Constitution in modern American governance.

[33] Alexis de Tocqueville, *Democracy in America*, Chapter 8, 118.

government bearing down on them but sacrifice services in an inefficient system.

BILL OF RIGHTS AND SCRIPTURE

In 1791 the first ten amendments to the U. S. Constitution were ratified and became law. It is a matter of the historical record that Bible-believing Christians had an influence on the creation of this Bill of Rights. The powerful Baptist pastor John Leland from Virginia had enough political clout to influence James Madison to pursue aggressively an amendment guaranteeing religious liberty.[34] In looking at the first ten amendments, it is instructive to see what content suggests any grounding in biblical teaching.

> 1 -- Congress shall make no law respecting an establishment of religion, or prohibiting the free exercise thereof; or abridging the freedom of speech, or of the press; or the right of the people peaceably to assemble, and to petition the Government for a redress of grievances.

Here the focus is on freedom of religion, the press, and the right to petition. For now we will highlight the aspect of the freedom of religion. One must note that the amendment language goes both ways. There is to be no established church under the Federal government (State governments are another matter settled elsewhere). The government does not appoint church leaders. Churches do not appoint government leaders. The language does not suggest that Christians have no right to speak publicly about political, ethical, and moral issues that affect the nation. However, influence should never morph into control.

---

[34] See J. M. Dawson, *Baptists and the American Republic* (Nashville: Broadman, 1956), 108-109.

The general passage that is at the center of discussion for this amendment is Matthew 22:21, "Render to Caesar what is Caesar's, and to God what is God's." Grudem gives the generally received understanding of this biblical text when he notes that Jesus "established the principle that there is one realm of activity under the authority of civil government and another realm of activity under the direct authority of God."[35] Second, in the book of Acts the reader readily notices that the Church is in no way connected to Rome, the empire of the first century. The domains are different; the organizations are not related. Thus, the Bible seems to support the content of the First Amendment which speaks to the relationship of the Church and the State.

> 2 -- A well-regulated militia, being necessary to the security of a free State, the right of the people to keep and bear arms, shall not be infringed.

The well-traveled debate over the right to bear arms centers on this particular amendment. If one chooses to emphasize an individual's right to bear arms, the Bible narrative shows that the disciples following Jesus carried a sword probably for protection (Lk 22:38). In this case the biblical narrative can serve as a precedent for the right to bear arms. If one chooses to emphasize a corporate right to bear arms in a corporate governmental way (some interpret the militia this way), then Romans 13:1-7 gives governmental authorities the right to bear the sword. Thus, in either reading of this text, one can see a biblical grounding of this amendment.

Amendments 3 through 7 below will be listed together since a similar principle governs the reading of each amendment.

---

[35] Wayne Grudem, *Politics According to the Bible* (Grand Rapids: Zondervan, 2010), 99.

Biblical Distinctions Applied 441

3 -- No soldier shall, in time of peace be quartered in any house, without the consent of the owner, nor in time of war, but in a manner to be prescribed by law.

4 -- The right of the people to be secure in their persons, houses, papers, and effects, against unreasonable searches and seizures, shall not be violated, and no warrants shall issue, but upon probable cause, supported by oath or affirmation, and particularly describing the place to be searched, and the persons or things to be seized.

5 -- No person shall be held to answer for a capital, or otherwise infamous crime, unless on a presentment or indictment of a Grand Jury, except in cases arising in the land or naval forces, or in the militia, when in actual service in time of war or public danger; nor shall any person be subject for the same offense to be twice put in jeopardy of life or limb; nor shall be compelled in any criminal case to be a witness against himself, nor be deprived of life, liberty, or property, without due process of law; nor shall private property be taken for public use without just compensation.

6 -- In all criminal prosecutions, the accused shall enjoy the right to a speedy and public trial, by an impartial jury of the State and district wherein the crime shall have been committed, which district shall have been previously ascertained by law, and to be informed of the nature and cause of the accusation; to be confronted with the witnesses against him; to have compulsory process for obtaining witnesses in his favor, and to have the assistance of counsel for his defense.

> 7 -- In suits at common law, where the value in controversy shall exceed twenty dollars, the right of trial by jury shall be preserved, and no fact tried by a jury shall be otherwise reexamined in any court of the United States, than according to the rules of the common law.

These amendments cover quartering soldiers (3), searches by authorities (4), and rules for trials both civil and criminal (5, 6, 7). In a general sense all of these are rationally thought out applications of limiting governmental authority in light of possible abuses due to depravity. So, perhaps we can assert that here is some level of common sense. However, it is also possible to notice that some biblical texts speak of a kind of due process which is the point of these constitutional texts. The treatment of property with respect as is found in the Mosaic legislation would be important (e.g., Lev 19:13, Ex 22). Appropriate rules for trials such as witnesses would also be significant (e.g., Dt 17:6, 19:15). The idea of due process found in such legal texts in the Bible informs such thinking for legislative priorities in Constitutional texts.

There are some cautions that need to be mentioned here. The United States is not a covenant nation like Israel. One has the right to ask what right we have to view Mosaic legislative texts as speaking to how nations should execute their laws today. We do not want to repeat the Christian Reconstructionist mistake.[36] As a dispensationalist, this present author would make sure to avoid the replacement theology of the Founding Fathers and an over-application of Old Testament texts to American life and experience. The best that one can do is to apply the text indirectly with dispensational sensitivity. There can be no direct application. A second caution comes from

---

[36] Greg Bahnsen, *Theonomy in Christian Ethics*, 3rd edition (n.p.: Covenant Media Press, 2002). In this work, Bahnsen argues for the application of the Old Testament text in exhaustive detail in today's culture. This cannot be harmonized with a dispensational understanding of Scripture.

Biblical Distinctions Applied 443

the presence in the Old Testament of examples where due process was not the case. One could ask the Canaanites or Amalekites if they experienced due process. Nonetheless, we learn from the examples of the Old Testament so that we can live better (e.g., 1Co 10:6). In that sense perhaps, it is possible that the due process of these particular amendments find an analogy in Scripture and protections against the potential expression of the depravity of governmental authorities.

> 8 -- Excessive bail shall not be required, nor excessive fines imposed, nor cruel and unusual punishments inflicted.

This amendment is probably the clearest example where Constitutional law finds clear precedent expressed in the biblical text. The statement concerns the fact that the judgment or punishment must fit the crime. A person who drives 56 mph in a 55 mph zone should not be executed for this crime! This teaching is expressed in Exodus 21:23-35, "But if there is serious injury, you are to take life for life, eye for eye, tooth for tooth, hand for hand, foot for foot, burn for burn, wound for wound, bruise for bruise." Jesus also addresses this text in his words in the Sermon on the Mount (Mt 5:38-42). Generally, this verse has been abused greatly as permission to carry out vengeance. But this would contradict teaching elsewhere in the Bible (Ro 12:19). The passage in its Old Testament context teaches that there are precise limits to punishment that is meted out. The Founding Fathers would have been aware of this biblical text and understood it appropriately.[37]

---

[37] Amendments 9 and 10 have already been covered in an earlier section of this chapter.

CONCLUSION

Any attempt to ground all of the Constitution in biblical teaching would be tricky business. The Founders were extremely educated men and well read. Their familiarity with history, philosophy, and political theory is easily demonstrated. As a result, many streams of influence combine to produce the document of the U. S. Constitution. However, most, if not all, Founders embraced the Judeo-Christian worldview. The Bible was respected, read, and used. Its application in such an important matter of life such as government would not have been dismissed easily. In light of the matters discussed above, especially the issue of depravity, the Constitution is a document designed to maximize protection against political abuse and to take full advantage of the blessings of liberty. In this light, it is safe to suggest that there is a biblical basis for the U. S. Constitution.

Chapter 16 – On Civil Liberties
The Origin of Individual Civil Liberties[1]
Christopher Cone

The Declaration of Independence makes the audacious claim that "all men are created equal ... endowed by their Creator with certain unalienable rights." This assertion of origin is rooted in a Judeo-Christian worldview – or more precisely, a Biblical one – and has been embraced by America's founding fathers and their philosophical progenitors. In contrast, Plato's ideal of Republic and its implementation in contemporary Marxist theory is rooted in an opposing understanding of the origin and scope of human rights. These two competing socio-political systems underscore the significance of human origin for practical aspects of societal structures and daily life within those constructs.

This chapter examines the Biblical roots of individual civil liberties, showing the importance of interpretive method applied to key passages. In literal grammatical historical renderings, the Declaration's unalienable rights claim is affirmed, while other hermeneutic devices allow for an ecclesiastic advocacy of the Platonic/Marxian alternative. Either system can be championed in the name of God, depending on the hermeneutic employed. This is, in the pursuit of a proper worldview, another key instance in which the importance of interpretive method is discernible, and dispensational

---

[1] Originally presented to the Council on Dispensational Hermeneutics as "The Biblical Origin of Individual Civil Liberties and Two Competing Views on Their Legitimacy and Implementation," September 16, 2020, also published in Christopher Cone, *Authentic Social Justice* (Lees Summit, MO: Exegetica Publishing, 2020), 7-27.

conclusions can be seen as having much greater (positive) reach than has been traditionally assumed by their critics.

PLATO'S PHILOSOPHER KING IDEAL VERSUS THE GENESIS-REVELATION DOXOLOGY

Plato (428-348 BC) asserts that the human *psuche* is comprised of three parts: appetite, spirit, and mind. The appetite represents the basic desires, and that which might ground an artisan to pursue his craft in order to meet those basic needs. Spirit is the passion that would drive a person toward justice and protection. The mind is that which undergirds a reflective and thoughtful approach to life. Each individual possesses all three elements, but one will dominate. If a person is primarily driven by appetite, that person will (and should) be an artisan – one of the business class. If a person is directed by spirit, that person would be well fitted to be a guardian – one of the military class – in order to help protect society. If a person is more shaped by mind, that person may be well fitted to be at the top of the guardian class as a philosopher king. It is only the enlightened mind-centrics who are qualified to lead society in this way. Because artisans and lower guardians have very limited perspectives and are not predisposed to examine life and understand how it all works, that the philosopher kings are the necessary rulers of society. Only they have the needed enlightenment to rightly govern and direct society. For society to flourish, the "organ of knowledge must be turned around from the world of becoming…until the soul is able to endure the contemplation of essence and the brightest region of being."[2] Only the philosopher kings were able to accomplish this correct understanding of reality. For Plato, then, there was little concern for individual rights – particularly in the oversight of

---

[2] Plato, *The Republic Books VI-X*, trans. Paul Shorey, (Cambridge, MA: Harvard University Press, 1935), (518c), 135.

society. His priority was the well-being of the Republic, and that could only be ensured when the philosopher kings were ruling. It is based on this metaphysical understanding that Plato despised democracy, for democracy represented a rule by those who were unenlightened and could not possibly govern well. Plato's anthropocentric, naturalistic elitism is a direct antithesis to Biblical conceptions of government and rule.

Genesis 1:26-27 records God's decree for the creation of humanity and the fulfilling of the decree. Unlike any other aspect of creation, the man and woman were created in the image of God,[3] and thus possessed the qualification and the qualities needed to govern His world as He prescribed.[4] It is evident that those qualifications and qualities were at least altered if not destroyed at the Fall,[5] leaving behind a human race imprinted with the image of Adam[6] – broken and separated from God. This new reality for humanity was one of fallenness and incapacity to fulfill the rule and subdue mandate. The mandate was redacted, or rescinded, and humanity was no longer expected to govern as initially prescribed (hence the concept of *redacted dominionism*).[7] Still God promised to provide a redemptive path for humanity,[8] and He fulfilled that promise in the person and work of Jesus the Christ.[9] Restoration and reconciliation with God was provided for all through belief in Him.[10]

While the provisions for redemption were put in place, the rule of humanity over creation was not restored. As Paul puts it, "the whole creation

---

[3] Genesis 1:27.
[4] Genesis 1:28.
[5] Genesis 2:17.
[6] Genesis 5:3.
[7] Cf., Genesis 1:17-28 and 9:7.
[8] Genesis 3:15, 12:1-3, 15:6, 22:10-18.
[9] Romans 5.
[10] Genesis 15:6, John 3:16, Ephesians 2:8-9.

groans and suffers the pains of childbirth together until now…"[11] One day when hope is fulfilled, the creation itself will be redeemed at His glorification. Christ Himself will fulfill the human mandate for governance,[12] as He is the only (untarnished) one with the qualifications and qualities to do so. Until the inauguration of His rule, human government is flawed and doomed to failure.[13]

God's redemptive plan for humanity is a central Scriptural theme but is not His highest goal. The redemptive plan serves His doxological purpose – to express His own glory and character.[14] The Bible underscores a redemptive plan for humanity's ultimate restoration, and that plan is designed and executed by God for the purpose of His own glory.

While Plato asserts that only the most enlightened of humanity should rule, and that quality for governance is measured by quality of mind, the Biblical model suggests that human government is inherently imperfect until the qualified King takes His throne. Plato's ideal is the philosopher king. The Biblical ideal is the Messianic King. Plato's socio-political system is anthropocentric. The Biblical model is theocentric. It is evident then that a Biblical model for human rights is undergirded by the doxological principle and derives human value not from human achievement, but from Divine design. It is for this foundational reason that the contemporary progressive socialist socio political tendencies reflect Platonic rather than Scriptural thinking, yet Plato's conclusions are found not only in atheistic elucidations of human rights (such as that of Marx and Engels), but also in some theistic models. It is especially in these cases that hermeneutic inconsistencies lead to socio political inconsistencies.

---

[11] Romans 8:22.
[12] Revelation 20.
[13] E.g., Daniel 2.
[14] As expressed in Ephesians 1:5,6,12,14.

FILMER'S ASSERTION OF SCRIPTURAL DIVINE RIGHT

Richard Filmer (1588-1653) describes and opposes a common seventeenth-century view, that "Mankind is naturally endowed and born with Freedom from all Subjection, and at liberty to choose what Form of Government it please: And that the Power which any one Man hath over others, was at first bestowed according to the discretion of the Multitude."[15] He characterizes the view as popularized by divines to minimize the king's authority and facilitate the Church's increasing influence and power.[16] By contrast, Filmer suggests, "the Scripture is not favourable to the Liberty of the People,"[17] that desire for liberty was the cause of Adam's fall, and was consequently as dangerous for moderns as it was for Adam.[18] Filmer assigns motive to Adam (desire for liberty), employing a theological hermeneutic, going beyond what is written, and effectively supporting the divine right view by that one supposition. Nothing in the Genesis text nor later texts dare assign motive to Adam. Rather the accounts and later commentary (including nine direct NT references to Adam) simply provide the historical facts of what occurred.

Filmer's hermeneutic maneuver allows him to view authority as imbued in a parental sense. He says, "I see not then how the Children of Adam, or of any man else can be free from subjection to their Parents: And this subjection of Children being the Fountain of all Regal Authority, by the Ordination of God himself; It follows, that Civil Power, not only in general is by Divine Institution, but even the Assignment of it Specifically to the

---

[15] Sir Richard Filmer Baronet, *Patriarcha: Or the Natural Power of Kings* (London: Richard Chiswell, 1680), chapter 1.
[16] Filmer, 1.1.
[17] Filmer, 2.1.
[18] Filmer, 1.1.

eldest Parents, which quite takes away that New and Common distinction which refers only Power Universal and Absolute to God; but Power Respective in regard of the Special Form of Government to the Choice of the people."[19] Authority, in Filmer's view is through parentage, and it is not a far reach for Filmer to connect parental authority with the authority of the king: "As long as the first Fathers of Families lived, the name of Patriarchs did aptly belong unto them; but after a few Descents, when the true Fatherhood it self was extinct, and only the Right of the Father descends to the true Heir, then the Title of Prince or King was more significant, to express the Power of him who succeeds only to the Right of that Fatherhood which his Ancestors did Naturally enjoy; by this means it comes to pass, that many a Child, by succeeding a King, hath the Right of a Father over many a Gray-headed Multitude, and hath the Title of Pater Patriæ."[20]

In Filmer's view the king had divine authority to govern as a parent of the people. While in some cases kings were removed or deposed, such was only accomplished by Divine will, even if unrighteous acts (such as rebellion) were employed by the people to accomplish regime change. Filmer asserts that, "If it please God, for the Correction of the Prince, or punishment of the People, to suffer Princes to be removed, and others to be placed in their rooms, either by the Factions of the Nobility, or Rebellion of the People; in all such cases, the Judgment of God, who hath Power to give and to take away Kingdoms, is most just: Yet the Ministry of Men who Execute Gods Judgments without Commission, is sinful and damnable. God doth but use and turn men's Unrighteous Acts to the performance of his Righteous Decrees."[21] This imbued authority was absolute and unconditional, and assured in every generation: "the Authority that is in any one, or in many, or

---

[19] Filmer, 1.4.
[20] Filmer, 1.8.
[21] Filmer, 1.9.

in all these, is the only Right and natural Authority of a Supream Father. There is, and always shall be continued to the end of the World, a Natural Right of a Supreme Father over every Multitude."[22]

Filmer provides no remedy for investable tyranny, as "The Father of a Family governs by no other Law than by his own Will; not by the Laws and Wills of his Sons or Servants. There is no Nation that allows Children any Action or Remedy for being unjustly Governed."[23] Still, natural law demands that the king seek to preserve his people. Thus the interests of the many necessarily outweigh those of the individual. The most significant implication of Filmer's divine right theory is that there simply are no individual rights, and Filmer justifies that principle as part of a system for human governance that is built on New Testament teaching: "If any desire the direction of the New Testament, he may find our Saviour limiting and distinguishing Royal Power, By giving to Cæsar those things that were Cæsar's, and to God those things that were God's…We must obey where the Commandment of God is not hindered; there is no other Law but God's Law to hinder our Obedience."[24] God limits royal power, but does not provide specific ground rules for its expression. There is a wall of separation then between God's sovereignty expressed in the affairs of humanity and the workings of human government, all by virtue of the first hermeneutic device – a theological imputation of motive to Adam.

JOHN LOCKE'S PERSONAL FREEDOM MODEL

John Locke's (1632-1704) model eliminates Filmer's wall altogether, as he directly castigates Filmer's view. Locke says after reading *Patriarcha*, that

---

[22] Filmer, 1.10.
[23] Filmer, 3.1.
[24] Filmer, 3.3.

he was "mightily surprised that in a book, which was to provide chains for all mankind, I should find nothing but a rope of sand."[25] In his first *Treatise* Locke seems bewildered at Filmer's willingness to see all humanity born enslaved, and remarks early in his work that "Slavery is so vile and miserable an estate of man, and so directly opposite to the generous temper and courage of our nation, that it is hardly to be conceived that an Englishman, much less a gentleman, should plead for it."[26]

As Locke critiques Filmer's divine right view, he first takes on Filmer's argument from Adam, summarizing Filmer's case and then lamenting that "the thing is there so taken for granted, without proof, that I could scarce believe myself, when, upon attentive reading that treatise, I found there so mighty a structure raised upon the bare supposition of this foundation."[27] Specifically, Locke challenges Filmer's assertion that Adam's authority was the basis of human government. Locke lambasts Filmer for not proving his assertion, nor even really arguing for it. But by making an assertion "drawn from the authority of Scripture,"[28] Filmer opened himself up to scrutiny for his exegesis. Locke responds as any good hermeneut should: "If he has in that chapter, or any where in the whole treatise, given any other proofs of Adam's royal authority, other than by often repeating it, which, among some men, goes for argument, I desire any body for him to show me the place and page, that I may be convinced of my mistake, and acknowledge my oversight."[29]

---

[25] John Locke, *Two Treatises on Government* (London: Printed for Thomas Tegg; W. Sharpe and Son; G. Offor; G. and J. Robinson; J. Evans and Co.: Also R. Griffin and Co. Glasgow; and J. Gumming, Dublin, 1823), 7.
[26] Locke, 7.
[27] Locke, 13.
[28] Locke, 14.
[29] Locke, 13-14.

Locke further challenges Filmer's assertion that Adam was given governmental authority over humanity at the creation, recounting in some detail the text of Genesis: "First, it is false, that God made that grant to Adam, as soon as he was created, since, though it stands in the text immediately after his creation, yet it is plain it could not be spoken to Adam till after Eve was made and brought to him; and how then could he be monarch by appointment as soon as created, especially since he calls, if I mistake not, that which God says to Eve, Gen. iii. 16, the original grant of government, which not being till after the fall, when Adam was somewhat, at least in time, and very much distant in condition, from his creation, I cannot see, how our [Author, referring to Filmer] can say in this sense, that, "by God's appointment, as soon as Adam was created, he was monarch of the world."[30] Filmer had asserted that Adam had royal authority over all *including humanity*. Locke suggests that there was no element of authority over humanity until – at the earliest, Genesis 3:16. In short, according to Locke, Filmer cannot assert exegetically that Adam had a natural sovereignty over humanity at creation. Locke adds that, "Whatever God gave by the words of this grant Gen. i. 28, it was not to Adam in particular, exclusive of all other men: whatever dominion he had thereby, it was not a private dominion, but a dominion in common with the rest of mankind. That this donation was not made in particular to Adam, appears evidently from the words of the text, it being made to more than one; for it was spoken in the plural number, God blessed them, and said unto them, have dominion."[31]

While Locke says much more against Filmer's assertion of Scriptural justification for divine right, this particular interchange is emblematic of Locke's approach. Whether one agrees with Locke's conclusions or not, it is evident that Locke is approaching Scripture with a literal grammatical

---

[30] Locke, 16.
[31] Locke, 23.

historical approach in these contexts – even making extensive appeal to the Hebrew vocabulary and grammar of the Genesis account – while Filmer is content to employ a theological hermeneutic allowing him to make self-justified suppositions. It is no coincidence then that Locke's conclusion would be such a stark contrast to Filmer's. For Locke, all humanity are equal; for Filmer, there is integral inequity, and slavery belongs to all at one point or another.

Once he had destroyed Filmer's divine right "fatherhood" explanation of governmental authority, Locke would argue at length in his *Second Treatise* that the basis of government was rooted in natural law as given by the Creator. This natural law has embedded within it the idea of universal equality and liberty and universal responsibility: "The state of Nature has a law of Nature to govern it, which obliges every one, and reason, which is that law, teaches all mankind who will but consult it, that being all equal and independent, no one ought to harm another in his life, health, liberty or possessions; for men being all the workmanship of one omnipotent and infinitely wise Maker; all the servants of one sovereign Master, sent into the world by His order and about His business; they are His property, whose workmanship they are made to last during His, not one another's pleasure."[32]

Locke identifies here such an important principle, that all humanity belong to God and for His own pleasure. It is because of this stewardship of life that life, liberty, and the pursuit of happiness have their true value. It is this foundational concept that guides Locke's perception of the grounding of authority, as this state of nature demands that all humanity collectively have "the right to punish the transgressors of that law to such a degree as may hinder its violation."[33] Locke's concept of government agrees with Genesis 9:6, which provides the first direct legislation of human enforcement

---

[32] Locke, 107.
[33] Locke, 108.

against unlawful activity (specifically, the violating of the image of God through the act of murder), and is consistent with Romans 13:3-4 which warns the reader that there is no need to fear authority if one does good, for authority bears the sword – as a servant of God – a punisher and wrath bringer against those who do evil.

Locke acknowledges the universal and natural freedom of all humanity, and that freedom cannot be infringed, because "This freedom from absolute, arbitrary power is so necessary to, and closely joined with, a man's preservation, that he cannot part with it but by what forfeits his preservation and life together."[34] Freedom under government is then that freedom to abide by a societal standard – standards agreed upon by those participating. Locke is hinting at a government of the people, by the people, and for the people. Slavery was another matter, and a totally unacceptable one. For Locke this meant that people must use their ability to reason as an expression of their freedom and to protect that freedom: "The freedom then of man, and liberty of acting according to his own will, is grounded on his having reason, which is able to instruct him in that law he is to govern himself by, and make him know how far he is left to the freedom of his own will. To turn him loose to an unrestrained liberty, before he has reason to guide him, is not the allowing him the privilege of his nature to be free, but to thrust him out amongst brutes, and abandon him to a state as wretched and as much beneath that of a man as theirs."[35] It is here that the responsibility of parental education is apparent. Whereas Filmer argued for parental rule as the foundation of government, Locke argues that parental authority is designed for education unto the appropriate use and preservation of individual liberty.

---

[34] Locke, 114.
[35] Locke, 131.

MARX'S AND ENGELS' ECONOMIC SOLUTION

Karl Marx (1818-1883) and Friedrich Engels (1820-1895) proposed that the human problem was borne of class struggle and the resulting oppression of one class by another.[36] That oppression was expressed through four epochs of world history, all representing the struggle between oppressor and oppressed: (1) primitive and communal, (2) slave, (3) feudal, and (4) capitalist. Marx and Engels argued that a fifth era – a socialist and communist epoch – would resolve the issue once and for all, bringing in a golden age of equality and justice. This solution was rooted in the view of all history as economic history, thus the problem was an economic problem, and the solution was likewise an economic one. That solution was "summed up in the single sentence: abolition of private property."[37]

Marx and Engels suggested that private property had already been abolished for most, as "private property is already done away with for nine-tenths of the population; its existence for the few is solely due to its non-existence in the hands of those nine-tenths."[38] The implications of the elimination of private property (as a tool of oppression) were broad, and necessitated the "abolition of the family,"[39] and the use of familial relations as engines of commerce. In order to rescue children from the evils of oppression, education would be made public and removed from the ruling class and their privatized education.[40]

The summary focus of this economic solution – socialism and communism – "abolishes eternal truths, it abolishes all religion and all

---

[36] Karl Marx and Friedrich Engels, *The Communist Manifesto* (New York: Penguin Books, 1967), 95.
[37] Marx and Engels, 96.
[38] Marx and Engels, 98.
[39] Marx and Engels, 99.
[40] Marx and Engels, 100.

morality, instead of constituting them on a new basis."⁴¹ These ends "can be attained only by the forcible overthrow of all existing social conditions."⁴² Because the problem is diagnosed simply as economic, there is no focus on the tethering of justice to anything other than an economic system – no justification of *why justice matters*. There is only an appeal to those dissatisfied by their current conditions to overthrow the economic powers of the day in order to seek their own betterment. Marx and Engels advocate a system that was in their time a modern expression of Plato's ideal city state governance – rule by the enlightened few to ensure that the common people are protected from themselves. "Communism sets out to free the human condition from the greed that so entangles us and that ultimately facilitates our own enslavement. Communism is most ambitious in its diagnosis of the human condition (greed, oppression) and in its prescription for redeeming the human condition (the abolition of all private property, and the dissolution of every societal force promulgated by the existence of capital). In communism, morality (albeit entirely redefined) is legislated to the utmost."⁴³

Because the communist ideal views the proper state of nature as the appropriate economic conditions to ensure the absence of oppression, individual liberties are not advocated. It is the very expression of those liberties that is perceived as creating the oppressive conditions. Rather than allowing people to independently and from parents learn to reason and express their freedoms and responsibilities well, the socialist communist agenda co-opts parentage and education in order to ensure that none pursue individualistic interests. Private property – that very thing that Locke

---

⁴¹ Marx and Engels, 103.
⁴² Marx and Engels, 120.
⁴³ Christopher Cone, "The Inherent Limitation of Government" in *Biblical Worldview Applied* (Fort Worth, TX: Exegetica Publishing, 2016), 195.

considered as a means of personal preservation and the preservation of liberties – cannot have a place if the collective is put before the individual. Of course the *Manifesto* makes no appeal to Scripture for its claims, for if it did, it would have to contend with the likes of Locke who would challenge the reliability of the exegesis and encourage the reader to use their own reason to assess and critique the system – choosing for themselves whether to participate or not.

ADAM SMITH'S PROPERTY AS EXPRESSION OF FREEDOM

Building on Locke's foundation, Adam Smith (1723-1790) viewed property and wealth as a necessary expression of individual liberty, not only for subsistence but for the well-ordered life: "Neither is wealth necessary merely because it affords the means of subsistence: without it we should never be able to cultivate and improve the higher and nobler faculties. Where wealth has not been amassed, every one being constantly in providing for his immediate wants has no time left for the culture of the mind; and the views, sentiments, and feelings of the people become alike contracted, selfish, and illiberal…The acquisition of wealth is, in fact, quite indispensable to the advancement of society in civilization and refinement."[44] Smith recognizes that society is able to flourish when the appropriate handling of wealth is in place. He suggests that, "The number and eminence of our philosophers, poets, scholars, and artists have always increased proportionally to increase of the public wealth, or to the means of rewarding and honoring their labors."[45] Smith even acknowledges that the concept of free trade allows the

---

[44] Adam Smith, *An Inquiry Into the Nature and Causes of the Wealth of Nations* (Edinburgh: Adam and Chalres Black and William Tait, 1837), xv-xvi.
[45] Adam Smith, xvi.

sharing of wealth, and that God spread out the resources of the planet so that there would be global and free trade among all: "For the God of heaven and earth, greatly providing for mankinde, would not that all things should be found in one region, to the ende that one should have need of another; that, by this means, friendship might be established among all men, and every one seek to gratifie all."[46] Because of this principle, Smith advocates for only minimal regulation of commerce. He postulates that "Had government been able to act according to its sense of what was most for the public advantage, without being influenced by the narrow views and prejudices of the manufacturing and commercial classes, there seem to be good grounds for thinking that there would have been, comparatively, few restrictions on industry."[47]

While Locke focused on the basic premises of government, Adam Smith delineates the expressions of appropriate government in economic contexts, specifically related to property and wealth. Smith's conclusions are directly contrary to those of Marx and Engels, as Marx and Engels are working from a Platonic platform of the elite making choices for the populace, while Locke and Smith are working from an altogether different platform that *the individual* rather than the collective is most important, because individuals are imbued by God with His image, and consequently, possess certain rights.

---

[46] From a 1553 letter to Sir Hugh Willoughby and Richard Chancellor, in Adam Smith, xxv.
[47] Adam Smith, xxv.

THE DECLARATION OF INDEPENDENCE: THE NECESSITY AND PRIORITY OF RIGHTS

The Declaration of Independence attributes the rights of individuals and government to "the Laws of Nature and of Nature's God."[48] By virtue of all humanity being created equal,[49] all equally are "endowed by their Creator with certain unalienable rights."[50] These rights are integral to human existence, and their description as unalienable means they *cannot* be removed from the individual. The Declaration orders the rights by logical priority: "Life, Liberty, and the Pursuit of Happiness."[51] Without life, one cannot have liberty, and without liberty one cannot pursue happiness. The order of these rights is no coincidence, and it is by failing to recognize the order of importance in priority that they are often violated. For example, the pro-choice platform argues that "the government should not intrude into an area of intimate, private decision-making…Instead, the government should remain neutral on the issue of childbearing and allow people to make their own decisions."[52] This thinking emphasizes the woman's personal liberty, which is at first glance a wonderful thing. However, the grave error is that it prioritizes the woman's personal liberty over the unborn's right to life. The current Democratic Platform includes this right to choose as an inherent need for the flourishing of women: "We believe that comprehensive health services, including access to reproductive care and abortion services, are vital

---

[48] The Declaration of Independence: A Transcription, https://www.archives.gov/founding-docs/declaration-transcript.
[49] Declaration of Independence.
[50] Declaration of Independence.
[51] Declaration of Independence.
[52] ACLU, "The Right to Choose at 25: Looking Back and Ahead," https://www.aclu.org/other/right-choose-25-looking-back-and-ahead/

Biblical Distinctions Applied   461

to the empowerment of women and girls."[53] On the other side of the aisle, the Republican Platform affirms that,

> The Constitution's guarantee that no one can "be deprived of life, liberty or property" deliberately echoes the Declaration of Independence's proclamation that "all" are "endowed by their Creator" with the inalienable right to life. Accordingly, we assert the sanctity of human life and affirm that the unborn child has a fundamental right to life which cannot be infringed. We support a human life amendment to the Constitution and legislation to make clear that the Fourteenth Amendment's protections apply to children before birth.[54]

The order of these rights matters immensely and violating the order of these rights violates the Declaration and the Constitution which guarantees and protects the three unalienable rights. Consequently, any violation of those rights represents tyranny, and reasonable justification for peoples to "dissolve the political bands which have connected them with another."[55] By implication no governing authority has the right to violate these rights and any authority that does so represents political bands which may rightly dissolved. In acknowledging these bands, the Declaration is asserting that no person has the right to rule over another in a way that violates these rights. Based on self-evident natural law created by God, the three essential human rights are the necessary condition for governmental authority. Natural law

---

[53] The 2020 Democratic Party Platform, 82, https://www.demconvention.com/wp-content/uploads/2020/08/2020-07-31-Democratic-Party-Platform-For-Distribution.pdf.

[54] The 2020 Republican Party Platform, 13, https://prod-cdn-static.gop.com/docs/Resolution_Platform_2020.pdf.

[55] Declaration of Independence.

supersedes governmental law, as governmental law is (or ought to be) an outworking of natural law.

Because God as Creator supersedes natural law, lack of submission to governmental powers that usurp these inherent human rights imbued by God is no violation of legitimate authority, and thus the Declaration can call upon people to "throw off such Government, and to provide new guards for their future security."[56] This is revolution without rebellion. The Declaration advocates governmental overthrow, and its authors knew full well Paul's mandate that "every person is to be in subjection to the governing authorities"[57] Perhaps they also understood the passage to come with an important qualification. Those who are governing (ὑπερεχούσαις) are not necessarily authoritative. Only those who are governing and actually *are* authorities (ἐξουσίαις) are subject to this kind of submission. Paul says nothing of tyrannical rulers or those who are usurping authority, but rather he addresses those who actually are authorities as having authority established by God Himself.[58] Therefore, the one resisting the authority (τῇ ἐξουσίᾳ) is resisting God Himself.[59] Nonetheless, we cannot read Romans through the lens of the Declaration, instead we must view the Declaration through the lens of Romans.

---

[56] Declaration of Independence.
[57] Romans 13:1a.
[58] Romans 13:1b.
[59] Romans 13:2.

BIBLICAL ASSERTIONS
OF INDIVIDUAL CIVIL LIBERTIES

It is evident that Paul wrote his Letter to the Romans during a time of tyranny and unjust rulership. He wrote the letter in 56-57,[60] during Nero's rule – one of the most oppressive administrations in Roman history. While he generally set a submissive and respectful tone, the trajectory of his entire ministry was impacted by a continuous civil disobedience on his part. First, before he became a believer in and follower of Christ, he was an enforcer against those who were violating the law in following Christ.[61] After his conversion, Paul was proclaiming the gospel of that very Christ, was imprisoned for doing so, and kept proclaiming the good news of Jesus anyway.[62] He encountered state and civil sanctions on numerous occasions,[63] yet remained undeterred. Like Peter who said, "We must obey God rather than men,"[64] Paul's own actions help provide context and qualification of his exhortation that believers be submissive to governing authorities. Paul understood both the Source and the nature of true authority, and he recognized that those two concepts were intertwined with the idea of individual liberties – both by nature, and in Christ.

Humanity was created uniquely in the image of God, and as such enjoyed a different relationship to nature than the rest of creation.[65] Animals were not described as being morally accountable for how they treated each other, but they were held morally accountable for their treatment of human

---

[60] Christopher Cone, *A Concise Bible Survey: Tracing the Promises of God,* 4th edition (Fort Worth, TX: Exegetica Publishing, 2012), 216.
[61] Acts 8-9.
[62] E.g., Acts 16.
[63] 2 Corinthians 11:23-26.
[64] Acts 5:29.
[65] Genesis 1:26-28.

life.[66] Further, humanity was mandated to enforce the sanctity of the *imago dei* in humanity.[67] It is in this context that we find the first mandate for human government, and it is directly connected with the sanctity of life *for every individual human*.

Within the Mosaic Law not only was God concerned with national interests, but He also paid close attention to individual interests. The last six of the Ten Commandments dealt with actions toward individuals.[68] In fact, God was so considerate of individual liberties – after establishing the individual's right to life, that He even protected their "right" to possess, without molestation, their own personal property.[69]

While God is sovereign over governments,[70] He also works through the vessels of human governments, appointing kings and holding them accountable.[71] When Jesus instructed His listeners to render to Caesar what was Caesar's, He wasn't taking a *laissez faire* approach to human government, rather He was illustrating how people could recognize the limitation of human government, not of His own. As had been prophesied long prior, there would be no end to His government.[72] In that future kingdom economy there is individual responsibility and individual blessing – happiness.[73]

In the present age individual liberties are expressed in the phrase "Love does no wrong to a neighbor."[74] Love cannot infringe on one's Biblical right to life,[75] nor on ones' personal liberty (or freedoms) except their own

---

[66] Genesis 9:5.
[67] Genesis 9:6.
[68] Exodus 20:12-17.
[69] E.g., Exodus 20:17b – "or anything that belongs to your neighbor."
[70] Job 12:23, Psalm 22:28, 47:8, 75:7, 82:8, Isaiah 40:15-17.
[71] E.g., 1 Samuel 13, Daniel 4, etc.
[72] E.g., Daniel 2:44-45.
[73] Jeremiah 31:29-30, 34-35.
[74] Romans 13:10.
[75] Genesis 9:6.

freedoms on behalf of another,[76] nor on one's pursuit of happiness – if happiness is defined as blessing, which comes from right relationship with the Lord and proper application of that position in relationship with others.[77] Even in the body of Christ which is one, there are many members, and each play a vital role,[78] and each have a manifestation of the Holy Spirit for the common good.[79] As Peter later explains, each believer is gifted for the purpose of glorifying Him through serving one another.[80] There is an incredible balance between personal liberties and personal responsibilities. Without the one, the other cannot be met.

In taking these passages at face value, we recognize that God first provides a platform wherein we can understand what He has said and what He intends (epistemology), then He has revealed to us the realities of which He wants us to be aware (metaphysics). Once we understand the realities and have confidence that we have understood Him, we can understand what we should do about all this (ethics), and how we should interact with each other (social political thought). For Plato, Filmer, Marx, Engels, and other thinkers who are not beginning with God as authoritative (Filmer begins with God, but enthrones himself as interpreter of Scripture), their understanding of the nature of the individual and their rights and liberties is distorted. On the other hand, with the literal grammatical historical understanding of Scripture, we end up with similar conclusions as Locke, Smith, and the writers of the Declaration – these who recognize that all humanity possesses unalienable rights to life, liberty, and the pursuit of fulfillment and blessing by knowing God and utilizing that which He has given to us.

---

[76] 1 Corinthians 11:23-24, 31-33.
[77] E.g., Matthew 18:6, 19:14.
[78] 1 Corinthians 12:12-27.
[79] 1 Corinthians 12:7.
[80] 1 Peter 4:10-11.

Chapter 17 – On Political Science
The Royal Psalms: Their Unique Contribution to a Christian Understanding of Political Science
Bruce A. Baker

DEFINITION AND METHODOLOGY

Definition

The crux interpretum of a biblical theology of the royal psalms is the problem of definition. Is there such a thing as a royal psalm, and if so, what are its characteristics? Gerhard Hasel is quite correct when he notes that

> there is inevitably a subjective element in all historical research worthy of the name. ... The historian will always be guided in his work by a principle of selection, which is certainly a subjective enterprise, and by a goal which gives perspective to his work, a goal that is equally subjective.[1]

This subjectivity is readily seen in such works as Claus Westermann's *Praise and Lament in the Psalms*.[2] By limiting himself to these two categories, he gives only a cursory nod to the royal psalms, noting (without evidence) that they are concerned with the "'re-presentation' of history."[3] The German words

---

[1] Gerhard F. Hasel, *Old Testament Theology: Basic Issues in the Current Debate*, 4th ed. (Grand Rapids: Eerdmans, 1991), 48.
[2] Claus Westermann, *Praise and Lament in the Psalms* (Atlanta: John Knox, 1981).
[3] Westermann, *Praise and Lament*, 245.

translated "re-presentation" express the ideas of "presenting to the mind" and of "actualizing or making relevant to the present."[4] Thus, there is no room for prophetic revelation about the messianic king in this schema. Westermann's principle of selection and pre-understanding of the nature of the royal psalms is a textbook example of the subjective element run amok.

While it may be impossible to remove the subjective element completely, any serious attempt toward establishing a biblical theology of the royal psalms must take concrete steps designed to mitigate its deleterious effects. Thus, a well-defined set of guidelines must be sought to provide as much objectivity as possible. Such guidelines, however, are more difficult to ascertain regarding the royal psalms than for other genres within the Psalter. For unlike more common genres, like praise or lament, there seems to be no common structure to the royal psalms.[5] Anderson, for example, finds two

---

[4] Ibid., 214.

[5] It should be noted that Leupold insists that too much has been made of form and structure of the various genres within the Psalter. The goal of placing the individual psalm in "its proper pigeonhole" does not constitute the last word on the nature of that psalm. He reasons as follows:

"It is frequently being overlooked that the pattern or type involved is not so much a matter of traditional form as it is a purely natural procedure that is bound to be followed whether the types involved are clearly in the mind of the writer or not. There is a kind of natural logic about some of these procedures. When a man is in trouble and gives poetic vent to his emotions in a literary production or, for that matter, in a free outburst of prayer, it may well happen that without any reflection or without being conscious of any pattern he describes his situation in detail to the Lord. After this a lament might quite naturally follow, laying bare his inmost feelings and bitter pain. Such a lament might be repeated or dwelt on at greater length, depending on the extremity of the situation in which the man is involved. Then quite naturally could follow petitions for relief from the great distress. This prayer might be long or short as the feelings of the moment dictate. There could then follow more lament, if the prayer had failed to raise the petitioner above the level of his distress. Or there might follow a note of restored confidence and even a word of thanksgiving for the comfort and help received from the Lord.

No one would deny that the sequence of parts in such a psalm could be arranged in almost any order. One and the same man might be praying in one fashion this year and in quite another fashion three years hence. In other words, the rigidity of pattern

different forms in Psalm 89 (89:1-37 hymn, 89:38-51 lament) even though he classifies its overall message as a royal psalm.[6] Therefore, their identification must be based upon subject matter and theme instead of organization or literary patterns. Bellinger argues,

> The psalms of lament and praise are literary types in the strict sense, but the royal psalms are not. Our list of these psalms includes a variety of literary forms. The common characteristic that holds the category together is the king; the psalms relate to different settings in the life of the Jerusalem king. Because the king held a distinctive and prominent position in the life of the worshiping community, and because this group of psalms makes its own contribution to our understanding of a variety of themes and concerns in the Psalter, it makes sense to treat these texts separately. So while 'royal psalm' is not actually a literary type, there is justification for including it in our treatment of the various classes of psalms.[7]

While there have been previous attempts to classify the psalms,[8] Leupold notes that after the publication of Gunkel's work in 1933,[9] commentators have, for the most part, followed his classification pattern.[10]

---

has been stressed too much." H. C. Leupold, *Exposition of the Psalms* (Columbus, OH: Wartburg Press, 1959), 11.

[6] Bernhard W. Anderson, *Out of the Depths: The Psalms Speak for Us Today*, rev. ed. (Philadelphia: Westminster, 1983), 241.

[7] W. H. Bellinger, *Psalms: Reading and Studying the Book of Praises* (Peabody, MA: Hendrickson, 1990), 106-107.

[8] "In his Summarien Luther listed five classes of psalms as being outstanding. There were in his opinion first of all those psalms that were prophecies about the Christ; then there were doctrinal psalms; then psalms of comfort; then also prayer psalms; and lastly psalms of thanksgiving. Almost every writer that commented on the psalms after him had his own particular pattern of classification." Leupold, *Psalms*, 10.

[9] Hermann Gunkel and Joachim Begrich, *Einleitung in Die Psalmen*, 2nd ed. (Göttingen: Vandenhoeck, 1966).

[10] Leupold, *Psalms*, 10.

As part of his general classification of the psalms,[11] Gunkel listed ten psalms (with the possible addition of Psalm 89) as royal psalms: 2, 18, 20, 21, 45, 72, 89, 101, 110, 132, and 144.[12] Bullock notes that this list has become "rather standard"[13] while Futato notes that "a fairly strong consensus" affirms Gunkel's list.[14]

While there may indeed be a "strong consensus," this in no way implies uniformity. Bullock, rejecting form criticism as a valid investigative tool, prefers to emphasize "messianic psalms" instead of the more restrictive category of "royal psalms." Still, he acknowledges that the "messianic psalms" may be divided into two types: 1) those dealing with the king and his rule (2, 18, 20, 21, 45, 61, 72, 89, 110, 132, 144), and 2) those that treat the man and his life generally (8, 16, 22, 35, 40, 41, 55, 69, 102, 109).[15] It is the

---

[11] "As Gunkel sees it, there are seven classes to be observed. They are 1) hymns, 2) enthronement of Yahweh psalms, 3) national laments, 4) royal psalms, 5) laments of the individual, 6) psalms of individual thanksgiving, 7) lesser categories. In this last class are to be found six subheads: a) words of blessing and cursing, b) pilgrimage songs, c) hymns of victory, d) hymns of thanksgiving, e) the legend, f) the law." Ibid., 10.

[12] C. Hassell Bullock, *Encountering the Book of Psalms: A Literary and Theological Introduction* (Grand Rapids: Baker Academic, 2001), 178.

[13] Bullock, *Encountering the Book of Psalms*.

[14] Mark David Futato and David M. Howard, *Interpreting the Psalms: An Exegetical Handbook* (Grand Rapids: Kregel, 2007), 181.

[15] C. Hassell Bullock, *An Introduction to the Old Testament Poetic Books*, rev. ed. (Chicago: Moody, 1988), 137. The careful observer will note that his first list is identical to Gunkel's with the exception of the addition of 61 and the omission of 101. Bullock notes that, of the latter category, every psalm is applied to Christ in the NT excepting 55. Bullock contends that these very human psalms find their "ultimate extensions and resolutions" in Christ. "David's cry of abandonment in Psalm 22:1 was used in its Aramaic form by our Lord on the cross (Mt 27:46), and the author of Hebrews applied 22:22 to Christ (Heb 2:12). Psalm 16 centers upon the importance of finding one's true identity in God. Peter quoted verse 8-11 in his Pentecost sermon to say that David's personal affirmation was fulfilled absolutely in Christ's resurrection (Ac 2:24-32). Our Lord Himself used Psalm 41:9 in reference to Judas' betrayal of Him (Jn 13:18), although the real situation was that the psalmist had experienced some illness because of his sin (v. 4). There was a definite sense in which the human dilemma described in these psalms could not exhaust their meaning, and was, in fact, only a relative fulfillment. The absolute satisfaction of the terms of the psalm was effected only in and

first of these two divisions—namely the king and his rule—that are generally seen as the subject of the royal psalms.

Methodology

Even though Gunkel's list is the result of his adherence to form criticism, a careful examination using objective criteria will show that this list is not without merit. Put another way, one does not have to accept the tenants of form criticism to accept the results of Gunkel's work, at least in this area.

As has been stated, the most common theme mentioned for the royal psalms is the king and his rule. While this is certainly descriptive of the psalms in question, a more exacting and objective criteria for identifying the royal psalms may be found in the Psalter itself.

Psalm 2 has pride of place in the Psalter as the first royal psalm in the collection and as one of the most quoted psalms in the New Testament.[16] In fact, it has been suggested that Psalm 1 and 2 were intentionally placed at the beginning of the Psalter as introductory psalms that dealt with two central tenants that constituted the core of Israel's belief system.[17] Therefore, since

---

by Jesus Christ." Ibid., 139. In contrast, only Psalms 2, 18, 45, and 110 are directly quoted in the NT, although there are numerous allusions to them. Ibid., 137.

[16] Willem A. VanGemeren, "Psalms," in *The Expositor's Bible Commentary* with the New International Version of the Holy Bible, ed. Frank E. Gaebelein (Grand Rapids: Zondervan, 1991), 65.

[17] Anderson, *Out of the Depths*, 22. "These two themes—the revelation of God's will in the Torah and the hope for the coming of the Messiah to inaugurate God's kingdom—constituted the two cardinal beliefs of the Jewish people at the time the Psalter was given its final form." Ibid., 22-23. While their placement at the beginning of the Psalter may or may not have been for introductory purposes, the paring of these psalms is almost certainly not accidental. Leupold notes that "similar situations or contrasting situations often lead to putting two psalms side by side. Quite frequently similar words and phrases that occur in two psalms seem to have led to placing them side by side whatever their character may have otherwise been. This similar use of words and phrases strikes us as having been one of the most common factors in determining the placing of two psalms side by side." Leupold, Psalms, 4. So in these two psalms, the parallels are quite striking. The blessed man does not stand (ע.מ.ד) in the way of the wicked (1:1) but the kings of the earth "take their stand" (י.ת.י.צ.בו·)

Psalm 2 is the first of its type and is placed in such a prominent position within the Psalter, it seems reasonable to conclude that the general theme of the royal psalms would be conspicuous within it. A careful examination shows this to indeed be the case.

The activity in Psalm 2 revolves around three major actors and a chorus.[18] The major actors are the kings of the earth (or more generally the "nations"), the LORD, and his "anointed one." The chorus consists of those who are allied with the king.

While the identity of the first two major actors is relatively obvious, one must engage in further study to determine the identity of the third major actor: the "anointed one" (מ.שׁ. יח.). To aid the investigation, it is helpful to note that the LORD also calls the anointed one (מ.שׁ. יח.) "my king," (מ.ל.כ. י. 2:6) and "my son" (ב. נ. י. 2:7) within the same psalm. While these three titles (anointed one, king and son) appear to be synonymous in Psalm 2, the king and the son have more than one referent elsewhere.

For example, Psalm 18:50 equates these three terms— the "king" (מ.ל.ך.), the LORD's "anointed One" (מ.שׁ. יח.) and "David and his seed forever" (ל.ד.ו.ד. ו.ל.ז.ר.ע.ו ע.ד־ע.ו.ל.ם)—as synonymous. It is the mention of David's offspring that shows a dual referent. One the one hand, the "anointed one" is David.[19] On the other hand, this "anointing" extends to the royal line of David forever. This, of course, is in keeping with God's covenant with David as stipulated in 2 Samuel 7:12–16. Solomon is clearly the referent of the pronoun in verse 7:13 ("He is the one who will build a house for my name..."; cf 1Ki 9:1-9). Yet it is the "greater son of David"

---

against the LORD (2:2). Both the righteous and the wicked are muttering their thoughts (ה.ג.ה.), only the content of their musing is different (1:2; 2:1). Likewise, both psalms end with the LORD making a judgment concerning the righteous and the wicked, with either blessing or destruction as a result (1:5-6; 2:11-12).

[18] This use of the word "chorus" harkens back to ancient Greek tragedies where a group of performers commented on the main action, typically speaking and moving together.

[19] It should be noted that at his death, David is specifically called the "anointed of the God of Jacob," (2Sa 23:1).

that is in view in verse 7:16 ("And your house and your kingdom shall endure before me forever; your throne shall be established forever."; cf Lk 1:32-33). Therefore, references to David or any of his offspring, including the future rule of "David's Son yet David's Lord"[20] may be referred to as the "king, or the "anointed one."

In the same way, Psalm 2 makes clear that the king is God's son by adoption (2:7). Once again, this idea hearkens back to the Davidic covenant. In 2 Samuel 7:14 God states that "I will be a father to him and he will be a son to me." It is vital to notice that this divine adoption is descriptive of the entire Davidic line.[21] The verse quoted above clearly refers to Solomon.[22] Yet in Psalm 89, David—who was anointed with holy oil (בְּשֶׁמֶן קָדְשִׁי מְשַׁחְתִּיו 89:20)—is also adopted as a son, and not only a son, but the firstborn (אַף־אָנִי בְּכוֹר אֶתְּנֵהוּ... 89:27)! In the same way, Jesus, the ultimate fulfillment of the Davidic covenant, is called a son by the apostle Paul (Ac 13:33) as he quotes Psalm 2:7.

Those allied with the king should be viewed as a chorus supporting the actions of the LORD and his king. They are described as either being the beneficiaries of the king's goodness and protection, or as praising the king for what he has done. Their actual activity is limited and often merely implied with the first person plural pronoun. The function of this chorus seems to be limited to highlighting the uprightness and strength of the king. Therefore, while they are present in each psalm under investigation, they are usually found to be the recipient of the actions of others, rather than initiators of actions themselves. In Psalm 2, this character group is described in the last verse as "all who take refuge in him" (כָּל־חוֹסֵי בוֹ).

---

[20] Taken from the hymn *Stricken, Smitten and Afflicted* by Thomas Kelly.

[21] The concept of adoption as sons of an entire group of people is not without theological antecedent. The entire nation of Israel was identified as the firstborn son of God (בְּנִי בְכֹרִי יִשְׂרָאֵל Ex 4:22). In the same way, the adoption of Israel serves as a precedent for the adoption of the church (c.f. Ro 9:4; 8:23).

[22] "[W]hen he commits iniquity, I will correct him with the rod of men and the strokes of the sons of men…" 2 Samuel 7:14 NIV.

Thus, the objective criteria sought after in this study may be found in the search for some mention of the LORD, the nations, and some combination of David, the king, the son, or the anointed one, and those allied with him. It should quickly be added that vocabulary alone is not sufficient to identify all the psalms with the appropriate theme. Just because a word is used in a psalm does not mean that the theme of the psalm is consistent with all other uses of the word. At the same time, the ideas expressed in these words may be communicated without employing the actual vocabulary being sought. Context, in addition to the mere vocabulary employed in a particular psalm, is an essential element in discovering its theme. Most concepts may be describe with a multitude of different words. For example, Psalm 2:1 speaks of the nations (גוֹיִ·ם)as a primary actor. This actor, however, is also described as the people (לְ·אֻ·מִ·ים 2:1), the kings of the earth (מַ·לְ·כֵ·י־ אֶ·רֶ·ץ 2:2), and the ones who rule (רוֹ·זְ·נִ·ים). Thus, a simple vocabulary search for the word "nations" (גוֹיִ·ם) is not sufficient. Likewise, ordinary words may be used to express extraordinary concepts. Psalm 2:4 speaks of "He who sits in the heavens" (יוֹ·שֵׁ·ב· בַּ·שָּׁ·מַ·יִ·ם). The word "sits" is an accurate translation of an ordinary word, but when used in the context of the LORD sitting in the heavens, it is just as correct to speak of him as "enthroned" as does the NIV. Nevertheless, one should expect some uniformity of description when the theme remains the same. [23] Thus, when all three of these actors appear in a particular psalm, it seems safe to classify this psalm as a "royal psalm" after the pattern set in Psalm 2. The mention of the chorus discussed above will add credence to such a classification.

When Gunkel's list is examined with this criteria in mind—that is, the presence of these three major actors along with the minor character group, regardless of the specific vocabulary—one finds his list remarkably accurate.

---

[23] If several strangers on a street corner witnessed an auto accident and were subsequently questioned by the police, it would be unusual indeed if there were no common elements or words to their eyewitness accounts.

The following is an examination of each psalm in Gunkel's list to see which of these characters are mentioned, if any.

INVESTIGATION

Psalm 2

Since this psalm was used as the prototype for classification purposes, it comes as no surprise that this psalm lists all four participants. In fact, the author records a dialog between the three major characters listed.

"Let us tear off their bonds (נְֽנַתְּקָ֗ה אֶת־מֽוֹסְרוֹתֵ֑ימוֹ) and fling from us their ropes" (וְנַשְׁלִ֖יכָה מִמֶּ֣נּוּ עֲבֹתֵֽימוֹ), cry the nations. Thus do the "kings of the earth" (מַלְכֵי־אֶ֗רֶץ) take their stand and the rulers (רוֹזְנִ֥ים) take council with one another against the "LORD and his anointed one" (עַל־יְ֝הוָ֗ה וְעַל־מְשִׁיחֽוֹ).

The one who "sits in the heavens" laughs (יִשְׂחָ֑ק) and scoffs at them (יִלְעַג־לָֽמוֹ) for this outrageous claim. His angry retort is that he has installed "my king" on Zion (וַ֭אֲנִי נָסַ֣כְתִּי מַלְכִּ֑י עַל־צִ֝יּ֗וֹן).

When the king speaks, he speaks only the LORD's words.[24] He calls him "My Son" (בְּנִ֥י) and speaks of his plans for the violent repression of the rebellion of the nations. With a "scepter of iron" (בְּשֵׁ֣בֶט בַּרְזֶ֑ל) he will "shatter them like pottery" (כִּכְלִ֖י יוֹצֵ֣ר תְּנַפְּצֵֽם). This concept of warfare by the LORD against the world will be a major theme of these psalms.

Interestingly, there are two possible destinies for the nations. These destinies are dependent, not upon their relationship with the LORD directly, but indirectly through their relationship with the Son. Verse twelve speaks of wrath against his enemies and blessing for those who take refuge in him. Here is found the chorus. It is those who "Serve the LORD with fear and rejoice with trembling" (עִבְד֣וּ אֶת־יְהוָ֣ה בְּיִרְאָ֑ה וְ֝גִ֗ילוּ בִּרְעָדָֽה).

---

[24] See this same pattern in John 8:26, 28; 12:49.

Thus we see in this psalm the LORD, his anointed one, the nations as enemies of them both, and those out of the nations that serve the Son and are blessed in their refuge.

Psalm 18

In this psalm, David calls himself the "servant of the LORD" (לְעֶבֶד יְהוָה לְדָוִד)[25] and spends the majority of his time giving thanks for the LORD's deliverance from his enemies (אֹיְבַי). These "enemies" were deadly ("the ropes of death surrounded me" — אֲפָפוּנִי חֶבְלֵי־מָוֶת) and their actions are described as "torrents of wickedness" (נַחֲלֵי בְלִיַּעַל). His enemies hated him (שֹׂנְאַי) and waited until the "day of my calamity" (בְיוֹם־אֵידִי) so that they were too strong for him (כִּי־אָמְצוּ מִמֶּנִּי).

While David calls himself the "servant of the LORD," the LORD calls him "his king," (מַלְכּוֹ) and "His anointed" (מְשִׁיחוֹ). These two titles belong to "David and his seed forever" (לְדָוִד וּלְזַרְעוֹ עַד־עוֹלָם).

This attack upon the anointed king causes the LORD to fly to battle. While most of the terms used to describe the LORD's salvation are associated with creation (lightning, darkness, clouds, hailstones, wind, many waters, and so forth), some are borrowed from the arena of warfare. For example, the LORD sent out "arrows" (חִצָּיו) so that the enemy was "scattered" (יְפִיצֵם) and "thrown into confusion" or "routed" (יְהֻמֵּם).

Not only are warfare terms used to describe the LORD's actions, they are also used of the enablement he gives to his anointed king. The LORD trains his hands for war" (מְלַמֵּד יָדַי לַמִּלְחָמָה) and "his arms can bend a bow of bronze" (וְנִחֲתָה קֶשֶׁת־נְחוּשָׁה זְרוֹעֹתָי). He gives him the "shield of salvation" (מָגֵן יִשְׁעֶךָ) and "girds him for battle" (וַתְּאַזְּרֵנִי חַיִל לַמִּלְחָמָה). Therefore David pursues (אֶרְדּוֹף) and overtakes (אַשִּׂיגֵם) his enemies, and destroys (אֲמִיתֵם) them. As

---

[25] 18:1 HMT.

a result of this violent confrontation, David is delivered from the "strife of the people" (מְרִיבֵי עָם) and is placed as the head of the nations.

The chorus is again seen as the beneficiary of the LORD's goodness. Described as an "afflicted people" (עַם־נַעֲנִי), they join in the praise of God with the king by proclaiming, "Who is a rock besides our God?" (וּמִי צוּר זוּלָתִי אֱלֹהֵינוּ —note the use of the first person plural). Thus, it is that the king is able to give thanks to God "among the nations" (בַגּוֹיִם).[26]

As in the previous psalm, all four characters—the LORD, the king, the nations, and the king's willing subjects—are present. Likewise, one of the main ideas expressed is the suppression of the peoples so that the anointed king my be installed as "head of the nations" (רֹאשׁ גּוֹיִם).

Psalm 20

Here as well, all four characters are present. In verses 1-4, the LORD is the subject of each sentence.

Verse five records a shift from the 3rd person singular pronoun to the 2nd person singular. This new referent is identified in verse 6 as "the LORD's anointed" (יְהוָה מְשִׁיחוֹ), and in verse 9 as "the king" (הַמֶּלֶךְ). Interestingly, there is an intercession on behalf of the king by his subjects in this verse. There are two short prayers in this verse, both dealing with deliverance from an unstated enemy. The first prayer requests salvation for the king, the second requests salvation for the people who follow the king— identified with the first person plural pronoun "us" (יַעֲנֵנוּ). This concept harkens back to Psalm 2:12, where a blessing is pronounced upon those who take refuge in the Son (אַשְׁרֵי כָּל־חוֹסֵי בוֹ).

The third major actor is not explicitly mentioned by any of the names one might expect (such as enemies, nations, rulers, peoples, etc.), but is unmistakably present nevertheless. This prayer to the LORD is offered when the king is "in the day of distress" (בְּיוֹם צָרָה). There will be singing

---

[26] Paul quotes this verse in Romans 15:9 to press home his teaching that the Gentiles may also glorify God because of his mercy.

when God grants the king "victory"[27] (יְשׁוּעָתֶךָ.) and banners (such as are carried in battle to identify the various tribes) will be set up (נִדְגֹּל). The questions these statements raise is over whom is the king granted victory? The answer is found in verse seven. It is those who boast in their military might instead of the LORD (אֵלֶּה בָרֶכֶב וְאֵלֶּה בַסּוּסִים). It is important to note that, once again, the concept of military defeat of the king's enemies is prominent. The enemies have either been subjugated (in that they have bowed down ... כָּרְעוּ) or they have been killed in battle (they have fallen ... נָפָלוּ). Thus, as before, the LORD, his king, his subjects, and their enemies are mentioned, along with the idea of military conquest over the enemies.

Psalm 21

One of the more difficult aspects of Psalm 21 is determining who is the subject in certain portions. In verses 1-6, the address is to the LORD with the king spoken of in the third person. In this section, all the actions of the LORD are for the benefit of the king. In fact, the blessings bestowed upon the king indicate that the recipient of these blessings is not David and his decedents, but the greater son of David himself, Jesus Christ. For example, he is given "length of days forever and ever" (אֹרֶךְ יָמִים עוֹלָם וָעֶד) and he is "blessed forever" (בְרָכוֹת לָעַד).

Verse seven acts as a hinge in the psalm where both the LORD and the king are spoken of in the third person. Understanding that when the subject of a sentence is a pronoun the referent to the pronoun is the subject of the preceding clause, verses 8-12 shifts the direct address to the king himself. Thus, the second half of this psalm recounts what the king is able to accomplish due to the LORD's enablement.

Once again we have evidence that the king is none other than the Lord Jesus due to the nature and extent of his judgment. The king will find "all

---

[27] This word could also be translated "salvation," but the question then becomes salvation from what? The only choice is salvation from his enemies.

[his] enemies" (כְּ‏לְ‏־אֹ‏יְ‏בֶ‏יךָ‏.). At the "time of his appearing" (לְ‏עֵ‏ת פָּ‏נֶ‏יךָ‏.), "he will swallow them up in his wrath" (יהוה בְּ‏אַפּ‏וֹ יְ‏בַ‏לְּ‏עֵ‏ם), and a "fire will devour them" (תֹ‏אכְ‏לֵ‏ם אֵ‏ שׁ‏). This language foreshadows later revelation concerning the second coming.

The behavior of the enemies is consistent with what has been described in the previous psalms. They "hate" (שֹׂ‏נְ‏אֶ‏יךָ‏) the king, "intend evil" (כִּ‏י־נָ‏טוּ עָ‏לֶ‏יךָ‏ רָ‏עָ‏ה) against him, and "purposed evil devices" (חָ‏שְׁ‏בוּ מְ‏זִ‏מָּ‏ה). They will "not be able" (בַּ‏ל־יוּכָ‏לוּ...) to accomplish their wicked schemes, however, because of the violent military intervention of the king who "aims [his] bowstrings at their faces" (מֵ‏יתָ‏רֶ‏יךָ‏ תְּ‏כוֹנֵ‏ן עַ‏ל־פְּ‏נֵ‏יהֶ‏ם.).

The subjects of the king close the psalm with a vow of praise. Again, they are bystanders observing the action of the main three actors.

Once again in the psalm, we find the theme of the violent overthrow of those who oppose the LORD and his anointed. This theme keeps reappearing because of the nature of the enemies and the nature of the LORD and his anointed one. The nations will not yield, so the LORD destroys them through overwhelming force.

Psalm 45

When read in a plain and ordinary way, Psalm 45 not only fits the criteria set above but also makes an important statement about the nature of the anointed king. The king is none other than God himself. This is easily shown by reading the divine commentary provided in Hebrews 1:8-9. But there is no reason to leave the immediate context of the psalm to illustrate this truth.

While these verses are composed for the king (45:1), the title of the psalm makes it clear that it is didactic in nature and intended for public worship. The phrase "of" or "to the Sons of Korah" (לִ‏בְ‏נֵ‏י־קֹ‏רַ‏ח) leaves it unclear as to whether they were the composers or performers of this song.

Nevertheless, their prominent position in the Psalter,[28] their responsibilities in the house of God (1Ch 9:19), as well as their readiness to lead in public worship (2Ch 20:19) demands this song be taken as part of the worship liturgy. Likewise, the descriptive title מַשְׂכִּיל (instruction) identifies this as a song designed for contemplation.

As one begins the investigation, one jarring difference sets this psalm apart from the others. This psalm alone among the collection does not use God's covenant-keeping name יהוה, but instead uses אֱלֹהִים. There is no question, of course, that these two names are synonymous with regard to their referent. But there does seem to be a different emphasis attached to each one. While doing a full-orbed study of these two names is beyond the scope of this study, one can hazard a guess as to the unique change in names for this psalm.

Psalm 45 is sometimes called a "marriage" psalm because of the instructions to the bride of the king given in verses 10-15.[29] While it is true that a royal wedding is being discussed in this song, the larger subject seems to be the character of the king himself. It is because he is "more beautiful than the sons of man" (יָפְיָפִיתָ מִבְּנֵי אָדָם) that she is to forget her people and her father's house (וּבֵית אָבִיךְ) and attend to the king's desires (כִּי יִתְאָו הַמֶּלֶךְ יָפְיֵךְ). In fact, the king is identified as at once God himself yet a person distinct from God.

This apparent paradox is found in verses 5 and 6, and these two verses have been troublesome to many commentators. Taken at face value, the throne of God (אֱלֹהִים taken as a vocative) is the subject of verse 6, where the insignias of royalty (throne, scepter, kingdom) are prominent. The throne could just as easily have been the king's, as the statements made about this throne are made elsewhere about the anointed one. Verse 7 continues talking about the same person (אֱלֹהִים) by using the second person masculine pronoun for the subject of the sentence. What makes this troublesome to

---

[28] Eleven psalms—42, 44–49, 84, 85, 87, and 88—are attributed to them.

[29] It is clear that the subject changes in the last two verses of the psalm due to the change from the feminine to the masculine pronouns employed.

some is that God (אֱלֹהִים), who is the subject of the sentence, is described as a separate person in the second clause. Inserting the vocative of verse 6 into verse 7 illustrates the construction:

> Your throne, O God, is forever and ever; a scepter of righteousness is the scepter of your kingdom. You [O God] have loved righteousness and hated wickedness; Therefore God, your God, has anointed you with the oil of joy above your companions.

The fact that some commentators find this difficult is not traceable to any unusual Hebrew construction, but to what can only be called an antiprophetic bias towards the psalms in general. Broyles' exception to the very plain statements of the text are typical:

> The phrase "Your throne, O God," is problematic because it appears to address the human king as divine…. While kings of Egypt and early Mesopotamia may have claimed divinity, the OT is elsewhere most explicit that this was not the case for Yahweh's appointed king. The closest the OT gets is in the language of Yahweh's "begetting" the royal "son," but this is simply a metaphor (see on 2:7 and 110:3)."[30]

Yet this explanation ignores the possibility that this composition could be primarily prophetic in nature. Additionally, any other translation other than the one proposed above, twists the Hebrew text like a wax nose. Kidner's understanding is much preferred:

> The RSV, NEB, and RP (but not JB nor Gelineau) have sidestepped the plain sense of verse 6 (which is confirmed by the ancient versions and by the New Testament) by reducing the words "Thy throne, O

---

[30] Craig C. Broyles, *Psalms, New International Biblical Commentary*, Old Testament Series 11 (Peabody, MA: Hendrickson, 1999), 207.

God" to something less startling. But the Hebrew resists any softening here, and it is the New Testament, not the new versions, which does it justice when it uses it to prove the superiority of God's Son to the very angels (Heb 1:8f). Adding to this, verse 7 distinguishes between God, your God, and the king who has been addressed as "God" in verse 6. This paradox is consistent with the incarnation, but mystifying in any other context. It is an example of Old Testament language bursting its banks, to demand a more than human fulfillment (as did Ps. 110:1, according to our Lord).³¹

The most natural reading, therefore, makes אֱלֹהִים both God and king, while maintaining God as a separate person who establishes the king. While it would be difficult to establish a fully fleshed-out trinitarian theology from the royal psalms, it is instructive to note that another name for the king is son. Thus, when understood prophetically, it is easy to see the identification of the LORD and his anointed one.

As before, the enemies present themselves and God (or possibly the king, as it is difficult to tell the referent of the "mighty one" (גִּבּוֹר)) establishes his military superiority over them. He straps on his sword (חֲגוֹר־חַרְבְּךָ עַל־יָרֵךְ) and with sharp arrows (חִצֶּיךָ שְׁנוּנִים) the heart of the enemies are pierced (בְּלֵב אוֹיְבֵי הַמֶּלֶךְ) so that the peoples fall beneath him (עַמִּים תַּחְתֶּיךָ יִפְּלוּ).

Those that remain are subjugated to him so that they seek his favor. The "daughter of Tyre" presents a gift (וּבַת־צֹר בְּמִנְחָה), and the richest men seek the king's face (פָּנַיִךְ יְחַלּוּ עֲשִׁירֵי עָם). In this case, the "daughter of Tyre" most likely represents the population of a city and not an individual.³² Tyre was considered one of, if not the, leading city of commerce

---

³¹ J. A. Alexander, *The Psalms* (1850; n.p.: reprint, Grand Rapids: Zondervan, n.d.), 203-204.

³² The "daughter of Zion" in Psalm 9:14 is another instance of the population of a city being referred to as a daughter.

during the time of David and Solomon. The many good that could be found in her markets as well as her trading partners are listed in detail in Ezekiel 27. It was natural, therefore, for those of David's day to refer to Tyre as a symbol for wealth and commerce in the world. The construction which places the "daughter of Tyre" epexegetically with "the richest men" adds support for this understanding. The prophetic nature of this psalm also supports this interpretation, for Isaiah 23:17-18[33] predicts that Tyre's wealth will go to the LORD's people, mentioning specifically "fine clothing" such as the bride is wearing here. Finally, if the "daughter of Tyre" were a part of the king's loyal subjects, this would be the only place in the royal psalms where those allied with the LORD and his anointed one perform an action other than prayer or praise.

As in the other psalms examined, the chorus—that is, those loyal to the king—are also present. While there are others mentioned—the virgin attendants and the bride's companions—it is the bride who receives the most attention. Interestingly, the bride has her origins from among the nations but has been selected by the king to be his bride. She is commanded to "forget her people and her father's house" (שׁ.כ.ח.י. ע.מ.ך. ו.ב.ית א.ב.י.ך J) and instead bow down (ה.שׁ.ת.ח.ו.י-לו) to her Lord (א.ד.נ.י.ך J). While most of the other royal psalms are alluding to the Davidic covenant, this instruction harkens back to the Abrahamic covenant as recorded in Genesis 12:1. The fact that the bride comes from among the nations, rather than from Israel, makes it difficult for those familiar with the New Testament to ignore what appears to be a foreshadowing of the king's relationship with the Gentile nations. While it goes too far to call this a prediction of the church, it does seem to be in line with other OT texts (such as Amos 9:11-12) that

---

[33] "And it will come about at the end of seventy years that the LORD will visit Tyre. Then she will go back to her harlot's wages and will play the harlot with all the kingdoms on the face of the earth. And her gain and her harlot's wages will be set apart to the LORD; it will not be stored up or hoarded, but her gain will become sufficient food and choice attire for those who dwell in the presence of the LORD" (Is 23:17-18 NASB).

predict a relationship between the future king in his kingdom and the Gentile nations.

It should also be noted that the bride and her companions do not initiate any actions. The bride is led (תּוּבַל) to the king. Her royal wedding garments seem to be a gift from him as well. This lack of action is in keeping with all the previous psalms.

Psalm 72

All the characters indicative of a royal psalm are present within the first four verses of this prayer by Solomon. The prayer is directed to God (אֱלֹהִים later identified as יהוה אֱלֹהִים in 72:18) on behalf of the king. He asked for the ability to reign righteously (requesting God's "judgments" (מִשְׁפָּטֶיךָ.) and "righteousness" (Ôצִדְקָתְךָ)) so that he may "vindicate the afflicted of the people" (יָשְׁפֹּט עֲנִיֵּי־עָם) and "save the sons of the needy" (יוֹשִׁיעַ לִבְנֵי אֶבְיוֹן).

Later in the psalm, those loyal to the king are described as "the needy" (אֶבְיוֹן) who "have no helper" (אֵין־עֹזֵר לוֹ). But it isn't merely economic justice that is being offered. The king rescues their lives from oppression and violence (מִתּוֹךְ וּמֵחָמָס) because "their blood is precious in his eyes" (יִיקַר דָּמָם בְּעֵינָיו). It should be noted that the reason the needy are afflicted is not because of inequities in the Law, but because of the actions of the enemy. Here the enemy is called the "oppressor" (עוֹשֵׁק). As a result of their deliverance, they are to pray for him continually and bless him all day long (...יִתְפַּלֵּל בַּעֲדוֹ תָמִיד כָּל־הַיּוֹם יְבָרֲכֶנְהוּ). Again, prayer and thanksgiving seem to be the only actions attributed to the chorus—those loyal to the king.

While the previous psalms have all touched on this theme, in Psalm 72 the major idea seems to be the world-wide rule of the king. The prayer is that he would reign "from sea to sea" (יֵרְדְּ מִיָּם עַד־יָם) unto the "end of the earth" (עַד־אַפְסֵי־אָרֶץ). This universal reign will have the following characteristics: 1) prosperity: even on the tops of mountains there will be grain (יָ.ה.ר.אשׁ בְ.עָ.רָ.א.ר.ב..ר.ב.תְ.סַ.פִּי.ה.י), health: the population center will "flourish like vegetation of the earth" (בְ.עָ.כָ.יר..עָ.מַ..צוּ.יָ יָ.ה.ר.אָץ), it will be eternal: as long as the sun and moon endure (עִם..שׁ.מֶ.שׁ..וְ.לִ.פְ.נִ.י..יָ.רֵ.חַ..דּ.וֹ.ר..דּ.וֹ.רִ.ים), it will be characterized by an "abundance of peace" (רֹ.ב..שָׁ.לוֹ.ם).

While it is the king who rules this kingdom, it is important to note that Psalm 72 is a prayer to God that this kingdom might be established. He is the one who grants these blessings to the king since he is the one "who alone works wonders" (עֹ.שֵׂ.ה..נִ.פְ.לָ.אוֹ.ת..לְ.בַ.דּ.וֹ).

Psalm 89

While the previous psalm emphasized the world-wide rule of the king, this psalm addresses the eternal nature of the covenant with David and his offspring. This theme is clearly seen in the opening verses. The word "forever" (עוֹ.לָ.ם) is used three times in the first four verses and the phrase "to all generations" (לְ.דֹ.ר..וָ.דֹ.ר) is used twice. It comes as no surprise, therefore, that the first thirty-seven verses discuss the everlasting nature of the Davidic covenant, quoting the stipulations of the covenant directly.

It should also be noted that three of the four actors are mentioned in this introductory section. The author is Ethan the Ezrahite. For this study it matters not the history or identity of this person. What is important is that it is a person not the king, yet loyal to the king. He sings of the LORD's great love (חַ.סְ.דֵ.י..יהוה) and faithfulness (Ô.א..מוּ.נָ.תְ.ךָ), both terms repeated in the second verse. The way these characteristics of the LORD are displayed is in the covenant he made with David—who is called "my chosen one" (בְ.חִ.יר.י) and "my servant" (עַ.בְ.דּ.י)—and his offspring (Ô.זַ.רְ.עֲ.ךָ) forever. Conspicuous by its absence is any mention of the nations or the enemy in the introduction.

The importance of the everlasting nature of the covenant is seen in verses 38-45, for the actual circumstances surrounding the composition of this psalm point to a different conclusion. It is in this section that the enemy is prominent. Surprisingly, however, the majority of the actions described in this stanza are not to the adversaries, but to the LORD. For example:

- you have spurned and rejected (וְאַתָּה זָנַחְתָּ וַתִּמְאָס), 89:38
- you have been full of anger with your anointed (הִתְעַבַּרְתָּ עִם־מְשִׁיחֶךָ), 89:38
- you have abhorred the covenant of your servant (נֵאַרְתָּה בְּרִית עַבְדֶּךָ), 89:39
- you have profaned his crown in the land (חִלַּלְתָּ לָאָרֶץ נִזְרוֹ), 89:39
- you have broken down all the walls (פָּרַצְתָּ כָל־גְּדֵרֹתָיו), 89:40
- you have brought our fortresses to ruin (שַׂמְתָּ מִבְצָרָיו מְחִתָּה), 89:40
- you have exalted the right hand of his adversaries (הֲרִימוֹתָ יְמִין צָרָיו), 89:42
- you have caused all of his enemies to rejoice (הִשְׂמַחְתָּ כָּל־אוֹיְבָיו), 89:42
- you have caused to return the edge of his sword (אַף־תָּשִׁיב צוּר חַרְבּוֹ), 89:43
- you have not caused him to stand in battle (וְלֹא הֲקֵימֹתוֹ בַּמִּלְחָמָה), 89:43
- you have put an end to his purity (הִשְׁבַּתָּ מִטְּהָרוֹ), 89:44
- you have cast his throne to the ground (כִסְאוֹ לָאָרֶץ מִגַּרְתָּה), 89:44
- you have shortened the days of his youth (הִקְצַרְתָּ יְמֵי עֲלוּמָיו), 89:45
- you have covered him with shame (הֶעֱטִיתָ עָלָיו בּוּשָׁה), 89:45

Because of these direct actions of the LORD, all who pass by on the road plunder the king (שַׁסֻּהוּ כָּל־עֹבְרֵי דָרֶךְ), and he has become a reproach to his neighbors (הָיָה חֶרְפָּה לִשְׁכֵנָיו). Thus, it would seem that the LORD has broken his covenant with the offspring of David.

That this is not the case is the main idea of this psalm. Not only is the introduction a reiteration of the eternality of the covenant, but verses 30-33 is an amplification of 2 Samuel 7:14. In 2 Samuel 7:14 the LORD includes, as a stipulation of the covenant, the promise to reprove (הֹכַחְתִּי) with the rod of men and the wounds of the sons of men (בְּשֵׁבֶט אֲנָשִׁים וּבְנִגְעֵי בְּנֵי אָדָם) the one in the Davidic line who commits iniquity (בְּהַעֲוֹתוֹ).

It is the tension between the promise of eternal love and faithfulness in the introduction of the psalm and the actions of the LORD on behalf of the king's enemies that makes poignant the cry in verse 46, "How long, O LORD? Will you hide yourself forever?" (עַד־מָה יהוה תִּסָּתֵר לָנֶצַח). While it remains unclear whether the personal masculine pronoun in verse 47 and following is referencing Ethan the Ezrahite or the king, what is clear is that the ones loyal to the king are included in the petitions. "Remember O Lord, the reproach of your servants" (זְכֹר אֲדֹנָי חֶרְפַּת עֲבָדֶיךָ), pleads the author.

It is also interesting to note that, while the king remains under the chastening of the LORD, he is still referred to as "your anointed one" (מְשִׁיחֶךָ). Thus we have curious position of the enemies taunting the footsteps of "your" anointed one (חֵרְפוּ עִקְּבוֹת מְשִׁיחֶךָ). While this was certainly true of the king under the reproach of the LORD due to his transgression of the Law, it also seems to foreshadow the greater son of David in his first advent.

Psalm 89, therefore, clearly meets the qualifications set forth as a royal psalm. All four characters are present, and they respond in a predictable fashion. The LORD is true to the Davidic covenant, even in the stipulations of discipline with the wounds of men. The king is in the line of David and still considered the anointed one even when enduring discipline. The enemies attack the LORD's anointed one and taunt his footsteps. Those loyal to the king cry out to the LORD for deliverance.

Psalm 101

Identifying the four characters in this psalm is slightly more difficult than in some of the others. A careful examination of the text, however, reveals the presence of each one.

The presence of the LORD (יהוה) is quickly seen as David makes his lovingkindness and justice (ח‗ס‗ד־וּ‗מ‗שׁ‗פ‗ט) the object of his praise. Likewise, the actions that David promises center in "the city of the LORD" (ע‗יר־יהוה).

The character of the king is expressed in several ways. First, David is listed as the author. This in and of itself is not conclusive due to the tenuous nature of the superscriptions in the psalms.[34] Nevertheless, when one considers the nature of his promised deeds, it becomes clear that the author is acting in a royal capacity, for only a king could accomplish such things.

For the first several verses, David speaks of his own personal holiness. Beginning with verse five however, he takes the seat of a judge, administering the lovingkindness and justice spoken of in verse one.

For example, his lovingkindness is demonstrated by choosing the one whose walk is blameless (ת‗מ‗ים) to minister (י‗שׁ‗ר‗ת‗נ‗י) before him. His eyes are on the faithful of the land (ע‗ינ‗י‗ב‗נ‗א‗מ‗נ‗י־א‗ר‗ץ), so that they may dwell with him (ל‗שׁ‗ב‗ת‗ע‗מ‗ד‗י). Here we find the presence of the chorus. As before, they are the passive recipients of the king's goodness. No action is attributed to them.

In contrast, his justice is expressed toward another major actor in the royal psalms: "all the wicked of the land" (כ‗ל־ר‗שׁ‗ע‗י־א‗ר‗ץ). This justice takes the form of capital punishment (lit. to cut them off ל‗ה‗כ‗ר‗ית). This

---

[34] Although this author believes them to be accurate unless convincing evidence is presented to the contrary.

is clearly a prerogative that belongs to the king alone. While this is behavior expected of a righteous king, what is interesting is the extent to which justice is administered. It is not limited to those who have committed open and obvious crimes but extends to those "who slander their friend in secret" (מְלׇושְׁנִי בַסֵּתֶר רֵעֵהוּ ...). While it could be this secret crime has become public, it seems more in keeping with the actual wording that this crime is indeed a secret one. Additionally, this is not normally considered a capital crime. Thus, it seems possible that David is writing the words of the ultimate king to come. When one considers the absolute nature of his promised character and compares that with his confessions of his own sin (Psalms 37 and 51 come to mind), this possibility becomes more likely.

Psalm 110

Psalm 110 stands apart from the other royal psalms in several respects. First, the authorship is an important issue that must be settled before one can honestly approach the psalm. Second, there are significant translation issues that must be faced. Third, the king is also called a priest, a distinction unknown in the other psalms. Fourth, the chorus could be seen as performing an action, although this is not at all certain.

Concerning the authorship, the New Testament witness concerning the author and character of Psalm 110 should be taken seriously. This in no way implies that one should allow the New Testament to reinterpret the Old Testament. The Old Testament should be allowed to speak on its own. Yet there are a number of places where the New Testament explicitly states certain truths about this psalm. This witness should be taken as authoritative.

Modern critics have tended to see this psalm as an enthronement oracle for either David or one in his line, written in the fashion of the enthronement oracles of the surrounding pagan nations by some unknown cultic official. For example, M. J. Paul informs us, "the majority of the exegetes regard the speaker in the psalm as a cultic prophet, or an unknown priest addressing the king. Only a small minority believes David to be the author."[35] This view has no support other than mere conjecture, and more importantly, as Kidner so eloquently notes, "Our Lord and the apostles, it is understood, were denied this insight."[36]

On our Lord's own authority, we know Psalm 110's messianic quality (Lk 20:41), its Davidic authorship (Lk 20:42), and its rightful place in the canon (Mt 22:43). Twice he used the phrase "David himself" to describe the speaker (Mk 12:36-37). Additionally, what is a superscription in the English translations (A Psalm of David) is the first line of the psalm in the Masoretic Text (לְדָוִד מִזְמוֹר).

Understanding David as the author answers another important question. Is the king in question an idealized portrait of what the human king should be or is he someone who is yet to come that is more than a mere man? Alexander answers these questions with the following unequivocal assertion: "The repeated, explicit, and emphatic application of this psalm, in the New Testament, to Jesus Christ, is so far from being arbitrary or at variance with the obvious import of the psalm itself, that any other application is ridiculous."[37]

While such confidence might be jarring to modern sensibilities, Alexander's conviction is not unfounded. The portrait painted by the psalmist is of such extraordinary stature that only the Messiah can fully meet the qualifications set forth. He is a king who is completely identified with the LORD. It is the king's scepter (110:2), yet it is the LORD who wields it from Zion (מַטֵּה־עֻזְּךָ יִשְׁלַח יְהוָה מִצִּיּוֹן). At some point in the future, the Lord (אֲדֹנָי), a title used in the psalm for the king, will shatter all other kings in the day of his anger (מָחַץ בְּיוֹם־אַפּוֹ מְלָכִים). He

---

[35] M. J. Paul, "The Order of Melchizedek (Ps 110:4 and Heb 7:3)" *Westminster Theological Journal* 49, no. 1 (Spring 1987): 195.
[36] Derek Kidner, *Psalms 73-150: A Commentary on Books Iii-V of the Psalms*, The Tyndale Old Testament Commentaries (London: Inter-Varsity Press, 1975), 392.
[37] Alexander, *Psalms*, 456.

will judge among the nations (בְּגוֹיִ‌ם יָדִין), filling them with dead bodies (מָלֵא גְוִיּוֹת). The actions assigned to the king in verses 5-7, are merely an expansion of what the LORD has promised to do for the king in verse 1: make his enemies a footstool for his feet (Ôם הֲדֹם אֹיְבֶיךָ שִׁית עַד־אָ‌ לְרַגְלֶיךָ). Again, the idea expressed is of both the LORD and the king working in tandem toward the same end. In the meantime, he is invited to sit at the right hand of God [38] while awaiting that day.

Not only is he a king, but he has also been appointed by God as a priest (verse 4). Yet his priesthood is unique in that it lasts forever and is after the order of Melchizedek and not after the Levitical line of the high priest Aaron (אַתָּה־כֹהֵן לְעוֹלָם עַל־דִּבְרָתִי מַלְכִּי־צֶדֶק). Clearly, no one in history has met the qualifications for either the king or the priest described here, let alone both. Only the Messiah, true God and true man, satisfies the description of the person David calls, "My Lord."

Some have contended that this is a description of David in his role as king and priest. Leslie Allen, for example, contends that this psalm describes a "divinely appointed successor to the dynastic line of Jebusite priest-kings," even though he admits that in practice there was very little use of this honor in a cultic capacity.[39] Yet this explanation must be utterly rejected. It is almost inconceivable that God would maintain a dynastic line of priest-kings in a nation that he commanded be utterly destroyed because of the way their sins had polluted the land (Dt 20:17, Lev 18:24).

---

[38] "To be at the right side is to be identified as being in the special place of honor (1Kings 2:19; Ps 45:9). Thus, the full participation of the risen Christ in God's honor and glory is emphasized by his being at God's right hand (Acts 2:33–34; Heb 1:3)." Leland Ryken, James C. Wilhoit, Tremper Longmann III, gen. ed., *Dictionary of Biblical Imagery*, ed. Colin Duriez, Douglas Penney, and Daniel G. Reid (Downers Grove: InterVarsity, 1998), 728.

[39] "From his Jebusite predecessors he inherited the title of priest to Yahweh the Most High God, as sacred mediator between God and his people." Leslie C. Allen, *Psalms 101-150*, ed. David A. Hubbard and Glenn W. Barker, Word Biblical Commentary (Waco: Word, 1983), 86-87.

Merrill, in contrast, adopts a more conservative approach in his defense of David as the priest-king described in Psalm 110:

> Being of the order of Melchizedek was also the basis of David's role as royal priest and of his selection of Jerusalem as the site of the ark and tabernacle. He understood that just as Melchizedek had been king of Salem, so he, as successor to Melchizedek, must reign from Jerusalem. And just as Melchizedek was priest of God Most High, so he, as successor to Melchizedek in an order that was superior to that of Aaron, could exercise the holy privilege of priesthood before Yahweh. Thus on theological grounds, David could establish Jerusalem as cult center as well as political capital....[40]

Yet this explanation must also be rejected. Merrill builds his entire case upon the role that David played in establishing Jerusalem as the center for worship, his leading the procession that carried the ark dressed in a linen ephod, and the absence of any mention of a priest during the following sacrifices. Such slight evidence cannot carry the weight of such a substantial assertion. Additionally, any person other than the Messiah who is assigned the role of "my Lord" in Psalm 110 must be placed there through a generous helping of hyperbole. What is one to do with such phrases as "sit at my (God's) right hand" or "crushing the rulers of the whole earth" if someone other than the Messiah is meant?

If one takes Psalm 110 in its most straightforward and natural sense, without resorting to hyperbole or conjecture, it becomes clear that the Messiah alone is the one being described. Thus, when Jesus uses these words

---

[40] Eugene H. Merrill, *Kingdom of Priests: A History of Old Testament Israel* (Grand Rapids: Baker, 1996), 265-266.

to confound his critics in Luke 20 and Peter uses them to point to the deity of Christ in Acts 2, both were using the psalm in its most obvious sense. [41]

Little needs to be said about the presence of the enemies. They are clearly seen throughout the psalm and meet the fate afforded to them in the other psalms. It is the role of the chorus that requires additional attention.

Verse 3 is the only verse that mentions those loyal to the king. The translation problems associated with this verse, however, makes it difficult to ascertain exactly what is being said about them.

The New International Version translates the beginning of verse 3 (עַמְּךָ נְדָבֹת בְּיוֹם חֵילֶךָ) as, "Your troops will be willing on your day of battle." While this rendering might capture the broader sense of the phrase, strictly speaking it fails as "translation" in that it completely ignores the Hebrew grammar. The word translated "willing" (נְדָבֹת) is a feminine plural substantive, not an adjective that modifies the masculine singular noun "your people" (עַמְּךָ). Instead, the plural noun is better translated "free-will offerings," since this is its common usage in the Mosaic Law and the Psalms.[42]

If one provides a correlative verb,[43] the text would read, "your people offer free-will offerings." While this is a possible rendering, the more common substantive verb[44] is to be preferred. Thus the text would read, "your people are free-will offerings." That the reflexive[45] use of the concept

---

[41] "It is plain that there can be no lower reference of the Psalm to David or any other Jewish monarch. It is a prediction, and a prediction of the Christ as the true King, as the everlasting Priest after the order of Melchizedek. Nor is there anything to startle us in such a conclusion, unless we are prepared to deny altogether the possibility of a revelation of the future." John James Stewart Perowne, *Commentary on the Psalms* (London: G. Bell and sons, 1878-1879; reprint, Grand Rapids: Kregel, 1989), 296.

[42] For its usage in the Law see Exodus 25:2, 35:29, 36:3; and Leviticus 22:23. This word is also used in Psalm 54:6.

[43] A correlative verb in this case a verb that would show causation by the subject.

[44] The substantive verb expresses existence, such as the singular "is," the plural "are," or the infinitive "to be."

[45] The reflexive use identifies the subject and the direct object as having an identical referent.

of free-will offerings is demonstrated in both the Old and New Testaments[46] give credence to this interpretation.

The next phrase "in the day of your strength" (Ô.ךֶ.ל.ֵי.חַ ם֙ו.י.ְ ב) seems to be an obvious reverence to the time described in verse 5 as "the day of his anger" (וֹ.פ.ַא־ם.ו.י.ְב). Thus, at some point during this military engagement, those that are loyal to the king offer themselves as free-will offerings to be used as he determines. What is not stated, however, is whether this offering takes place at the beginning of the conflict, in the midst of the conflict, or after the engagement has finished. This lack of detail makes the expositor's job more difficult. For knowing the timing of the offering would go a great way in determining the task to which they offer themselves. Since this information, however, is not given, other clues must be sought.

The next phrase "in the majesty (or ornaments) of holiness" (שׁ.ֶד.ֹק־יֵ.ר.ְד.ַה.ְב), seems to be the key. In order to understand this phrase, two questions must be answered. First, does this phrase modify the first half of the verse or the second? In other words, are the people in "the ornaments of holiness," or is it the king that possesses the "majesty of holiness"? Second, should one take ה.ַד.ָר.ִי in a spiritual sense (majesty or glory), or in a physical sense (ornaments or decorations)? The way one answers the second question determines how one answers the first.

Searching the Scriptures for precedents is, in this case at least, unfruitful. This phrase is found, in addition to the passage under investigation, in Psalm 29:2; 1 Chronicles 16:29; and 2 Chronicles 20:21. In each case the NIV translates the phrase "the splendor of his holiness." Only in Psalm 110:3 does the NIV break this pattern, by translating the phrase "in holy array." Still, even with this variation, the phrase is consistently used to describe God

---

[46] A reflexive use of the same verbal root can be found in 2 Chronicles 29: 14, 17, and with reference to military duties in Judges 5:2, 9 and 2 Chronicles 17:16. The concept of presenting yourself as a free-will offering is also found in Romans 12:1 and Philippians 2:17. The idea of giving oneself to the Lord is also found in 2 Corinthians 8:5.

himself. In contrast, the NASB routinely translates this phrase as "in holy array," or "in holy attire." Adding to this confusion is the fact that the NASB consistently uses this phrase to describe those who worship the LORD, except in this passage, where they punctuate the sentence so that this phrase is modifying the second clause. Clearly the definition of this phrase and the one being modified by it remain in doubt.

If the phrase בְּהַדְרֵי־קֹדֶשׁ is best translated as ""the splendor of his holiness," so that it describes the character of the king, then those loyal to the king appear to be offering themselves as willing combatants in the military campaign being waged. Of all the royal psalms, this would be the first and only instance of potential activity on their part other than prayer or praise. This being said, even though they offer themselves as willing soldiers, there is no evidence that these troops are actually deployed in combat. Nor is there any need for their assistance because it is the LORD who is crushing the rulers of this earth and heaping up the dead. Thus, this interpretation is consistent with the rest of the psalms under study.

If, on the other hand, the phrase בְּהַדְרֵי־קֹדֶשׁ is best translated "in holy attire" and modifies those who are loyal to the king, then it seems best to take this as a reference to sacerdotal garments, with those wearing them performing the function of priests. The garments of the priest are specifically called "garments of holiness" (בִגְדֵי־קֹדֶשׁ) in Leviticus 16:4. This interpretation would indicate that, when the ultimate king (Jesus Christ) is installed at the beginning of the kingdom, those loyal to him—who will be primarily from the nation of Israel—will finally be serving the purpose for which God called them. They will indeed be a "kingdom of priests" (מַמְלֶכֶת כֹּהֲנִים Ex 19:6). While this function is broader in scope than has been seen formerly in that it would include leading organized worship, it is still in line with the limited activities previously assigned: prayer and praise.

In either case, it remains clear that the role of those loyal to the king is limited to worship. No activity is required on their part to bring justice to this world or to suppress those who remain in violent opposition to the LORD and his anointed one.

Psalm 132

Psalm 132 easily divides into two stanzas. The first (132:1-9) recalls David's zeal for finding a dwelling place for the ark of God. The second (132:10-18) is the prayer of one in the Davidic line requesting the LORD God not to forget the promises he made to David and to his house.

Stanza one mentions three of the four actors common to the royal psalms. The LORD and David are prominent in these verses as David brings the ark to "your resting place" (Ô.מ.נו.ח.ת.ךָ) in Jerusalem. Those loyal to the king—referred to as "your priests" (Ô.כ.ה.נ.יךָ) and "your pious ones" (Ô.ח.ס.יד.יךָ)—rejoice in this action.

The irony inherent in the Davidic covenant is played out in stanza two. While David was seeking resting place for the LORD, the LORD, in turn, establishes a place for David's offspring to "sit" (... י.שֵׁ.בו) "forever and ever" (ע.ד.י.עַד).

As has been seen in previous psalms, there is an identification between the LORD and his anointed one in stanza two. The LORD states that he will place one of David's offspring on his (David's) throne forever and ever (132:11-12). Yet at the same time, the LORD also states that he will sit at his resting place forever and ever "because I have desired it"(D.כ.י.א.ו.ת.יה. 132:14). This "resting" is not merely an habitation, however, because the LORD takes upon himself an active role in the well-being of the people. He will bless Zion with abundant provisions (J.צ.יד.ה.ב.ר.ך.א.ב.ר.ךְ) and will satisfy the needy with bread (א.ב.יו.נ.יה.א.שׂ.ב.יעַ.ל.ח.ם). Nevertheless, the LORD causes a "horn for David" (א.צ.מ.יח.ק.ר.ן. ל.ד.ו.ד) and for him will cause to flourish a crown (א.צ.מ.יח.ק.ר.ן. ל.ד.ו.ד).

It is only in the last verse that one see a reference to "his enemies" (או.י.ב.יו). That this mention is so brief seems to be significant. If one didn't know that the last verse of the psalm was written, the entire song could be read without noticing any significant loss. In other words, one could cut verse 18 from the psalm and have no clue that it was missing. This seems to indicate that a mention of "enemies" is a necessary component to this type of psalm. If this is true, then understanding and acknowledging the existence of enemies to the LORD and his anointed one is crucial to understanding the world as it currently exists and what will be necessary for the LORD to establish the reign of David's offspring.

Psalm 144

Psalm 144 is somewhat unique in that the first two-thirds of it are quotes from other psalms. Put another way, the only new material is found in verses 12-15. This being said, these quotations were arranged in a particular order so that the author could express his intended meaning, so they shouldn't merely be dismissed. Part of the editorial decision-making was the acrostic form (dividing verse 13 into two parts) the author chose.

David begins this psalm with a note of praise to "the LORD my rock" (יְהוָה צוּרִי). He then continues with praise, piling on descriptor after descriptor in his attempt to enumerate what God has done for him. He has "trained my hands for battle" (הַמְלַמֵּד יָדַי לַקְרָב) and "my fingers for war" (אֶצְבְּעוֹתַי לַמִּלְחָמָה). He is "my lovingkindness and my fortress" (חַסְדִּי וּמְצוּדָתִי), "my stronghold and the one who delivers me" (מִשְׂגַּבִּי וּמְפַלְטִי), "my shield and the one in whom I take refuge" (מָגִנִּי וּבוֹ חָסִיתִי). He is the "one who subdues peoples under me" (הָרוֹדֵד עַמִּי תַחְתָּי).

Knowing these things to be true of the LORD causes David to see himself and all mankind as they really are: "like a breath" (לַהֶבֶל דָּמָה) or "a passing shadow" (כְּצֵל עוֹבֵר). It is because God is who he is and man is what he is that David confidently calls upon him to rescue him from "the hands of the sons foreigners" (מִיַּד בְּנֵי נֵכָר). In other word,

David realizes his own helplessness in the face of danger as well as the impotence of all mankind to stand opposed to God.

Three of the four characters have been mentioned in the quoted section of this psalm. David is the author and thus the one uttering the praise. He is also mentioned by name in verse 10. The LORD is the main actor, being described in his personality and as the object of David's petitions. The enemies of David are described as ones whose mouths speaks vanity (א ֶֽו ְשׁ ־ר ֶב ִד ם ֶהי ִפּ) and whose right hands deceive (ן ִימ ְי ם ָניִמ ְי ר ֶק ָשׁ verse 8).

The new material describes the blessings that come upon those "whose God is the LORD" (וי ָהֹל ֱא הוהי ֶשׁ ם ָע ָה). The promise of healthy children (144:12), abundant food (144:13-14), and domestic tranquility (144:14) belong to those who follow him. It is important to notice that the people are the recipients of these blessings even though no actions are ascribed to them other than trust in the LORD.

Evaluating Gunkel's List

This brief review seems to have established the validity of Gunkel's classification. What is important to note, however, is that higher critical methods and assumptions are not necessary to arrive at this conclusion. A simple reading of the texts in question in a normal, every-day, socially-designated fashion is sufficient to verify the shared characteristics of the collection.

These shared characteristics are important because they exclude as well as include. Put another way, the three major actors and the chorus being present in every psalm under consideration provides workable boundaries to help establish what may be considered a royal psalm. For example, each of the psalms in Bullock's list of messianic psalms which speak of the man and his life generally (8, 16, 22, 35, 40, 41, 55, 69, 102, 109)[47] fail to meet these

---

[47] Bullock, *Old Testament Poetic Books*, 137.

qualifications. While there is little doubt that these are indeed messianic psalms, in most cases they portray the coming one in his suffering rather than in his glory as king.

One possible addition to Gunkel's list may be Psalm 61 as it does meet many of the qualifications mentioned above. There is a prayer raising up to God (אֱלֹהִים 61:1) for protection against the enemy (אוֹיֵב 61:3). The king (61:6) is said to dwell in the presence of God forever (יֵשֵׁב עוֹלָם לִפְנֵי) אֱלֹהִים 61:7). There is even mention of those who fear your name (יִרְאֵי שְׁמֶךָ).

Despite these qualifications, the psalm doesn't quite raise to the level of the other psalms in this study. God (אֱלֹהִים) is addressed, but the LORD (יהוה) is not. This is not automatically disqualifying as this is also true of Psalm 45. Yet in Psalm 45, there is an exegetical explanation for the change in address which is lacking here. Additionally, while there is the promise of the king dwelling in the presence of God forever, there is no mention of God actually placing him on the throne. This would make this psalm unusual in this category. Finally, the chorus is there but is not there. The first person singular pronoun is used to the exclusion of the first person plural pronoun. Much like Mrs. Grundy,[48] the chorus is mentioned, but remains off-stage and mute.

While these differences may seem minor, in the list assembled by Gunkel the characters act with a uniformity that is not replicated here. Therefore, one must conclude that this psalm should not be classified as a royal psalm.

---

[48] Mrs. Grundy is a fictional character from the play "Speed the Plough" (1798) by Thomas Morton. In the play, Mrs. Grundy is often referenced but never seen. Her main role is to show the tyranny of conventional propriety, as one of the lead characters—Dame Ashfield—is heard asking "What will Mrs. Grundy think?" or "What will Mrs. Grundy say?" at every turn of events.

THEOLOGICAL AND PRACTICAL INFERENCES

The consistency with which the royal psalms recount the relationship between the four characters enables the interpreter to draw several theological and practical truths.

The Nature of the World's Governments

The fact that the mention of enemies is a requisite for inclusion in this classification is evidence that evil exists and often prospers. This should surprise no one. What makes teaching of the royal psalms unique is that this evil is specifically applied to the governments of this world. Even though the governments that exist have been established by God (Rom 13:1-5), they are continuously taking their stand together against the LORD and his anointed one (Ps 2:2). As a result, those loyal to the Davidic king should recognize that, while they owe obedience to government in its role as a minister of God, the government they serve is in open rebellion and hostility towards their true sovereign. Thus, patriotic nationalism has no place in the worship of God.

The people that follow the LORD and his anointed one must often endure the oppression of the lawless because of the wickedness of the world system and its governments.

The Perpetuity of the Davidic Covenant

When the LORD established his covenant with David, he made provisions for punishing the wickedness of the human heart that would manifest itself within the royal line. Nevertheless, the Davidic covenant is a perpetual covenant that will establish one of David's sons upon the throne of Israel and even the entire world forever. Psalm 89 makes clear that no transgression perpetrated by the Davidic dynasty would be enough to abrogate the covenant.

The Re-establishment of the Kingdom

The kingdom is consistently portrayed in the royal psalms as a single unit, not a series of parts. When the ultimate king is placed upon the throne, his kingdom is the natural extension of the covenant that God cut with David and his offspring. Thus, there are not two kingdoms, but one. The re-establishment of the kingdom will not be an event that is entirely new, but will be a rebuilding of what has already been. These psalms make clear that there will be certain changes that will take place. Nevertheless, those changes are what should be expected when the king reigns in perfect righteousness.

Since this king will reign in perfect righteousness, he will be the champion of the oppressed. Those loyal to the king will ultimately receive the vindication and blessings of his reign, even though they were forced to endure the oppressor's aggression for a time.

The re-establishment of the kingdom will only be accomplished by the power of the LORD and not by human effort. Those loyal to the king perform no actions that help establish the king's reign. Instead, it is through violent, devastating, and overwhelming military conquest that the LORD puts down the governments of this world (which remain consistent in their rebellion against the LORD and his anointed one) so that the kingdom may be inaugurated. Until this military campaign is completed, the king remains a king in waiting (Ps 110:1).

The Nature of the Ultimate King

Even though the right to reign flows through the generations of David's offspring, it remains clear that one special king will appear. He will be different than the ones that preceded him. David himself calls this son "Lord" (Ps 110:1). His rule will encompass the whole earth and will continue forever and ever.

Amazingly, these psalms teach that the LORD and his anointed one are the same, yet distinct (Ps 45:6-7). He is God himself and yet serves God in some mysterious way that foreshadows the teachings of the New Testament but is left unexplained in these songs.

CONCLUSION

Ultimately, of course, these psalms speak to the future reign of our Lord Jesus. They teach of his divine nature, his human descent, his perfect righteousness, and the extent of his rule. These songs provide hope to the oppressed by reminding them of a future day when the LORD overthrows the wicked governments of this world, establishes his king on the throne, and pours out his blessings on the earth. Understanding and applying their teachings enables those currently loyal to the king to live in a world hostile to him by looking to the future when all the LORD's promises to David are fulfilled.

www.ingramcontent.com/pod-product-compliance
Lightning Source LLC
Chambersburg PA
CBHW062005180426
43198CB00037B/2386